W9-CLH-205

THE ARTICULATE PERSON
Second Edition

A Guide to Everyday
Public Speaking

Bruce E. Gronbeck
The University of Iowa

Scott, Foresman and Company
Glenview, Illinois

Dallas, Tex.   Oakland, N.J.   Palo Alto, Cal.
Tucker, Ga.   London, England

An instructor's guide, *Suggestions for Using the Articulate Person: A Guide to Everyday Public Speaking,* Second Edition, is available from your Scott, Foresman representative or by writing to College Division, Scott, Foresman and Company, 1900 East Lake Avenue, Glenview, Illinois 60025.

Library of Congress Cataloging in Publication Data

Gronbeck, Bruce E.
   The articulate person.
   Includes bibliographical references and index.
   1. Public speaking.   I. Title.
PN4121.G747   1983   808.5'1   82–20477
ISBN 0–673–15628–1

Photograph on page 1 by Robert Gumpert.
Photograph on page 83 © Doug Miller/West Stock, 1980.
Photograph on page 247 © 1982 Jim Markham.

1 2 3 4 5 6 RRC 87 86 85 84 83 82

PREFACE

The Second Edition of *The Articulate Person*, like the first, calls for articulate public speakers: those who can present appropriate, relevant, and clear ideas to their listeners in a direct, open, and convincing manner. It assumes that effective public speaking produces significant changes in audiences and therefore is an important social force. It argues that success in public speaking is achieved through the development of specific skills together with an awareness of the cultural expectations which surround various speaking occasions.

Thus, this edition presents and extends the principles and applications which characterized the first edition:

• Each part of the book begins with a Preview. These previews provide the communication theory and the cultural foundations for the chapters which follow.

• The first part, Understanding, provides an expanded presentation of public speaking principles and speech preparation skills.

• Beginning with the second part, Informing, the book is organized by speech type or occasion, so that students can focus their thinking, reading, and preparation on the concrete challenges of specific speech occasions.

• Each chapter is self-contained to provide maximum flexibility in the course curriculum.

• Extensive, detailed sample outlines and speech texts are included and are marginally glossed to show the rhetorical choices that have been made.

• Each chapter ends with exercises organized into Pre-Performance, Performance, and Post-Performance activities; these exercises, together with the "Tips" sections which conclude each applications chapter, reinforce the performative content of the book.

• The book is written in a contemporary idiom and the examples are drawn primarily from the students' educational and social environments.

Material new to this edition has been added according to the advice of teachers using the first edition:

• The discussion of audience analysis has been expanded and recast into a step-by-step format.

• A new Chapter 4 offers a frank discussion of speech fright and includes a program of physical and psychological techniques for reducing apprehension and gaining self-confidence and self-control in public speaking situations.

• Advice on wording speeches has been expanded and clarified.

• The discussion of organizational patterns is emphasized in each of the applications chapters with a major section devoted to organizing that type of speech.

• Coverage of persuasive speaking has been increased and a new chapter on "Reinforcing Old Beliefs and Values" has been added to the third part, Persuading.

• Material on group discussion and leadership appears in a somewhat briefer form in the Appendix for those wishing to keep a group discussion component in the course.

Moreover, because we are recognizing the importance of communication rituals and ceremonies in contemporary social life, a new fourth part, Celebrating, which has been added, draws from concepts inherent but undeveloped in traditional "speeches for special occasions" chapters. I believe the fourth part will enrich your students' experience and appreciation of celebratory speaking in the basic course, and will help tie the course to the real world of public communication.

A detailed Instructor's Manual, prepared by Harry Sharp, Jr., and David Henry of California State Polytechnic University at San Luis Obispo, will help you build your course around this book. It includes suggestions for organizing, teaching, and grading the course; sample syllabi; and additional assignments and activities, references, and sample test items for each chapter.

I am grateful to many people who contributed to this book, and especially to the critic-evaluators whose keen sensitivity, balanced judgment, and sound advice guided my efforts: Gary Collier, California State University at Chico; Alan Friedman, Belleville Area College; Richard Nitcavic, Ball State University; Larry Schnoor, Mankato State University; Michael Sedano, California State University at Los Angeles; Harry Sharp, Jr., California State Polytechnic University at San Luis Obispo; and William Thompson, Corning Community College.

At Scott, Foresman and Company, Michael Anderson directed the revision; Barbara Muller's good sense and good eye combined to clarify the prose and sculpt the in-text examples; and Linda Bieze worked on final manuscript preparation and production. I am grateful for Scott, Foresman's expertise in speech communication.

I appreciate also the teachers who answered our nationwide questionnaire: Ruth M. Cimperman, University of Wisconsin at Milwaukee; Dorothy Lawrence Franzone, Texas Southern University; Earline Grizzle, Victoria College; Fran Hassencahl, Old Dominion University; Joyce E. Henry, Ursinus College; Mark Isham, The University of Iowa; Caryl Krannich, Old Dominion University; Julie McNellis, St. Xavier College; Gail M. Morrison, Midlands Technical College; Eilene C. Pierson, College of Boca Raton; Phyllis Scharner, Milwaukee Area Technical College; B. R. Smith, Marshall University; and Bill Snider, Valencia Community College.

It is now up to you, the teacher of public speaking, to go about the business of preparing articulate persons, persons capable of making this society a more open, a more comprehensible, and a more exciting place in which to live and speak.

Bruce E. Gronbeck

CONTENTS

INFORMING

UNDERSTANDING

Today's
Articulate Person

As America moved into the last two decades of the twentieth century, it was sheathed with 62,000,000 English language daily newspapers and over 53,000,000 Sunday papers. Approximately 20,000 different magazines and journals, led by *TV Guide* (over 19,000,000 copies weekly) and *Reader's Digest* (over 20,000,000 copies monthly), filled coffee tables and waiting rooms. Some 7,300 radio transmitters were reaching 402,000,000 receivers, and over 1,000 TV stations were broadcasting to 76,300,000 households (98 percent of U.S. homes). According to the Recording Industry of America, in 1979 some 502,200,000 LPs and singles were shipped to record retailers—worth some $3.7 billion. The United States Post Office was handling almost 90 billion pieces of mail, including approximately $8 billion worth of direct-mail advertising, almost equal to the money spent on television advertising. By 1981, there were about 20,000,000 subscribers to basic cable TV, and about 9,000,000 households willing to pay extra bucks for special pay-TV channels; one of those channels alone, Home Box Office's movie and entertainment channel, was grossing a half-a-billion dollars a year. Mass media were big business enterprises.

In a time when the mass media bombard and, at times, overwhelm your daily life, why bother with a book on public speaking? Because, amidst the tons of paper and billions of kilowatts, in rural community halls as well as metropolitan neighborhood gatherings, comes the steady, sincere voice of a living human being—the articulate person.

Even in the face of all the mass media—from skywriting to buried cable—the public speaker has a single, unbeatable advantage: *The speaker is there.* The articulate person uses limbs, face, eyes, lips, tongue, and sound to bring appeals, ideas, and feelings to life. No other medium of communication offers you this advantage—the chance to put skin and bones on ideas. Even if you stumble around, interjecting those resounding "ahhh's" in the middle of sentences, even if you leave your speech notes at home, even if you think your voice sounds like Big Bird's—no matter what, a speaker always has the advantage of human-to-human, in-person communicative contact. When the bets are laid, the articulate person can outduel television sets, FM rock stations, and window envelopes with special offers inside. Even today, humanness still wins.

That which we call a "society" or "culture," after all, was born in orality. You learned what there was to learn about living and about people's expectations for you through oral words. Sure, maybe your parents occasionally left you notes, but they did most of their nurturing, directing, encouraging, and reprimanding through talk. Sure, maybe your elementary school had a few technological aids which accelerated your absorption of math facts, but teachers did most of their teaching, admonishing, ordering, and correcting through talk. And so did the preacher. And Aunt Matilda. And the YMCA-YWCA activities director, not to mention the soccer coach, your first employer, and the policeman. You have been conditioned by experience in this society to receive your most important ideas aurally; and, in turn, you probably transmit your own most personally held feelings orally as well.

WHO IS THE ARTICULATE PERSON?

The word *articulate,* for many, may call forth images of the polished, magnetic public speaker—people such as Winston Churchill and Martin Luther King, Jr.—who have moved millions with their words. To others, *articulate* may bring to mind the nineteenth-century Fourth of July orator, who stood in the full glory of his metaphors and measured sentences, spewing forth patriotic platitudes which communicated little but his own vanity to itchy audiences waiting impatiently for the fireworks. Or, the word may conjure up specters of speakers who *over*articulate, those whose speech is too stiff, too formal, too hollow for modern tastes.

Obviously, most of us don't aim for any of these images of articulateness. You probably are taking a public speaking course, not to become a "public speaker," but to learn to speak in public. You know that there will be many occasions, both formal and informal, in which you will be expected to express your ideas to others. And, on these occasions you wish to speak confidently and clearly.

The articulate person visualized in this book, then, is probably not a professional speaker. Perhaps this person only occasionally addresses a full audience, and certainly not for money. The articulate person this book describes is one who talks out once in a while at PTA meetings, political rallies, study groups, and organizational recruitment drives; one who perhaps gives demonstrations to co-workers at the office; one who sometimes introduces the "real" speaker of the evening, and maybe says a few words when presented with a service award. The articulate person speaks appropriately, with some measure of confidence, in both formal and informal speaking situations.

This person gets a bit fidgety when asked to speak, and may be attacked by a sinking feeling when told he or she will speak tomorrow, preferring—if public talk is necessary at all—to do it on the spur of the moment. Preparing to speak, this person may have sweaty palms, may work valiantly to remove the lump in the throat, and may wonder a good deal whether knee joints were really meant to bear up under the burden of "a speech." Yet, in spite of such natural reactions, the articulate person speaks and speaks effectively.

The articulate person chooses to speak publicly because there is something to say of interest, use, or relevance. This person speaks publicly because, in times of inquiry, problems, celebration, or inspiration, there is no replacement for a thinking, communicating human.

CHARACTERISTICS OF THE ARTICULATE PERSON

Today's articulate person is able to find interested, appreciative audiences even in an age of technology. But to keep an audience, a speaker must be in tune with it. As people and society have changed over the last few years, tastes in speaking styles have changed as well. The stiff, formal speaker finds few eager audiences. The wildly gyrating, overly aggressive salesman produces more chuckles than sales. Certainly a contemporary audience demands many of the same qualities demanded of public speakers for centuries. Yet other audience expectations of "proper" speaking style reflect the mood of our times:

Authenticity

The articulate person is open and honest. The so-called "me-ism" movements of the last two decades have wrought a personalization revolution, not of guns and dollars, but of consciousness-raising, sensitivity training, Transcendental Meditation, *est,* primal screams, and "I'm OK—you're OK" mentalities. This personalization revolution has affected our expectations for how speakers ought to "sound." Most important, it has made nonmanipulation and authenticity prime communicative values. Most audiences in America today are not looking for silver-tongued spellbinders; they are seeking sympathetic, understanding persons of solid integrity. Verbal gymnasts, of course, still have their places at political conventions, in revivalist halls, and on used car lots; but most of us will not speak publicly at those sites. We will talk at school board meetings, fund drive rallies, and business meetings—where openness, honesty, and candor are called for.

Appropriateness   *The articulate person has a visible concern for audiences and occasions.* Speaking appropriately simply means adapting your message to the given audience and the given occasion. A person discussing your neighborhood's free medical clinic would not present the same speech in the same way to a fourth-grade class, a group of parents, and a meeting of the American Medical Association. An appropriate speech comes from giving thoughtful consideration to the *knowledge* and *needs* of the audience as well as to the *demands* of the situation:

1. How much does this audience know about my subject? Need I start at the simplest level, or can I assume some basic background?
2. What attitudes do audience members hold about themselves, my subject, me, and this occasion? How should I take them into account when speaking?
3. Are there traditional expectations—in an important sense, "social rules"—governing this occasion? What will those expectations or rules demand of me and my speech?

We shall explore some of the answers to these crucial questions throughout the rest of the book. Once you can answer them reasonably well every time you say "Thanks for giving me a minute to say what's on my mind," you will understand what is meant by "appropriate" remarks.

Relevance   *The articulate person speaks for a purpose that is interesting and relevant to the audience.* Now, there undoubtedly will be times in your life when you speak publicly for self-centered reasons—to impress a boss, to bring cheers from your friends, to win acclaim for your wit or your acumen. Certainly speakers talk, in part, for selfish reasons. But, speakers could not survive long in the company of friends and audiences without having something to say that is relevant to the needs of others. If I am perplexed about zoning in my community, I certainly do not want to hear a blow-hard prattle on for twenty minutes about his personal virtues and the community growth index, in vague generalities telling me nothing relevant for the problem which *I* face in *my* neighborhood. I want to hear something which sheds light on the problem, which recognizes the integrity of my living situation, and which, with luck, indicates how I can improve it. Listeners want speakers who have *interests* in their situations, with ideas that have *relevance* to their problems. A purpose that is *audience-centered* is demanded of almost every speaker on almost every podium in the country.

Clarity   *The articulate person delivers a focused, well-structured message.* Ours is an age dominated by article and book abstracts, computerized summaries of information, and five-steps-to-success pamphlets. Ours is a time when people seek ordered, concise, packaged information. Speakers also are expected to concern themselves with *oral packaging.* Life is too short and time is too precious in the planning committee, the student senate, and the political rally to let speakers wander endlessly through their own muddled minds. Audiences have come to expect speakers to tell them, in an orderly fashion, *what* is being discussed, *how* it is relevant to some problem, *why* it should be listened to. "Order" is one touchstone here, and "clarity" is the other. The speech that clearly moves—even marches—through a topic is greatly preferred to one that beclouds understanding or meanders down too many mental paths.

Oral Simplicity

The articulate person uses straightforward, simple, direct language. We prefer to read poetry in the quiet of a solitary evening in a soft chair. Abstract philosophy, too, is meant to be consumed by reading and rereading. For complicated, technical information, we study charts, slides, or films. In a speech, however, most people want a minimum of flighty language, abstract generalizations, and technical data. In most speaking situations, Americans prize understandable, concrete, simple language.

A speaking style is markedly different from a writing style. Technically, the speaker's syntax, vocabulary, and organizational patterns are much simpler than the writer's. The public speaker who fully writes out a speech—usually in a written style, replete with complicated sentences—and then reads the thing *at* an audience inevitably violates a fundamental speaking principle. Talking *with* an audience, simply and clearly, concretely and understandably, creates a kind of eloquence which makes maximum use of the person-to-person communicative moment.

Naturalness

The articulate person speaks in a natural, spontaneous, relaxed style. "Back to nature" is a hallmark of this age—natural foods, organic gardening, backpacking and hiking, environmental preservation. America has been in a perpetual state of Herbal Essence since the early 1970's, and that desire for naturalness affects people's views of speakers as well. *Conversational, spontaneous speech* has become the public platform's ideal. Speakers now attempt to capture the moods, vocal patterns, and sense of commonality we associate with more intimate person-to-person talks. Audiences want speakers to talk "their" language, in their speech patterns and rhythms; they want to feel that speakers are speaking spontaneously, speaking their minds and hearts openly; they desire a sense of interpersonal relationship, of relaxed relationship, with their speakers. Hence, we seldom say that we are "giving a speech" anymore, because we associate "speechiness" with artificiality, bombast, and breast-pounding. We are more likely to say: "I'm going to give a talk to the Student Coalition Against the Draft next week"; or "I've got to do an oral report in class tomorrow"; or "Today I want to discuss with you a problem important to those of us with Hispanic cultural backgrounds." *Talking, reporting, discussing*—these are words we associate with interpersonal communication, with natural voices and tones, with spontaneous interactions between mutually respected equals. You are much more likely to get a sympathetic hearing from an audience if you are *you* than if you are playacting the role of a *speaker.*

Cultural Awareness

Overall, the articulate person meets this culture's expectations for public communication. This pretty well sums up all that's been said so far. You have an *obligation* to conform to the culture's *rules for communication.* Public speaking is a *social act.* It is carried on through a language given to you by this culture. It addresses concepts, processes, or problems important to this society. It is presented to other thinking, caring members of this society. Because it is a social act, public communication carries with it the basic obligation to be "polite"—to speak as society expects you to and to meet in particular this society's demands for honesty, interest, and relevance.

• Just as you do not eat mashed potatoes with your bare hands in social settings, so must you be aware of—and take steps to conform to—the social graces involved in talking.
• Just as you do not want charlatans to sell you "miracle cures" for every conceivable disease for only $5.95 plus shipping, so must you be honest with audiences.
• Just as you expect a demonstration on gun safety to actually teach you how to handle the weapon safely rather than to present you with a harangue against bleeding hearts who are trying to "disarm the nation," so must you as a speaker keep in mind an audience's actual reasons for listening as you discuss problems with them.

This is not to say, of course, that you must go through your communicative life telling audiences only what they want to hear, always sacrificing your personal integrity to the pressures of group conformity. Obviously not. The "social rules" for oral communication certainly do not dictate *what* you must say, for that would make you nothing but a prisoner-of-culture. Rather, the "rules" in fact are social, concerned with the ways in which you treat other people, respect their needs and cultural traditions, and conform to their general expectations. Communication rules tend to deal with *how,* not *what*—with your relationship to audiences as equals rather than subordinates, with your respect for members of the opposite sex or of varied cultural backgrounds, with your willingness to carry out announced purposes and to observe situational demands. Ultimately, to be aware of your culture is to be considered an articulate person, even by people "different" from you socially and intellectually.

Authenticity, appropriateness, relevance, clarity, oral simplicity, naturalness, and cultural awareness—if you meet these societal measuring rods, you are likely to reap the rewards of effective public speaking: the achievement of interpersonal understanding; the joy you feel when you realize that a complex process is now comprehended by listeners who were befuddled; the realization that you have clarified a problem for someone; the knowledge that a solution has been accepted by others; the self-satisfaction which comes from personal knowledge of having exercised your own thinking and talking skills.

METHODS FOR IMPROVING YOUR SPEAKING SKILLS

Before you can maximize your speaking skills, you probably have to improve them; you presumably are taking this course to do just that. Your skills will be sharpened markedly if you work on them in five basic ways:

1. *Understand the fundamental process of public speaking.* The next four chapters will seek to ground you in that understanding. Chapter 1 presents basic models of communication processes, explaining how they function. Chapters 2, 3, and 4 discuss the basic steps in preparing and delivering most kinds of speeches. The special communication principles that apply to informative, persuasive, and celebratory speaking will be presented in Previews II, III, and IV; they should help you understand the psychological and social factors that affect you and your audiences when you seek to present information and to influence minds and actions.

2. *Examine typical speech structures.* At least since the fifth century B.C., when the Greek orator-teacher Antiphon prepared sample speech outlines for his students, instructors have shown students sample structures of "ideal" speeches. Such sample outlines, of course, have their limitations. A sample speech is adapted to only one kind of subject matter; it cannot apply to every situation a speaker may face; and it is, after all, only one person's conception of the ideal. Nevertheless, sample outlines are useful, especially to beginning speakers and to others unsure of what is expected of them. Think of the outlines as basic *recipes.* The fledgling cook first goes to standard recipes for pie crust, vegetable soup, or chicken kiev, preparing those dishes often enough to master the basic techniques and to gain an understanding of some basic principles for mixing ingredients. Only then does the cook begin to alter and vary the recipes, adding personal touches and variations to reflect personal taste.

While public speaking is not so easily reduced to steps or recipes, we still can speak of basic structures or basic approaches to different kinds of speeches. Throughout the working chapters of this book you will find long outlines which can function as basic recipes. Keep in mind, though, that these are offered as illustrations of ways entire speeches of a given type can be put together. You would *never* actually speak from such long, complicated outlines, however, for (a) you would be tempted to read the whole thing (and hence lose valuable eye-and-soul contact with audiences), and (b) you would lose a good deal of flexibility and spontaneity (and hence couldn't adapt your stream-of-words to feedback you're getting from your listeners). When you present a real speech, you'll have to condense your "working" outline into a "speaking" outline—probably a series of brief notes, phrases, key words, and a few quotations and statistics. In this book, then, we'll present long sample outlines so you can visualize clearly how a type of speech "works"; but, to actually make one work, you'll have to shorten and recast it.

3. *Carefully think through the choices you have to make on each occasion.* Once you have gained the basic skills demonstrated in the speech outlines that follow, you then can vary them to suit the needs of specific situations and your own talents. Just as the good cook varies recipes, so will you need to alter your approach in light of the situation, your audience, and yourself.

Actually, adapting your communication to the occasion is a skill you have practiced since you were a baby. You already have learned that you must speak one way to Uncle Henry, another way to your immediate family, and still other ways to your work groups, to friends, and to strangers. Now, you make most of those decisions and adjustments without much thought, through habit. One of your goals as a student of public speaking is to bring those decisions back into consciousness. This book will help you make your communication choices consciously. Each chapter will present not only the outlines, but also discussions of situational, social, and personal factors you must consider in each speaking occasion. Each chapter will include a section on "tips" or advice to help you make these factors your *decision points.*

Often, the advice given in this book will seem like common sense. It ought to, because you often have made the kinds of decisions you'll be asked to make here. Now, though, the object will be to always make your speaking decisions with forethought—with awareness, with systematic planning. Only then will you be speaking in strategically sound ways.

4. *Practice, practice, practice.* Just as the cook seldom produces perfect egg rolls on the first try, speakers seldom achieve maximum impact on an audience in their first speeches. Indeed, a feature of most introductory public speaking courses is a structured series of speech assignments that forces you to try, to fail, to try again and again. Such practice fixes basic speaking principles in your mind; it allows you to explore your own strengths and weaknesses as a speaker; it lets you work on your speaking skills, one at a time. It offers you a variety of speaking challenges in which to try your hand at influencing others. So, take the speaking assignments seriously, and you'll learn more about speaking—and about yourself.

5. *Listen, too.* Use your speech class as a laboratory to learn about public speaking through *critical listening.* By "critical" we do not mean listening to find fault with someone else or to accept or reject their ideas on the basis of your own preconceived notions. That sort of practice is

better termed *defensive* listening. In critical listening, you listen not only for ideas but also for techniques: Did the speaker's cute anecdote fall flat because it simply wasn't funny or because it wasn't appropriate to the subject matter, audience, and occasion? Did another speaker make particularly good use of an analogy to clarify an abstract concept? Did someone draw up an especially clear and hard-hitting visual aid? How about the person who looked carefully and directly at each audience member when calling for them to act?

By making mental notes of effective (or ineffective), honest (or dishonest), thrilling (or embarrassing) communicative techniques, you can make a speech course work for you. In a class, say, of twenty-five people, you may give five or six speeches; but you will listen to 125–150 more. Use those other speeches to educate yourself. A good speech class will illustrate a wide range of rhetorical techniques you will want to employ in your own talks; and, it may also teach you how to be on guard against unscrupulous or degrading speaking practices.

As you listen both in class and out in the "real" world, you can identify effective and ineffective speaking techniques by asking yourself a series of questions. Asking such questions will help you develop your critical listening skills.

Listening to Understand Ideas

a. Can you identify the speaker's major or leading *ideas?*
b. Are ideas *arranged* in a clear, orderly fashion?
c. Are ideas *supported* and developed with appropriate and interesting illustrations, statistics, and comparisons?
d. Overall, do the ideas *make sense* as you think about your own knowledge and experience?

Listening to Evaluate Speaking Techniques

a. What were the speaker's general and specific *goals* in the speech? Were those goals appropriate to the situation?
b. What did the speaker do to arouse and maintain your *interest* and *attention?*
c. Did the speaker *support* ideas with evidence strong enough to be considered "proof"?
d. What were the speaker's *attitudes* toward you? Were you addressed as a thinking and feeling human being, or as a mindless lump of clay to be molded?
e. How *credible* was the speaker? Did you feel that the speaker was a competent, knowledgeable, sincere, friendly human being?
f. Overall, do the proposals offered *make sense* based on your knowledge, experience, and understanding of communication principles?

You will be able to refine and expand these listening questions as you read through the book, practice your own speeches, and listen to others. But, beginning with these basic questions will put you on the road to improving your critical listening skills.

In an age when too many people have surrendered the responsibility for important social, political, religious, educational, economic, and ethical decisions to the mass media, becoming an articulate person is admittedly no easy task. If you approach that task, however, with eagerness and openness, you can enhance your personal development and self-reliance, and contribute to decision-making in your society as well. We will succeed if we make you sensitive to one dominating idea: *Each time you rise to speak, on each "speech occasion," there are certain social expectations for communication you will attempt to meet.* And, as you think about that idea, you ought to, as well, keep a second one in mind: *You have the resources to meet those social expectations.* You can be "articulate" if you put yourself to work, gathering and assembling materials, practicing to improve your delivery skills. That's our job. Let's get on with it.

CHAPTER 1

Understanding Public Speaking

The word *communication* itself provides important clues as to what we are after when we say we are communicating with others. The prefix *com-* came from the Latin *cum* meaning "with." The root *munus* referred to service performed for the society. The Latin word *communis* meant "common." All of these meanings are involved in the word *communication:* the idea of sharing experience with others for the common good. In a sense, therefore, *communication systems* are organized efforts for working together to achieve society's goals. *Communication processes* are the operations we perform to make the systems work. If communication systems function properly, a state of shared experience or commonness or *communion* is achieved.

For centuries philosophers have debated over what distinguishes human beings from other animals. What is their defining characteristic? Are humans rational animals? ethical animals? tool-using animals? animals distinguished by an opposable thumb? Perhaps in our century we have answered that query most decisively by saying that *human beings* are *communicating animals.*

We know, of course, that other animals have ways of sending signals to one another. Bees "dance" in order to signal routes to fields of clover. Robins sing out the boundaries of their territories, and bears rub on trees for the same purpose. Baboons scream warnings of impending invasions. Dolphins emit a vast array of sounds to signal food, shelter, even affection.

But humans go much, much further when they communicate. They respond not only to signals; much more importantly, they respond to symbols. *Symbols* are specialized, complex meanings attached to words, pictures, color combinations, building shapes, arrangements of objects, and the like.

Thus, while all animals need food for sustenance, humans attach many other symbolic meanings to food. A banquet, holiday meal, or other food ceremony may carry meanings of friendship, family love, sharing, generosity, or success. Every beast of the field needs shelter, but only humans attach ideas of beauty or affluence to their houses, religious symbolism to their churches, and political idealism to the architecture of their public buildings. Our clothing not only protects us from the elements but also communicates to others. Uniforms tell our occupations; materials symbolize our affluence; formal or informal dress suggests our current activities; cut and design indicate our fashionableness.

Hence, while every animal we know of has a *signal system* for indicating the state of its glands and its external environment, human beings have multiple *symbol systems* for attaching complex meanings to their experience and their environment. Humans are able to communicate past experiences; to predict future consequences; to sort experiences into "goods" and "bads;" to institutionalize government, church, education, pleasure. This full range of experiences that make up human culture can be shared. Human beings can achieve communication.[1]

And that's what this book is about. It's about you sharing your experiences with other members of your culture. You have at your disposal a number of communication systems. There is the one-to-one sharing we call *interpersonal* communication. There are systems of sharing among several people which we call *group* communication. There are various forms of *mass* communication: telephone, telegraph, radio, TV, cable that make up *electronic* communication; books, magazines, newspapers that form the *print* media. There are even skywriting, clothing systems, and on and on.

We will concentrate upon one particular communication system here—*public speaking*—and your purpose will be to sharpen your skills in using this particular system. We hope you will become a more confident and expert public speaker, able to meet the challenges of a variety of public speaking tasks. Before you begin, however, it would be wise to step back a bit first, to see how communication systems function. In that way you'll be aware of these processes as you face the challenges and satisfactions of becoming an articulate person.

MODELS OF COMMUNICATION SYSTEMS

A model is nothing more than a picture or representation of a thing or a process. A model identifies the key parts or elements and indicates how each element affects the operation of all the other elements. A communication system can be reduced to such a model—in fact, to many models, depending upon what aspects of communication are of principal interest.

For example, one of the earliest definitions of communication came from the Greek philosopher-teacher Aristotle (384-322 B.C.). He defined communication, then called "rhetoric," as "the faculty of observing in any given case the available means of persuasion" (*Rhetoric* 1335b). With his stress upon "observing in any given case the available means" and with his long lists of things a speaker might want to say when talking in the Greek law courts and assemblies, his was a *speaker-centered* model of communication. Translating some of his Greek concepts into more contemporary language, his model looked essentially like this:

FIGURE 1.1 Aristotle's Model[2]

A SPEAKER discovers logical, emotional, and ethical proofs,

    arranges those materials strategically,

       clothes the ideas in clear and compelling words, and

         delivers the resulting speech appropriately.

As time passed, more and more rhetoricians or communication theorists became less concerned with the speaker or writer, and more concerned with types and contents of actual messages. For example, in the late eighteenth and nineteenth centuries the so-called "belletristic" approach to communication education developed in the schools. After learning as much as they could about language—its origins, its main elements, and its eloquent use—students were put through a series of exercises. These began with the construction of relatively simple descriptive passages, then moved on to more complicated historical narratives, and culminated in the writing of argumentative, persuasive, and literary works.

All of this emphasis upon preparing various kinds of messages led to *message-centered* theories of communication, theories which could be used to describe both oral and written discourse. The simplest and most influential message-centered model of our time came from David Berlo:

FIGURE 1.2   **Berlo's Model**[3]

A **Source** encodes a **MESSAGE** for a **Receiver** who decodes it,
or, the **S-M-R** model

The little model was useful for the post-World War II world of communication study for several reasons: (1) The idea of "source" was flexible
enough to include oral, written, electronic, or any other kind of "symbolic" generator-of-messages. (2) "Message" was made the central element;
that is, the transmission of *ideas* could be stressed. (3) The model
recognized that "receivers" were important to communication, for they
were the targets. And (4), the notions of "encoding" and "decoding" put
stress on the problems we all have (psycholinguistically) in "translating"
our own thoughts into words or other symbols and in deciphering the
words or symbols of others into terms we ourselves can understand.

The model was (and still is) popular. It does, however, tend to stress the
manipulation of the message—the encoding and decoding processes; it
almost implies that human communication is like machine communication, like signal-sending in telephone, television, computer, and radar
systems. It even seems to stress that most problems in human communication can be solved by technical accuracy—by choosing the "right"
symbols, preventing interference, and sending efficient messages.

But the problems of human communication are not as simple as that.
Even when we know what words mean and choose the right ones, we still
can misunderstand each other, because we all have different experiences
and interests in life. Even when a message is completely clear and
understandable, we often don't like it. Problems in "meaning" or "meaningfulness" often aren't a matter of comprehension, but of reaction, of
agreement, of shared concepts, beliefs, attitudes, values. To put the *com-
back* into communication, we need a *meaning-centered* theory of communication. While there are many such theories, perhaps one of the simplest
was that offered by theorist Wilbur Schramm in 1954:

FIGURE 1.3 **Schramm's Model[4]**

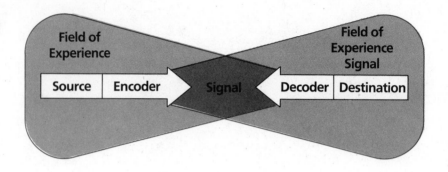

This model is elegant, in that it pictures the meaning-sharing process simply and graphically. It essentially argues that, in any given signal (message), you and I will comprehend and understand each other to the degree that our "fields of experiences" (interests, feelings, values, goals, purposes, information, ideas) overlap. That is, we can communicate in any given situation only to the degree that our *prior* experiences are similar.

Now we're getting somewhere. But before we assume we have frozen interhuman communication in a simple process, we must take into account three other aspects of people-talk: feedback, context, and culture.

Feedback First, we must remember that communication is usually a two-way path. Most communication systems these days allow receivers to feed back or return messages to sources.

We all have been taught a multitude of ways for sending messages back to communicators. Some of these methods are very *direct*, as when you talk in direct response to someone. Others are only *moderately direct*; you might squirm when a speaker drones on and on, wrinkle your nose and scratch your head when a message is too abstract, or shift your body position when you think it's your turn to talk. Still other kinds of feedback are completely *indirect*. For example, politicians discover if they're getting across by the number of votes cast on the first Tuesday in November; commercial sponsors examine sales figures to gauge their communicative effectiveness in ads; teachers measure their abilities to get the message across in a particular course by seeing how many students sign up for it the next term. Direct, moderately direct, and indirect feedback all offer opportunities to make a communication system work in both directions.

Context   A message may have different meanings, depending upon the specific context or setting. The message "Let's get out of here" has one meaning when uttered cooingly by a member of the opposite sex at a dull party, but quite another when snarled angrily in front of a waiter who has been providing bad service. Shouting "Fire!" on a rifle range produces one set of reactions—reactions quite different from those produced in a crowded theatre. Meaning depends in part on context or situation.[5]

Culture   Finally, a message may have different meanings associated with it, depending upon the culture or society. Each culture has its own *rules* for interpreting communicative signals. A hearty belch after a dinner in Skokie, Illinois, is a sign of impoliteness; but it is a supreme compliment to the host or hostess in other cultures. Negotiating the price of a T-shirt at Macy's is unheard of; yet it is a sign of active interest in an Istanbul bazaar or a neighborhood garage sale. Communication systems, thus, operate within the confines of cultural rules and expectations to which we all have been educated.

When we add the ideas of feedback, context, and culture to some of the other elements of communication we have been discussing, we come up with a model which looks like this:

FIGURE 1.4   A Contextual-Cultural Model

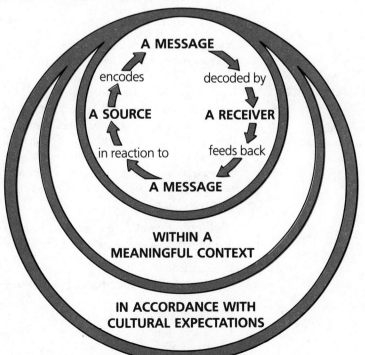

Our model now includes all the elements of a communication system that we need. To understand how systems operate, though, you also must keep in mind some of the characteristics of the elements we have alluded to:

1. *Sources* and *receivers* hold differing bundles of beliefs, attitudes, values, expectations, skills.
2. *Messages* are encoded into a variety of symbol systems (words, gestures, tones of voice, pictures, bodily postures).
3. *Contexts* or situations provide almost innumerable cues that help receivers interpret what is being said or done.
4. *Cultures* provide even more complex rules for offering and interpreting messages.

PUBLIC SPEAKING AS A COMMUNICATION SYSTEM

The model we have built can be applied to any sort of communication system—interpersonal, group, print, electronic, and so on. It is now time to narrow our scope and examine the peculiarities of public speaking as a communication system. Focusing a bit will help you examine the special relationships between you as the source/speaker and the receivers/audience. These peculiarities affect you every time you stand up for a few minutes to say what's on your mind.

Let's look again at the communication model we have built and see how its various elements function in the communication system of public speaking:

A source encodes a message for receivers who decode it within a meaningful context in accordance with cultural expectations.

A source . . .

Most important, the source in public speaking is a breathing, feeling, sometimes unsure yet concerned human being. When you speak publicly, you are a living idea. You literally stand for what you say. That's why there's often no good substitute for a public talk. Other media are too impersonal, too sterile; and they can't be talked back to in quite the same way. Public speaking will never disappear, even in the Age of Electricity and the Era of Xerox. A speaker has "oral presence." Learn to use it effectively.

Encodes . . .

Another feature of public speaking is that it is a *multimedia* communication system. Messages are sent to audiences via four primary channels:

1. Linguistic—words
2. Paralinguistic—sounds and tones of voice that add feelings and emphasis to words
3. Nonverbal—gestures, facial expressions, postures
4. Visual—flipcharts, chalkboard drawings, illustrative objects, and the like

In addition, audiences can react to messages that come through *secondary media:* fashion (the way you're dressed and its appropriateness); aromatics (yes, the way you smell for audience members close in); touch (it's not only for showmanship that evangelists touch their congregations). The speaker, therefore, bombards an audience with a series of messages across a number of channels.

One of your principal tasks, indeed, is to make sure that all of your messages reinforce each other. What you say and how you say it ought to tell an audience the same thing. Are your words angry but your voice unsure? Are you telling your audience to get involved while you hide behind a lectern? Such contradictory messages confuse an audience. Thus it's your job to coordinate your messages as you encode them into words, sounds, gestures, and visuals.

A message for . . .

You are speaking, after all, because you have something to say. A speech or talk exists because you, as one human being, know something, feel something, think something, wish to interpret something, want to argue or disagree with someone else, hope to persuade someone, or desire to move someone to action. Because you know/feel/think/wish/want/hope/desire, you build a message in the form of a speech. You could, of course, have chosen some other form—a telegram, a letter, or a TV ad. But you have chosen a speech: It allows you to address a fair number of people—with any luck at all—in a relatively inexpensive, open atmosphere. Because you, in a sense, are intruding upon those audience members, a speech as a message normally has certain characteristics.

A *speech-message has form.* It has a beginning, a middle, and an end. It starts by engaging an audience's interests, curiosity, feelings, and mind; it then moves into the information, ideas, arguments, and images that form the body of the message; and it finishes with final appeals, summaries, challenges. With a beginning, a middle, and an end, a speech-message carries an audience along through a coherent, structured thought.

A *speech-message is primarily verbal.* Even though you use all four channels mentioned earlier, a speech's main strength is its words. Words have the power to encapsulate ideas, visualize problems and solutions, hammer out arguments for or against. Language is an amazingly flexible instrument of communication, and hence is the speaker's main weapon.

A *speech-message has a purpose.* The audience attending an art show may ask, "I wonder what the artist meant by that?" But the audience listening to a speaker usually has some idea of the message's purpose. The setting may suggest the purpose (e.g., you generally know what a preacher's purpose is on Sunday morning). The purpose may be suggested by the speaker's reputation. On many occasions the purpose is publicly announced in a statement or in publicity for the speech. Even if the audience is unsure of the purpose, it can ask—something it can't do to a television set.

Receivers . . .   It is tempting to think of the speaker's receivers, the audience, in terms of a football analogy. If only we could visualize the speaker-quarterback throwing the message-football to the audience-receiver. If that were all there is to speaking, any reasonably sensitive speaker would throw a touchdown pass every time. But alas, an audience is not a passive, homogeneous pass-receiver. Strictly speaking, there is no such thing as "an audience." There is, instead, a collection of individuals—you and I and he and she and us and them and others. Each person sitting out there is an individual much like you, with his or her own experiences, hopes, desires, shortcomings, virtues, vices, and life to live. Some of them are wishy-washy, willing to believe almost anything you say. Others are bullheaded, immune to the most eloquent pleas and the most hard-nosed factual evidence. Most are somewhere in between these extremes.

Perhaps your primary job as a speaker is finding ways to target a speech to the interests and needs of the many individuals and groups that make up an audience. You can never reach everyone in a speech. You'd have to talk with them one at a time, interpersonally, to do that. About all any speaker can hope to do, therefore, is to make a decent impression on at least a significant number of them.

As we move through this book, we will have a good deal more to say about audiences. Because audience analysis is an essential step in speech preparation, we will suggest ways of identifying audience interests and needs, and adapting your speech to them. With forethought and planning, and with sensitivity to the people in your audience, you can improve your chances to actually communicate—to share experience.

Who decode it . . .   If encoding a speech involves casting a message into the four primary channels of public speaking (linguistic, paralinguistic, nonverbal, and visual), then decoding calls for reversing the process. To decode a message, a listener must—

- Perceive—observe the speaker's words, gestures, tones of voice, and visual aids;
- Reconstruct—blend those minimessages into the overall message;
- Expand—try to fill in the parts that were missed when the listener looked out the window or thought about what happened last night;
- Judge—decide what was meant and whether the message is acceptable or unacceptable, useful or useless, reasonable or unreasonable, and so on.[6]

Decoding, then, is a highly complex psychological process, involving *perception, reconstruction, expansion,* and *judgment*—all going on at the same time. It is no wonder that teachers discover at exam time that their explanations were misunderstood; that politicians often have to explain and re-explain what they meant; and that world leaders discuss the same problems perennially. Decoding is a process that can break down in a lot of ways. Words can be misheard. A significant vocal tone (e.g., of irony) may not be blended in. A key phrase can be missed when minds wander. Or prejudice can get in the way of interpretation. Because these and other psychological processes and problems—often called "communication noise" in theoretical essays—are extremely important to you as speaker, the previews in this book will help you think a bit about basic psychology.

Within a meaningful context . . .

Earlier we talked about context in terms of particular settings. In preparing speeches, you need to think of the traditions or rules that apply in each particular context. Then you must adapt your speech and yourself to them. If you are a nurse talking with a group of patients ready to start a physical therapy program, then you must be sensitive to ways nurses are supposed to talk in that setting. In a professional setting, we expect nurses to be sympathetic, knowledgeable about procedures but deferent to doctors, helpful, cheerful, and "clean." That's a heavy stereotype for them to carry around. Yet if they do not reflect those behaviors and ideals in their professional communications, they'll be less effective as a result. The same holds true in innumerable other settings—city council chambers, student newspaper offices, political rallies, schoolrooms, courtrooms. To one degree or another, all contexts contain rules for "proper" communication by "proper" speakers.

We can think of "contexts" in another way, too. As you scan the Table of Contents for this book, you'll notice words like "defining," "demonstrating," "explaining," and so forth. These words represent, not the physical contexts, but the *communicative contexts* for public speaking. They're contexts in the sense that audiences habitually *expect* certain things from, say, a definer—things that are different from the expectations audiences have for a reporter or an arguer or a leader of a group meeting.

Think, for a moment, of public messages you have heard recently. Do you ever think a TV reporter is doing a good or a lousy job? Have you noted that Mr. Jones was a pompous, tyrannical chairperson? Have you said, "That was the best sermon I've heard in years!" or "If that instructor expects me to understand, he'll have to explain that in plain English"? When you make remarks of this kind, you're demonstrating your own sensitivity to "proper" communication in particular communicative contexts, at least in part. You are already aware of many of the "rules" for demonstrating, reporting, leading, explaining, and arguing. Indeed, this book's major purpose is to make you even more sensitive than you already are to communicative contexts and their rules. Being aware of audience expectations in various contexts—and adapting yourself and your message to those expectations—is what this book is all about.

In accordance with cultural expectations.

For now, at least, you are operating within the culture of twentieth-century America. Communication in this culture is different from that of nineteenth-century America, as well as from communication in Near Eastern bazaars and Japanese councils. The general expectations for the articulate person described in Preview 1 are the cultural expectations you are trying to live up to, regardless of physical or communicative context.

This is not to say, however, that encoding a message for receivers this year is simply a matter of following the seven advisory points in Preview 1. Remember that the United States of America is not quite the "melting pot" we once imagined it to be. Rather, we are a diversified set of cultures, a society marked by cultural pluralism. Those cultures are sometimes defined by age, sometimes by sex, sometimes by educational level, sometimes by ethnic background, and sometimes by money, by power, by professional title and achievement.

With some topics, the different groups to which we each belong will affect what we expect from speakers. So, if I'm listening to a speech on day-care centers, my membership in the social group called "parents" is a pertinent factor. If the subject is governmental spending for education, my job as a university professor comes into play. If the subject is immigration laws, my childhood experiences of picking potatoes and hoeing sugar beets with Chicano "migrant" workers and of working with Chicano community leaders on agricultural housing and clothing projects will spring to mind. And the same with other topics: my economic position, if the topic is revision of welfare programs; my Norse background, if the subject is genealogy or the settling of the Midwest; my life in Iowa, if the subject is agribusiness and the family farm. Faced with the diversity of cultural groupings in our society, a speaker often needs to adapt a message to cultural experiences and expectations.

In recognizing the cultural pluralism of our society, remember that there are few universal rules for adapting your speeches to that fact. Should you always speak in "street language" to teenagers and in a more reserved, respectful idiom to the elderly? Must a classroom speech or lecture always be formal? Should a black politician or a Latino precinct captain always try to appear conciliatory—to appear "white"? The answer to these questions, of course, is that *it depends*—upon you, upon your relationship with the audience, upon your topic, and so on. The bottom line is this: watch these and other groups in action; talk to members of these groups; listen to other speakers address them; and be sensitive to the behaviors (verbal and nonverbal "feedback") of audience members. If you are alert and observant, you usually can discover whether you're meeting cultural expectations. If you watch, talk, listen, and feel, you're liable to be more accommodating and effective.

Public speaking, therefore, has its own challenges, strengths, and weaknesses as a communication system. As you use this system, you will be affected by many of its special characteristics: (1) the *source* is present in person; (2) *encoding* is a multi-channel process; (3) the *message* is formal, verbal, and purposive; (4) the *receivers* are diverse, yet one; (5) *decoding* depends upon the state of mind of the audience; (6) both *physical and*

communicative contexts set the rules for success; and (7) *cultural expectations* affect the way the message is received. If you think about these factors
all at once, you can be scared to death. You can, however, sit back,
consider them one at a time, and review specific parts of your speech with
each one in mind. If you carefully plan your speeches in this way, you can
overcome such fears. Planning and preparation, practice and self-respect
can combine to make you an articulate person.

This book is designed to help you achieve that goal. Chapters 2, 3, and
4 will present the steps involved in planning and preparing for a speech,
attempting to demystify that process. These chapters preach hard, systematic work as the way to gain self-confidence and to maximize your chances
for talking successfully in public. Previews II, III, and IV provide basic
information on the use of language, audience psychology and reasoning,
and American rituals. These will prepare you for speaking to offer
information and to affect the minds and actions of others. Each part
contains a series of chapters concentrating upon what we have called
communicative contexts. They also provide the sample outlines or "recipes" we talked about in Preview I.

If you engage in the hard work, master the sample forms, and think
about expectations each time you rise to speak, we're confident you will be
ready to help your society through its confusion and troubles. You will be
an articulate person.

NOTES

[1] For a sophisticated-yet-enjoyable discussion of the differences between "signs"
and "symbols," see Susanne K. Langer, *Philosophy in a New Key: A Study in the
Symbolism of Reason, Rite, and Art* (Mentor Book, 1942; new ed. New York: New
American Library of World Literature, Inc., 1951), Chap. 2, "Symbolic Transformation," pp. 33–54.

[2] Aristotle's speaker-centered model received perhaps its fullest development in
the hands of Roman educator Quintilian (ca. 35–95 A.D.), whose *Institutio
Oratoria* was filled with advice even on the full training of a "good" speaker-
statesman.

[3] Simplified from David K. Berlo, *The Process of Communication* (New York:
Holt, Rinehart, and Winston, 1960).

[4] From Wilbur Schramm, "How Communication Works," in *The Process and
Effects of Communication*, ed. Wilbur Schramm (Urbana: Univ. of Ill. Press,
1954), pp. 3–26.

[5] For an expanded *situational* theory of communication, see Lloyd Bitzer, "The
Rhetorical Situation," *Philosophy & Rhetoric*, 1 (Winter 1968), 1-14, as well as his
expansion of his original ideas in "Functional Communication: A Situational
Perspective," in *Rhetoric in Transition: Studies in the Nature and Uses of Rhetoric*,
ed. Eugene E. White (University Park: Penn. State Univ. Press, 1980), pp. 21–38.

[6] For an enlarged discussion of these psychological processes, see Douglas
Ehninger, Bruce E. Gronbeck, Ray E. McKerrow, and Alan H. Monroe,

Principles and Types of Speech Communication, 9th ed. (Glenview, Ill.: Scott, Foresman and Co., 1982), Chap. 2, "Listening: Speaker-Audience Interaction."

[*One final note:* We have drawn upon relatively simple communication models in this chapter to illustrate only the most basic features of public talk. Those wishing the intellectual challenges of deciphering and discussing sophisticated models are urged to see C. David Mortensen, *Communication: The Study of Human Communication* (New York: McGraw-Hill Book Company, 1972), Chap. 2, "Communication Models."]

CHAPTER 2

Preparing to Speak

In an era when companies try to hold down the costs of manufacturing by only partially assembling the lawn mower or the child's toy oven, and in a time when many of us are seized by do-it-yourself-in-six-easy-steps thinking, the notion of building a speech should not be a strange one. By now, you have participated for many years in our insert-Tab-A-in-Slot-1A23 culture. You probably have even overcome your natural fear of inserting the right tab in the wrong slot. Of course, you could hire a person to put together the lawn mower or pay a higher price for a preassembled oven. Similarly, you could go through life hiring ghostwriters to put together your speeches. You'll probably do that, however, only if you're an extraordinarily busy or rich public person—a politician, a corporate executive, a pressure group's mouthpiece. Most of us must build our own talks. Therefore, the purpose of the next two chapters is to take you step by step through the speech-building process.

There will be no magic formulas presented here. The task occasionally will be irksome and frustrating. At other times you'll speak on the spur of the moment, without the luxury of planning. And, of course, because you are you and not someone else, you might not always go through the following steps in precisely the order suggested. Nevertheless, the discussions in the next two chapters can be both useful and demystifying, if you use the directions for what they are—a checklist of factors you should consider when you build a speech. Anyone who can insert tabs into slots also can insert ideas into speeches.

We will discuss ten basic steps in the preparation of a speech:

1. Selecting a topic
2. Determining the purposes
3. Narrowing a topic
4. Analyzing the audience
5. Finding materials
6. Selecting actual materials
7. Organizing the speech strategically
8. Wording the principal ideas and appeals
9. Preparing to deliver the speech
10. Practicing the presentation

Here in Chapter 2, we will discuss the first five steps, which focus on general preparation. In Chapter 3 we will examine Steps 6 and 7, which involve actual construction of a speech. Finally, Chapter 4 will take up the matters of wording, delivery, and practice.

SELECTING A TOPIC

Through most of your adult life, selecting a topic is no problem. If you're speaking at a public hearing on a proposed rezoning of your neighborhood, you don't select a topic; it is built into the meeting. Or, if you are asked to give a monthly sales report, your boss has chosen the topic for you.

Yet, there are some occasions when you will have to do some choosing. In a speech class such as this one, of course, you must do it. Or, if you're invited to talk about your college major at a Rotary Club, should you discuss communication training and the business world or liberal arts education and preparation for life? If you are invited to the campus Environmental and Research Group, should you stress its collective lobbying power, its ability to launch a more effective informational campaign across the community, or the efforts each individual can make to clean up a local river? When talking with a local church group interested in helping to settle recent Southeast Asian immigrants, should you address short-range needs such as food, clothing, shelter, and befriendment, or such long-range requirements as jobs, the maintenance of dual-cultural identity, education, and community acceptance? In such settings, you have some selecting to do.

Selecting a topic, then, is your first decision-point. Among all the possible topics, how do you choose a workable one? A good topic normally must meet three tests for appropriateness.

Source Test

First, the topic must be appropriate to the speaker—you. It must be a subject you are interested in, committed to, and knowledgeable about. Because you are a living embodiment of your speech, your enthusiasms, feelings, ideas, and beliefs must show through. Spend a little time searching your own heart, mind, and experience for a topic that means something to you. You'll be spending a fair amount of time on your speech, so give yourself and your listeners the advantages of dealing with material that you're concerned about.

Receiver Test

Next, the topic must be appropriate to your audience. You must decide if it's possible to get the listeners interested or excited. Actually, that *if* should be thought of as a *how*:

- How can you tap the listeners' *interests?*
- How can you *motivate* them to listen, tapping their hopes, fears, daily or long-range concerns, beliefs, attitudes, or values?
- How can you extend their present *knowledge* in useful ways?

For example, you may believe that scuba diving is the sport of the century, but here you are, with an audience no closer than 120 miles from a decent-sized body of water. What can you do to make the presentation interesting? Show and demonstrate the equipment? How about trying to motivate them to try the sport themselves: Tell them about instruction and rental? Show them underwater slides? Stress the healthiness of the activity? And, what do they need to know? If they have no background in scuba diving, what do they need to know first? second? third? As you probe these and other questions, your eye always should be on the concept of *relevance*: If you absolutely cannot relate the topic in some significant way to the lives of your listeners you'd better not use it.

Occasion Test

Finally, the topic must be appropriate to the setting and occasion. While it might be fun to see a president-elect do a James Cagney imitation during an inaugural address, it would definitely flunk the occasion test. By now, we all have rather firm ideas about what is and is not appropriate at inaugurations. Or, when introducing a guest speaker to the Chicano Student Union, you know you are expected to talk about that person's background and accomplishments, not your own. And, if a city council is discussing a no-smoking ordinance, you would commit both a social and a parliamentary faux pas if you gave a little speech on chuckholes in Main Street. That, too, would flunk the occasion test, because the subject would not be appropriate to the announced purpose of the meeting.

Selecting a topic, in other words, is more than just dreaming up a subject. It's a matter of examining your own talents and interests, the interest and knowledge levels of the audience, and the traditions and rules governing the occasion.

DETERMINING A PURPOSE

Once you know what you want to talk about, the next question you face is "Why?" Actually, there are many *whys*. Why do you want to talk about this subject? Why would anyone want to hear you talk about it? Why might your ideas and plans be able to help some audience through a difficult question? These are tough questions. But, frankly, if you're going to have something to say *worth* sharing with people already deluged by too many messages, then you'd better discover some answers. You can answer those questions by thinking first about general speaking purposes and then about more specific purposes.

General Speaking Purposes

General purposes are the basic types of communicative acts public speakers perform. When speaking publicly, one usually has in mind one of three main general purposes or reasons for speaking: One can speak to *inform*; one can speak to *persuade*; one can speak to *celebrate*.

Informative Speaking Informative speaking is characterized primarily by "newness." It attempts to present concepts, processes, or ideas that an audience does not yet know or understand, or to demonstrate processes and procedures audience members do not know how to carry out. In informative speeches, speakers may define or outline new ideas, demonstrate unfamiliar procedures, offer reports on matters of importance, or explain something unknown to others. Thus, *definitional* speeches, *demonstrative* speeches, *reportive* speeches, and *explanatory* speeches represent four primary types of informative speeches. These will be the general types of informational messages we will discuss in Chapters 5 and 6. Overall, your job as an informative speaker will be to assemble and package information so that it is clear, coherent, and relevant to audiences.

Persuasive Speaking Persuasive speaking is marked basically by "change." It attempts to reshape, rebuild, or reorient the beliefs, attitudes, values, and behaviors that are already in the audience. In persuasive speeches, speakers may attempt to argue for an idea, refute the ideas of others, change people's attitudes, or move them to action. *Argumentative*, *refutative*, *attitudinal*, and *actuative* speeches are four major types of persuasive speeches, which will be treated more fully in Chapters 8, 9, 10, and 11. In addition, there is a special type of speech which is half informative, and half persuasive; it is the speech often presented to friendly audiences, reminding them of what they already know and believe and often asking them to act positively on that knowledge and those beliefs. It's called a *reinforcement* speech; because it relies on little new knowledge but on a good deal of psychological motivation, it will be treated as a type of persuasive speaking in Chapter 7. In general, then, your job as a persuasive speaker will be to change your listeners' minds about beliefs, attitudes, values, and actions you deem misguided or inappropriate.

Celebratory Speaking Celebratory speaking is marked basically by "tradition," even "oldness." Societies, and groups in societies, hold fundamental beliefs and attitudes, even values and ideologies or myths, which define what it means to be members of those societies or groups.

FIGURE 2.1   **General Speaking Purposes**

Inform
Build new definitions of concepts (*defining*)

Demonstrate new or unfamiliar techniques or processes (*demonstrating*)

Report information or policy alternatives (*reporting*)

Offer rationales or explanations unfamiliar to audiences (*explaining*)

Persuade
Emphasize the importance of acting upon old beliefs and values (*reinforcing*)

Change the audience's basic beliefs, attitudes, or values (*changing attitudes*)

Change the audience's behavior by getting them either to begin or to stop
doing something (*moving to action*)

Argue for some belief, attitude, or policy (*arguing*)

Argue against a belief, attitude, or policy offered by someone else (*refuting*)

Celebrate
Honor a person (*Offering tribute*)

Honor ideals (*dedicating*)

Honor group membership and goals (*keynoting*)

Honor a new leader (*inaugurating*)

Societies and organizations occasionally stop what they are doing, to
celebrate themselves and who they are by dedicating a statue to a
community leader, by ritualistically reciting their fundamental tenets as in
Fourth of July or Martin Luther King Day ceremonies, by electing new
leaders or standard-bearers as in political conventions. Public speeches
inevitably play a major role in ceremonies and rituals, perhaps because we
still believe almost magically in the Power of the Spoken Word, as did the
ancient Greeks and Hebrews. In Chapter 12, especially, we will discuss
several types of celebratory addresses, such as *dedications*, *tributes*,
keynotes, and *inaugurals*.

This book treats informative, persuasive, and celebratory speaking
separately because they have relatively distinct general purposes, even
though they all overlap in many ways. For example, an "informative"

speech on the sodium nitrate content of bacon may persuade several audience members to change their behavior—to quit eating processed bacon. Or, a "persuasive" speech on the desirability of building city bike paths undoubtedly will contain information new to some listeners. And, a good keynote address should serve such persuasive goals as getting the party-faithful to work during the general election campaign or getting big spenders to support a candidate financially.

Even though a speech may, in effect, *serve* more than one purpose, we can usually speak of it as *having* a dominant focus. The point is not to neatly categorize speeches. Rather, identifying a basic or general or primary purpose is useful because that purpose determines your principal strategies and speaking techniques. Audience members bring different *sets of expectations* to bear on you and your message, depending on whether you're defining, demonstrating, reporting, explaining, reinforcing, arguing, refuting, changing attitudes, moving to action, or celebrating. Thinking about general purposes alerts you to the special communicative challenges of each kind of speech—to the materials and strategies you'll need to choose as you move through the other preparatory steps.

Specific Speaking Purposes   A second important way to think about purposes is to consider specific purposes—the goals you set for a particular speech on a particular topic before a particular audience on a particular occasion. Specific purposes are *the concrete goals you are attempting to achieve.* Even for a single speech, you can have several different kinds of specific purposes.

Suppose, for example, that you decided to inform members of your food cooperative about the virtues of baking your own bread by demonstrating how it's done. Your *general purpose* would be informative, achieved by doing a demonstration speech. But, you might well have many specific purposes (concrete goals) as well:

Some of your goals might be *public* (related to the audience); others might be *private* (related to your sense of personal achievement):

• PUBLIC GOALS: "I want to demonstrate a quick, easy, foolproof way of making healthful, delicious, homemade bread."
• PRIVATE GOALS: ("I want to demonstrate that I can make a successful presentation. I hope members of the co-op will know me better and be more impressed with me after this speech.")

Some of your goals might be *short-term*, and some, *long-term*:

• SHORT-TERM GOALS: "I want all of you to immediately go home, with bags of flour, sugar, natural vitamin supplements, and yeast, and try out this recipe before you forget it!"
• LONG-TERM GOALS: "We all must change our food-buying and food-consuming habits if we are to save money and avoid the potentially harmful food additives in processed foods."

And, some purposes might be *goal-directed*, some *group-directed*:

- GOAL-DIRECTED: "I want to show you how to bake bread."
- GROUP-DIRECTED: (Often unstated: "I want us to feel a sense of group solidarity from participating together in a warm mini-society in this co-op. Mutual projects benefit us all.")

A speech, then, can have any number of concrete purposes. Some may even seem contradictory, as when a parent is firm or even angry with a child as a way of showing love. Keep in mind, further, that *all* of these kinds of specific purposes can affect the way you talk in public. Some of your private purposes can occasionally threaten to destroy your grandiose public purposes. For example, an overpowering focus on proving your skill as a speaker, on proving yourself, can take your attention away from your public goal of helping an audience learn something. Or, while you may not really feel much satisfaction from achieving a short-term purpose (getting a bunch of incoming freshmen to fill out a computerized registration card properly), you could find enormous pleasure in helping them because you know of potential long-term effects on them—a college degree, increased self-confidence, perhaps a better life. And, even though you might think your goal-directed purpose is minor, you must never forget the meaning of the word *communication*, the idea of sharing experience for the common good. Every little shared experience—even a lot of seemingly unimportant ones—adds a few ounces of humanity to those who listen. All of these specific purposes get stirred together when you stand up to speak, and to various degrees they all affect the impact of your message.

You need to explore both general and specific purposes, therefore, before you start to shape the actual speech and its materials. Clearly setting your general purpose helps you select materials and structure them. Being aware of your specific purposes allows you to come to grips honestly and consciously with your own motives and actions, and with their effects on what you say and how you say it.

NARROWING A TOPIC

Armed with a topic and a hatful of purposes, you are ready for the next step: to think about limits on what you're going to say. Obviously, you cannot possibly say all there is to say about something in a few short minutes, so you must narrow your topic. In deciding how to do that, three primary factors should be taken into account:

1. TIME LIMITS: Fit the "size" of the idea to time restrictions. How many ideas, facts and figures, and illustrations can you orally present to an audience in five minutes? ten minutes? fifteen minutes? Even if there are no time limits to a presentation, you still might want to heed the wise old preacher's advice: "If you don't strike oil in twenty minutes, quit boring."

2. PURPOSES: Think about your specific purposes in narrowing a topic. Suppose you're attacking the mythical savings that "10¢ off" food coupons provide consumers. If that's your purpose, you certainly don't need to talk about how grocery stores get their refunds, how the quaint little old ladies of White Bear Lake, Minnesota, make an excellent living sorting out those coupons for food companies, or how various companies code the coupons in order to determine their best advertising strategies. You may know a lot about those topics, but they're irrelevant to your specific goal.

3. AUDIENCE BACKGROUND: Take into account the audience's level of previous knowledge in narrowing your topic. If you're doing an informative travelogue on Mexico aimed at inexperienced travelers, you might generally describe different kinds of tourist attractions throughout the country. But, for an audience of people who have been to Mexico you might wish to concentrate and provide much more specific details, say, only on the Baja peninsula area.

Narrowing a topic, in other words, involves chopping away materials which, however interesting, do not fit your time limits, your purposes, or your audience. So, how do you actually go about narrowing a topic? Suppose you were going to talk informatively about vegetable gardening. That's a big topic, one that could generate any number of narrower topics, including the following:

- the growth of private gardening over the last decade (facts and figures on clubs, seed sales, expanded fertilizer and canning industries)
- methods for preserving homegrown vegetables (canning vs. freezing vs. drying vs. salting)
- enriching the soil (types of natural and artificial fertilizers available, the virtues and problems of each)
- factors to consider when selecting vegetables to plant (questions of plot size, family eating patterns, amount of time available for tending, availability and cost of supermarket vegetables)
- selecting among the varieties of any given vegetable (considering such factors as geographic location, length of growing season, kinds of regional pests and bacteria, storage considerations, germination and hardiness of varieties)
- kinds of literature available on gardening (library books, government pamphlets, magazines, seed catalogs, fertilizer company brochures)
- kinds of gardening tools (inexpensive hand tools, medium-cost hand-powered machines, expensive power machinery)
- year-round gardening (window box gardening, "grow" lights, cold frames, hot frames, greenhouses)

Each of these topics, in turn, could be further narrowed, depending upon time limits, your purposes, and audience background. And, notice one more thing about most of these: Within each are several different subtopics, which help you narrow even more. So, for example, instead of discussing all five kinds of year-round gardening, you could concentrate only upon types of background greenhouses or types of cold frames which can be made for under $100.

ANALYZING THE AUDIENCE

The most crucial step in speech preparation is audience analysis. Selecting the topic, setting the purposes, and narrowing the topic have all taken the audience into consideration; and, most of the decisions you will make in the remaining steps follow as well from audience analysis.

Audience analysis is important for two reasons: (1) As the speaker or "source" of the message, you want to be able to forecast listeners' possible reactions to your ideas. (2) And, as a communicator interested in affecting others, you want to be able to guess at people's knowledge level or their psychological state so that you can adapt what you have to say to them; after all, you are speaking, most of the time, to have an effect on others.

How do you analyze your audience? Traditionally, speakers have engaged in essentially two kinds of audience analysis: *demographic analysis* and *psychological profiling*. This is because human beings have been studied both as members of (demographic) groups and as self-sufficient (psychologically independent) individuals. That is, people exist in a series of easily identifiable *roles* (male or female, parent or child, banker or educator, rich or poor person, Legionnaire, Presbyterian) and yet also exist as individual *beings* (who have unique personal experiences, beliefs, feelings, desires, attitudes).

As a speaker, then, you are interested in your audience as both a group and as individuals. Hence you must attempt to analyze audience members in both ways if you are going to have as much information as possible about your listeners.

Analyzing the Audience Demographically

Especially if an audience is composed of strangers, it is perhaps easier to begin with a demographic or group-related analysis, simply because you can often directly observe demographic characteristics. You can easily identify gender, age, ethnic background, group memberships (often), and the like. In doing a comparatively simple demographic analysis, you could ask such questions as the following:

Age Are there primarily young, middle-aged, or older people in the audience?

Gender Is the audience predominantly male or female?

Education Are many audience members likely to be well informed on my subject? And, do they have the educational background which should allow them to learn easily and quickly?

Group Membership Do these people represent or belong to groups that are known to possess certain kinds of information and attitudes?

Cultural and Ethnic Background Are audience members predominantly from identifiable cultural groups?

The key to demographic analysis for the speaker is not simply to answer these and similar questions. Rather, *the key here is to decide how, if at all, any of these demographic factors will affect people's ability and/or willingness to accept and understand what you want to say.* The key is to figure out which, if any, of these factors is *relevant*; if any are, you will want to *adapt* your message to it (or them).

For example, if you are addressing a group of four-year-olds at a pre-school, you obviously are going to (1) talk simply, (2) use many, many clarifying examples, and (3) be sure you do not try to present them with too many ideas at once. Or, if you are addressing a group of college-age females, you would be more than foolhardy if you employed sexist language, called them "girls," and assumed they all planned on being "homemakers." When President John F. Kennedy addressed a German audience when he visited the Berlin wall, he made sure he incorporated references to German history and used bits of German phraseology.

Group membership is often a particularly important factor. Occasionally, you may address homogeneous groups—a local nurses' society, the Chamber of Commerce or Rotary Club, a church congregation. If you do, you often can assume that members of your audience will hold several important beliefs, attitudes, and values in common, and that many of those affect their perception of and reaction to your message.

For example, suppose you are speaking for a Tenant's Union that would like financial support from your community's United Way campaign. The United Way Board of Directors is composed of people who, as a group, generally think that (1) local programs deserve local financial support, (2) human services should be delivered to those who need them as efficiently as possible, (3) unpaid volunteers help local organizations provide low-cost services, and (4) major support of an organization from prominent members of a community is a sign that the organization is healthy and valuable. Knowing that the Board of Directors generally is committed to these tenets will help you select and phrase the arguments which comprise your plea for financial support. You will increase your chance for success if you are able to argue convincingly that your Tenant's Union is local and not a puppet of some national organization; that your overhead costs as a student organization are low; that volunteers provide almost all the counseling and help for tenants in need; and that well-known law offices in the community are involved in helping your organization.

Demographic analysis, then, is one important analytical tool for the speaker, because it will help you select appeals or arguments and determine how to phrase key ideas.

Analyzing the Audience Psychologically

We will discuss audience psychology more completely in Part III. At this point, however, we need at least a rudimentary vocabulary for discussing audience psychology. Social scientists and professional analyzers often find it useful to divide people into psychological groups on the basis of fundamental beliefs, attitudes, and values. Because we will use those three terms throughout this book, we need to define them carefully.

Beliefs A belief is essentially a proposition or "fact" thought to be true or false. It has been accepted by people on such bases as first-hand experience, evidence they have read or heard, authorities who have told them it is true, or even blind faith. When we use the word "fact" to characterize our beliefs, we are saying a good deal about our *certitude*; that is, when we say "It's a fact that John is six feet tall" or "It's a fact that cuts in government spending will reduce inflation," we are telling our listener that we're very, very sure of those beliefs (even though the *actual* truth or falsity of those beliefs might be open to debate, as in the second proposition).

People's beliefs and their belief-structures, of course, are most important to their lives. If we did not believe such things as "The sun will rise tomorrow," "Honesty is the best policy," "What goes up must come down," and "The way I treat people today will affect the way they treat me tomorrow," we wouldn't function very well in this world. These sorts of beliefs are often *fixed*, are almost impossible to change.

Other beliefs, however, because they have been based on authority or faulty evidence or all-too-blind faith, are susceptible to change. You may believe that cuts in government spending will reduce inflation; that is a complex, causal belief that you probably learned from authorities or a basic economics course. If, however, a speaker is able to document several instances in various countries where government spending cuts actually increased inflation, then your belief may well be altered. Some of our beliefs, therefore, are "soft" or *variable. Indeed, one of the speaker's principal tasks in audience analysis is to determine which beliefs are fixed, and which are variable.* Only in that way will the speaker know which of the audience's fixed beliefs to use in defense of a case, and which of their variable beliefs might be changed to fulfill his or her purpose.

Attitudes Attitudes may be defined as feelings of positiveness or negativeness about some belief. They often are defined as predispositions to respond positively or negatively to some person, object, or idea; they express our preferences. Attitudes are expressed in such statements as "My dog's *better* than your dog," "Abortion is *wrong*," "I *hate* liars," "Cheating is *immoral*," "The Mona Lisa is a *beautiful* painting," "Public speaking is a *useful* course."

Because attitudinal statements express our preferences, our predispositions, our reactions, and our basic judgments, they represent the core of our psychological makeup. They often control our behavior, because we tend to do things we like or prefer and avoid things we dislike or hate. Also, we're only human, so most of us avoid even thinking about things (the suffering of others, death) we dislike or fear; we prefer instead to contemplate beautiful sights (a summer sunset), positive beliefs (a sense of our own goodness), and preferred associates (a close friend or lover). A speaker, therefore, is well advised to attempt to assess the dominant attitudes of audience members. That, of course, is often hard to do, for seldom are you able to give audiences a pencil-and-paper attitude "test" to discover precisely their preferences or predispositions. But, often, you can talk to a group leader, ask questions of several individuals who will be in the audience, or simply watch a group over a period of time as it discusses important matters; if you do these things, you probably can guess at important attitudes.

Values   Values may be defined as basic orientations to life—habitual ways of looking at the world or responding to problems. Values, in a sense, are psychologically "larger" than attitudes. Whereas attitudes represent particularized judgments about specific persons, objects, or ideas, values include broad categories into which many specific attitudes are grouped mentally. Thus, for example, a person may hold a specific attitude about abortion:

Attitude: "Abortion is wrong."

That attitude probably is held, however, because of the way the person conceives of abortion, because of the valuative category into which the person psychologically "puts" abortion:

Values: Abortion is primarily . . .

- a medical question [*scientific* value].
- a moral question [*religious* value].
- a question of a woman's right to control her own mind and body [*psychological* value].
- a matter of allowing groups in a society to make their own decisions without being dictated to by others [*sociological* value].
- something to be thought of only in life-or-death situations [*pragmatic* value].
- something to be decided by a nationwide referendum [*political* value].

Thus, a person's attitude, "Abortion is wrong," might be held because the person values scientific evidence which suggests a fetus can survive as a human being; because of religious authority which calls abortion murder; because the person thinks sociological, psychological, or pragmatic questions are irrelevant to abortion; or, because, politically, most people in this country may be opposed to abortion legislation.

Knowing, or trying to find out, what values members of your audience habitually bring to bear on issues you are discussing, then, is a most important part of audience analysis. Knowing, for example, that members of the Board of Directors of United Way are strongly motivated by sociological concerns (concerns for needy groups in society) and by pragmatic concerns (concerns for fiscal efficiency and responsibility) will help you construct your speech in support of the Tenant's Union.

In psychological analysis, then, as in demographic analysis, your main concern always is to discover, if possible, *relevant beliefs, attitudes, and values*. Obviously, you need not do a complete psychological inventory of everyone in the audience; rather, you are attempting to understand what beliefs, attitudes, and values might affect the ways listeners perceive and respond to your speech. Once you have decided what demographic and psychological characteristics are important to you and your purpose, you can write up audience analyses such as those in Figure 2.2.

FINDING MATERIALS

The final step in the general preparation for constructing a speech is to find the materials which actually will form the primary content of the speech. Many different kinds of materials might be useful to you. You might want to include:

- *quotations* from experts or from wise social commentators
- *statistical summaries* that describe a problem in quantified terms or that point to trends

---

FIGURE 2.2 **Sample Paragraphs Doing Audience Analysis**

Analysis of an Audience for a Speech on Gardening: To Inform

I am addressing a 4-H club [*group membership and age factors*]. Therefore, I probably can assume most have been exposed to the basics of gardening [*area with well-formed beliefs*], and probably even enjoy it [*positive attitudes*]. I can skip over the basics like planting and move to a more advanced topic about which they know less [*area with few beliefs*], such as various methods for preserving foods grown at home. I will review the four principal methods [*belief-goal*], and suggest the strengths and problems of each [*attitude-goal*].

Analysis of an Audience for a Speech on Food Chemicals: To Persuade

I am addressing food co-op members [*group membership factor*], which means most of these people probably are interested in economy, environmental issues, and "natural" methods [*basic beliefs*]. Furthermore, most probably are in favor of saving money rather than time, and are suspicious of "artificial" chemicals, fertilizers, and food additives [*basic attitudes*]. And, because the people all belong to this collective and have engaged in letter-writing campaigns before [*political and sociological values*], I can effectively advocate that we write to newspapers and legislators in support of State Senate Bill 1234 to regulate the use of chemicals in commercial food-processing [*persuasive purpose of the speech*].

- *various examples—*
short examples, often called *specific instances*, which are usually just listed quickly (as when you point out the seven fastest-growing cities in the country)

middle-sized examples, usually just called *examples* or *samples*, which are offered to an audience two or three at a time (as when you describe two or three "typical" types of students who are enrolling in a particular course)

extended examples, called *illustrations*, which serve as systematic, well-developed case studies (as when you use your own trip to France as a travelogue to describe five or six hazards to avoid in foreign travel)
- *both sorts of analogy*
literal analogies (or *parallel cases*), which compare point-by-point two similar cases (as when you urge your hometown public library to install videotape by reviewing the system operating in another town very much like yours)

figurative analogies, which compare things metaphorically (as when the universe is compared to a clock or the human body is described as a machine)

Because the uses of supporting materials are best discussed in connection with specific types of speeches and their demands, at this point we will not describe in detail ways to use these materials. Rather, when you are generally preparing to speak, your initial concern is simply to find possibly-usable materials. The question you face, for now, is: *Where* can I find good quotations, statistics, examples, analogies?

You as a Source   Start with yourself. If necessary, begin a list of what you know, believe, like, dislike, and value in relation to your topic. Especially if you engage in a topic-narrowing process (like the one we did on gardening), you'll find several areas about which you know a lot and have firm attitudes. Of course, starting with yourself has another virtue: it clarifies what you *don't* know and will need to learn.

Interviews   Talking with others is one of the principal ways of finding information—and one most of us forget about. If you need to know what your county is doing to help battered children, arrange an interview with a county social worker. If you would like background on the T-shirt craze, talk with the manager of a local iron-on shop. An owner of a bookstore undoubtedly would be glad to tell you about trends in fad diet books. Most "experts" such as these are really quite happy to grant you a brief interview; we all like to talk about ourselves and to be seen as authorities. To make the best use of an interview, know precisely what you want to ask. This preparation keeps you from wasting the person's time and helps you gain the precise information you want. It is also wise, if possible, to verify facts and figures given to you during the interview by consulting other sources.

Letters and Questionnaires

To gain some systematic information, you could make up a questionnaire or conduct a series of street interviews. That's kind of fun, really, and potentially very profitable. Suppose, for example, you were going to talk about the nuclear power plant proposed for construction in the county next to yours. Suppose, too, that you wished to include public attitudes toward it. To get at those attitudes, you could collect information in several ways: (1) stand on a street corner for a couple of hours, asking people how they feel about it; (2) go door to door in a few different neighborhoods, conducting your own survey; or (3) mail a one-page questionnaire (the shorter they are, the more likely they'll be returned) to members of certain groups, to city or county officials, or to people randomly selected from the phone book. If you start all this far enough ahead of time (and if you include stamped, self-addressed envelopes), you'll probably get some interesting, concrete information for your speech. Comparing responses from the general public with those from officials could even be startling.

Print Resources

The world of print can be a terrifying maze of books, magazines, reference works, documents, pamphlets, newspapers, and reports. Yet, it probably contains almost anything you might wish to know. The only way you can effectively use these resources is to choose print resources in terms of types. Different types of print resources are principally useful for finding different kinds of information.

Newspapers are primarily a source of information on current events, opinions, and "facts" about who/what/why. The larger newspapers have indexes to help you find accounts of people and happenings of national interest. The *New York Times*, for example, has a good index that goes back to 1913.

Magazines can also put you in touch with current materials. Newsmagazines, such as *Time* or *Newsweek*, report on the state of culture, politics, and the world week-by-week. Other magazines, such as *The Nation, Fortune,* or *The New Republic,* will background current economic, political, and social questions. *Popular Science, Scientific American,* and *Popular Mechanics* will describe in readable fashion scientific advancements or questions. And so on. With a specific topic or research problem in mind, you can go to a city or school library, consult either the *Readers' Guide to Periodical Literature* or a reference librarian, and undoubtedly find several magazine articles of use.

Yearbooks and encyclopedias are useful primarily for factual summaries: U.S. coal production, electoral results, crime statistics, Academy Award winners, and the like. In particular, *The Statistical Abstract of the United States* covers most subjects on which the federal government collects data. Other topics (Olympic medal winners, birth dates of famous people) are covered in more popularized yearbooks such as *World Almanac, Information Please, The People's Almanac,* and a host of others. Encyclopedias also can give you facts, but chiefly, they offer generally intelligible background information on what a thing or concept is, where it came from, and its current state. Keep in mind, though, that even good encyclopedias are often dated, and hence cannot be your only source.

Documents and reports are extremely useful for finding the opinions and policy recommendations of officials and authorities. The government documents section of your school library probably has a sizable collection of hearings, debates, and records. A librarian can help you find interesting expert testimony. City libraries usually have good collections of special reports issued by various institutions, commissions, institutes, and lobby groups, such as the Carnegie Foundation, the Hoover Institution, "Nader's Raiders," Common Cause, the U.S. Chamber of Commerce, the World Council of Churches, and the like. Such reports typically summarize or give background for problems. They are a rich source of policy recommendations. And they certainly are quotable.

We could go on, naturally, talking about **books** (look up your topic in a card catalog); **pamphlets** (your library probably has a *Vertical File Index,* which will indicate what sorts of pamphlets are available); **major reference works** (such as *Who's Who* and *The Essay and Literature Index*); and the like, but perhaps you get the idea.

Your run through print resources won't be exhausting if you practice these principles: (1) know what you need to find out; (2) use librarians and indexes for help; and (3) classify sources by the type of information they're especially good at supplying. Using this research process has another virtue: it will keep you from becoming a victim of the *Reader's Digest* Syndrome—a terrible disease which causes people to think they can learn all there is to know from a single source. A variety of print and nonprint resources will keep your mind active and keep your mouth from saying watered down, one-sided nonsense.

Finally, when doing research, remember one more very important rule: Carefully record what you find and where you find it. Carefully! On note cards, sheets of paper, or anything else you can easily store and shuffle, write down the information, the quotations, background materials. Include the title, author, publication information, date, and page numbers. Then you can always go back to a source easily if you find you missed something. And if anyone questions you on the information or opinions you mention, you can point that person to the same source.

SUMMARIZING THE RESULTS OF YOUR GENERAL PREPARATION

You have now finished the first five steps of speech preparation. You know your topic, and have some idea why it's relevant to you, your audience, and the occasion; you have cast both its general purpose and various specific purposes as guides to actual speech construction; you've narrowed the topic to a point where you think you're covering just the right amount of ground, given time limits, audience knowledge, and the like; you've assessed the audience's demographic and psychological characteristics as well as you can, hoping you have discovered relevant factors which might affect your listeners' perception of and reactions to your speech; and, you've diligently recorded facts and figures, quotations and analogies, and tons of examples on notecards or sheets.

You have worked hard in all this. You've had to think seriously about who you are, who your listeners are, and what you're really going to talk about. You've also assembled mounds of materials, materials that sit there in random fashion awaiting careful selection and shaping.

A lot of work? Yes. Will it be worthwhile? Emphatically yes, because once you've gone through these general preparations, actually building the speech will be comparatively easy. If general preparation is done well, constructing and shaping your talk will become essentially a creative affair; you'll be able to act the part of the artist, molding your materials into a speech you can give with pride.

ASSIGNMENTS

Pre-Performance

1. To help you recognize how communication affects your life, your instructor may ask you to keep a communication journal. Your instructor may give periodic special assignments or may suggest that you make regular entries pertaining to communicative experiences. In either case, the instructor will want to read your journal at intervals during the term.

The following special assignments can help you make initial self-evaluations and observations about your communicative experience:

a. Evaluate your skills as a public speaker. How much experience do you have in speaking? In what ways are you a particularly able speaker? What aspects need improvement? What do you hope to get out of this course?

b. Describe a speaking encounter which demonstrates how feedback from others has affected your self-concept. How has your own use of feedback possibly affected others' self-concepts?

c. Ask some students in a class other than this one to aid you in "testing" how speakers respond to feedback. In particular, arrange to have fellow students give positive feedback to one of the instructor's movements (such as walking to a specified side of the classroom, sitting on a table, or moving in front of the podium). What effects did this feedback seem to have on the professor's behavior? Why did the professor respond this way?

2. If you were invited to deliver the commencement address to students of your former high school, how would you go about selecting the topic, determining the purpose, narrowing the topic, and analyzing the audience?

3. The following list contains the names of persons who may be considered experts in their respective fields. Plan a hypothetical interview with one of these experts to obtain information for a speech that you might give in an area related to their expertise. Decide on the specific purposes of your interview. How do they differ from the specific purposes of the projected speech? Next, prepare a set of questions for the interview which are keyed to the information you wish to obtain.

Jerry Falwell	Geraldo Rivera	Pete Rose
Paul Harvey	Chris Evert	Jane Fonda
Alexander Haig	Phyllis Schlafly	Barbara Jordan
Johnny Carson	Billy Graham	Garry Trudeau
Jerry Brown	Roger Staubach	Ralph Nader

Performance

1. Short speeches given at the beginning of the term should be positive experiences which help students get acquainted and get a feel for future speaking assignments. One short speech assignment might be to discuss a pet peeve and indicate why you feel so strongly about this subject. Or you might present your feelings about what worries you most in the world today. The theme of "Fantasy Island" provides a third general approach. Explain a fantasy you would like to live and tell why the fantasy is significant to you.

2. As a means of getting acquainted and initiating a feeling of cooperativeness, the class could take part in a series of interviews. Each person will spend five to seven minutes interviewing another classmate. The assignment can be structured so that each student will interview one classmate and be interviewed by another (e.g., A interviews B, B interviews C . . . Y interviews Z, Z interviews A). Although interviewers should prepare questions in advance, they should attempt to conduct free and friendly exchanges rather than recite inflexible lists of questions.

Post-Performance

1. Your instructor will probably not give detailed criticisms of early speeches (such as those in Performances 1 and 2 above), so between class sessions make a special effort to exchange helpful comments with some of your classmates.

CHAPTER 3

Building the Speech

In a sense, of course, it is naive to speak of "building a speech," for the task little resembles the one faced by a builder who constructs a house. The same sort of precision in materials selection, measuring, fastening, and erecting is not possible for the speaker; there are too many unpredictable elements involved in the speaking situation. Yet, in another sense, the metaphor of building is an apt one: like a carpenter, the speaker is choosing raw materials and forming them into a utilitarian whole. And like the building of a house, the construction of your speech will depend for success on your good sense, previous knowledge, and even creativity. That's a tall order, but, if you have done an adequate amount of preparation, the task of building a speech is less formidable.

Building a speech demands two tasks of you: (1) selecting the ideas and materials which will make up the substance or content of the talk, and (2) organizing those ideas and materials in strategically clear and sound ways. These are the matters this chapter will address.

SELECTING ACTUAL MATERIALS

Let us suppose that you followed the advice given in Chapter 2 on finding speech materials. If you did, you're surrounded with disorganized material which apparently has no pattern; and, you have much too much of it. What do you do? You try to boil it down, to decide on some pieces for inclusion in your actual speech. How do you do that?

That's a tougher question. Part of the answer will depend specifically upon the type of speech you're delivering. As we'll see in later chapters, certain types of speeches seem to demand certain kinds of materials: end-of-the-year reportive speeches demand statistics; speeches defining unfamiliar concepts certainly can use analogies; celebratory speeches very often contain beautifully phrased quotations which capture the mood. You'll find help, therefore, on selecting specific materials in those later chapters. But, for now, it is worth our while to review some general principles which apply to virtually *all speeches*. Whenever you are selecting materials for any speech, you should be sure that your materials meet the standards of attention, variety, rationality, and concreteness.

Attention Do you have interesting material that will gain and sustain your listeners' attention? Anyone listening to a speech is tempted to tune out occasionally, to think about the weather or the evening's entertainment or a shrinking bank account. A principle of public speaking as old as the twentieth century itself is this: "Attention determines response."[1] If people do not attend to—that is, perceive and make sense out of—what you are saying, they simply will not respond to it in ways you want them to. Now, you can attempt to hold their attention through vocal or physical dynamics; but because, after all, you normally are more interested in having them attend to your ideas than to you personally, you have to find materials which will rivet them to your subject-matter. You will find that audiences often respond attentively to *anecdotes, comparisons* (especially *figurative analogies), jokes, metaphors,* and *startling statements or facts;* also well-phrased *quotations,* humorous or otherwise, can periodically be worked into a speech.

Variety A second standard for selection, one closely related to the matter of attention, is variety. People probably will find a speech that is made up of one statistic after another boring and hard-to-follow; unrelieved strings of examples, while they are interesting at first, tend to become monotonous; a speech loaded with quotations will sound like a bad sermon. Intermixing different kinds of materials will keep boredom or monotony from setting in; further, coming at an idea from more than one direction usually helps to clarify it. Suppose, for example, that you are preparing a speech on the growth of cable television in the United States. You might use the following variety of supporting materials to discuss the spread of cable TV operations:

I. Cable television has almost quadrupled its coverage of the country in the last decade. *[assertion]*
   A. That growth can be seen in the number of households subscribing to cable TV. *[statistical trend]*
      1. In 1971, 5.3 million households had cable.
      2. In 1975, the number had grown to 9.8 million subscribers.
      3. By the spring of 1981, that number rose to 19.7 million— almost four times the number of households that had cable ten

years earlier. *[completion of the statistics, with a "translation" into a multiplying factor]*

B. Another way to understand this growth is to think about it in terms of population percentages. *[a translation of the statistical trend into another form]*
   1. In 1971, less than 9 percent of the U.S. households were wired for cable.
   2. By 1975, almost 15 percent had cable.
   3. But as the new decade opened, over a quarter—26 percent, one out of four households—were paying cable fees; that's a 150 percent growth in a decade.
C. Over the same period, we must keep in mind, regular over-the-air television broadcasting grew by only 1-2 percent. *[comparison]*
D. In the words of Robert Welna, President of Media-Watch, Inc.: "The growth of cable television in the '70s represented not only technological innovation of unimaginable proportions, but, more important, it meant that cable TV was beginning to significantly change the lives of many, many Americans." *[quotation from an expert]*
E. It is that change in your everyday lives that I want to discuss today. *[purpose statement and transition]*

In this speech introduction, you can see variety at work. While the main idea needs support from statistical analyses, the speaker has been careful to (1) translate the statistics into different forms in hopes of making audience members understand them, and (2) offer comparisons and testimony in hopes of making the idea compelling, of making it seem "important" enough to think about.

Rationality   In addition, you always need to apply certain tests of rationality or reasoning to the speeches you present. If some pieces of supporting materials don't reasonably or logically support your assertions, then you must throw them out. Suppose you are arguing that your city consumer advocacy office is doing a bad job. To prove your point, you decide to cite examples of people who have been ill-treated. To check if your argument is reasonable, make sure that you have a *sufficient number of examples* to make your point; that the examples are *typical* of the experience of other people; and that someone else couldn't simply *counter* your argument by pointing out even more examples of effective advocacy by the same office. Or, suppose you're offering a demonstration speech on how to build your own picnic table; be careful not to skip any *essential steps* in that process. Or, if you're relying upon expert testimony when arguing that supermarkets which offer giveaways are unnecessarily raising the price of other foods, make sure your "expert" is one your audience would *accept* and *trust*, and be ready to cite evidence he or she has used in arriving at that conclusion. In sum, rigorously "test your evidence," for if you don't, someone else will! (See the Preview to Part III for further tests of reasoning.)

Concreteness

Because a speech is oral, it often presents certain problems of comprehension for audiences. People can reread a difficult paragraph in a newspaper or replay a stereo record to catch a particular lyric; but they normally cannot reread or replay your speech. You therefore must help them comprehend your message the first time through.

Concrete ideas and examples make it easier for listeners to understand you. Use *specific stories or anecdotes* to demonstrate what you're saying, *hard-hitting numbers*, an apt *analogy*, a vivid *illustration*. Make sure you have enough concrete materials, rather than only general statements and opinions, to help your audience comprehend your messages. And, don't be afraid to *restate or rephrase ideas* occasionally; sometimes different words help clarify abstract notions.

Addressing the problems of attention, the desirability of variety, the need for rationality, and the value of concreteness will help you select specific materials to include in your speeches. In addition, each type of speech places its own demands on materials; we'll cover the criteria for each type of speech purpose in later chapters. For now, remember to leave yourself enough time during the preparation period to make careful and useful selections among materials as you get ready for the next step.

ORGANIZING THE SPEECH STRATEGICALLY

Once you have selected materials, you must mold them into a speech that has purpose and form. We've already talked about purposes, so we will move directly to form. A speech needs form at two levels: a speech must have an *overall form*—an introduction that raises questions and suggests a focus, a body of materials that answers questions or expands ideas, and a conclusion that rounds out the message. And, more specifically or narrowly, a speech also needs an *internal form* or structure; it needs to be built in a "pattern" which is recognizable and appropriate to your subject-matter.

Because your focus normally is first and foremost on your subject-matter, we'll begin by talking about internal structures—so-called organizational patterns. Then we'll discuss briefly types of introductions and conclusions to complete the overall form of your speech.

Organizational Patterns: Internal Structures

If ideas are presented to listeners in seemingly random or disconnected ways, they are likely to be unintelligible; and, from your point of view, they're likely to lose impact. Some sort of structure or pattern, therefore, should be discernible when you talk to people about ideas that matter. A useful organizational pattern has four virtues:

1. A useful pattern is *recognizable*. Ever since you were a child, you've learned to see patterns in your experiences. You've learned that some

events (effects) are "caused" by others; you know that some events follow each other "temporally"; you've learned that some things make sense when you picture them "geographically" or "spatially"; you learned what some ideas mean by "contrasting" or "comparing" them with similar ideas. Much of your basic learning in life has been patterned; you use basic patterns or structures matter-of-factly, almost without thinking. As a speaker, then, learn to employ common or everyday patterns-of-thought which are familiar and understandable to others, because you, too, are trying to teach people something about ideas and actions when you rise to speak.

2. A useful pattern is *coherent*—it makes sense. That is, patterns-of-thought are important primarily because they associate ideas with each other in important ways. We need to think about causes and effects in order to predict what will occur in situations or to stop something from continuing; "cause-effect" structures clearly do that for us. Or, if we're trying to understand where some idea or phenomenon came from, we almost automatically use a chronological sequence ("First this happened, then this, and then . . .") to describe the evolution of ideas, institutions, or events; "temporal" or "chronological" structures clearly explain our strings of experience. Any useful organizational pattern, therefore, has power if it clearly and coherently associates something with something else.

3. A useful pattern is *appropriate to your purposes*. Different patterns are more or less useful for different purposes. For example, suppose you wanted to tell your class what the college's Career Planning and Placement Service is and what it does. You may well figure out that a comparison-and-contrast pattern makes the best sense, for it allows you to compare that service to state and/or private employment agencies; or, you might decide that a topical pattern will best allow you to discuss specific services offered by Career Planning and Placement. But, if you were trying to persuade class members to actually use the service, then you might use a problem-solution pattern, first discussing problems students have in finding jobs after graduation and then talking about career planning and placement as a good way to solve those problems. Select specific patterns by taking into account (a) your purposes and (b) audience responses you are seeking.

4. And, a useful pattern is *appropriate to the occasion*. You're expected to observe the "rules" operating in many situations; and, sometimes at least, there are "communication rules" which tend to dictate what organizational patterns you should use. A presidential inaugural, for example, almost inevitably must be in a problem-solution format, with the speech first identifying the major national and international problems facing the country and then pointing to the kinds of solutions this administration plans to offer. Weather forecasters "have to" use geographical or spatial patterns because that's how people normally think about weather. And,

college professors know they are expected by good notetaking students to use topical patterns for definitional or orienting lectures, and problem-solution or cause-effect patterns for most of their interpretive lectures. Various expectations, therefore, make particular organizational patterns appropriate.

Basically, all organizational patterns fall into four categories:

- *Sequential patterns* place ideas in temporal or physical order.
- *Causal patterns* specify intellectual or physical forces and their results.
- *Topical patterns* divide a subject into its constituent parts or subordinate concerns.
- *Special patterns* meet particular circumstances or audience needs.

We all respond to *sequential patterns* since all human existence occurs in time and space. In fact, *chronological and spatial sequences* provide our *primary orientations* to living.[2] Speakers attempting to give audiences orientations to ideas, institutions, or the dynamics of growth and development, therefore, find the two major sequential organizational patterns extremely useful.

Look at the two sample outlines in Figure 3.1. In the first, the speaker wants listeners to sense three different kinds of growth—growth in size, cost, and purpose or responsibility. A chronological pattern is perfect for this task, because one is able to chart the increments of growth temporally, and to demonstrate simultaneously the reasons why growth took place. And, in the second, the speaker wishes to offer a rationale for varied zoning laws in a community; it is only natural, then, that the person would employ a spatial pattern, for it allows different geographical regions to be discussed separately. Thus the audience is given a picture of or an orientation to community actions via a spatial pattern.

Causal Patterns are normally used in different kinds of situations. Because human beings are capable of abstract thought—capable of *explaining* occurrences in their environment and of *predicting* future occurrences—various kinds of causal analyses are important to them. Further, because people often are able to intervene in cause-effect situations—to apply remedies or to take preventive actions—some causal sequences are *solution-oriented*. Thus, the three principal causal sequences are cause-effect, effect-cause, and problem-solution.

Those three causal sequences are illustrated in Figure 3.2. In a cause-effect pattern, normally the emphasis is upon the effects; this pattern is used in situations where the audience is well acquainted with the cause (here, the federal funding cutback) but is unsure of the effects (for example, how it will affect certain groups of people). The reverse is true of the effect-cause pattern; in our example, presumably the audience has read in the newspapers about effects (such as the budgetary overruns in the Public Works Administration) and is wondering about the cause (why that

FIGURE 3.1   **Sequential Organizing Patterns For Speeches**

Sequential Patterns: organize ideas temporally or spatially

I. *Chronological Pattern* (time order)

    A. *[assertion]* Over the last ten years, the Human Relations Department of our city government has grown in complexity and size.

    B. *[original situation]* Ten years ago, Human Relations was responsible only for basic city employee training, which we accomplished with two part-time employees and a minimal budget.

    C. *[first major change]* Then, in 1974, Human Relations was asked to monitor all city affirmative action, equal opportunity, and governmental contract compliance procedures for the city, demanding a doubling of the Human Relations staff and of the department's budget.

    D. *[second major change]* In 1976, the department became responsible for two more major governmental functions—developing an annual and long-range city pay plan, and investigating all discrimination complaints in the city—creating a need for three more employees and a 40 percent budgetary increase.

    E. *[conclusion]* Therefore, the Human Relations Department now is the fifth-largest department in the city, is a major budgetary item, and has both inter-departmental and public responsibilities. *[growth and development have been charted via chronological sequence so as to explain or justify the bureau]*

II. *Spatial Pattern* (physical order)

    A. *[assertion]* Our city's Home and Community Environment Program is developing the river areas under its jurisdiction in several different ways.

    B. *[geographical area #1]* As the river enters our community from the west, it flows through a natural floodplain, which demands that we create a natural "free space" or preserve to protect our water supply.

    C. *[geographical area #2]* In the center of our community we find river sites useful for both parks and multiple-family dwellings.

    D. *[geographical area #3]* The hills rising from the river on the east edge of town have no drainage problems and hence are suitable for residential platting and housing.

    E. *[conclusion]* Therefore, the Home and Community Environment Program has sought to keep commercial and residential building programs out of the west, has asked the Zoning Commission to rezone the central portion of town for apartments, and will support construction projects on the eastern borders, thereby giving controlled growth where the river justifies it. *[demonstration of rationale for different treatments via a spatial pattern]*

happened). Effect-cause patterns place primary emphasis on causes rather than effects. The problem-solution is simply an extended causal pattern; it is based on the assumption that human beings, when faced with undesirable effects, wish to stop them from happening. Thus, the problem-solution organizational pattern goes a step beyond effects with a strong

---

FIGURE 3.2 **Causal Organizing Patterns for Speeches**

CAUSAL PATTERNS: interrelate causes, effects, and/or solutions

I. *Cause-Effect Pattern* (clarify or predict relationships)
   A. *[proposition]* There's going to have to be a serious cutback in our city's Human Relations staff.
   B. *[cause #1]* Reduced revenue-sharing funds from the federal government hits hardest our human services budgets.
   C. *[cause #2]* The budget of the Human Relations Department is one of the few where we have discretionary funds, and hence it must bear the brunt of the reduction.
   D. *[effect #1]* Discrimination complaints will not be investigated as quickly as in the past *(give examples)*.
   E. *[effect #2]* There will be a freeze on all new training programs *(with examples)*.
   F. *[effect #3]* The heads of other city departments will be asked to handle their own personnel problems *(with examples)*.

II. *Effect-Cause Pattern* (explain why something has occurred)
   A. *[proposition]* There are reasonable explanations as to why our Public Works Administration overspent its budget by eight percent last year.
   B. *[effect-to-be-explained]* The Public Works Administration was $37,500 over budget during the last fiscal year.
   C. *[cause #1]* The extraordinarily cold temperatures of last winter caused twice as many streets to break up, and hence we more than doubled the cost of street repair.
   D. *[cause #2]* Public outcry after the death of an eight-year-old demanded that we install an electronic traffic light at the corner of First and Sycamore, a $75,000 expenditure we had not budgeted for.
   E. *[cause #3]* The heavy spring flooding severely damaged the river dikes in Central Park, and unanticipated repair cost us another $45,000.
   F. *[conclusion]* Therefore, in the face of unexpected expenditures of over $175,000 last year, it's amazing the Public Works had a budgetary overrun of only $37,500. *[explaining the effect and even minimizing it via an effect-cause pattern]*

III. *Problem-Solution Pattern* (advocate changes)
   A. *[proposition]* Overtime pay for clerical support services to City Council members is a problem we must solve.
   B. *[problem]* City Council member requests for services from the city's clerical staff last year cost us $15,500 in overtime pay.
   C. *[solution #1]* The Council could request reduced support for other executive and operating departments to free up help for themselves (but that might increase inefficiencies in those departments).
   D. *[solution #2]* Council members could file their requests for services farther ahead of time so they could be worked into regular routines (although that might inconvenience Council members).
   E. *[solution #3]* Council members could seek clerical help from private sources which might donate services (although some might see that as a hidden tax or business cost). *[proposing solutions and indicating effects of each proposal via a problem-solution format]*

---

concern for solutions—actions which will interrupt or alter causal occurrences in society. In general, we can say that (1) cause-effect and effect-cause sequences are particularly useful in speeches of report and explanation, and that (2) problem-solution sequences are valuable for persuasive and actuative speeches.

Topical Patterns, by contrast, are especially useful for definitional and explanative speeches; this is because the speaker is attempting to *describe* and *clarify* the specific aspects or parts of some notion or thing, to offer specific information about some thing, object, or process. We use topical patterns because they break down something that's complex into more understandable aspects or units.

In Figure 3.3, notice that there are fundamentally two kinds of topical patterns—complete and partial enumeration. *Complete enumeration* is used in situations (1) where it is actually possible to describe exhaustively all parts or subtopics, and (2) where audiences are demanding full disclosure. In the sample outline on state sources of city revenue, presumably it is possible for people to comprehend six sources of money and presumably anyone interested in state funds would not want you to skip one or two sources. In contrast, *partial enumeration* is usually employed either when complete enumeration is impossible or when only some aspects of something are relevant to an audience. Thus, in Figure 3.3, partial enumeration is used in the speech given to senior citizens because complete enumeration of all a city manager's duties would only be confusing and because only three of the person's responsibilities directly affect audience members.

A final comment on topical patterns: Many beginning speakers, especially, are tempted to *overuse* topical patterns because they seem so "easy"; after all, one need only think up two or three things to say, and then simply announce them as "topics." Actually, remember that the very ease with which topical patterns can be used means they *may not* be your best choice of pattern. If your list of two or three topics doesn't seem coherent or relevant to audience members, then you'll have defeated the purpose of using patterns in the first place. Always make sure, especially when employing partial enumeration, that the subtopics "hang together" (literally) and that they represent areas of primary listener interest and concern.

Finally, we come to *special patterns*, so named because they represent sequences used only in special circumstances dictated either by your *particular purpose* or by your *audience's special needs*. Actually, we could offer a much longer list of special patterns and, indeed, some other ones will be offered in later chapters, but the three here—comparison and contrast, question-answer format, and elimination order—illustrate the basic principles underlying special patterns. One principle is, "Your specific purposes may call for a special pattern"; and, the other is, "Your audience's informational or psychological state may require a special pattern."

FIGURE 3.3   **Topical Organizing Patterns for Speeches**

Topical Patterns: divide subjects into constituent parts or subtopics

I. *Complete Enumeration Pattern* (full description)
   A. *[topic]* Our city receives money from the state in six ways.
   B. *[source #1]* The Bank Franchise Tax returns $60,000 to our community.
   C. *[source #2]* The state's Police and Fire Retirement Fund pays us $50,000 for law enforcement and fire personnel retirement plans.
   D. *[source #3]* The State Transit Assistance Act provides a $200,000-per-year subsidy of our city bus system.
   E. *[source #4]* The State Liquor Commission returns ten percent of its gross profits from area stores to us, providing our general budget with a quarter of a million dollars.
   F. *[source #5]* The State Municipal Assistance Act is a state revenue-sharing plan which raised us $330,000 last year.
   G. *[source #6]* And, the State Road Use Tax is shared with us, bringing in almost a million and a half dollars last year. *[complete enumeration is possible here because of the limited number of actual parts]*
II. *Partial Enumeration* (selection to highlight some aspects)
   A. *[central idea, when speaking to senior citizens]* While I as City Manager have many different duties, three of my responsibilities affect you directly.
   B. *[subtopic #1]* Working with the Home and Community Development Commissioner, I help plan and administer the low-cost retirement complex on Fourth Avenue.
   C. *[subtopic #2]* Three times a year, I meet with other members of the state's City Managers Association as we lobby the state government for increased social services and the federal government for continued "Meals on Wheels" subsidies for the elderly.
   D. *[subtopic #3]* Once a month, I hold "office hours" in the city's three main retirement complexes so that you can express your concerns directly to me. *[partial enumeration used to develop subtopics relevant to the particular audience being addressed]*

In Figure 3.4, both of those principles are illustrated. The comparison and contrast sample exemplifies both principles, actually. Presumably, the speaker is in the short-run attempting to give listeners information about budgeting, and, in the long-term, probably seeking to achieve a more personal, political goal—that of justifying budget hearings and the city's allocation of funds to various programs. Comparisons and contrasts work effectively for both purposes because they tie "new" knowledge to "old" knowledge (here, public finances to personal finances) and because the tie-in to previous beliefs and attitudes will make future persuasive efforts easier to undertake.

The question-answer format is one particularly suited to instances when

FIGURE 3.4   **Special Organizing Patterns for Speeches**

Special Patterns: meet particular needs of subject or audience

I. *Comparison and Contrast Pattern* (clarify similarities/differences)
   A. *[central idea]* You can best understand city budgeting if you compare and contrast it with your own attempts to grapple with money.
   B. *[comparisons]* Like you, we in the city have some very ordinary budget problems—fixed income, many fixed expenditures, some unexpected expenditures *(illustrate)*.
   C. *[contrasts]* But, we also have some budget problems you don't face—constant changes in income (thanks to yearly changes in state and federal allocations), governmental regulations that often control what we can spend money on, dozens of different constituencies in our "family" demanding increased support *(illustrate)*.
   D. *[conclusion]* Knowing these comparisons and contrasts may help you understand better our next annual public hearings on the budget. *[using a comparison with the well-known problems of personal finance to clarify the technical, perhaps misunderstood, problems of city finance]*

II. *Question-Answer Order* (address primary audience concerns)
   A. *[central idea]* Today, I'll answer the three main questions most citizens of our community ask me repeatedly.
   B. *[question-answer #1]* How come the city simply threw asphalt in the chuckholes on my street, but completely repaved the next street over? *(give answer)*
   C. *[question-answer #2]* Why does the city spend so much on streets, buildings, and salaries, but so little on direct social services? *(give answer)*
   D. *[question-answer #3]* What's the difference between the City Manager and the Mayor? *(give answer)*
   E. *[conclusion]* Those, then, are the answers, but if you have additional questions, I'll be happy to answer them at our next meeting. *[respond to audience concerns via a direct question-answer approach]*

III. *Elimination Order* (eliminate some proposed solutions so that only *your* proposed solution remains when urging action)
   A. *[proposition]* There is only one feasible solution to the problem of spring floods along Ralston Creek.
   B. *[faulty solution #1]* Some argue we should build a dike along the creek, but that would destroy the aesthetic appeal of the park and harm the wildlife of the area.
   C. *[faulty solution #2]* Some say we should cut an overflow channel from the creek to the river, but that would require purchase of expensive private property and relatively large construction costs.
   D. *[preferred solution]* Therefore, the only solution which meets both aesthetic and economic criteria is the construction of a series of mechanically controlled dams along the creek. *[cutting off counter-proposals via an elimination order]*

an audience all but cries out for a certain body of information or for reduction of psychological fears; when people are asking for information or attitudinal-valuative responses, the question-answer is the sequence that directly attacks those problems. In contrast, note that the elimination order is more purpose-centered than audience-centered. It is used in persuasive or actuative speeches when your purpose is to clear the air of competing ideas or actions. To use it well, you must be able to (1) convincingly eliminate the competitors, and (2) actually demonstrate that your preferred idea or solution is suitable to the problem at hand. If you can do those things, the elimination order is a powerful communicative weapon.

Before we leave organizational patterns for now, keep in mind three important admonitions about their use:

1. *Select organizational patterns by considering, not your subject, but your purposes and your audience.* Notice that *all* of the sample outlines presented deal with the same subject-matter—city government generally, from the viewpoint of the city manager in particular. We've done that to hammer home the crucial communicative point that you and your audience determine together what patterns will work best in a speaking situation. Organizational patterns are not "natural"; rather, they are human inventions built to serve human purposes.

2. *Because organizational patterns serve communicative purposes, don't be afraid to adjust them to your own purposes.* You may think, for example, you want to use a topical pattern for a speech on the role of various local officials (doctors, social workers, law enforcement agents) in preventing child abuse, but then discover during your research a lot of interesting information about the social and personal causes of child abuse. If you do, you'll want to change patterns, moving to an effect-cause pattern; make that adjustment rather than trying to force a complete discussion of causes into a topical pattern. Or, if you have enough time, go to a problem-solution pattern, where you (1) survey the problem, (2) enumerate the causes of the problem, and (3) then discuss steps doctors, social workers, and law officers can take to solve it.

Often, too, you can—carefully—mix various patterns. For example, you may try to use one pattern as the *overall* organizing structure and then a second pattern as an *internal* pattern.

    A. Development of Cause #1
        1. Origin of cause
        2. Growth of cause
    B. Development of Cause #2
        1. Origin of cause
        2. Growth of cause
    C. Effects

In this hypothetical example, a cause-effect sequence provides the overall organizational pattern, but a chronological pattern is used on the two main subpoints. Make sure, however, that when you mix and match sequences your audience will be able to follow you; if necessary for clarity, explain what you're doing, as in "First, I'll deal with the principal causes of X, giving you background on the historical development and growth of each one. Then we should be in a good position to see how they have effected Y."

3. *Work extra hard to make your speeches' structures unmistakably clear to an audience.* If a pattern has no apparent coherence, people will get lost. To keep them from wandering, you can use three primary verbal techniques for clarifying the pattern:

Forecasting—telling your audience what you're going to talk about and how you'll deal with it. ("Today I want to explain three causes of declining enrollments in our city's elementary schools and two actions we can take to counteract those causes.")

Signposting—indicating to an audience where you are in the development of this speech. ("The first cause, then, is a decline in city growth over the last decade; let us now consider another cause, the decline in this county's birthrate.")

Summarizing—demonstrating the completeness of your analysis by restating main ideas. ("So, we've looked at three causes of declining enrollments—the stoppage of city growth, the reduction of the birthrate, and the addition of a popular private school in town. We've also discussed two possible solutions: industrial expansion in order to bring more school-age children into our district and a plan for redistricting the city.")

Organizational Patterns: Beginnings and Endings

Once you have shaped the main body of your speech, you can reasonably think about introductions and conclusions—ways to get in and get out.

An introduction to any speech can serve several functions: (1) It can get the audience accustomed to listening, paying attention, tuning in; (2) it ought to pique their curiosity and interest, making them want to hear more; (3) it probably should state your public purposes as clearly as possible; and (4) it often should, especially for a longer talk, orient the audience (tell them how you're going to proceed so they can more easily follow you). There are, of course, many standard ways to accomplish these functions. Consider the following techniques:

Reference to the Subject "You may have marveled at the skill of Navajo artists who make the striking sand paintings you see in people's homes and doctors' offices. Well, if you can sketch and cut glass, you too can make them, and today I'm going to show you how."

Reference to the Occasion "This is the first public discussion this council has had of the Black Coalition for Citizen's Action petition, and I'm pleased to be a part of it. It shows that our city is willing to face controversial human rights issues squarely, and. . . ."

Personal Reflection "I'm more than pleased to be speaking to you tonight. I've been interested in parents' school associations for years, having had three kids go through the elementary schools of this town. So, I find it a special pleasure to come back, not as an angry parent, but as a concerned school board member."

Startling Question or Statement "How would you like to get out of college in three years instead of four? That's possible if our school adopts a trimester plan—the plan I want to advocate tonight."

Quotation " 'It was the best of times, it was the worst of times, it was the age of wisdom, it was the age of foolishness, it was the epoch of belief, it was the epoch of incredulity, it was the season of Light, it was the season of Darkness, it was the spring of hope, it was the winter of despair, . . .' With those words Charles Dickens described the era of the French Revolution, nearly 200 years ago. But he could just as well have been talking about today and tomorrow. We live in a similar age of contradiction and turbulence, in an atmosphere which threatens to destroy every institution, including this church. Today, I . . ."

Humorous Anecdote "I came home the other night to find my eight-year-old son ready with a joke. 'Daddy,' he said, 'what's green and red and goes a hundred miles an hour?' 'I don't know,' I said wearily, 'what?' 'A frog in a blender!' he shouted triumphantly. That time of the evening, the story merely turned me green. Upon reflection, however, it has caused me to think about the ways in which modern technology—right down to the blender on the kitchen cupboard—has invaded our thinking, our values, yes, even our humor. And tonight, I want to. . . ."

Look over these techniques carefully. Not only do they accustom an audience to your voice, perhaps pique curiosity, move the speaker into the subject-matter, and offer some orientation; but, they also put the speakers' emphases in different "places" of our communication model.

Quotations and references to the subject tend to emphasize the *message*, the subject-matter. References to the occasion call attention (by definition) to *context*, while personal reflections stress *speaker*. Most startling questions or statements are *audience-centered*, in that they usually project the listeners into the topic via direct address (the use of the word "you"). And, humorous anecdotes—depending upon who or what is featured in the story—can emphasize any element. That is, you can tell funny stories about yourself, about the place where you're talking, about your subject-matter (as in our example), or even about the listeners. The point is this: different techniques of introduction are more or less useful for different specific purposes you have. Think about your purposes, about what you seek to stress at the beginning, when you select one or another of these tactics for opening your talks.

Because we already have talked about the second element in the overall structure, the body of the speech, let us move to the final element—the conclusion. A good conclusion (1) summarizes the main point; (2) leaves the audience in a mood to do whatever thinking or acting you wish them to do after the speech; and (3) strikes a note of finality and firmness. Some of the following types of conclusions are often used:

Challenge "In closing, then, I hope by now that it's abundantly clear you're more than a student while you attend this school. You're still a full-fledged, card-carrying member of the human race and of this society. You don't leave your humanity behind when you're in school. In fact, you become more sensitive to your social obligations to your culture-mates as you study history, sociology, psychology, communication, and anthropology. I challenge you to drop your books for a little while, reassert your humane obligations, and attend tomorrow's Nuclear Disarmament rally."

Illustration "There's a wonderful story about a five-year-old in Sunday School which captures the spirit of what I've been trying to say tonight. The child was busily drawing a picture, and the teacher asked what it was. The five-year-old replied, 'It's a picture of God.' 'But,' protested the teacher, 'nobody knows what God looks like!' 'They will when I'm done,' came the reply. It's that sort of self-assurance, creativity, and naive willingness to take on big projects I'm talking about. You can turn your own life around if. . . ."

Personal Commitment "I personally believe very strongly in the beautification project I've defended today. As a matter of fact, I believe in it fervently enough to make two commitments to you. First, I will contribute twenty-five dollars to start off the fund we all know we need. And second, I will devote myself to a month of Saturdays, helping with the cultivation, planting, and care of seedlings. If each of you will make a similar commitment, this city will be on its way to reviving a sense of civic pride long absent from our community. Here's my check."

In addition, of course, many conclusions also contain *summaries* of the main points ("I've explained tonight three main features of . . ."); *quotations* ("in the words of . . ."); additional *inducements* ("If none of the foregoing reasons are enough to move you to action, consider one more fact: . . ."). Whatever tactic you use, make sure you are ready to end the talk with point, power, and a sense of finality. Again, notice that different concluding strategies tend to put your final emphasis in different places. Challenges are directed explicitly at *listeners' actions*; illustrations are used primarily to clarify or give power to the *ideas* in your message; and, expressions of personal commitment are *speaker-centered*, and tend to be used when the speaker is a highly credible person. So again, then, select the strategy which reflects the sort of focus and purpose you have.[3]

"Building" a speech, in summary, is not a mechanical process. It is a matter of selecting and organizing your materials to construct a purposive, clear, comprehensible, interesting, even compelling structure-of-ideas.

SAMPLE SPEECH:

INFORMING

Pre-Speech Analysis

We now have reviewed enough of the steps in the speech preparation to need a good example of the results. Following is a text of Joyce Chapman's speech, "The Geisha," which she delivered when she was a freshman at Loop College, Chicago. It illustrates well most of the virtues of careful speech preparation discussed thus far: (1) Its general purpose, to inform, is unmistakably clear; (2) her specific goals—both for herself as an Asian and her audience as misunderstanding individuals—likewise show through; (3) her topic has been narrowed sufficiently to make it possible for her to convey enough information without simply bombarding listeners; (4) she has found historical and contemporary details capable of being molded into a coherent speech; (5) she uses a topical pattern for the main outline, with each of the three main topics developed chronologically for clarity; and (6) she works especially hard in the introduction to use personal references and topical forecasts to orient her audiences well. The results of those decisions are clearly visible in the text.

Speech

The Geisha[+]
Joyce Chapman

Introduction

Personal reference

As you may have already noticed from my facial features, I have Oriental blood in me and, as such, I am greatly interested in my Japanese heritage. One aspect of my heritage that fascinates me the most is the beautiful and adoring Geisha.   /1

I recently asked some of my friends what they thought a Geisha was, and the comments I received were quite astonishing. For example, one friend said, "She is a woman who walks around in a hut." A second friend was certain that a Geisha was, "A woman who massages men for money and it involves her in other physical activities." Finally, I received this response, "She gives baths to men and walks on their backs." Well, needless to say, I was rather surprised and offended by their comments. I soon discovered that the majority of my friends perceived the Geisha with similar attitudes. One of them argued, "It's not my fault, because that is the way I've seen them on TV." In many ways my friend was correct. His misconception of the Geisha was not his fault, for she is often portrayed by American film producers and directors as: a prostitute, as in the movie, *The Barbarian and the Geisha*, a streetwalker, as seen in the TV series, "Kung Fu," or as a showgirl with a gimmick, as performed in the play, *Flower Drum Song*.   /2

Central idea

A Geisha is neither a prostitute, streetwalker, or showgirl with a gimmick. She is a lovely Japanese woman who is a professional entertainer and hostess. She is cultivated with exquisite manners, truly a bird of a very different plumage.   /3

Orientation

I would like to provide you with some insight to the Geisha, and, in the process perhaps, correct any misconception you may have. I will do this by discussing her history, training, and development.   /4

Body

First point: history

The Geisha has been in existence since 600 A.D., during the archaic time of the Yakamoto period. At that time the Japanese ruling class was very powerful and economically rich. The impoverished majority, however, had to struggle to survive. Starving fathers and their families had to sell their young daughters to the teahouses in order to get a few yen. The families hoped that the girls would have a better life in the teahouse than they would have had in their own miserable homes.   /5

During ancient times only high society could utilize the Geisha's talents because she was regarded as a status symbol, exclusively for the elite. As the Geisha became more popular, the common people developed their own imitations. These imitations were often crude and base, lacking sophistication and taste. When American GIs came home from World War II, they related descriptive accounts of their wild escapades with the Japanese Geisha. In essence, the GIs were only soliciting with common prostitutes. These bizarre stories helped create the wrong image of the Geisha.   /6

Second point: training

Today, it is extremely difficult to become a Geisha. A Japanese woman couldn't wake up one morning and decide, "I think I'll become a Geisha today." It's not that simple. It takes sixteen years to qualify.   /7

At the age of six a young girl would enter the Geisha training school and become a Jo-chu, which means housekeeper. The Jo-chu does not have any specific type of clothing, hairstyle, or make-up. Her duties basically consist of keeping the teahouse immaculately clean (for cleanliness is like a religion to the Japanese). She would also be responsible for making certain that the more advanced women would have everything available at their fingertips. It is not until the girl is sixteen and enters the Maiko stage that she concentrates less on domestic duties and channels more of her energies on creative and artistic endeavors.   /8

The Maiko girl, for example, is taught the classical Japanese dance, Kabuki. At first, the dance consists of tiny, timid steps to the left, to the right, backward and forward. As the years progress, she is taught the more difficult steps requiring syncopated movements to a fan.   /9

The Maiko is also introduced to the highly regarded art of floral arrangement. The Japanese take full advantage of the simplicity and gracefulness that can be achieved with a few flowers in a vase, or with a single flowering twig. There are three main styles: Seika, Moribana, and Nagerie. It takes at least three years to master this beautiful art.   /10

During the same three years, the Maiko is taught the ceremonious art of serving tea. The roots of these rituals go back to the thirteenth century, when Zen Buddhist monks in China drank tea during their devotions. These rituals were raised to a fine art by the Japanese tea masters, who set the standards for patterns of behavior throughout Japanese society. The tea ceremony is so intricate that it often takes four hours to perform and requires the use of over seventeen different utensils. The tea ceremony is far more than the social occasion it appears to be. To the Japanese, it serves as an island of serenity where one can refresh the senses and nourish the soul.   /11

One of the most important arts taught to the Geisha is that of conversation. She must master an elegant circuitous vocabulary flavored in Karyuki, the world of flowers and willows, of which she will be a part. Consequently, she must be capable of stimulating her client's mind as well as his esthetic pleasures.   /12

Third point: development

Having completed her sixteen years of thorough training, at the age of twenty-two, she becomes a full-fledged Geisha. She can now serve her clients with duty, loyalty, and most important, a sense of dignity.   /13

The Geisha would be dressed in the ceremonial kimono, made of brocade and silk thread. It would be fastened with an obi, which is a sash around the waist and hung down the back. The length of the obi would indicate the girl's degree of development. For instance, in the Maiko stage the obi is longer and is shortened when she becomes a Geisha. Unlike the Maiko, who wears a gay, bright, and cheerful kimono, the Geisha is dressed in more subdued colors. Her make-up is the traditional white base, which gives her the look of white porcelain. The hair is shortened and adorned with beautiful, delicate ornaments.   /14

As a full-fledged Geisha, she would probably acquire a rich patron who would assume her sizable debt to the Okiya, or training residence. This patron would help pay for her wardrobe, for each kimona can cost up to $12,000. The patron would generally provide her with financial security.   /15

The Geisha serves as a combination entertainer and companion. She may dance, sing, recite poetry, play musical instruments, or draw pictures for her guest. She might converse with them or listen sympathetically to their troubles. Amorous advances, however, are against the rules.   /16

Conclusion

So, as you can see the Geisha is a far cry from the back-rubbing, streetwalking, slick entertainer that was described by my friends. She is a beautiful, cultivated, sensitive, and refined woman.   /17

NOTES

[1] "Attention determines response" became the battlecry of students of James Albert Winans at the turn of the century. His textbook, *Speech-Making* (New York: D. Appleton-Century Co., 1915), devoted three whole chapters ("Interest," "Methods of Interesting," and "Composition and Interest") to attention. Psychologist Floyd L. Ruch provides a contemporary definition of attention: "From among the many stimuli which are within range physiologically, we select—and consciously react to—only those that are related to our present needs and interests. . . . Most psychologists regard attention as having three interrelated aspects, all of which are part of a single complex act. Attention is (1) an adjustment of the body and its sense organs, (2) clear and vivid consciousness, and (3) a set toward action." In *Psychology and Life*, 7th brief ed. (Glenview, Il.: Scott, Foresman and Co., 1967), pp. 295, 572. Because, then, it is our ability to attend that "connects"

stimuli (things-around-us) to our needs and interests, it obviously is crucial for speakers to constantly renew it.

[2]   For much fuller discussions of temporal-spatial patterning and its importance to our sense of orientation and well-being, see Edward T. Hall, *The Silent Language* (1959; rpt. New York: Fawcett World Library, 1966), esp. Chaps. 3, 9, and 10; and, Albert E. Scheflen, *Human Territories; How We Behave in Space-Time*, with Norman Ashcraft (Englewood Cliffs, N.J.: Prentice-Hall, Inc., 1966).

[3]   These and additional introductory and concluding strategies are developed at much greater length in Douglas Ehninger, Bruce E. Gronbeck, Ray E. McKerrow, and Alan H. Monroe, *Principles and Types of Speech Communication*, 9th ed. (Glenview, Il.: Scott, Foresman and Co., 1982), Chap. 10.

[4]   "The Geisha" by Joyce Chapman, *Communication Strategy: A Guide to Speech Preparation* by Roselyn L. Schiff et al. Copyright © 1981 by Scott, Foresman and Company.

ASSIGNMENTS

Pre-Performance   1. In the following speaking situations what techniques might you use as a "starter" or introduction for your speech? Be specific.

Anniversary of the death of Martin Luther King, Jr.

Meeting of the foreign students association

Public gathering on the Fourth of July

Barbecue to kick off a political campaign

Opening session of a convention of women in management

Banquet sponsored by Fellowship of Christian Athletes

Meeting of a group of trial lawyers

Noon luncheon to begin a United Fund drive

Session of a men's consciousness-raising group

2. The divisions between introduction and body and between body and conclusion are not absolute. Read five speeches and comment on how it is sometimes difficult to isolate these as three distinct components. You can find speeches printed in several sources including the following: the magazine *Vital Speeches of the Day*, the *Congressional Record*, the *New York Times*, and *Representative American Speeches* (an anthology of contemporary speeches published annually).

3. Work in groups of four or five class members. Each group should draw up a questionnaire that considers all the information about your classmates you believe would be valuable in preparing speeches for this specific audience. Select one member of your group to work with a representative from each of the other groups. The representatives should combine the ideas included in each group's questionnaire into a master questionnaire. Your instructor will print copies and summarize the data after the class fills out the forms. The master inventory should elicit some psychological, as well as demographic, information about the class.

4. Conduct a brief survey to discover what your classmates consider the

main problems they are facing. Use the results to help you determine topics for future speeches.

Performance

1. The instructor will divide the class into three groups and assign a single, controversial topic for all three groups. Each group should write an introduction for a speech on that topic and choose one member to deliver the speech introduction. Group 1 should prepare a speech introduction for a supportive audience; Group 2, for a hostile audience; Group 3, for an indifferent audience.

2. Your instructor will develop a card file of impromptu speech topics: a set of challenging quotations, topics of interest and common knowledge, current events, and the like. Each student will draw two cards from the file, quickly make a choice, and return the unused card. Students have one minute to think before beginning their talks. On the first round of impromptu speeches, your instructor may want to limit talks to two or three minutes. Utilize the organizing patterns for speeches outlined in the chapter as methods for developing impromptu speeches. At first, it probably will be best to select only one of the patterns rather than to combine patterns.

Post-Performance

1. After the speech introductions in Performance 1 have been delivered, the class should discuss their effectiveness. Did each introduction meet the challenge presented by the audience attitude (supportive, hostile, or indifferent)? How did the speakers attempt to establish common ground with the audience in each situation?

CHAPTER 4

Giving the Speech

When people think of public speaking, they often bring to mind images of fast-talking politicians, moralistic (and boring?) sermonizers, or condescending corporate supervisors who start off each year with an empty little talk on why ABC Businesses, Inc., is a place for teamwork. "Giving a speech," to many of us, is an exercise in false eloquence or dull recitation.

You will serve yourself and your audiences well by clearing those images out of your head. As we noted in Preview I, today's Articulate Person is anything but a silver-tongued, dull, snooty Orator. *Giving a speech is a matter, ultimately, of sharing ideas and perspectives of worth.* If you keep that in mind, then actually "giving" a speech loses some of its frightening aspects. Not that you won't be frightened or at least apprehensive most of the time—of course you will. (As a matter of fact, at the end of this chapter we'll confront the problem of communication apprehension head-on.) If, however, you prepare to deliver the speech carefully and specifically, the paralyzing dimensions of that fright will disappear.

In this chapter, then, our goal is to finish your preparations by considering the last three steps as outlined in Chapter 2: (1) wording the principal ideas and appeals; (2) preparing the delivery of the speech (encoding); and (3) practicing the presentation.

WORDING THE PRINCIPAL IDEAS AND APPEALS

As we noted in Chapter 1, the linguistic channel is public speaking's primary medium-of-communication. Most of the important meanings you communicate to others depend upon your ability to cast thoughts into words. The bits and pieces of language you use in your speeches serve three important communicative functions:

- *Forming images.* Your language creates an image of "who" you are. It gives an audience a sense of what kind of person you are and how you feel about yourself, your subject, the occasion, and your listeners.
- *Structuring ideas.* Your use of language tells an audience what the central concepts or propositions are, and indicates how those concepts or theses are related to each other.
- *Conveying emotions.* Your language communicates to an audience how they ought to feel (angry, sad, happy, frustrated, interested) about your subject matter and ideas. Words can both denote (refer to something) and connote (add evaluative meanings to that something).

Let us consider language strategies which help you fulfill these three functions.

Forming Images of Yourself

An audience's perception of you—of your ethos or credibility as a source of ideas and judgments—depends in good measure on some of your word choices (and secondarily, as we'll see soon, your voice). That's a scary thought, but true: unless your listeners already know you, they form pictures of your *trustworthiness*, your *dynamism*, and your *self-confidence* largely from the way you use language.[1] Some of your linguistic choices are especially crucial in other people's judgments about who you are and to what extent you should be believed and trusted:

Qualifications Do you frequently use qualifiers (perhapses, maybes, probablys) in your conversation? Qualifications tend to indicate that you are a deliberate, guarded, careful (perhaps even overly cautious) person. Using a few necessary qualifiers may suggest that you are accurate and realistic. Too many qualifiers may suggest that you are unable or unwilling to take a definite stand.

Shadings Do you add shadings of meanings that properly convey your intentions? "You could do that," "You can do that," "You might do that," "You may do that," "You should do that," "You must do that," "You will do that," and "You shall do that" are sentences exactly the same except for the auxiliary verbs. But the meanings are different. At the extremes, *could* conveys that you're unsure or tentative, while *shall* indicates you're a strong, order-giving person. You reveal parts of yourself through your selection of auxiliary verbs and the shadings they add. Through them you create a particular relationship with your audience.

Dynamism You communicate a sense of your own dynamism in your selections of verbs, adverbs, and metaphors. "I think that's bad" isn't nearly as forceful as "I think that's a disgrace." "That's ugly" states your opinion; but you'd demonstrate yourself to be a more involved and reacting human being if you said, "That's a blight on the neighborhood." Using striking words and metaphors builds an image of you as a dynamic, active, lively person.

Hesitancies Is your speech punctuated with an inordinate number of "umms," "ahs," "It's, well, like . . . ," and "ohs"? Now, we all tend to use these and other hesitancies while speaking, and they usually don't bother an audience. They're a part of oral language. But consider a sentence which runs on like this: "What I'm, ah, trying, uh, to say, like, is, umm, that you, ah, oh, let's see, oughta think about, like, well, my, oh, proposal, and, ah . . ." Sometimes it's better to simply let a little silence creep into your talks as you choose the right words. There's nothing wrong with some hesitancy, but speeches limping along with hesitancy suggest you are unsure or unprepared and they reflect negatively upon you as a speaker.

Vocabulary Do you tend to use words that are appropriate to the audience and the occasion? Are you forced to say "That what-cha-ma-call-it," or do you know the precise word ("a lathe," "a restraining order") when you need it? While long strings of abstract or technical words can confuse an untutored audience, you reveal yourself to be a careful, knowledgeable person by being able to use language which conveys your exact meanings.

As you phrase your speech outline, then, pay attention to language that reveals your "self." As an audience listens to the string of words which comprise your speech, they are forming an image of you. And the image they hold of you affects the credibility you have with them. An audience will more readily accept information and advice from speakers they find trustworthy, dynamic, personable, and knowledgeable; and those impressions are in part conveyed by your word choice.

Structuring Ideas

A second important job your language ought to accomplish in public speaking is to carefully set out your major ideas. An audience can't go back and reread a speech. It's flowing by rapidly, and you must do all you can to help them absorb it the first time through. The words you choose, and the way you arrange them, will help accomplish this.

Simplicity Use simple language to make ideas understandable. While you sometimes need to use technical or "big" words in order to convey precise meanings, at the same time you need to keep the language and sentence structure as simple and short as possible. In a speech on supermarket foods, you could say, "the meat is undergoing a process of chemical transformation which causes decomposition"; or you could say, "the meat's rotten." You could say, "Serious, controlled experimentation has presaged the demise of civilizations which surrender ethical-scientific decision making to dwellers in the ivory towers"; or you could state, "Studies show that countries that leave all important ethical and technical decisions to university professors get into trouble." Simplicity as a speech virtue refers both to vocabulary and to sentence arrangements. Short, direct, hard-hitting sentences with a minimum of ponderous language usually work best.

Repetition Normally you're better off if you phrase an idea in more than one way when speaking. Because an audience can't reread, it needs repetition or redundancy. So you might say: "Today I want to talk about 'pass-fail' grading. That is, I want to discuss some of the advantages of a school grading system which has only two marks—'pass' and 'fail'—instead of the 'A-B-C-D-F' grades you're used to seeing." In this simple piece of repetition, the basic idea is given twice and is made more explicit the second time. This is a common way of restating an idea without subjecting an audience to exact and boring repetition. Internal and final summaries are other forms of repetition that fill out your ideas and help an audience remember.

Connectives Connective phrases serve oral communication in much the same way that punctuation and paragraphing serve written communication. They show structure, thought divisions, and relationships between ideas. Learn to link the parts of your speech with phrases like the following:

- In the first place. . . . And second, . . .
- In addition to . . . notice that. . . .
- Now let's look at this problem from a different angle.
- That last point raises another question. . . .
- Turning now. . . .
- Not only . . . but also. . . .
- More important than this is. . . .
- In contrast, I. . . .

Simplicity, repetition, and connectives all give shape to your ideas and aid an audience in the important task of comprehending what you're trying to say.

Conveying Emotions The third major function of language in a speech is to convey a sense of your feelings, and of the feelings you hope your audience will have in reaction to what you are saying. Some important ways to create emotions are by using imagery, intense language, and metaphors.

Imagery One quality which articulate persons often have is the ability to make an audience "see" or "feel" or "hear" what they're talking about.

Images—verbal pictures—allow listeners to project themselves into a situation you're describing, letting them see/feel/hear/smell/taste the experience. So a speech on the need for stronger pollution control standards for your city might begin with imagery like this:

"I don't know how many of you have driven through the factory district in this town, but if you haven't, you should. You'll see flower gardens and backyard laundry covered with the gray grime of coal and oil ash; dirty children trying to play street hockey along gutters filled with the overflow of lime trucks; skies that are never truly blue because smoke hides the clouds. You'll smell the 'rotten eggs' of sulphur processing, the nose-burning odor of chlorine, the decay of settling ponds. The roar of smelters, knitting machines, and steel-pounding will be deafening. If you can take all of this for more than five minutes, you're a better person than I am. And, to think that hundreds of families are subjected to. . . ."

You can get carried away with flights of images, of course, but a good, realistic dose can awaken a complacent audience.

Intensity The English language, like any other, is rich in synonyms. You usually can choose among several words that have almost the same meaning. Some of these words are stronger, more intense, than others. You can call the person who presides in city hall "the mayor," "a political hack," or "a greedy grafter." You can label the person teaching this class "a purveyor of wisdom," "an instructor," "a speech teacher," or "an intellectual snob." You can say someone "talked to," "lectured at," or "harangued" you. The stronger or more intense your language, the greater the possibility of creating strong positive or negative feelings in an audience. Only take care that your language is not *too* intense, for it may turn off an otherwise sympathetic hearer.[2]

Metaphors Just as metaphors tend to create an image of you as a colorful person, they also can serve to color your subject matter. Some, such as sports metaphors, add a sense of dynamism and involvement: "If we play ball with central administration, they're going to. . . ." Others, such as sexual metaphors, put a definitely negative cast on some fact: "This country has been raped by unchecked, greedy developers." A strong death metaphor creates a sense of impending doom and destruction and makes an audience feel a sense of urgency: "The cancer of . . . will eat away our . . . unless we as a society use radical surgery to. . . ." Again, a caution is in order: Metaphors that are gruesome or disgusting can revolt an audience, so be careful with them. Used well, however, metaphors can associate positive or negative feelings with your ideas.[3]

Your primary concern in encoding your message, then, is effective use of language. Obviously, you don't want to carefully choose every single word, sentence by sentence. That would produce a whole manuscript which you'd be tempted to read, and most of us are not good oral readers. You'll rarely be as effective reading a manuscript as you'll be speaking directly with an audience. As you phrase some of the key ideas in your outline, however, attention to words and sentence structures at the main junctures will pay off. It will create the audience's vision of you, strengthen your ideas, and build an appropriate emotional atmosphere.

ENCODING YOUR SPEECH: USE OF VOICE

In public speakers, this culture currently prizes one particular vocal quality—a sense of *conversationality*. The most successful speakers of our time have cultivated the ability to make an audience feel that they are directly, even intimately, addressing each person. Conversational quality is an art which involves, primarily, convincing yourself that you have in front of you, not a group of programmed robots you're speaking "at," but a group of living, breathing human beings who want to be talked "with." Your principal concern in using your voice is developing a mental attitude rather than using a physical technique.

There are, however, a few observations worth making about the physical use of your voice. Because voice (like language) is so important in conveying impressions of you, in getting concepts across, and in emotionally coloring your ideas, we should review some general characteristics of a "good" voice. A good speaking voice has intelligibility, variety, oral stress, and an appropriate quality.

Intelligibility

"Speak clearly!" "Speak up!" "Slow down!" All of us have been subjected to these vocal commands most of our lives. Essentially, people are asking us to be more intelligible, more understandable. In everyday, person-to-person conversation, we all tend to articulate our words a bit sloppily and to speak in relatively quick and quiet tones: we can do this in conversation because the other person usually knows us pretty well and because we usually are only three to five feet apart. But in public speaking, you often are addressing people who don't know you, and you can easily be twenty-five or more feet away from your listeners. In such a situation, you become harder to understand. To become intelligible at that distance, you have to speak slowly, clearly, and loudly.

Slow Down Instead of jabbering along at 250-300 words per minute, as you often do in animated conversation, you have to slow down to 150-225 words per minute. Obviously, you can't go around timing your speaking rate, but you do have to consciously reduce your rate, especially if you come from the northern and western parts of the country.

Enunciate Clearly Because most of us are "lip lazy" in normal conversation, many speakers have to physically form their words more carefully, putting on the beginnings and endings of words and filling in syllables we often skip in conversation. You may have to force yourself to say "going" instead of "go-in," "just" instead of "jist" (which can be mistaken for "gist"), "govern-ment" instead of "guv-mnt." Obviously, you can *over*articulate, *over*enunciate, and hence sound artificial. Practice, however, will help you find a happy medium.

Speak Loudly You also have to increase your volume. In a large room, especially, your sounds tend to get lost in the high ceilings and dissipate over the space they must cover. If you notice audience members straining forward in their seats, cupping their ears, or frowning, you'll know your volume probably could be increased a bit. Although you can wear out an audience if you shout incessantly, most of us can stand to increase our volume.

One of the reasons, frankly, that public speaking seems unnatural to many people is because rate must be slowed, articulation must be more precise, and loudness must be increased. Public speaking tends to seem too slow, too artificial, and too loud to the speaker's own ear. Just remember that you're inside your own head; keep in mind the people who are outside. As you speak more and more often in public, your own sense of unnaturalness will be reduced. Then you'll become more intelligible, and happy that you are.

Variety As you move from intimate conversation to public speaking, you may also find yourself subject to the charge of monotony—a monotonous sound, a monotonous rate. You'll sometimes discover that you are lulling an audience. In conversation, you can get by with very little variety in sound and rate because people are in a position to "read" your face and body, to talk back and forth (and hence break up your discourse), and to catch subtle vocal cues. That's not true in a speech, however. And hence you must compensate by adding variety in your voice.

Pitch In normal talking, you usually employ only a few "notes" in your speaking range. In a speech, you usually must have higher "highs" and lower "lows." A narrow pitch range tends to communicate that you are bored or uninvolved. You must expand your range, being careful only not to go too far, with an artificially sing-song, up-and-down pattern.

Rate Not only must most of us slow down, but we all could profit from varying the rate at which we speak. Variety in rate communicates our intentions and our emotions. You may speak more quickly when you are excited or hurrying over less important material, more slowly when you want to emphasize key ideas. You may even want to mark your notecards before speaking, to remind yourself when to slow down to stress important points.

Pauses In everyday conversation, you put in appropriate pauses or breaks, little intervals of silence you include naturally. When many of us get behind a lectern, however, because we are nervous and because we know the material, we tend to charge forward without those natural breaks.

Don't be afraid to include some silence and a few pauses. Pauses allow time for key ideas to sink in. They can also be used to heighten audience anticipation, as when you say, "And now, notice how John Jones characterizes city planning when he says, and I quote: . . ." A slight break between that statement and the actual quotation adds variety and increases suspense.

Changes in pitch and rate, and pauses can, of course, be overdone, leaving the impression of mechanical delivery and a sense of artificiality which destroys your credibility. As you practice making speeches, however, you'll soon discover a level of variety in these three vocal factors that is effective.

Stress   A third significant voice characteristic involves stress patterns, the way you accent or "hit" words. By stress we mean those points in a sentence which you hit with increased vocal energy. Important to the good speaking voice is "proper" (usually nonrhythmical) stress, putting the emphasis on the right words or syllables to accurately convey meanings. Consider the simple sentence "Our friends are in the living room." Depending upon which word you stress, you change the meaning of the sentence. Stressing *our* indicates that *their* friends aren't here; *friends,* that our enemies aren't around; *are,* that another person's assertion ("they aren't") is wrong; *living room,* that they're not in the kitchen. (Try it!) Stressing the right words communicates your meanings accurately.

Questions of stress are relatively subtle concerns for most beginning speakers. If you try too hard to lay out your speech like a musical score, you'll go crazy. It never hurts, however, to underline or capitalize key words or phrases in your notes, to remind yourself of what you want to stress.

Voice Quality   The fourth characteristic of a good speaking voice is a quality appropriate to the speaker, the audience, and the occasion. *Voice quality* refers to fullness or thinness of the sound, the degree of harshness, nasality, breathiness, deepness of tones, and the like. Voice qualities are produced by highly complex adjustments of your vocal mechanism—lips, jaw, tongue, roof of your mouth, voice box. We usually describe the results of such adjustments with words such as *yelling, moaning, whining, screeching, groaning, wailing, pleading, threatening,* and so on. Voice qualities are aspects of your sound that you rarely think about, yet they are extremely important to the way people interpret you. Just ask the parent who practices varying the degree of threateningness in his or her voice when giving orders to a child.

A good speaking voice matches vocal qualities to the speaker, the audience, and the occasion. If your words are angry but your voice quality is hesitant, an audience will be confused. If you're telling an audience to take it easy while your voice is strained and tight, you'll be sending two different messages to the listeners. If what you say and how you say it don't jibe, you're in trouble. There is no magical way of producing the "right" voice quality. About all you can do is react to feedback and later ask observers how you sounded. You certainly do want to create appropriate "emotional sounds," though, as you deliver the speech.

What we have been saying about voice, then, is this: there is no need to concern yourself with creating a perfect speaking voice, for after all, naturalness and general conversationality are the primary virtues of voice. Yet there are things you can do to make sure your voice accurately portrays your own feelings, carefully packages your ideas, and overlays the emotions you want to generate in hearers. By watching for intelligibility, variety, stress, and appropriate voice qualities (without getting too technical and carried away), you'll make your voice do its job as a channel of communication.[4]

ENCODING YOUR SPEECH: USE OF BODY

A balanced approach also applies to your use of body—movements, gestures, facial expressions. If you start thinking about each and every little quirk you have as a human being—a twitch here, a squiggled nose there, more right-arm than left-arm gestures—you'll be distracted and never get on with your talk. Keep in mind that most listeners will accept you for who you are, an individual. You should, however, be conscious of the fact that your whole body communicates with an audience. "Body language" has received so much attention in recent years that you ought to think a bit about the four categories of body language of most concern in public speaking: facial expressions, gestures, stance and posture, and use of space.

Facial Expression

Your face is an important aspect of body language, or nonverbal communication. Your face provides an audience with many key cues to your feelings. Working together with your words and your voice qualities, your face "tells" your audience—

- whether you are being straight or ironic or satirical;
- whether you are mad, sad, stern, relaxed;
- whether you're open to them as individuals or a closed, tight person with your mind already made up.

Especially important are your eyes. While, obviously, most audience members can't see your eyes clearly at a distance of twenty-five feet or more, they generally can tell whether or not you're looking at them. If you deliver your speech to the back wall or out the window or at the ceiling, or if you constantly stare at your notes, you break eye contact. Instead, look directly at individual members of the audience, moving from front to back, from side to side. Such eye contact is extremely important in this culture. An audience judges your earnestness, sincerity, and forthrightness on your willingness to look people in the eyes.

Good eye contact has another important virtue: it allows you to "read" the audience, to get feedback. By looking at individuals, you can tell if you're getting through—whether you need to slow down, speed up, add examples, subtract material, repeat yourself.

There is, of course, no "perfect" way for a speaker's face to look; and you certainly cannot stand up in front of an audience and control every little facial muscle. But you can think about your feelings and how they are traced across your face; and you can make sure, especially, that you establish a visual bond with your audience.[5]

Gesture   You do have more control over the second aspect of nonverbal communication, gesture. In normal conversation, most of us are animated, moving our heads and arms appropriately; we gesture freely in informal situations. Sometimes, however, we freeze when we stand up to say a few words. We may feel naked in front of an audience, and hence tend to hold our arms down and in, to forget that we communicate with our whole bodies. To make full use of your body as a speaker, you can employ three sorts of gestures:

Conventional Gestures are signs or symbols that function as visual "words" in our culture, such as the hand gesture meaning "stop," the "V for Victory" sign, or two raised fingers for the number 2.

Descriptive Gestures depict the idea you're communicating, such as holding the hands apart to show length, holding thumb and index finger close together for smallness, or moving hands and arms to indicate shape.

Emotional Gestures suggest feelings, such as pounding a table in anger, throwing up your arms in disgust, or pointing a finger to threaten.

All of these gestures are important for describing both ideas and feelings to audiences. Using them while giving a speech is sometimes hard for a beginner; but gestures are necessary if you want to be a totally communicating public talker. To help yourself make full use of your arms and hands especially, you might follow these suggestions:

Keep arms and hands in a ready position. If you're standing behind a lectern, let your arms rest comfortably on it, so that you easily can gesture above it or beside it when moved to do so. If you're standing beside a lectern, you might let your arms rest gently by your sides or stand with your hands at about belt level so that you can gesture smoothly from the elbow. Or if you're seated on a table or behind a desk, you might want to rest your hands in your lap or on the table top, ready to move. If you can forget about how awkward your arms and hands feel, you usually will get them into your act naturally.

Practice with full gestures. When you practice your speeches, make sure you practice in ways you'll actually deliver them. Quietly sitting at a desk or table, mumbling to yourself with hands limp, does little to improve your gestures. Gesturing during a practice session can seem awfully dumb (especially if anyone catches you doing it!); yet it is invaluable as a way of warming yourself up and making gestures seem more natural during the actual delivery of the speech.

Stance and Posture

A third aspect of body language is how you stand and hold your body during a speech. Some speakers slump informally over a lectern; others stand erectly and stiffly behind it. Some are almost perfectly immobile, while others are constantly running around the room, back and forth, side to side. Again, while there are no rules for stance and posture, it is important to realize what stance and posture can communicate about you and about your feelings toward an audience. The speaker who stands still and erect behind a lectern is saying, in effect, "This is a formal occasion and message, and I am a serious person." The one who leans forward over a lectern, gesturing in front of it, is saying, "I am interested in you, and want you to understand and accept my ideas." A constantly changing stance and posture is a sign of nervousness and excitement.

To be sure, you more or less naturally slip into habitual postures and stances while actually giving a talk, but some thought in advance will help you use your habits productively. By considering the formality of the occasion, the kind of relationship you are seeking to establish with the audience, and the attitudes you hope to embody, you can at least make some general decisions on your posture and stance.

Use of Space

Another aspect of body language is your use of the space around you. Your use of space works along with your stance and posture in creating the relationship between you and your audience. In the usual speaking situation in which there is a lectern in front of an audience, a speaker has to choose how to use the space around the lectern.

Behind the Lectern You can stand directly behind the lectern, hands clasping it on each side. This is the most formal stance. It puts the most physical and psychological distance between you and the audience.

Beside the Lectern This is a little less formal. Many speakers will put their notes on a lectern or table, referring to them when necessary, yet leaving themselves free to move and gesture.

In Front of the Lectern By standing in front of it, other speakers make sure the lectern doesn't present a barrier between them and their audiences. The lectern can be used for "storing" notes that way, but it doesn't psychologically block direct communication.

Seated Position The most informal posture is to sit on the front edge of a table. Sitting communicates a sense of relaxation and openness (assuming the audience likewise is seated). This is at present an "in" way to use physical space; but keep in mind that it is almost too informal and freewheeling for some situations. You may lose some power and authority, too.

Normally, the situation or occasion determines the way you use space in public speaking. If you are delivering a formal eulogy to a friend, you probably don't want to sit on the front edge of a table. But, if you are trying to calm the fears of an anxious audience, you may find that the informality of sitting helps you achieve that goal. If you're going to talk only a minute or two in a large meeting, standing at your seat is an appropriate way to use space; but if your remarks are going to be longer, you may well want to walk to the front of the room and assume the lectern, so the audience won't break their necks trying to see you for several minutes and so they can hear you better. Your best use of space, then, is dictated by the situation and by the kind of psychological relationship you're setting up with your audience.[6]

In planning body movement before your actual speech, you may want to check out room arrangements to make sure you can be seen; to decide whether you want to stand behind, alongside, or in front of a lectern; and to remind yourself to keep your eyes on the audience, your arms high enough to be of use, and your body loose enough to respond to what you're feeling.

The study of body language has become a kind of parlor game today. Obviously, you can become too hung up on every little nuance of emotion you potentially convey with every adjustment of face, gesture, stance, and space. As with both language and voice as channels of communication, so too with body: *You* are much more highly aware of your own foibles than the audience is. That audience is busily taking in the whole message, the *combination* of language, voice, and body. Unless you have some extraordinarily weird or unusual words, vocal characteristics, or gestures, audiences probably won't even notice how you sound or look. Your central concern is not "doing it right," but "doing it effectively"—conveying via words, sounds, and movements the messages *you* want to get through. Effective use of language, voice, and body can help you meet the expectations for an articulate person—openness, honesty, naturalness, conversationality.

ENCODING YOUR SPEECH: USE OF VISUAL AIDS

The fourth channel of communication in public speaking is the use of visual aids. These include flipcharts, chalkboards, actual objects, slideshows, films, and the like, which often accompany oral talks. A picture is worth a thousand words because it can show and reveal. It can show complex operations better than you can ever describe them, and it can reveal nuances and details. That's why travelogues include films. Television, film, and color photography have made ours a society that relies upon visual communication. In such a visual society, you are advised to consider how you might enhance your talk with pictures, handouts, graphs, objects, and other visual aids. We will take up this subject in more detail in Chapter 5, "Introducing New Concepts and Activities." If you're going to use visual aids in a speech before getting to that chapter, feel free to skip ahead for advice on making the best use of them—to see what some of the possibilities are. Using good visual aids can save you both words and frustrations.

PRACTICING THE PRESENTATION

The final step in preplanning and preparation is practicing the speech out loud. For those occasions when you have the time and forewarning, practicing will make you feel better prepared, especially the first few times you talk publicly. You probably don't need to go to the extremes the great Greek orator Demosthenes did, shouting into the ocean's roar for six months with his mouth full of pebbles. But you should do a few run-throughs to increase your self-confidence, to set some of your principal ideas and phrases clearly in mind, and to vocally smooth out any potentially rough spots. There are few foolproof rules for practicing, but the following methods can help:

1. *Work from your actual speaking outline.* If you have prepared a long, technical outline of the type which appears in this book, cut it down to a "speaking" outline—to something you can work with easily, unobtrusively. A big outline lets you visualize the whole speech; a small outline allows you to communicate with others directly and forcefully.
2. *Practice full voice.* Don't huddle away in a bedroom, whispering to yourself. Work in a fairly large room, and talk more loudly than normal. That will help you get used to your own voice coming back to you, to get used to taking the deeper breaths you need, and to get your rate under control.
3. *Work on your "look-up."* Don't just read over your notes or manuscript, word by word. Practice looking up most of the time. An audience wants to be visually bonded to a speaker, so you simply must get away from your notes to communicate with the audience.
4. *Use a mechanical aid* if you're gutsy. Work with a tape recorder, for example. Your voice may sound strange to you because you're used to hearing it from "inside" your head and not from an "outside" machine. Once you overcome that reaction, listen to your rate, your phrasing, and your pauses to make sure an audience can follow you easily.
5. *Practice with someone else* if possible. If you can successfully deliver the speech to a close, critical friend, you can deliver it to anyone! Working with another person will give you direct feedback, condition you to watch for reactions, and allow you to work "full body," using arms, stance, and face in a way you normally wouldn't by yourself.

After you give a speech in class, seek out additional feedback on how you're coming across—that's one of the reasons you're in a classroom. To allay your fears (*or* to discover really problematic areas for improvement), talk with people you can trust—a speech communication teacher, a friend, a supervisor, or whatever. If you find a consistent pattern of comments upon your language, voice, body, or visuals, think of ways of improvement. Just don't overreact to criticism; use it positively to improve your skills.

Practice may not make perfect. If it does, you've *over*practiced and are in danger of losing the sense of naturalness, spontaneity, and conversationality we've discussed. But practice will prepare you to seize the opportunity with confidence and control. And that's what it's all about.

OVERCOMING SPEECH FRIGHT

Now that we have completed our review of the ten basic steps in speech preparation, we need to discuss something that runs through everyone's mind before standing up to talk: speech fright.

Most people—at least 60 to 75 percent according to surveys of college students—suffer from speech fright or what some experts call "communication apprehension." It's a complex psychophysical state, really, that arises from psychological stress (fear of public failure, feelings of inadequacy) and from physiological overloads (increased flow of adrenalin in times of expectancy or fear, increased heart rate and blood pressure, excessive muscular tension). Speech fright is a perfectly natural reaction of your mind and body to stress. Although the reaction varies a good deal from person to person, it tends to produce sweaty palms, throaty tension, bodily rigidity, and vocal hesitations ("ahs," "ahms," half-words, rephrasings).

Keep in mind, though, that for the vast majority of us, speech fright is simply a fear which must be overcome in ways we overcome most of our other fears. These include actually engaging in the activity often enough to discover it's not fatal, talking through our fear with others to see how they control it, and attacking it physically and psychologically.[7] Many students of public speaking have found the "tricks" listed on Figure 4.1 to be useful.

Keep in mind, too, another feature of communication apprehension: it can be *used positively* by most speakers. Speech fright tends to make you a more alert, energetic person as you seek physiologically to dissipate the extra adrenalin coursing through your veins and as you psyche yourself up for meeting the challenge of public address. This extra energy gives you an edge—like being up for a game. And remember, too, that because speech fright often is an *anticipatory reaction*, something you go through mainly before you talk, it tends to decline naturally as you talk. The very act of talking aloud physiologically "uses up" the adrenalin; and, as well, two to three minutes into the speech you discover that, as a matter of fact, people *are* listening, *are* interested, and hence you psychologically comfort yourself as well.

So, yes, you probably will feel nervous about getting up to give a speech. And yes, you will have to do a fair amount of work—physical and psychological—to overcome it. But, no, it will not keep you from being an

FIGURE 4.1   **Methods for Coping with Speech Fright**

Not all of the following methods for coping with speech fright will work for everyone, although some undoubtedly will help you control your worst fears.

I. *Take Precautions to Prevent Problems Ahead of Time:*
   1. Rehearse aloud, and be sure to use several different wordings to give yourself flexibility.
   2. Use legible notes, well spaced for easy reference; number your pages.
   3. Be familiar with the setting—size of room, closeness of audience, amplification equipment—so you're not surprised.
   4. Even while practicing, focus on your ideas—what you'll be saying first, second, third, etc.—rather than your fears of "how you're doing."
   5. Also during practice, remind yourself of things you're doing very well—marshalling materials, varying your gestures, and so on.

II. *Search and Destroy Your Hidden Fears:*
   1. *Information:* What's your shakiest piece of information or your least well-supported claim? Can you improve it?
   2. *Audience:* Who's going to be there? Whom do you most dread facing? Why? Can you overcome that dread through better preparation? through convincing yourself that the dread is unfounded?
   3. *Visualization:* Can you visualize yourself giving a successful speech? If not, why not? Keep working on that psychological picture until you look good to yourself.
   4. *Questioning:* What's the one question you hope no one will ask? How will you answer it? (Remember that presidents of the United States prepare for press conferences by practicing answers to all the nasty questions the Press Corps is likely to ask.)
   5. *Appearances:* Are you worried about looking young? inexperienced? poorly or inappropriately dressed? awkward? How can you compensate for those worries in what you do, wear, or say?
   6. *Disasters:* What's the worst thing that could go wrong during the speech? What can you do to prevent it?
   7. *End of Your Career:* What's the worst thing that could happen to you as a result of this speech? Will it happen? Is it really the end of the world?

III. *Prepare Yourself Physically To Speak:*
   1. As your time to speak nears, take several deep breaths, holding them and then slowly releasing them.
   2. If your mouth has a tendency to dry out (that's called "cottonmouth"), keep a glass of water handy; drink water before and even during your speech.
   3. Just before you rise to speak, tense the muscles in your legs, arms, chest, stomach, buttocks, and face (if you can without others seeing you!). Tensed muscles must relax for a while after forced tension.
   4. Just before you utter your first word, take one last deep breath, and perhaps tense your hands and arms if you can do so unobtrusively.
   5. And remember, the act of speaking will drain off excess energy within a minute or two, especially if you remember to move during the introduction of your speech.

effective public speaker; in fact, it can be used to add extra "punch" to your presentation.

CONCLUDING THOUGHTS AS YOU GET READY TO BEGIN

We've now been through all the steps and activities of preparing, building, and delivering a speech. Ten easy steps? Not really, of course, because no one is a natural orator, and because everyone who's willing to think carefully about speeches must make dozens of pre-speech decisions. But, a principle which underlies Chapters 2, 3, and 4 must be underscored once more: *The more carefully you plan your speeches, the more confident you'll be about your own chances for success.* The more conscious and systematic your preparation, the more likely you are to be an Articulate Person.

Keep telling yourself that, over and over, as you charge into Parts II, III, and IV of this book.

NOTES

[1] For a near-exhaustive listing of ways in which you can increase your credibility and in which your credibility can affect audiences, see Stephen W. Littlejohn, "A Bibliography of Studies Related to Variables of Source Credibility," *Bibliographic Annual in Speech Communication: 1971*, ed. Ned A. Shearer (Falls Church, Va.: Speech Communication Association, 1972), pp. 1–40. See also Ronald L. Applebaum et al., *Fundamental Concepts in Human Communication* (San Francisco: Canfield Press, 1973), pp. 123–146.

[2] John Waite Bowers has cautioned speakers to remember, however, that overly intense language can affect an audience negatively. On a scale of one to seven (with "one" being extremely intense negatively and with "seven" being extremely intense positively), if your audience is at the "five" position—i.e., fairly positive about something—you should pitch your words either at "four" (if you want them to be less positive) or at "six" (if you want them to be more positive). Going too much farther in either direction is likely to produce what's called a *boomerang effect*; that is, the audience is likely to go in the direction opposite from the one you're advocating. See John Waite Bowers, "Language and Argument," in *Perspectives on Argumentation*, ed. G. R. Miller and T. R. Nilsen (Glenview, Il.: Scott, Foresman and Company, 1966), esp. pp. 168–172.

[3] On the use and effectiveness of sexual and death metaphors, see John Waite Bowers and Michael M. Osborn, "Attitudinal Effects of Selected Types of Concluding Metaphors in Persuasive Speeches," *Speech [Communication] Monographs*, 33 (June 1966), 147–155. On obscene metaphors and language in general, see R. Bostrom, J. Basehart, and C. Rossiter, "The Effects of Three Different Types of Profane Language in Persuasive Communication," *Journal of Communication*, 23 (1973), 461–475, and Anthony Mulac, "Effects of Obscene Language Upon Three Dimensions of Listener Attitude," *Communication Monographs*, 43 (November 1976), 300–307.

[4] For general analyses of the vocal aspects of oral communication, see W. Barnett Pearce and Bernard J. Brommel, "Vocalic Communication and Persuasion," *Quarterly Journal of Speech*, 58 (October 1972), 298–306, and Howard H. Martin, "The Prosodic Components of Speech Melody," *Quarterly Journal of Speech*, 67 (February 1981), 81–92. And, much of the research on judgments people make

about your voice is summarized in Mark L. Knapp, *Nonverbal Communication in Human Interaction*, 2nd ed. (New York: Holt, Rinehart & Winston, Inc., 1978), esp. Chap. 10; Judee K. Burgoon and Thomas Saine, *The Unspoken Dialogue* (Boston: Houghton Mifflin Co., 1978), Chaps. 3 and 8; Randall P. Harrison, *Beyond Words: An Introduction to Nonverbal Communication* (Englewood Cliffs, N.J.: Prentice-Hall, Inc., 1974), Chap. 6; and Dale G. Leathers, *Nonverbal Communication Systems* (Boston: Allyn & Bacon, 1976), Chap. 6.

[5]   An excellent review of the face and its role in communication can be found in Leathers, Chap. 2. For a fuller treatment see Paul Ekman, Wallace V. Friesen, and P. Ellsworth, *Emotion in the Human Face: Guidelines for Research and an Integration of Findings* (New York: Pergamon Press, Inc., 1972).

[6]   Discussions of posture, positioning, and use of physical space can be found in: F. Deutsch, "Analysis of Postural Behavior," *Psychoanalytic Quarterly*, 16 (1947), 195–213; W. James, "A Study of the Expression of Bodily Posture," *Journal of General Psychology*, 7 (1932), 405–436; Albert Mehrabian, "Significance of Posture and Position in the Communication of Attitude and Status Relationships," *Psychological Bulletin*, 71 (1969), 359–372; and Edward T. Hall, *The Hidden Dimension* (New York: Doubleday & Company, Inc., 1969), Chap. X, "Distances in Man."

[7]   Programs in systematic desensitization were launched in various parts of the country following the publication of James C. McCroskey, "The Implementation of a Large Scale Program of Systematic Desensitization for Communication Apprehension," *Speech Teacher [Communication Education]*, 21 (November 1972), 255–264. Other "programs" have been tried as well: R. J. Fenton et al., "The Use of EMG Biofeedback Assisted Relaxation Training to Reduce Communication Apprehension," paper presented to the Western Speech Communication Association convention, Seattle, 1975; Kim Giffin and K. Bradley, "An Exploratory Study of Group Counseling for Speech Anxiety," Research Monograph 12, Lawrence, Ks.: Communication Research Center, University of Kansas, 1967; G. M. Phillips, "Rhetoritherapy versus the Medical Model: Dealing with Reticence," *Speech Monographs*, 35 (March 1968), 34–43.

ASSIGNMENTS

Pre-Performance

1. Find a paragraph in a newspaper editorial or letter to the editor or other piece of writing that uses inflammatory or intense language. Revise the paragraph by substituting less intense words and phrases for those that would likely create strong negative feelings.

2. Read at least one speech by each of three recognized speakers (e.g., John F. Kennedy, Abraham Lincoln, Martin Luther King, Jr., Clarence Darrow). Compare the language in these speeches by giving special attention to factors discussed in this chapter:

simplicity	colorfulness
repetition	vocabulary
coherence	imagery
qualifications	intensity
shadings	metaphors

3. In your communication journal make a list of expressions, excluding hesitancies, that are overused by members of your class. Are a few expressions used repeatedly?

To understand how these expressions slip into our speech, you may want to experiment with coining a new word and seeing if it will catch on and become overused by your friends or family. Choose an adjective or adverb (remember "peachy keen," "cool," "far out," "swimmingly"?) and use it frequently. If you are asked what the word means, give a definition, but do not reveal the nature of your experiment. How long does it take for the word to be picked up by others? Who started using it first? How rapidly or slowly did the word spread? How fast did the word fade?

4. *Paralanguage* relates to the way vocal sounds (intelligibility, variety, stress, and voice quality) interact with words to produce meaning. To increase your awareness of the significance of paralinguistic dimensions in communication, divide into groups of four or five and complete the following exercise. Sit in a circle that is wide enough to prevent classmates from touching each other. Each member should be blindfolded during the five- to ten-minute conversation which the groups will conduct. These rules apply to the actual conversation:

   a. Members are to speak only with numbers.

   b. Conduct the conversation by varying the pitch, rate, volume, stress, and quality of your voices.

   c. The nature of conversation suggests that members of the group share talking time.

After the conversation discuss whether feelings and emotions were conveyed without conventional sentences and even though blindfolded. Were some of the members able to develop particularly meaningful vocal variations? What did you say to each other?

5. Form three-member groups. One member should draw a geometrical figure; a second member should then attempt to describe the drawing to the third member who attempts to reproduce the figure. Observe these rules:

   a. Do not show the drawing to the third member.

   b. Do not use gestures.

   c. State the directions only once.

   d. Do not allow any questions.

What were the major difficulties in completing this project? What specific implications does this exercise suggest to the public speaker?

6. In his book *Power! How to Get It, How to Use It* [New York: Ballantine Books, 1975, p. 26], Michael Korda suggests that a person can assert power by moving into another's territory. For example, the next time you have dinner with a friend, deliberately set some object of yours (a glass of water, a purse, a cigarette lighter) on your friend's portion of the table. Slowly move the object further into your friend's territory as you use it and put it down again. Watch your friend's reactions and record them later in your communication journal. What does this power play suggest to the public

speaker? What happens to the speaker who stands in front of the lectern and gradually closes in on the audience?

Performance

1. Following the steps outlined in Chapters 2 and 3 for constructing a speech, prepare a three- to four-minute speech on a subject of your choice which your instructor approves. A day or two before delivering the speech in class, meet in groups of two or three for the purpose of practicing your presentation. Trade advice, perhaps by referring to the questions for listeners that are listed in Preview I. Your instructor may want to make an audio- or videotape of the actual presentation.

2. Prepare a short speech relating to communication. For instance, you might discuss suggestions for conversing with a physician, a speech that you will always remember, or a technique of saying no to telephone solicitors. These speeches, of course, will depend upon you as a personal resource rather than on outside research.

Post-Performance

1. After one of these early speeches, your instructor likely will comment on intelligibility, variety, oral stress, and quality. Fellow students also might complete brief vocal analysis forms after listening to a classroom presentation. If possible, listen to a tape of one of these early presentations and make self-evaluations.

2. If your instructor made a videotape of one of your speeches, analyze your video image and your audio image and consider how well they mesh.

3. Immediately following a day's round of speeches, form groups of two or three for the purpose of giving each speaker feedback about language, body movement, and vocal patterns.

INFORMING

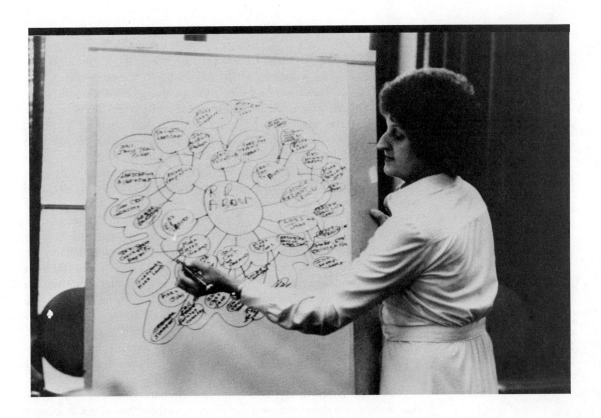

Information Transfer

"Information," "data," "the scoop," "the lowdown," "background (or foreground)," "the whys and wherefores,"—"the facts . . . the facts . . . the facts." We are a society which has come to almost worship "the facts." The development of the electronic media, photostatic printing of written materials, computerized data storage and retrieval systems, the invention of the transistor and other miniaturized circuits, improved telephonic transmissions of both voice and image—all have conspired to launch this culture into the Era of the Information Explosion. That explosion has facilitated fact-based decision-making, but it has also knocked the walls out of libraries, overloaded electronic circuits, and guaranteed that no one human being ever again could be called a "Renaissance man," capable of knowing all there is worth knowing.

Amidst the tons of paper and the kilowatt hours of electronic signals, however, stands the oral communicator, armed with a few little facts, an opinion or two, and a hope that someone might take a few minutes from reading and watching in order to listen. A speaker can offer something no other medium of information transfer can. As a human being, you embody information, giving it life, personality, experience, and feelings. As a sensitive person, furthermore, you can react to your listeners, expanding an idea when someone looks puzzled, hurrying along if others appear bored. No other medium of data input can compete with you in that arena.

All of this is not to say, of course, that human, face-to-face information transfer is not sometimes difficult, is not subject to failure. It is more than a matter, as we shall see, of "just the facts, ma'am." Yet with a little forethought and audience adaptation, you can adequately meet the challenge of informing an audience. In the chapters that follow, we will be dealing with four types of informative speeches: defining, demonstrating, reporting, and explaining. The "recipes" laid into those chapters will offer you techniques for presenting information and will facilitate your prespeech planning.

Before looking at those recipes, let us briefly stop to think about how information is transferred from one human being to another. Knowledge of the linguistic, social, and psychological processes involved, while a bit theoretical, should clarify the general problems you may face when you seek to inform.

WORDS, WORDS, WORDS

When Shakespeare asked, "What's in a name?" and then smartly replied, "That which we call a rose by any other name would smell as sweet," he missed the point. Gertrude Stein's "Rose is a rose is a rose is a rose" didn't help our understanding of names, either. The French Academy's attempt in the seventeenth century to draw up a list of "proper" words (with the blessing of King Louis XIII no less) was doomed from the beginning, as is every grammar school teacher's demand that kids use dictionaries. Words are not static objects which neatly correspond to "the facts." Their meanings are affected by all manner of personal idiosyncrasies and social-cultural pressures. *Words are slippery, dynamic, changing media of interhuman communication.* You're lucky to be able to communicate at all!

To better understand the changing quality of words, let us begin with the word *cow*. A cow? Everyone knows what a cow is! Wrong. To a child on an Iowa farm, a cow is a friend to be cared for when it is weaned, a means of economic livelihood, and a source of sex education. Some of these cows have distinct personalities, especially those raised for a 4-H show; others are mere objects to be bought and sold, to be regulated by the government and turned into cash. In contrast, to a child reared in inner-city New York, a child raised on pavement, a cow is a wild animal kept in zoos along with lions, tigers, and tapirs. Milk, after all, comes in cartons and meat comes in monofilament plastic from a grocery store. A cow is a mere animal, to be examined quizzically and to be ridden by cowboys (weird word) on TV. And to a Hindu child of India, a cow has a religious meaning. Linked with the divinity Krishna, who was a cowherd, the cow is a sacred animal to be venerated and to be worshipped in some religious ceremonies.

A cow? Everyone knows what a cow is? Not really. The essence of "cowness" cannot be captured in a mere word, for three reasons:

1. *Society—your "culture"—dictates how mere words are to be taken.* "Society" tells you what meanings—what objects, ideas, feelings, values —you are to associate with words such as *cow*.

2. *You further complicate the process by assigning your own meanings to words on the basis of your individual experiences.* No matter what your society in general says, you add on other meanings to words, depending upon where and when you are raised, your family, your friends, your teachers, your experiences in the world. As a private person, indeed, you often are placed in a double bind. Your society, for example, may say that *democracy* is a system of government wherein elected officials respond to mandates from the people in order to make decisions based on equality, fairness, equal access, the rights of majorities and minorities, and a series of other principles recorded in constitutions and statutes. If you live in an economically and politically deprived neighborhood, however, your own life experiences teach you that *democracy* is a system of oppression that is insensitive to individual needs, strangled in red tape, prone to over-promising and underdelivering, and personified in the figures of the political boss and overworked social agencies. Words—they have to be elastic enough to hold all of the meanings and associations that both you and your society dump into them.

3. *And, to make matters even worse, the meaning and force of words vary a good deal from context to context.* Take another word, *promise.* The three-year-old who tells his mother that he promises "never to lie again" in all probability will stretch the truth on future occasions, and that fib may be responded to with no more than another admonition to honesty. But the person who promises "to love, honor, and keep" may face a set of moral and legal sanctions if that promise is broken, as will the people who "hereby promise to pay the Last National Bank, ninety days hence" or who "promise faithfully to execute the office and duties of President of the United States" but do not. The meaning of words, then, can vary a good deal depending upon many factors within a context: (a) who you are in that context (a kid, an adult, a peer, a subordinate); (b) who the audience is (people who respect your authority or those who don't know or care who you are); and (c) the setting in which the words are uttered (an informal social relationship or a formal or legal situation).

Thus the meanings of words cannot really be captured in a dictionary or frozen in a *Reader's Digest* "Increase Your Word Power" listing. Meanings of words—the media of information transfer—change with the times, the place, the culture, the person, and the situation.

SYMBOLS AND INFORMATION TRANSFER

Before you cry yourself to sleep, however, let us pull out of this morass of universal misunderstanding and noncommunication. We do, after all, actually manage to convey a fair amount of information to others. We can achieve an amazingly high level of communication, in spite of the slipperiness of words, if we ever so carefully use our words and other symbols to chunk up, package, and convey "the facts." Information can be transferred orally through the four language processes which undergird interhuman communication: *naming, showing, interrelating,* and *signifying.*

Naming

Enough of cows for now. Let' move to *war.* How in the world can you explain to a child of five what a war is? You could tell the kid to look it up in the dictionary, but then the poor dear might be faced with: "1. armed conflict between groups within a society or between social or cultural units. 2. military combat as the study of maneuvers and tactics, or as an institution within a government. 3. hostility and/or overt aggression; contentiousness; ill will: as the *war* between science and religion. . . ." This sort of definition would only replace the word *war* with a host of other difficult notions—"armed conflict," "maneuvers and tactics," "cultural units," "aggression," "contentiousness." *You and I do not learn our basic concepts from a dictionary; we learn through direct or indirect experience.*

We often learn such concepts as *war* through metaphors and analogies. So the five-year-old never has marched off to battle. Still, you can teach a child something about war by comparing war to a fight between neighbor kids. (Technically, their fight is metaphorically similar to "real war," as when you say, "There's a full-scale war going on in the back yard!") You might also say, "War is like two dogs fighting over the same soup bone." (Technically, any fight over an object, right, or territory is a war no matter who or what engages in the fight.)

The first process, *naming,* is a matter of finding *references* (experiences or objects with which an audience is familiar) so as to tie a word together with a thing or event.

Showing

While naming refers or points to objects and experiences, showing goes even further by actually presenting objects and processes to an audience. If a picture is worth a thousand words, presumably the actual object or some detailed representation of it (a diagram, drawing, or model) is worth double that. The carnival hawker of vegetable-chopping machines or universal-Swiss-Army-knives-with-sixteen-blades is not content to verbally describe the glories of gourmet salads or the macho-mania you can feel with such a weapon lashed to your belt. The hawker "shows" the product, letting you hold it, pound it, cut with it, and admire its genuine, guaranteed-for-the-life-of-the-machine stainless steel blades. The person speaking to a group of antique buffs at the local craft center does not merely lecture on the art of caning chairs. Weaving cane across a chair seat involves a five-step process (soaking the cane, cleaning out the holes, weaving the cane through the holes, tying it off under the chair seat, and lacing a heavier piece over the holes to cover the work). Merely talking about those processes would undoubtedly only confuse the audience. But demonstrating—showing the process step by step with some cane, a chair, and a series of diagrams—would get them ready to go.

Our second process, *showing,* thus is as important as naming, because visualization can put flesh and meat on complicated information. Showing makes information accessible to a listener's sense of sight as well as sound.

Interrelating

Basically, interrelating makes mental connections between separate (and perhaps seemingly unrelated) pieces of information. Your sensory equipment—eyes, ears, hands, tongue, and nose—is constantly bombarded by sensory stimuli. To make sense out of your surroundings, you are continually engaged in sorting those stimuli into groups, labeling them and describing in your own head the relations among them. When the articulate person is one of those stimuli, he or she has an obligation to help the audience connect and structure ideas. Potentially, an audience needs such interrelating of ideas in at least two situations:

Filling Informational Gaps Sometimes, an audience needs a bridge of data to get it from one point to another. So the audience at the craft center knows that you have to start with a bundle of cane and a chair frame, and knows what the final product ought to look like; but it has no sense whatsoever of how to actually get from one to the other. Or a person knows she is in Minneapolis and knows she wants to get to Chicago, but needs to know the best route between them. Or, think of the person about to embark on a degree program in night school; the person is faced with a bewildering catalog description of core or required courses and options, of majors and concentrations, of departments and programs, of degrees, of residency and fee schedules, and then, of lists of courses offered now and in the future for actually occupying time while on campus. Until an advisor or orientation officer actually leads this person by the hand through that maze of regulations, interpreting the words and concretely describing a structure of experiences, the student will be totally lost. One of the structures or interrelationships an oral communicator is called upon to provide, therefore, is one which bridges informational gaps.

Suggesting Rationales Some people, however, even when given structured information, are bold enough to ask "Why?" Why is cane laced in particular patterns across chair frames? Why is Interstate 94 a better way into Chicago than Highway 10? Why are there required courses and variable fee schedules? These questions ask for more than informational bridges; they demand *rationales or explanations.* They demand causes tied to effects, needs tied to solutions—reasons for doing something, or going somewhere, or thinking about some idea in a particular way. Some of these reasons are simple enough to provide. The chair caner can show that a particular pattern of weaving provides structural support from one strand of cane to another. The AAA representative can explain that Interstate 94 is faster, subject to more stable weather, and shorter than Highway 10. Some reasons are astronomically more complicated, however, as when a historian tries to explain how the Thirteen Colonies came to a state of open rebellion and revolution over a dozen-year period. The pattern of explanations and reasons—the structure of ideas—involved in this discourse can demand volumes if carried to its fullest. But when an audience wonders why, when it seeks to remove bewilderment, the articulate person must rise to the verbal challenge of interrelating complex information into a coherent, understandable, rational package.

Our third social-psychological process, *interrelating,* perhaps represents the speaker's greatest informational challenge. Interrelating or structuring information makes it whole, puts it into a comprehensible package.

Signifying

Even after an audience has been given definitions, demonstrations, and complex explanations, however, it still can ask, "So what?" It can wonder, "What does it all mean to me?" "To what effect?" "When and to whom?" "Why should *I* care?" Unless all of that defined/demonstrated/interrelated information is made to seem *relevant to the individual*—to each person's hopes, fears, dreams, sense of reality, needs, wants, or aspirations—the data may be thrown into a mental garbage can.

Junk mail provides us with a good analogy to the oral communicator's need to make information significant. If you're a healthy, involved American adult whose name has been sold by one mailing list to all of those others, your mailbox undoubtedly contains a torrent of information weekly—on three-days-only sales, on hungry children in Africa, on one-time-only magazine subscriptions, on limited edition plates, on church missionary finances, and on and on. Which of those multipage appeals do you read? The ones in which the computer has put your name into the text? The ones which say, "Only YOU can stop. . . ."? The ones in which the last paragraph starts, "WHAT DOES ALL OF THIS MEAN TO YOU?" The purveyors of third-class salvation and sacrilege are getting smart, at last, now that computer technology and motivational research is catching up with them: They are seeking out tactics of *personalization.* They package information on sales and suffering and outrage and adventure—and then tell you what it means to YOU, John or Jane Doe of Everytown, U.S.A. They *signify* by relating the information, not just to the whole world, but by putting the message in terms of your individual situation.

And so must the articulate person. Nobody in that audience will ever cane a chair until you relate the finger-slivering process to their desire for

FIGURE II.1   **The Four Processes of Information Transfer**

Language Function	Verbal Act	Audience Response
Naming	This is a cow.	What is referred to in my environment?
Showing	Here's how cattle are raised and marketed.	That's the way it works, huh?
Interrelating	The price of beef is affected by many factors.	No wonder the cost of meat fluctuates.
Signifying	So, when you buy ground beef in a supermarket, you are paying for . . .	I'll remember that my next trip uptown, and better understand . . .

creativity, to their appreciation of primitive or folk art, to their pride in being able to display grandpa's century-old chair redone in all its splendor. They'll never enroll in another course in school unless they think the time and money they'll expend are worth it in outcomes they can understand—scholarly knowledge, a better job, closer friends, keener understandings . . . a fuller life. The facts do not speak for themselves, ultimately; *you* must speak for them. You must provide their human and humane significance. Making the facts significant for the audience is the essential process that makes naming, showing, and interrelating information both possible and useful. Signifying completes the interhuman transfer of information.

The examples presented in Figure II.1 demonstrate how the linguistic-socio-psychological process of information transfer works. It all looks innocent and easy enough when seen as simple statements in a chart, in much the same way that assembling the bicycle looks simple enough as you scan the kit's directions. Once you actually start to insert a shaft from the blue package into the hub marked IX34C with groove V2 in a two o'clock position, however, you may find that the three-page diagram seems woefully inadequate. So, too, with the acatual, waord-by-word transfer of information in a public speaking situation. Often you are tempted to spend the few extra bucks and go to a bike shop for a completed ten-speed whizzer; and, in a meeting, you occasionally will yield to your communicative fears and have someone else give the talk or say, "Tell you what. I'll type up a ditto and hand it out next week, OK?" (Once you try to type it up, you find out that's not so easy, either; but that problem belongs in another course. . . .)

But putting your fears and frustrations aside, you *can* build a better bike—and a better speech. Each of the chapters that follow will lead you through the actual construction of speeches in more detail—through definitions, illustrations, sample speech outlines, and advice.

Chapter 5 will concentrate upon introducing new concepts and activities to an audience; hence, it will be most concerned with naming and showing, with definitional and demonstration speeches. Chapter 6 will deal with packaging and clarifying ideas, with oral reports and explanatory speeches; it will describe interrelating and signifying.

It is time to pass from descriptions of the process to the real thing. Turn the page and get on with it!

CHAPTER 5

Introducing New Concepts and Activities

The growth of technological and sociological specialties has filled our lives with jargon—"lem," "synergy," "black holes," "microprocessors." And, in the late 60s and early 70s, we all were bombarded with "back-to" advice for living; we were told to get back to Nature, Folk Arts, and Basics, to seize every opportunity to do something for ourselves—make our own yogurt, cook our own Chinese meals, and tat our own doilies.

These rapid shifts in what we are asked to *think about* and to *do* have produced their own disease, what Alvin Toffler and many futurists since him call "future shock." Disorientation occurs in the face of future shock, for accepted explanations of what one is to do and how one is to behave get lost. In the face of future shock, the psychiatrist does a booming business.[1]

To reduce some of that despair and to lessen stress-levels, what most of us need is someone—yes, an articulate person—to discuss those new ideas sensibly and clearly and to show us how to do new things we might want to do. We need someone to introduce the new concepts and activities to us. Speeches of this nature are the subject of this chapter.

THE OCCASION AND THE AUDIENCE: WHAT, WHO, WHEN, WHY

Fundamentally, speeches introducing new concepts and activities fall into two categories: *definitional speeches* and *demonstration speeches*.

A definitional speech is one in which a speaker offers an audience a vocabulary for dealing with concepts it already knows, or offers a vocabulary that identifies some aspect of the world the audience knows little about. Thus, a definitional speech can either ask an audience to re-examine *something familiar* or to think about *something unfamiliar*.

Almost everyone gives and listens to definitional messages with great regularity. When you start college, someone tells you what an Associate of Arts degree or core requirement is; when you have your first parent-teacher conference in elementary school, the Iowa Tests of Basic Skills are described; or, when you buy your first house, someone explains what earnest money is. These are definitional messages that give you the words—the concepts—for dealing with ideas unfamiliar to you. Or, in a high school science class, a teacher discusses weather changes you've seen by referring to the jet stream, high and low pressure domes, and the relationships between discomfort and the Humidity Index; a television talk show guest urges that you think of children, not as private possessions, but as pre-adults having the same basic rights and responsibilities as older people. These people are busily trying to get you to look at familiar objects, people, and processes in a new light.

Hence, a definitional speech is appropriate any time you think an audience lacks a prerequisite vocabulary for dealing with their surroundings. This type of speech is necessary when an audience does not have a clear set of concepts to deal with their environment, and could possibly better handle some aspects of life if they possessed ideas you know.

Demonstration speeches are closely related to definitional speeches. A demonstration speech is one in which a speaker communicates a series of steps, as well as the physical and mental skills required, for carrying out a procedure of relevance and interest to an audience. The resulting message should be carefully structured and segmented to help an audience follow and remember it. Demonstrations come in two varieties: the *show talk*, in which the speaker actually manipulates or constructs the object or process; and the *tell talk*, in which the speaker relies primarily upon verbal description, analogies, and perhaps visual aids to set some procedure in the audience's minds.

Unless you are planning to live in social isolation for the rest of your life, you undoubtedly will be involved often in showing and telling. At work, new employees or subordinates will need you to lay out office or on-site procedures. At home, your kids will ask you to show them how to make a dragon for the Chinese New Year celebrations. At play, a soccer team member will want you to demonstrate the proper technique for a side-foot cross-field pass. The list could go on and on—and will.

The basic rationale for the demonstration speeches is simple: much of our learning comes through imitation or *modeling*.[2] You began that practice as a baby, honed your imitative skills on the playground, and have continued imitative learning into your adulthood. The demonstration speech represents quite a special relationship between speaker and listener. It is one of those rare moments in life when people voluntarily surrender their undivided attention, good will, and hopes to another human being, in order to be given prepackaged knowledge.

RAW MATERIALS FOR DEFINITIONAL AND DEMONSTRATION SPEECHES

Given what we have said about speech purposes and audience needs, it should be clear that five kinds of raw or supporting materials are normally used in definitional and demonstration speeches. These materials are: *motivational statements, definitional statements, examples, analogies,* and *visual aids.*

Motivational Statements

As we noted in Preview II, "information" is simply raw data until someone perceives that it is *useful* or *relevant* to life. A speaker, therefore, cannot simply throw it up and serve it to audiences like a tennis ball. Rather, you must tell audience members how and in what ways your topic and its ideas can make some sort of difference in their lives. You, in a word, must *interest* them. We will have a good deal more to say about motivation in Part III of this book, but for now think about four common strategies informative speakers can use to motivate people to listen:

Health, Happiness, Prosperity, Security Some definitional speeches focus on concepts which, you can argue, affect your listeners' basic psycho-physical needs for self-protection and self-fulfillment. So, you can urge them to listen to a speech on cardiopulmonary resuscitation (CPR) because of its benefit to health. (See the outline which follows.) Or, you can promise that your speech on different strategies for job-seekers will make them more employable and successful in job-hunting. A speech describing Transcendental Meditation techniques might potentially increase their self-satisfaction and self-control.

Solutions to Recognized Problems A second way to improve listener interest is to show how your topic can provide solutions to particular problems. Suppose, for example, a group you belong to is looking for ways to raise money; you might do a speech defining "direct advertising" techniques, showing how they will solve the money problem better than any other promotional scheme. Or, a definitional speech on the capabilities of home computers could be made attractive by discussing the range of personal problems and needs which can be handled by microprocessors.

Newness and Timeliness Because most of us want to be "in-the-know" when it comes to technological and/or social innovation, a useful motivational strategy is one which stresses newness and timeliness. A speech on videotape systems and public libraries certainly could use this appeal, as more and more public libraries in fact are building in videotape systems, and some are even checking out video discs to patrons who own such machines. Or, any citizen knows that he or she simply must have more information about "supply side economics" in order to understand pending legislation. Hitting popular technological, political, social, or economic trends as they are growing makes for an effective motivational appeal.

Controversy and Conflict of Opinion Similarly, you often can convince people to listen to your speech by noting how controversial the topic is; if it does generate conflict, people may well wish to know more about it so that they can express their opinions in bull sessions and social banter. So, in a speech on proposed legislation which might change the Fairness Doctrine as it applies to television news broadcasting, you might say: "In the January 1982 issue of *American Film* magazine, NBC Vice President Corydon Dunham and Michigan Congressman John Dingell expressed sharply different views on the Federal Communication Commission's so-called 'fairness doctrine.' Dunham argued . . . while Dingell replied that. . . . As you can see, the Fairness Doctrine is surrounded by political controversy, and the resolution of this issue by Congress this spring may well determine what sort of political coverage the networks will provide of this fall's national election. Therefore, today I'd like to tell you what the 'fairness doctrine' is, explain how it works, and discuss three issues which arise from it as they affect information you'll be receiving about politics."

Overall, then, almost any informative speech—whether it is defining concepts, demonstrating procedures, or even explaining or reporting events—demands motivational statements which give listeners reasons-for-listening.

Definitional Statements

In most speaking situations as well, audience members need fundamental definitions-of-concepts. You cannot expect them to understand, to comprehend, ideas if they're unfamiliar with the words you are using *or* if they're using words in a manner different from your own understandings. Eight sorts of definitions are useful to speakers:

Defining from Dictionaries When you think of definitions, you probably first think of *reportive definitions*, the kind found in dictionaries. Dictionary definitions put an object or concept in a category and specify its characteristics: "An orange is a *fruit* [category] which is *round, orange* in color, and of the *citrus family* [characteristics]." Actually, dictionary definitions are fine for learning unfamiliar or technical words, but they often are not too helpful in speeches. Usually the kinds of words you need to define for an audience are not especially clarified by such definitions. Thus, a dictionary might define *socialism* as "a system or theory of production and distribution of goods in a society wherein ownership, operations, and transportation systems are controlled by the society or community at large rather than by individuals or private corporations." That definition simply defines one abstract word in terms of other abstractions; an audience unfamiliar with socialism would not get much out of it. Dictionary definitions can provide you and your audience with a general orientation to an idea and its dimensions, but normally must be followed by other kinds of definitions that more effectively clarify a concept.

Defining in Your Own Words Occasionally, a word has so many definitions in common parlance that speakers have to indicate which definition they wish to use. In that case, you must use a *stipulative definition*—one that stipulates the way you will use a word: "By *speech* I mean the act of offering a series of ideas, arguments, and prods to action to a group of hearers in a face-to-face situation." Such a definition, if done well, orients the audience to your subject matter. Furthermore, if you think an audience respects an authority or expert, you can use that person's stipulative definition (an *authoritative definition*): "Hyman Smith, president of this school, defines a *liberal arts education* as one in which students are taught, not merely technical operations and job-related skills, but rather ways of thinking and reasoning. Today, I want to explore that definition and what it means to you in your four years here." Use a stipulative definition whenever you want to narrow meanings in a particular way or whenever it will reduce ambiguity of a word that has several meanings.

Defining Negatively Further clarity can be added by telling an audience how you are *not* going to use a term or concept—by using a *negative definition*. Along with the stipulative definition of *speech*, for example, we could have said: "By *speech*, I do not mean to refer to the production of the 'correct' sounds and words of the English language, even though that is a common meaning of the word; rather, I will mean. . . ." Defining negatively can clear away possible misconceptions. Using a negative definition along with a stipulative definition is a technique that is especially useful when you are trying to treat a familiar concept in a novel or different way.

Defining from Original Sources Sometimes, you can reinforce a series of feelings or attitudes you wish an audience to have about a concept by telling them where the word came from: "*Sincere* comes from two Latin words, *sine* meaning 'without,' and *ceres* meaning 'wax.' In early Rome, a superior statue was one in which the artisan did not have to cover his mistakes by putting wax into flaws. That statue was said to be *sine ceres*—'without wax.' Today, the term, a 'sincere person,' carries some of that same meaning. . . ." This is called an *etymological definition* when you trace a word's meaning back into its original language. It's termed a *genetic definition* when you explain where the idea rather than the word comes from. You could, for instance, explain the American concept of "freedom of speech" by looking at important discussions of that idea in eighteenth-century England, and then showing how the American doctrine took its shape from our ancestors' British experiences. Defining from original sources, either of the word or of the idea, gives an audience a sense of continuity and at times explains certain nuances of meaning we cannot explain in any other way.

Defining by Examples Particularly if a notion is unfamiliar or technical, one of the best ways to define is an *exemplar definition*—one that simply points to a familiar example: "Each day, most of you stroll past Old Capitol on your way to classes. That building is a perfect example of what I want to talk about today—Georgian architecture." Be careful only to pick defining examples that your audience members will be familiar with.

Defining by Context You also can define a word or concept by putting it in its usual context—through a *contextual definition*. This can be done verbally, as when a speaker says: "The difference between the words *imply* and *infer* is best understood in this way: The person generating a message *implies* a meaning: an observer *infers* an interpretation. Thus, you imply some idea or feeling in what you say, while I draw inferences about what you meant." A contextual definition also can go beyond such verbal descriptions, and, like a definition which uses examples, can point to a "real" context: "While there are many possible meanings to the word *revolution*, today I want to use it to describe the kinds of events which produced the American Revolution." You then would go on to specify those sorts of events. Defining by context gives an audience a sense of meaningfulness in presumably familiar situations; it thus is a good tactic for making certain kinds of concepts concrete.

Defining by Analogy Still another means for making technical or abstract notions easier to understand is the *analogical definition*. An analogy compares a process or event that is unfamiliar or unknown with something that is familiar or known: "Perhaps you can better understand this school's registration procedure if you think of it as an assembly line. First, raw materials (student identification cards, registration forms, lists of available classes and times) are brought into the plant (our fieldhouse). Then, those materials are shaped by skilled craftsmen (advisors, departmental representatives, and you). Next the needed adjustments are put together to make the product (your schedule). And finally, the completed product is checked by quality control people (representatives of the dean's office). Let's go through these steps one at a time." By relying upon a familiar concept or process, the analogical definition can make the unfamiliar idea much easier to grasp. Be sure, however, that the essential features of the two compared objects or processes are more similar than different. Don't confuse an audience with an analogy that doesn't fit.

Defining by Describing Operations Some words or concepts are best defined by reviewing the operations or procedures used in making or measuring something—by offering an *operational definition*. For example, we have no good way of defining *intelligence* with words. Rather, we usually define it in terms of how it is measured: "*Intelligence quotient* is a person's score on the Wechsler-Bellevue Intelligence Test compared with the scores of other members of the population." Or, we often define a process by explaining the steps involved: "*Chair caning* is a process of weaving strands of reed or bamboo across a series of holes drilled in a chair frame; basically, chair caning involves five steps. . . ." You then would go on to specify them. Along with exemplar and analogical definitions, operational definitions are especially good for making an audience "see" an idea or process.

These, then, are the most commonly used kinds of definitions. From them you can choose the kinds that would most clearly explain the particular ideas you wish to define. The effective speaker often combines them, approaching a concept from various angles, in the hope that one method or another will clarify the concept for various individuals in the audience. Your obligation to approach all speeches—including the definitional speech—from the vantage of the audience's needs and condition should be foremost in your mind.

Examples

As we suggested in Chapter 2, examples come in three main varieties— short examples (specific instances), middle-sized ones (simply called examples, usually), and fully developed descriptions (illustrations). Let us look at each type.

Specific Instances

Specific instances are *undeveloped* examples. Instead of describing something in detail, one merely mentions or points to instances of the object or event in question. Specific instances may be used singly or, more often, in longer lists. So, you might say, "In our community the best examples of federal period architecture are the First Methodist Church, the Fourth Street Elementary School, the Historical Society, and the Civic Center."

Examples or Samples

In examples proper (often called samples), speakers usually develop their illustrations a bit more fully, offering more details which, in turn, should increase comprehension. For example, if you were to give a speech dealing with the variety of "do-it-yourself" educational opportunities in your community, you might introduce it as follows:

While most of you are familiar with the regular, semester-long courses offered at this college, you may not know much about the great number of do-it-yourself short courses and workshops available to you. For example, five times a year, our community college offers five-week sessions on Chinese cooking in the evenings; these courses introduce you to the world of the wok, to Chinese cutting and cooking methods, to oriental vegetables and seasoning, and to meal-planning. Every two months, the Women's Action and Resource Center of the college offers a free, six-session workshop on assertiveness training for women (and even men); in the workshop, you learn much about yourself and your own stereotypes, and practice talking to others openly about your concerns and ideas. And, through our town's Department of Parks and Recreation, each spring you can take a free, five-session walk-and-talk course on wild flowers, strolling through Hanson Arboretum, learning to identify wild flowers, and gaining an appreciation of natural flora we seldom even see. These are just three examples of course opportunities. Today, I want to discuss several more with you.

In using examples such as these, be careful (1) to make sure that your sample is *representative* of the concept or opportunities you want to discuss, and (2) to select your examples with your *specific audience* clearly in mind. One would *not*, probably, want to discuss a short course on mountain climbing or some other rigorous physical activity with senior citizens, or a course on beginning drafting with a group of architects!

Illustrations A detailed narrative example of an idea or statement you wish to support is called an illustration. Sometimes an illustration describes or exemplifies a concept, condition, or circumstance; sometimes it shows or demonstrates the results which have been obtained through the adoption of a plan or proposal. Thus, illustrations can be used either to clarify new ideas or to prove the soundness of some proposal. For example, the following illustration was used by Margaret Harrison of Western Kentucky University in a speech on the cost of chronic illness:

But how much does chronic illness cost in America today? Let me give you a personal example. My mother has rheumatoid arthritis, not an uncommon disease, for most of us as part of the aging process will suffer some stiffening and inflammation of the joints. My mother, however, has been an arthritic for the last twenty-eight years, and for the past nine has been confined to a wheelchair. During the years '62–'71 she was in and out of the hospital nine separate times and spent a total of thirty-seven weeks between hospital walls. Her hospital bill (even back then) amounted to over $14,200. And that figure does not even begin to include regular visits to her physician, prescribed medication, and physical therapy stretching back over the last twenty-eight years. Now my father is not a rich man, and as a young couple they did not plan on her chronic illness, but he works for a company with an excellent group health insurance plan that pays 80 percent of his medical expenses.

We were lucky. But there seems to be something inherently wrong with a health-care system that can inflict such financial burdens on the consumer. [3]

From here, Ms. Harrison goes on to describe newer models for health coverage. She has used an extended illustration—which she believes is *typical*—to launch her discussion of other plans. Illustrations take up speaking time, but are valuable if you can pack all of your informational details into a single example. (The speech on tombstone dabbing which follows shows how to use a single illustration to undergird a demonstration speech.)

Overall, examples provide definitional and demonstration speeches—and other types as well—with vehicles of *concreteness*. Audiences have trouble with mere abstract, verbal definitions and descriptions, but they usually can get their heads around particular examples.

Analogies and Comparisons

We noted earlier that analogies (literal and figurative) as well as more extended comparisons form a common kind of supporting material. This is because, psychologically, all of us regularly learn about new ideas or unfamiliar concepts by relating them to old ideas or familiar notions, a process called *association*. Associative learning is a particularly good mechanism for learning new ideas and procedures, because it works from base knowledge you already have. Indeed, I. A. Richards, a great communication theorist from the first half of this century, argued that associative learning is *the* basic mode by which you acquire new ideas.[4]

Figurative Analogies Figurative analogies are especially helpful for speakers who want to make ideas or distinctions *clear*, comprehensible, to an audience. Notice how Dr. Louis Hadley Evans, minister-at-large for the Presbyterian Church, used figurative analogies to clarify the distinction between the terms *deist* and *theist*:

> *To you the world is what: a clock or a car? Is it a huge clock, that God once made, that He wound up at the beginning and left to run of itself? Then you are a deist. Do you believe that it is rather a car that God once made, but that does not run without His hand on the wheel, without His ultimate and personal control? Then you are a theist.*[5]

Notice that the figurative analogy here (clock:deist::car:theist) doesn't "prove" the existence of God; rather, it is employed to make understandable the differences between two often-confused concepts.

Literal Analogies More useful as methods of proof are literal analogies or parallel cases, which compare *like* phenomena. So, you might try to convince a neighbor to plant rhubarb Swiss chard this year by pointing out how well it grew in your garden last year (and, as well, by indicating how similar your soils and gardening methods are). Or, state legislators seeking to defend a new plan for corporate capital gains taxation are likely to show how effectively the plan worked in two other states very much like their own. *If the cases are actually parallel*—if conditions are similar, if there aren't different forces acting in the two situations—then literal analogies can be powerful modes of proof.

Comparisons and Contrasts Generally, comparisons and contrasts are simply extended analogies, but with one important difference: Speakers not only look for *likenesses*, but also for *differences*. As we saw in Figure 3.4, comparisons and contrasts can be used to organize an entire speech—especially a definitional speech. But, they can be used on a smaller scale as well, often to demonstrate the complexity of some problem or idea. Such was the purpose of Henry Thornton, a student at Kirkwood Community College, in a speech outlining the problems of providing mass transit systems in smaller cities:

> *Because a city such as ours cannot develop more than one kind of mass transportation, the question of providing a maximally useful system is difficult to answer. Consider three typical citizens. Joe Paterson and his family live in the suburb of Center Point; he works downtown, his eldest son goes to school here, and the family comes into the city for shopping and entertainment. The Paterson family would love to see money put into a commuter rail system, as it would save them the hassle of driving and parking. Eileen Rolphe and her two daughters live just south of the river. With an efficient bus system, she could put her kids on the Lancaster Street bus heading to their school, and then hop one herself to the corner of 4th Avenue and Grand, where she works. And then there's Adolph Frank, a retired widower. He doesn't get out much, because he's a bit lame. His physical impairment makes train-hopping and bus-changing almost impossible, so he would like to have our transportation dollars spent on a subsidized taxi system, like the one they have in Strawberry Point. Then he could have door-to-door service when he goes shopping or to the doctor.*
>
> *The variety of economic and social needs, of neighborhood features, and of individual plights enormously complicates the mass transportation problems facing a small city.*[6]

Visual Aids The fifth material resource of definers and demonstrators, of course, includes visual aids. Visual aids are tremendously important to speeches introducing new concepts and activities because "seeing" is not only believing but, more important, is knowing as well. If ideas and activities can be given visual shape, they become measurably more concrete; and, as we have stressed through this section of the book, *concreteness* is one of the keys to information transfer.

In Figure 5.1 you will find a list of common visual aids and their general uses. Study the list and think about which ones you can employ profitably in your next speech; indeed, you'll want to refer to the list every time you talk, for even if a picture really isn't worth a thousand words to you, it is to your audience members.

FIGURE 5.1 **Types of Visual Aids**

Here, briefly, are some kinds of visual materials that you may use to support and enhance the ideas in a speech.

Objects. The object itself (such as a microscope or an antique clock) has strong immediate impact and intensity.

Models. You may use either *small-scale models* of large objects (a model racing car) or *large-scale models* of small objects (a model of the structure of a molecule). Models help show the operation of an object or device, as well as its basic structure.

Slides. Slides, of course, require that you obtain projection equipment. Since they must be shown in a darkened room, the speaker becomes obscured. Yet slides usually add interest and help the audience understand.

Movies. Showing movies also requires projection equipment and a darkened room, but has the great advantage of showing action.

Maps. Maps should be large enough to be seen easily by everyone in the audience. The maps used should emphasize those details that relate to the point being made.

Chalkboard Drawings. Prepare chalkboard drawings before the audience assembles, and make sure that the chalk marks are heavy enough to be seen by everyone. Keep chalkboard drawings covered until you are ready to refer to them, so that the audience is not distracted by them while you are talking.

Graphs. You may use several different kinds of graphs. *Bar graphs* show the relationship of sets of figures. *Line graphs* show two or more variable facts. *Pie graphs* show percentages in a proportionately divided circle. *Pictorial graphs* show relative amounts by the size or the number of symbols.

Diagrams. Diagrams can range from the very simple to the very complex. *Cutaway diagrams* of an object show its inner workings as well as its external appearance. Diagrams which show a *three-dimensional* view are especially helpful.

Charts and Tables. These are useful for showing statistical information. *Organizational charts* or *tables of organization* can illustrate the parts and the structure of a business or agency.

Handouts. Mimeographed, dittoed, photocopied, or printed information can be handed out to an audience. Handouts can be used to present statistical information, to give suggestions to be followed up later (such as addresses of people to write to), or to provide brief or full descriptions of the steps in a complex process.

1. Objects

2. Models

3. Slides

35mm color transparency

4. Movies

5. Maps

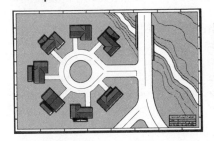

6. Chalkboard Drawings

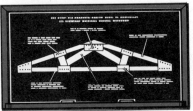

7. Graphs

HOUSING STARTS 1983

8. Diagrams

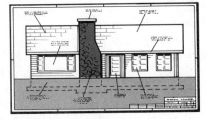

9. Charts or Tables

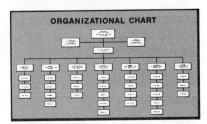

ORGANIZATIONAL CHART

10. Handouts

Build A

HOW TO BUILD YOUR OWN HOME

While other sorts of materials (authoritative quotations, statistical trends, historical narratives, etc.) occasionally appear in speeches introducing new concepts and activities, these five forms—motivational statements, definitional statements, examples, analogies, and visual aids—certainly are the most commonly used supporting materials.

ORGANIZING DEFINITIONAL AND DEMONSTRATION SPEECHES

How can you usefully put together these materials into coherent speeches? As you review the organizational patterns described in Chapter 3, you'll perhaps note that some of them are especially well adapted to the tasks of defining and demonstrating. *Chronological patterns*, with their stress on backgrounding and development, often are used when speakers want to show the growth or spread of ideas and, of course, when they are doing "show" and/or "tell" talks which lead an audience through sequential steps in a process. (The sample outlines which follow will use a chronological pattern; the first will offer historical background, and the second will use chronological development for the entire speech.) Similarly, *spatial patterns* can be used by speakers needing to geographically orient audiences; a speech describing your library's services, for example, could profit from a spatial pattern.

Naturally, *topical patterns* are often employed when you're trying to develop clearly for an audience not only a primary concept but also its subparts. Thus, in Figure 3.3 the speaker used a topical pattern to clarify, not just state tax policy, but rather distinctions between different sorts of state taxes. And finally, speakers use *comparison and contrast patterns* as well as *question-answer sequences* in definitional speeches, especially. Comparisons, as we have been saying, are most appropriate when you can tie the new knowledge to old knowledges, and question-answer formats allow you to focus directly on audience needs and interests. So, a speech explaining new degree requirements probably is best encased in a comparison-and-contrast formula, while one describing a new major is best offered via question-answering (What is the new major? What are the requirements? What sorts of career opportunities are available for students taking it?).

Let us look at a couple of sample speech outlines to see how definitional and demonstration speeches work. The first outline defines an unfamiliar concept; the second is a "show" demonstration speech. Throughout this book, each major sample outline will be preceded by a section called "Pre-Speech Analysis," to remind you of some of the ways in which audience analysis and self-analysis can help you plan your procedures. Notice, too, that some of the outlines in the chapters which follow are quite long—almost full speech texts presented in outline form. Obviously, you will seldom (if ever) work from such full outlines. We are using lengthy illustrations so that several different tactics can be described.

SAMPLE SPEECH:	**DEFINING**

Pre-Speech Analysis

Subject:	Cardiopulmonary Resuscitation (CPR)*
Audience:	A gathering in a church, a club, a dorm, an athletic organization
Situation:	The audience may have heard of CPR through television public service announcements or newspaper ads, but is unsure of what CPR is.
Purpose:	To define CPR clearly enough to help the audience understand what CPR training involves
Speaker:	The speaker has gone through the usual half-day training session and has read the literature on CPR.
Strategies:	1. Most people are aware of their own ignorance of first aid, are embarrassed by it, and perhaps fear they may be called upon to give help. The speaker plays upon those hidden fears.
	2. Most people are too lazy to spend much time learning about medical helps for others. The speaker tries to overcome that resistance.
	3. The audience does not have a clear concept of the techniques of CPR. The speaker fills out the idea vividly enough to interest the audience in attending a training session.
	4. This short speech does not allow for full demonstration. The speaker attempts only, therefore, to (a) define it, (b) offer its rationale, (c) underscore its importance, and (d) indicate where it's taught.

Outline

The ABCs of CPR

Introduction

Briefly states the problem

I. About 1,000,000 persons in the United States experience acute heart attacks each year.
   A. More than 650,000 die annually.
   B. About 350,000 of these deaths occur outside a hospital, usually within two hours of the onset of symptoms.

Isolates a need of the audience, to make the speech relevant to their lives

II. The tragedy is that a large number of these deaths could have been prevented by prompt, adequate, on-the-spot treatment—treatment most of us have not learned how to give.
   A. Most of us are ignorant of basic first aid appropriate for heart attack, drowning, electrocution, suffocation, or drug intoxication victims.

Adds a personal anecdote

   B. I don't know about you, but I used to fear that I'd stumble across someone on the sidewalk or in a store and not know what to do.

* Information for this outline has been taken from "Standards for Cardiopulmonary Resuscitation (CPR) and Emergency Cardiac Care (ECC)," Supplement to *The Journal of the American Medical Association* (February 1974). Copyright © 1974 by the American Medical Association. Reprinted by permission of the American Heart Association, Inc.

1. I thought only doctors, nurses, and other medical professionals could help.
2. That's when I heard about CPR—Cardiopulmonary Resuscitation—and the half-day training sessions anyone could attend.

Suggests a solution to the problem

III. I went through a CPR workshop last spring, and I want to tell you about it.
  A. For only a dollar, the cost of materials, I gained the knowledge necessary to save a life.
  B. With only a couple of hours of reading and a four-hour training session, you, too, can gain the skills—and the confidence needed to put your skills into action.

Provides transition and forecasts what will be discussed

IV. For you to clearly understand what CPR is, I'll first offer a bit of background on its phenomenal growth over the last decade. Then, I will discuss its ABCs. And finally, I'll tell you how to gain the satisfaction of knowing you can be better prepared to help your fellow human beings for only a small investment of your time.

Body

Engages the audience's curiosity

I. Let me give you some background on CPR.
  A. [Optional: Review of ancient methods of resuscitation: flagellation and heat in the Middle Ages; fumigation, inversion, and the barrel methods of the eighteenth century; the Russian and trotting-horse methods of the nineteenth century; and artificial respiration as taught in the twentieth century. These would be especially interesting if they are illustrated with slides.]

Genetic definition that tells the origin of the idea

  B. In 1966, the National Academy of Sciences-National Research Council sponsored a Conference on Cardiopulmonary Resuscitation.
    1. It recommended training medical, allied health, and paramedical personnel in CPR.
    2. Its recommendations resulted in widespread acceptance of CPR and training programs throughout the country.
  C. That conference was followed in 1973 by the even larger American Heart Association and National Academy of Sciences-National Research Council sponsored National Conference on Standards for CPR and Emergency Cardiac Care.

Cites authorities and experts to justify the concept

    1. Participating in the 1973 conference were over thirty-five national medical, governmental, and service organizations; American Heart Association chapters from thirty-seven states; and representatives from thirty medical schools.

General description of the recommendations

    2. In part, the 1973 conference made several recommendations:
      a. That professional and public education programs be developed to increase awareness of heart attack symptoms and emergency treatment;
      b. That the public, particularly, become more involved in basic life-support training; and
      c. That communities integrate emergency cardiac care as part of a

comprehensive medical services program, making it available throughout entire communities.

Suggests specific methods for carrying out the recommendations

3. To carry out the recommendations, the 1973 conference argued that—
    a. Professionals such as police personnel, fire fighters, and lifeguards be immediately trained in CPR;
    b. High-risk industry workers and families of cardiac patients be trained next; and
    c. Then the training to be extended to school-children and the general public.

Transition

D. And, that's where I—and I hope you—come in.

II. What, then, *is* CPR?

Dictionary definition

A. Technically, CPR is a series of actions for basic life support, in which you recognize airway obstruction, respiratory arrest, and cardiac arrest, and properly apply, singly or with another person, a series of measures for alleviating those problems.

Analogical definition compares the process to a more familiar situation

B. CPR can be compared to procedures used by traffic controllers when they are faced with a blocked interstate highway.
    1. First, they must open sideroads or remove the blocking vehicles from the highway.
    2. Second, they must signal the stopped vehicles to get moving.
    3. Third, they must bring in rescue or tow trucks to restore cars which have overheated during the tie-up.

Operational definition concretely lays out the steps in the process

C. Likewise, CPR is as simple as ABC.
    1. A stands for "airways."
        a. If you come upon a collapsed person, first you shake the person, shouting, "Are you all right?"
        b. If there is no answer, you put the person on his or her back.
        c. Then you lift the neck or chin to open the airway, looking for chest and stomach movement, listening for sounds of breathing, and feeling for breath on your cheek.
    2. *B* stands for "breathing."
        a. If opening the airway does not start spontaneous breathing, you must provide rescue breathing.
        b. The best method is the mouth-to-mouth technique.
            (1) Pinch off the nose with one hand, holding the head in a tilted position with the other.
            (2) Immediately give four quick, full breaths in rapid succession.
        c. Then check for a pulse along the carotid artery. [Demonstrates where it is.]
    3. *C* stands for "cardiac compression."
        a. Pressing on the person's chest in the right place [demonstrates where it is] will start to provide artificial circulation.
        b. To force the heart to pump, you must set up a rhythmical, rocking motion to ensure the proper amount of pressure and relaxation.
        c. You then start a procedure whereby you alternate chest compress-

ions and mouth-to-mouth breaths; the ratios are on the card I have given you. [Holds up the card.]

4. These techniques, basically, are continued until help comes, until you are exhausted, or until there are unmistakable signs that the person will not recover.

Quickly reviews the basic steps

III. I have outlined the basic ABCs—airways, breathing, and cardiac compression —the CPR techniques you use when coming upon an unknown victim.

Warnings about special techniques

A. Remember, though, that there are variations in techniques if you are dealing with a child rather than an adult, a drowning or electrical shock victim, or someone with a fractured neck.

Limitations of what the speaker is offering

B. My job today is *not* to teach you CPR, but rather to tell you what it is, to let you know it can and ought to be learned by everyone in this room.

Conclusion

Program review

I. Almost every community in America, through the American Red Cross, school programs, YMCAs, clubs, hospitals, and other groups, has CPR training available.

A. It usually involves only a few pennies for the materials, a few hours of preparation, and about four hours of training.

B. Periodic refresher courses, of shorter length, are available for those who are afraid they will forget it; and cards such as this one [holds the card up] can be carried around as reminders.

Restates the general purpose

II. The ABCs of CPR, especially when they become integrated within community-wide emergency cardiac care programs involving mobile cardiac units and special area facilities, undoubtedly will significantly cut into those three-quarters of a million deaths annually.

A. With heart attacks still the number one killer in this country, everyone must get involved.

Mild attempt at shaming the audience into acting

B. You can, of course, try to buy off your conscience with a few dollars to the yearly Heart Fund drives, but you also can overcome some of your fear and hesitation by directly training yourself as well.

Suggests how to take the first step

C. On that card I gave you is the name of the nearest CPR workshop center in this area. Now that you know what CPR is, contact the center and attend the next training session.

D. If *I* ever have trouble, I want *you* trained!

This speaker has introduced an unfamiliar concept to an audience. Notice the care taken to (1) relate the concept to felt needs; (2) orient the listeners with enough background material to make the concept seem important; (3) employ enough different types of definitions to engage the minds of various sorts of listeners; (4) use a memory device (A = airways, B = breathing, and C = cardiac compression) to help listeners retain the information; and (5) describe follow-up procedures which prod the listeners to act upon their newly acquired concept. In other words, this speaker has tried to make sure that the idea is clear and that it potentially can become a part of the audience members' lives. Any good definitional speech ought to meet those two criteria of clarity and relevance in order to be effective.

Our second sample outline is a demonstration speech. It illustrates a series of decisions speakers have to make, decisions on how much detail to include, which steps in a process to demonstrate fully and which to only suggest, and what sorts of motivational statements to build into the speech.

SAMPLE SPEECH: **DEMONSTRATING**

Pre-Speech Analysis

Subject:	Tombstone dabbing
Audience:	A meeting of a historical society, a genealogy study group, a D.A.R. chapter, a night class
Situation:	Audience members, by coming, have shown interest in studying and preserving samples of our earlier culture. Some may desire tangible evidence of their family trees, while others may be more interested in retaining accurate cemetery records or in constructing interesting wall hangings. None of them, however, has tried any sort of tombstone rubbing.
Purpose:	To introduce the steps involved in dabbing (one of the basic techniques for doing a tombstone rubbing) through demonstrating those steps on sample stones borrowed from a stonecutter
Speaker:	The speaker began making rubbings several years ago. She is now skilled at what was a trial-and-error hobby.
Strategies:	1. By displaying and using the materials needed for dabbing, the speaker can give the audience an idea of the basic techniques and the investment involved.

2. At least one finished dabbing will be on display for illustration and motivation. The speaker will refer to it during the speech.

3. To help the audience in watching, the speaker uses stones large enough to view clearly, but small enough to be transported. The speaker uses two stones (one partially prepared) to avoid delays in the preliminary drying stage.

4. Since the audience has an interest in preserving historical items, the speaker can spend less time justifying the activity and more time showing the process.

5. In this brief speech the speaker (1) explains why she's chosen to demonstrate this particular technique; (b) displays the items needed for dabbing; (c) introduces each of the seven basic steps in the dabbing method; and (d) discusses specific points for trouble-shooting while completing the individual steps.

6. The speaker distributes a dittoed handout that lists the supplies and briefly describes the steps. The handout will help the audience remember what is involved.

Outline	**Gone But Not Forgotten**
	Introduction
The speaker hands out the dittoed sheet and displays the final product to generate curiosity and interest.	I. [Display a completed dabbing which reads: James E L Son of TN & HN Gracy Born March 16, 1847 Killed & skelped by indians April 9, 1862 Aged 15 years & 24 days]

Presents the subject from the larger perspective	A. This is a rubbing I made ten years ago in a cemetery in my small Texas hometown.
	B. Only recently I learned that the portion of the cemetery where I made this rubbing has been marked for urban development.
	  1. Fortunately, the local historical society has formulated a plan to move the stones from this older section to another part of the cemetery.
	  2. Because the stones could be damaged during the move, I'm glad that I have records of several of the stones on these early graves.
	  3. And I've been able to decorate my living room with fascinating conversation pieces.

Basically defines and describes the process and presents several techniques for achieving the final product Motivation: offers advantages of rubbings	II. A rubbing is a reproduction of a design or printing carved on a surface such as stone or wood. We can obtain a negative print of the design through either of two basic techniques: by placing a piece of paper over the surface and rubbing wax, charcoal, crayon, or some other rubbing element; or by dabbing the paper with a wet element such as watercolor or ink. A. Rubbings provide far better details than photographs, and may highlight features that are overlooked or difficult to see by simply looking at the surface. B. So whether you want to record your city's history, provide evidence of your family tree, or just create an artwork, rubbing is something you'll want to learn.
	Body
Definition	I. Although there are several techniques for rubbing, I'm going to demonstrate the wet method, called dabbing. The dabbing method is suitable for most surfaces, including the weathered marble or limestone you're most likely to encounter in local cemeteries. A. The dabbing method is so named because the element used to obtain the negative print is actually applied with light strokes (as in painting) rather than passed over the surface with pressure, as in dry methods using wax,

crayon, or charcoal. These dry methods are more useful in working with slate stones.

Reviews materials
displayed on a working
table, pointing to them
as they are
mentioned

   B. To use the dabbing method you need the materials I have right here.
     1. A relatively stiff-bristled brush
     2. Fairly lightweight Japanese rice paper
     3. Masking tape
     4. A plastic spray bottle filled with clear water
     5. Tubes of liquid watercolor
     6. A damp washcloth
     7. Dabbers—sponge balls tautly covered with soft cotton
     8. A jar lid
     9. A large plastic jar filled with clear water, along with cloth for cleaning the stone and your hands
     10. A portfolio for storing paper and finished rubbings
   C. Of course, it also takes a stone you want to copy. The stones I'll use here are practice stones I borrowed from a local stonecutter.

Demonstration

Props up the stone so
the audience
can clearly see its
surface

Caution

II. There are seven steps in completing a dabbing similar to this one. Now, let's actually do a dabbing.
   A. To begin with, it's important to clean the stone with a relatively stiff-bristled—but not wire—brush.
     1. Make sure the stone is clean of lichen, bird droppings, and other debris.
     2. Do not be too rough in cleaning. You don't want to damage the stone. Some impurities may remain; but if smoothed down, they will not harm your project.
   B. Second, center the paper on the stone and tape it in a couple of places to hold it in position.
   C. Third, spray a little water near the center of the paper and gently pat the paper with the dampened washcloth to make it adhere to the contours of the stone.

Speeds up the process
here, suggesting
how it is done
without actually
completing
the task

     1. Try to work out air bubbles and wrinkles.
     2. Continue this process, beginning in the center and working outwards, until the paper is completely pressed to the stone. This step will actually take longer than I have time to show you today.
     3. You'll need to take your time. This step is important for successful dabbing!
   D. Fourth, let the paper dry.
     1. Because I'm using tube watercolor, itself a wet medium, I want my paper dry or very nearly dry.

Uses a shortcut to
control time

Pours in full view so
audience can see the
consistency

     2. Rather than wait for this paper to dry, I'll now switch to a second stone on which the paper is pressed and dried.
   E. The fifth step is to prepare the dabber.
     1. Squeeze some of the watercolor into the jar lid.
     2. Dilute with a little water to form a soupy paste.

Pauses after saying each step to actually complete it

Caution

3. Soak some color onto a dabber.
4. Remove the excess color on the edge of the lid.
F. In step six, you begin to dab.
   1. Remember three things:
      a. Do not rub as you would in a dry method. Simple brush gently or lightly pat the paper with the dabber.
      b. And don't let the dabber rest on the paper or you'll have a blot on it and perhaps on the stone.
      c. Work very carefully around the recesses such as the carved-out spaces within letters. You may even want to use a smaller dabber in these areas.
   2. Repeat the dipping and dabbing procedure until you've covered the entire stone.

Shows all of these operations slowly, and displays a previously made dabbing of the practice stone

G. Finally, when your dabbing is done, let the paper and watercolor completely dry. Then carefully remove the paper in an even, gentle motion. Step seven is completed when you safely place the finished product in your portfolio.

Conclusion

Reviews the steps in the procedure and involves the audience by having them read along

I. Let's briefly review the seven steps in the dabbing technique. Please follow along on the dittoed sheet I've prepared.
   A. First, gently clean the stone with a relatively stiff-bristled brush.
   B. Second, center the paper on the stone and tape it lightly in place.
   C. Third, spray a little water and pat the paper. Do this by areas, from the center outwards, until the paper completely adheres to the stone.
   D. Fourth, let the paper dry.
   E. Fifth, prepare the dabber.
   F. Sixth, dab, dab, dab and gently dab some more until you've covered the paper's surface.
   G. Seventh, when the paper and watercolor are dried, carefully remove the paper and prepare it for transport.

Bolsters and motivates by telling personal experiences while learning

II. Now you're ready to dab, but don't be discouraged if it takes several practice runs to perfect your dabbing technique.
   A. Believe me, I've done several dabbings of a single stone just to learn how soupy I want my watercolor paste or how to dry the paper.
   B. Occasionally, I goof and blot the paper—even the stone.
      1. But, because I use watercolor rather than oil or dye-base inks, I can spray a little water on the stone and easily clean it.
      2. Then I can begin again to record the surface of some gravestone, confident that though time may deface the stone, I won't spoil it with my watercolors.
   C. I'll then have a treasure I made myself.

Note carefully in the preceding outline the attention to motivation and confidence. The speaker gave the audience a *cultural* reason for learning the technique (preservation of history); an *aesthetic* reason (a fine specimen suitable for display at home); an *economic* reason (low-cost supplies); and the general encouragement that comes from actually viewing the whole process. Especially in the conclusion, the speaker also encouraged the audience, through the personal example of the speaker's own skills and little traumas, to overcome initial failures and to press on to final success.

The speaker controlled the time needed for the process in two ways. First, the speaker kept the audience's attention by not taking the time needed to complete step three (wetting the paper to make it adhere to the stone). Then the speaker skipped over step four (the drying stage) by switching to a stone on which the paper was already dry.

You'll also notice that the audience did not directly participate. For one thing, it would have taken a headstone for each person, which probably would have produced a roomful of hernias. And for another, the group most likely would have become bogged down on step three (adhering the rice paper to the stone), causing the speech to come to a full stop at that point. Our speaker made the shrewd choice of keeping the audience watching instead of doing, so they first could get a sense of the whole process. They could actually wrestle with the wetting and adhering on their own time, in the privacy of their own cemetery.

TIPS FOR INTRODUCING NEW CONCEPTS AND ACTIVITIES

Advice on Speeches of Definition

All speeches introducing new concepts and activities must be clear, efficient, and comprehensible. In addition, however, definitional and demonstration speeches demand particular talents in their presentation. As we close this discussion of speeches introducing new concepts and activities, therefore, we ought to review some advice successful speakers with these purposes usually follow.

■ *Keep your audience in mind at all times.* It is often tempting, after you have studied a concept or idea and worked with it awhile, to assume that everyone can comprehend it as easily as you did. Remember, people often have difficulty understanding especially abstract and unfamiliar notions merely by listening to them. Always start your speech preparation on the assumption that someone is going to get confused if you are not careful.

■ *Avoid sounding lecturish.* It is very easy to turn a definitional speech, especially, into a dry, abstract lecture, full of high-sounding phrases and preachy advice. But most listeners want a conversational tone to public speeches, a sense of contact between equals. Don't leave the impression that you are cramming something down their throats, and don't be condescending toward them as human beings.

■ *Balance general ideas and concrete examples.* In a sense, your definitional speech is a balancing act. On the one hand, you are trying to get an audience to comprehend the broad contours and implications of an idea or process (to generalize it). On the other hand, you want them to see its specific aspects (to concretize it). It is for that reason that oral communicators tend to rely on several kinds of definitions. To generalize concepts, dictionary, stipulative, negative, genetic, and contextual definitions are useful. To add specific detail and visual appeal, etymological, exemplar, analogical, and operational definitions are effective. Search out ways of achieving a balance between those two aspects of defining.

Advice on Speeches of Demonstration

■ *Work hard to instill motivation and confidence.* While many people are interested in learning a craft, skill, or process, they're often afraid to actually do it, because they think it is costly or demands a high degree of artistry, and because they fear failure. In a demonstration speech, therefore, you are not only an expert but also a cheerleader. You must inspire both confidence in yourself as an expert and confidence in the audience members themselves as potential artisans. Your goal is to leave the audience with the impression that if you could learn to do it, so can they.

■ *Be sensitive to questions of rate.* Most of us have seen TV shows that demonstrate skills and crafts. Especially when they are showing how to do something that takes a little time, you'll notice that these public demonstrators inevitably fall back on strategies for *controlling time.* You may, for example, see the TV baker whip up the batter for the cake, pour it in the pan, but instead of baking it, pull out one already baked and hurry on to the next step—icing the cake. When one process that takes a good deal of time has to be completed, you can simply shift the demonstration to an object already at that stage. Using such time-controlling strategies will help you keep the attention of the audience.

■ *Think through the problem of detail.* Another difficulty you often face is caused by the size of objects and processes you are showing. Often, you are demonstrating relatively small, subtle techniques being applied to little objects. Other times you are teaching techniques for working with objects too large to use practically in your demonstration. The obvious solution to the problem of scale is the use of visual aids.

How, for example, can you show various embroidery stitches to an audience of twenty? One sort of help would be pieces of poster board, illustrating various stitches on a larger scale. Another and even better aid would be a three-by-four-inch piece of cloth stretched over a wood frame; using an oversized needle and yarn instead of thread, as well as stitches measured in inches instead of millimeters, you could more easily make your techniques visible. In other situations, you could employ a chalkboard, hand out a sketch, record the steps on a flip chart, bring in a cutaway diagram, or show slides or even a short film or videotape.

■ *Select an appropriate level of audience involvement.* How much do you have an audience actually do while you are talking? When you are deciding whether to involve the audience, remember that direct involvement tends to facilitate learning, so use it when you can. But also remember that there are limits; in some situations audience involvement is impractical. So if you're trying to teach an audience how to tie six or seven different everyday knots, give each person a couple of pieces of rope so they can tie along with you. But it would be more than impractical, when demonstrating fiberglass lamination, to have each audience member build a boat.

There is, too, another practical question to consider. Sometimes audience participation slows you down, and the audience begins to lose sight of the forest for all of the trees. When a process is particularly long and complicated, or when some steps in the process require time and practice, it is usually best to keep the audience watching and listening. Then they can develop an understanding of the whole process before attempting to work through it. Thus the advice we give is simple: think about the possibilities for audience participation, think about the potential pitfalls, and from there on, use your innate good sense to avoid the pits.

■ *Carefully coordinate the verbal and visual aspects of the demonstration.* Let's face it: it's difficult to coordinate your flow of words and your sequence of movements. The pitfalls are numerous. The chart you're using falls down, needles break, bulbs burn out, the yarn tangles, and the paste sets up while you're busy answering a question. What do you say to an audience in your flustered condition? You must remember Murphy's Law ("Anything that can go wrong, will") and be ready to cope. To make the "show" and the "tell" work together, plan some extra things to say, enough midprocess reviews to keep an audience up with you. Practice your actual physical movements for key points in your presentation. Our best advice is to find some poor sucker to sit through a rehearsal, commenting and asking questions. Such a trial run will aid your confidence—and coordination—tremendously.

If you follow all of this sage advice, you will have helped produce a more sensible world of information.

NOTES

[1]   See Alvin Toffler, *Future Shock*, Bantam Books (1970; rpt. New York: Random House, Inc., 1971), esp. Chap. 16.

[2]   On "informal" or imitative learning as one of three major ways you acquire ideas (along with "formal" and "technical" learning), see Edward T. Hall, *The Silent Language*, Fawcett Primier Book (1959; New York: Fawcett World Library, 1966), Chap. 4, "The Major Triad."

[3]   From "Medical Care" by Margaret Harrison. Reprinted from *Winning Orations* by special arrangement with the Interstate Oratorical Association, Larry Schnoor, Executive Secretary, Mankato State University; Mankato, Minnesota.

[4]   I. A. Richards, *The Philosophy of Rhetoric*, Galaxy Book (1936; rpt. New York: Oxford University Press, 1965), esp. Chap. 1, and also Chaps. 2 and 3. "Associationism" has been a part of most learning theories at least since eighteenth-century British philosophers—notably John Locke and David Hume—built entire theories of mind on the principle of association.

[5] From "Can You Trust God?" by Dr. Louis Hadley Evans. Reprinted by permission of the author.

[6] From a speech given at Kirkwood Community College, Cedar Rapids, Iowa, spring term, 1979. Reprinted with the permission of Mr. Thornton.

ASSIGNMENTS

Pre-Performance

1. In Preview II we noted that naming is an important social-psychological process for transferring information. Sometimes, different names suggest alternative ways to view the same phenomenon. For instance, the *war* in Vietnam was described by some as "aggression from the North," and by others, as "civil war." Different terms which describe such potentially ambiguous concepts tend to be used in favorable/unfavorable pairs: *conscientious objector/coward, thrifty/miserly, self-confident/arrogant.* The use of favorable and unfavorable names occurs frequently in language designed to differentiate between the sexes; the negative effect more often tends to be associated with the female terms, hence *bachelor/old maid* and *aggressive/pushy.* Can you think of other examples where the names applied to a single concept are more favorable for one sex than for the other?

2. List and define three words for which you think members of your speech class hold a common meaning. Meet in small groups; present your words and allow each member of the group enough time to write down a meaning for each word. Collect the definitions that your classmates have written for your words, and compare their meanings with your own. Each member in the group should follow the same procedure. Are there significant variations in meaning? What types of words seem to call forth the most variance in definitions?

3. Work in groups of two or three to develop a series of definitions for *communication.* Attempt to formulate a definition of each of the ten types of definitions (including subtypes) discussed in this chapter. How do these definitions compare in difficulty, length, precision, and interest?

4. The instructor should develop a five- to ten-piece puzzle made up of geometric figures and duplicate enough pieces so that two-thirds of the class members each can have an envelope containing all the pieces of the puzzle. The instructor will divide the class into groups of three. Two members of each group will sit back to back. One of them will assemble the puzzle and then tell the other how to arrange the puzzle in the identical way. The person receiving the directions cannot speak. Nor can the receiver set about to solve the puzzle. Rather, the receiver must try to follow the directions of the first member. The third member of the group should observe the activity and be prepared to suggest how to improve the instructions.

5. Assume that you are to speak on the subject "How to Build a Plant Terrarium." Analyze each of the following audiences, and indicate what

special steps you might take in developing a speech that meets the needs of each particular audience:

a third-grade class

members of the Hoe and Hope Garden Club

your speech class

a group of senior 4-H'ers

Performance

1. Prepare a two- or three-minute speech in which you define some word or phrase that is in common use, such as *feminism, violence, carcinogens, amateur athletics,* or *property tax*. Use one or more of the methods for defining described in this chapter. Be prepared to explain why you chose this manner of defining a relatively familiar concept.

2. Hold a definition bee. The class should set ground rules before beginning competition. Sample rules may be similar to these: Each participant must announce the type of definition to be given; participants will be allowed one minute of thinking time; a panel will be established to make judgments in disputes about the clarity and precision of definitions. The instructor should provide terms for the exercise.

3. Deliver a two- to four-minute demonstration speech requiring specific physical action. You might demonstrate such things as how to conduct traffic or how to do simple magic tricks. Practice gestures, but try to avoid a "mechanical" appearance.

4. Present a three- to five-minute speech in which you describe a relatively complex process. Depend upon language rather than upon gestures and visual materials.

Post-Performance

1. To make sure that your definition of an unfamiliar or familiar concept is clear, the instructor may wait until the end of the day's performances and randomly call upon a student to repeat a definition to the speaker's satisfaction. The class should be listening carefully to the round of speeches but not taking notes.

2. From your observation of speakers in Performance 3, list speakers' actions which distracted your attention from what they were saying. Prepare to discuss this list in class.

3. "Test" whether listeners grasped the complex process you described in Performance 4. After your presentation, ask someone to enumerate the steps in the procedure.

CHAPTER 6

Packaging and Clarifying Ideas

Two forces in our society have made explanations extremely important forms of communication. First has been the staggering growth of things, ideas, and policies needing explanation. Simply put, ours has become an enormously complex society, second to none perhaps in terms of innovations in technology, the institutionalizations of special interests and voices demanding to be heard, and webs of often conflicting policy choices. The fact, furthermore, that newspapers, inexpensive paperback books, films, radio, television, and newsletters and other bulk mailings all bring new products, techniques, and problems into our homes means that few of us can escape such complexities.

The second force is in part the result of the first: as "new" authorities, institutions, and ideas/processes/objects come into existence, they tend to erode the power of the old ones. Ours is a "throwaway" society; we not only toss out last year's Christmas present, but also last year's solution to our economic crises, our identity crises, the crime problem, medical-ethical decision-making, and the like. Faced by so many discordant voices in religion, government, and culture, our natural reaction is to put less faith in any one of them, and to cry out, "What?", "How?", and "Why?" with increasing frequency. We need solid, sensible explanations.

We all, therefore, need communicators who can bring order to disorder, and who can reduce the seemingly innumerable decisions we must make to a few key ones. In a word, we all need skilled speakers and writers capable of *packaging* ideas, and thus clarifying our ideas and our decisions.

THE OCCASION AND THE AUDIENCE: WHAT, WHO, WHEN, WHY

"Packaging" and "clarifying" are, in the terms we used in Preview II, a matter of interrelating pieces of information and of signifying that information's causes, effects, and implications. The sorts of speeches which package and clarify ideas are *reports* and *explanations*. Though closely related, these two speech types have identifiably different rhetorical characteristics.

Reports

We normally speak of "reporters" as persons who are responding to some *duty* or *charge*. Most reporters operate within prescribed limits—limits set by the body of persons who hired or delegated authority to the reporter in the first place. Thus, each morning a news reporter is given events to cover by an editor or producer; the person preparing the monthly sales report on South Dakota marketing has a very specific charge for the staff meeting; the fraternity which sends a brother to scout out the best restaurant for the spring banquet knows what it wants. Reporters, in other words, are born of a need to delegate tasks when there is too much informational or evaluative ground to be covered by busy people in too short a time, or when too many people need to share the information to demand practically that they all go out and get it.

Hence, a *reportive speech* is one which assembles, arranges, and interprets information gathered in response to an actual or perceived charge or expectation. In some cases, it focuses primarily upon the assembled information; the *factual report* is such a report. In other cases, it includes recommendations for acting upon the information; the *advisory report* offers such suggestions.

Both sorts of reports are prepared for relatively cohesive audiences which have asked for them. The reporter faces, usually, a "command" or "charge" comprised of three sorts of instructions:

- *Goal.* The kind, quantity, and quality of information needed by the audience normally is specified.
- *Time Line.* A single deadline for reporting may be set, or, the audience or group may ask for different sorts of information at different stages. So, for example, business managers are expected to present their offices with monthly totals of expenditures and outlays, quarterly reports comparing this year's expenditures and outlays to date with the projected overall budget, and annual reports comparing this year with last year and projecting next year's budgets.
- *Form.* Many groups, as well, not only indicate goals and time lines but also specify the forms it wishes the report to take. So, a journalistic reporter may be asked to do, say, a "background" piece, a "straight" informative report (on who/what/when/where/how), or a "feature." Or, a "blue ribbon task force" may be asked by the school board either to describe categorically various courses offered in junior high schools across the community or to make recommendations for changes in the junior high curricula.

In sum, reportive speechmaking involves considerations of comparatively particular audience expectations on the one hand, and of ways one can best meet those expectations by clearly and effectively packaging the desired information on the other. Packaging for the reporter becomes a matter of (1) finding the "right" material, (2) organizing it in clear ways, and (3) ultimately meeting the group's goals and charges on time.

Explanations   In one sense, explanative speeches are very much like reportive speeches, in that one is organizing and interrelating information for audiences. Explanative speeches, however, are not controlled by "commands" in the same way reports are. Explanative speeches can be called for on many more occasions.

An explanative speech is one in which a speaker either (1) makes clear the nature of a concept, process, thing, or proposal, or (2) offers a supporting rationale for a contestable proposition or claim. The notion of "making clear" means that explanative speeches have much in common with definitional speeches, because the purpose of a definition is to clarify. Normally, though, an explanative speech is less concerned with the word or concept—the "vocabulary"—than it is with connecting one concept with a series of others. While a definitional speech on political corruption might concentrate upon the term and its positive or negative meanings, an explanative speech would likely go into more depth, indicating what sorts of social conditions are likely to foster corruption or what methods are available for eliminating it. Thus, definitional speeches are more concerned with the process of *naming* concepts; explanative speeches are more concerned with *interrelating* ideas or phenomena.

Actually, the key to most explanative speeches lies in the second notion—"offering a rationale." Most explanations do their explaining from a particular point of view. Suppose, for example, you were giving a lecture on the causes of the American Revolution. You could offer, potentially, a great number of explanations, depending upon your point of view. One explanation might be *economic*, stressing American-British disagreements over trade and taxation policies. Another might be *political*, noting that Americans felt a strong need for self-governance. A third might be *social* or *cultural*, for surely the Revolution could not occur until the colonists had a strong sense of their own social identity as separate from the Mother Country. You could even offer a *rhetorical* explanation, arguing that the separation could not come about until this country had newspapers, printers who put out pamphlets and broadsides, and great orators able to enflame the citizenry. The point is, each of these explanations is "correct," even "useful"; each explains how the Revolution evolved and what events comprised it. They differ primarily in their perspectives.

Keep in mind that varied vantage points are a characteristic of this culture generally. By now you've probably heard economic, sociological, and political explanations of urban decay; political and technological ramifications of shutting down the space program; moral, educational, and sociological explanations for America's high divorce rate; and every explanation possible of the effects of excessive TV viewing.

People want explanations whenever they feel *confused* or *ignorant*. They want reports when they have particularized informational goals; but they want explanations any time concepts are fuzzy, information is only partial, or competing claims need negotiation. So, a group of parents may have heard of the concept of "alternative schools," but still can be puzzled by what an alternative school is like in terms of day-to-day school activities. Or, a group of students might be faced with a choice between a Bachelor of Arts and a Bachelor of General Studies, but won't know why to select one over the other until someone explains in detail and indicates what each might be good for.

Although each has different specific purposes, reportive and explanative speeches are called for whenever people need information packaged and clarified.

RAW MATERIALS FOR REPORTIVE AND EXPLANATIVE SPEECHES

Because both reportive and explanative speeches, of course, seek to inform audiences in ways similar to definitional and demonstration speeches, they also make use of the raw materials discussed in Chapter 5. *Motivational statements* are especially important in explanative speeches; while audiences for reports generally "know what they want," those attending explanative lectures and talks often need motivational prodding, statements telling how their attendance will decrease their ignorance or reduce their mental confusion. Both reports and explanations may require precise *definitions*, especially if the report deals with technical matters or if the explanation offers specialized rationales. *Examples*, of course, are so important to all informative speeches that we will discuss them again, in somewhat different ways, shortly. Almost all reports use *comparisons*, especially statistical comparison (see below), and both reports and explanations can profit from clarifying *analogies*. Finally, *visual aids* are frequently a must for technical reports, and may add a kind of physical presence to some explanations.

Given audience expectations, however, reportive and explanative speeches often require additional materials: *classifications*, *statistical summaries*, *examples (case studies)*, *criteria for judgment*, *various types of explanations*, and *resolutions*. Let us examine each.

Classifications

A requirement in a good many reports is that they classify data in ways useful to the group.

For example, a weather reporter normally discusses climatological conditions *geographically*, both to show people from various regions what their weather is going to be and to predict longer range developments based on the generally eastward movement of air masses.

The manager of a music store could arrange a report on trends in popular music *chronologically*, in order to identify tastes in music as they come into vogue, peak, and trail off; in that way the store can make reasonable decisions on what sorts of records and sheet music to order.

If a city manager is directed by the city council to report on the state of city services, he might classify data in a *cause-effect* pattern, indicating that a variety of causes has led to a series of effects. Double the average annual snowfall (cause) has led to the breakdown of snowplows and increased overtime wages to workers (effects). The drying up of federal funding (cause) has led to a decrease in revenue available for childcare centers (effect). A strike (cause) has created lagtime in the construction of low-income housing (effect). In this way, he can explain why many city services are in serious trouble.

Many business supervisors classify their data *topically*; that is, with categories which divide business concerns in traditional ways: figures on sales and returns, assets and debits, orders filled and orders backlogged, productivity measures, employees hired/retired/fired/laid off/absent. Good reporters check the scene around them, to discover appropriate methods for classifying and presenting the information they are asked to assemble.

Statistical Summaries

Many times, a person delivering a factual report is asked to display statistical data in summary form (such as lists, tables, or charts). Statistical summaries help audience members digest the information and allow them to examine it later on. The reporter, in such a situation, usually hands out the information and then orally presents only the highlights and a few implications.

Suppose you were asked to give a report on trends in grades (distribution of *As*, *Bs*, *Cs*, etc., as well as grade point averages) in sections of a basic speech communication course at your school. You might build a handout something like Figure 6.1 on the next page. In the actual oral report, you then could make the following points:

1. Within the sections offered during the fall term in 1981, the average grade for each class ranged from 2.05 to 2.76. This is a difference of almost three-quarters of a grade point. Perhaps different instructors are grading on quite different criteria.

2. For the fall term of 1981, most of the variance among sections was accounted for by two instructors (Jones' sections having the lowest grade average and Smith's sections having the highest). Because they are the newest members of the staff, perhaps they were not oriented to the grading criteria used by the other instructors.

3. Overall, the grade point average (GPA) for this term is the same as in 1980, but is down slightly from the averages in the preceding four years. (Often GPA's decrease when the size of classes increase; but in this case, enrollment is holding steady.)

FIGURE 6.1   Sample Statistical Summary

SPEECH 1: FALL 1981 GRADES

Instructor	Section	Enrollment	As	Bs	Cs	Ds	Fs	Inc.	GPA*
Jones	1	21	2	3	12	2	1	1	2.15
Smith	2	16	3	5	6	2	0	0	2.56
Hanson	3	17	1	6	7	3	0	0	2.29
Smith	4	17	6	2	8	1	0	0	2.76
Hanson	5	21	1	8	6	2	1	3	2.33
Roland	6	18	3	4	9	2	0	0	2.44
Roland	7	21	2	9	9	4	0	0	2.43
Jones	8	21	1	4	12	1	2	1	2.05
FALL 1981:		152	19	41	66	17	4	5	2.38

PREVIOUS YEARS

FALL 1980:	151	24	38	58	16	8	7	2.38
FALL 1979:	143	30	31	58	8	10	6	2.46
FALL 1978:	141	29	34	56	9	11	2	2.44
FALL 1977:	138	33	35	51	12	3	4	2.62
FALL 1976:	143	28	49	49	12	2	3	2.64

GRADE POINT AVERAGES FOR ALL FRESHMAN COURSES

FALL 1980:	2.45	*To calculate grade point averages, let A = 4.0, B = 3.0, C = 2.0
FALL 1979:	2.53	D = 1.0, F = 0.0, and discount "incompletes."
FALL 1978:	2.55	
FALL 1977:	2.50	
FALL 1976:	2.57	

4. The downward trend is consistent from 1976 to the present, but it is a steeper downward trend than that which exists in other freshmen courses at this school.

From this statistical summary, you also could go beyond factual reporting to advise or make recommendations to the group receiving the report, if you were asked to do so.

Examples (Case Studies)   In many reports and explanations, speakers need to include examples or case studies to highlight a point they are trying to drive home, for two reasons. Many reports and explanations tend to become highly general or abstract, especially if they are previewing alternative rationales or a lot of statistical data. Also, both types of speeches demand that people make sense of complex material primarily by listening. Thus, examples help make abstract ideas concrete and help listeners understand and remember what they hear. Two types of examples or case studies appear in these sorts of talks:

Typical Cases Suppose a large organization with a multitude of branch or regional offices wants a report on how a new procedure is working out. Instead of just presenting the "big picture" across the country, the reporter might instead look at a typical office, say, in Cleveland. The example could examine in some detail the Cleveland employees' reactions (positive and negative) to the procedure, as well as the Cleveland office's consequent increase or decrease in productivity resulting from the procedural change. Typical cases, in reports especially, function as prototypes that can be analyzed concretely. They are valuable, of course, only insofar as they are *actually typical*. If they represent more the exception than the rule in the audience's experience, the analysis will be biased and the reporter will be in trouble.

In many explanative speeches, typical cases function essentially as elements in an *inductive* analysis or argument. Suppose, for example, you were doing an explanative speech on ways in which inflation affects undergraduate students at the University of Minnesota. You might choose to discuss three "typical" students—a student who depends solely on home support, one who works full-time alternate quarters, and one who depends primarily upon scholarship monies and loans. So long as the case studies in fact seemed typical to your listeners, you could use the examples to support a generalization: no matter what kind of financial base students have, the astronomical increases in tuition, room and board, books and fees, and entertainment are threatening to drive undergraduates out of universities.

Extreme Cases There are times, though, when a reporter especially wants to investigate the extreme cases. Suppose a metropolitan city has mounted a number of youth training programs in business, recreation, public service, and technical skills. Because the training program is made up of so many different kinds of activities, it would be difficult to generalize about the program from one example. No cases could really be considered typical. To evaluate the program, a reporter might instead go to extreme examples—those centers which have "graduated" the most and the least number of trained youths. The reporter could gather data on several factors (time in program, kinds of youths recruited for it, background of instructors, facilities, location within the city). In that way, the city might be able to figure out which factors seem to predict success and which seem to predict failure.

Whether you set out typical examples or extreme examples, make sure your audience knows the basis for your selection—that you in fact can argue, if questioned, for why you selected the cases you did.

Criteria for Judgment

In advisory reports—those in which you are making recommendations—you usually are asked to justify those recommendations. And, in many explanations, you can be required to justify the rationale or perspective you have assumed: why are you looking at the American Revolution in economic terms rather than, say, sociological ways? Why should we be more worried about the psychological effect than about the political effects of excessive TV viewing? Or, better, by what "measuring rods" can we determine if TV viewing is "excessive" at all? Remember that the facts do not speak for themselves; you speak for them. So, as you draw implications from the facts, audience members will want to know why you infer what you do. And, when you make advisory recommendations, people will expect a rationale.

If you are proposing a course of action, you might be asked to tell why you think that action is *valuable*, *practical*, and *feasible*. Thus, your criteria for judging possible courses of action would be "intrinsic value," "practicality," and "feasibility." Say, for example, that you are recommending that the student government council set up a summer orientation program for incoming transfer students and freshmen. You might make that recommendation by saying that it is the kind of service the student government's constitution calls for (it is valuable); that programs such as this have worked at other schools like your own (it is practical); and that the council has enough money in its treasury to run the program (it is feasible). Think through such a list of appropriate criteria for judgment whenever you are asked to recommend actions.

Kinds of Explanations

Because there are essentially three purposes served by explanative speeches, we can talk about offering three kinds of explanations: *explanations-what*, *explanations-how*, and *explanations-why*.

Explanations-What "What is it?" is a question raised whenever something unfamiliar or confusing is introduced to us. The question "What?" is a signal that someone wants a concept related to events or things in the "real world." Sometimes that question is asked when we're unsure what concept to apply to some event, thing, or object. So, when looking at a tree in your friend's backyard, you might inquire, "Is that a sugar maple or an American maple?" You're really asking that friend to indicate what the characteristics of each are, so that you can distinguish between them and decide which concept to apply to the real tree standing there. At other times, we know the concepts well enough, but are unsure what the actual conditions are, so we cannot apply the "right" concept to the situation. So, we may know the difference between a liberal and a conservative, but aren't sure what characteristics Abraham Lincoln possessed that made him one or the other. When we don't know what something is—either because we don't know the concepts or because we don't know the facts in the situation—explanations-what are called for.

Explanations-How "How did it come about?" is another frequently asked question. How was it that Richard Nixon could be written off completely after his gubernatorial defeat in 1962, only to be elected President in 1968? Did he change? Did conditions in the country change? Or how did the commercial-residential zoning mess come about in the west end of town? neglect? maliciousness? opportunism? And how does the Federal Reserve Board go about making decisions on interest rates, on tight and loose monetary policies? What factors do they consider? Whom do they listen to? Explanations-how are attempts to trace through a series of events, stages, or actions in order to find a rational pattern or logic in those events. Explanations-how link causes with effects, those effects with other effects, and on and on until we see the pattern. They are normally presented from a particular point of view, as in the case of the several explanations-how which we offered for the American Revolution.

Explanations-Why More complex are answers to the question "Why did it happen?" At first glance, that question seems like "How did it come to be?"; that's true only because in this culture the word *why* has so many different meanings. We are going to use its most comprehensive meaning here, however, to refer to explanations which depend upon some *universal generalization*. When someone asks, "Why did my temperature rise when I got sick?", it's possible to refer to universal biochemical laws which

---

FIGURE 6.2   **Kinds of Explanations**

	Answers the question	**For example**
Explanation-what	*What* is it?	The strife in the Middle East is a cultural as well as a territorial struggle.
Explanation-how	*How* did this come about?	The Middle East situation is the result of events that have been occurring over thousands of years. As early as. . . .
Explanation-why	*Why* did this happen?	Such struggles are the result of every society's needs to maintain its social, political, and religious institutions and to maintain its territory.

explain that phenomenon. Similarly, we know that most cultures hit by revolution have social-political-economic conditions in common, and that laws regarding planetary motion explain the regular reappearance of Halley's Comet. Explanations-why, of course, often are highly technical. And for many occurrences we still have not formulated precise laws or generalizations. (If we had, we could predict suicides, earthquakes, political victors, and the like.) Yet scientists, social scientists, historians, and many other academic experts spend their lives attempting to discover generalizations capable of giving us solid explanations-why. During your lifetime of communicating, you probably will call upon many of them—when you explain to your neighbor why wood has to be cured before being used in construction, and to your politically naive friend why a person has to scream to get city hall to move. Many of our more common generalizations even become enshrined as pieces of folk wisdom: "Squeaky wheels get the oil," and "A stitch in time saves nine."

Ultimately, then, the three kinds of explanation represent the three dominant purposes of explanative speeches. Explanations-what are attempts to clear away confusion by offering *conceptualizations* which we can relate to some particular part of our world. Explanations-how order or *pattern* that world according to some point of view or logic. And explanations-why account for *regularities* in our world.[1]

Resolutions   Some reports require that you formally present recommendations in the form of *motions* or *resolutions*, especially if your group functions under parliamentary procedures. Formal motions are often required in political groups (like city councils), in many business and professional meetings (boards of directors and school faculty meetings), and in some other organizations (like the PTA or PTO). Motions are formal statements that either specify an action or sanction a particular belief or attitude. "I move that we spend $700 on a new typewriter" and "I move that we endorse Jane Smith as candidate for city comptroller" are examples of motions. If called upon to offer a motion or a resolution, take the trouble to write it out beforehand. And, if the resolution or motion is complicated, distribute copies of it among the group members. It will be much easier to comprehend, and it can be amended more efficiently.

In summary, reportive and explanative speeches, in addition to the types of materials we discussed in Chapter 5, may require classificatory schemes, statistical summaries, typical or extreme case studies, criteria for judgment, explanations-what, -how, and -why, and even formal resolutions or motions. These raw materials, in most ways, are a good deal more complicated in their mental demands upon listeners than materials we examined in Chapter 5. As a reporter or explainer, therefore, you must pay attention to packaging and clarifying the details. Not only must your reportive and explanatory language be clear and concrete whenever possible, but you must package it all shrewdly—our next concern.

ORGANIZING REPORTIVE AND EXPLANATIVE SPEECHES

While all of the organizational patterns we discussed in Chapter 3 are potentially useful to reporters and explainers, a few are especially well suited to their tasks.

Reportive speeches perhaps most frequently use *topical patterns* so that important information can be grouped under subheadings. Thus, a journalistic reporter often assembles information under the headings of "who," "what," "when," "where," and "how." Or, year-end financial reports can be put together by considering "expenditures," "income," "reasons for changes from last year," and "future projections." The reportive speech which follows will be organized by two topical summaries and a body of recommendations.

Other patterns, however, are also utilitarian. A *chronological pattern* is used in background reports. A *spatial pattern* provides a fine structure for, say, marketing reports which treat activities in different portions of the country or territory. When a committee or other group has asked for answers to particular questions, then of course the *question-answer format* is a natural.

Explanative speeches, given what we said about explanations-what, -how, and -why, most often employ a *cause-effect, effect-cause,* or even a *problem-solution sequence.* This is because these patterns represent the ways human beings normally interrelate facts; most of the time, when asking for explanations, we are seeking answers to the questions, "Where did it come from?" "What are its effects?" "How can we stop something harmful from continuing?" But, as well, a *comparison and contrast format* is particularly applicable to speeches wherein one is actually comparing the power of alternative explanations. Introductory physics lecturers use this format every time they explain the differences between "wave" and "particle" theories of light; so do economists who contrast "trickle-up" and "trickle-down" taxation and spending policies. Finally, of course, *topical patterns* can be used almost anytime; indeed, it is the pattern we'll use in the sample speech outline on marriage contracts simply because the clauses which can be written into such a contract are best discussed via partial enumeration.

To see how reportive and explanative speeches can be assembled, a sample speech and a sample outline are presented for your careful study.

SAMPLE SPEECH: **REPORTING**

Pre-Speech Analysis

Subject: Report on an elementary school's after-school program
Audience: The Henry Louis Elementary School's Parents Association
Situation: The Parents Association launched an after-school program of activities for students in order to extend the school day, to take pressure off working parents (who need kids taken care of until 5:00 p.m.), and to introduce students to new crafts, arts,

and activities. The program is now being evaluated by a three-person committee which is recommending changes for the next year.

Purpose: To assess last year's program and to make recommendations for the coming year

Speaker: The speaker chaired the committee.

Strategies: 1. The speaker establishes credibility by demonstrating a clear grasp of the statistical summaries (in useful categories), by citing testimony from other affected parties (school staff, parents, outside helpers), and by offering clear rationales for proposed changes in the program.

2. The speaker sets out criteria for judgment based on the special interests of these affected groups.

3. The speaker helps the Parents Association see the total picture through the use of visual aids.

4. Because the program is still considered experimental and depends upon volunteers, the speaker suggests ways of implementing recommendations which will not increase significantly the workloads of interested parties.

Speech

Report on the After-School Program
Andrea Michaels

Orientation: reviews the charge, explains the method

At our last meeting you requested that three of us review last year's after-school program and make recommendations for next year's offerings. To carry out the review, we went over the school's records, interviewed the principal, and talked with the parents and others who helped run the program.   /1

Previews the criteria for judgment used in making recommendations

After the committee reviewed the offerings and examined the viewpoints expressed by the principal, parents, and other helpers, we settled upon our recommendations by considering three factors: (1) student interest in various activities; (2) the amount of support from teachers, parents, and other helpers; and (3) the improvement of curricular-type activities through this program or others.   /2

Forecast

In this report, therefore, I will review our findings, and then offer our recommendations and our rationales for those recommendations.   /3

Highlights aspects of the statistical summary

First, then, pick up Table 1 and follow along as I discuss the students' use of various crafts, arts, and activities. The first column shows the number of students who signed up for each activity at the start of the term. Students did not register for daily drop-in activities, and some offerings were dropped when an insufficient number of students registered for them. The second column shows the actual number of students attending after such adjustments were made.   /4

You'll notice in both terms apparently high demand from kids for projects involving crafts and activities that aren't treated in the regular school curriculum— sewing, cooking, model-building, videotaping, and chess. And you'll see consistent interest in a potential curricular subject—foreign languages. And finally, you'll find that interest in other areas—notably macrame, dance, coin collecting, and new games—varied from term to term.   /5

Uses examples

Why the variance? There seem to be a couple of explanations. Some of these activities—macrame and coin collecting, for example—are activities in which students needed only good starts by experts. Once started, kids could continue these on their own, so they didn't need to participate for extended periods in groups. And the other two activities—folk and modern dance—are available in physical education classes. Students seemed to go to those only when they ran out of other challenges—primarily during the second term.   /6

Table 1—Student Enrollments in Various Activities

Activity	Fall Term		Spring Term	
	Students originally registered	Students actually attending	Students originally registered	Students actually attending
Crafts				
Macrame (Mon.)	11	12	4	0
Sewing (Tues.)	13	16	10	9
Cooking (Wed.)	10	10	12	14
Models (daily)*	—	aver. 9	—	aver. 11
Woodworking (daily)*	—	0	—	0
Arts				
Folk dance (Mon.)	2	0	7	8
Modern dance (Tues.)	0	0	4	5
Videotaping (Wed.)	7	7	9	10
String art (daily)*	—	aver. 7	—	aver. 5
Watercolor (daily)*	—	0	—	0
Activities				
Chess (Mon.)	8	8	8	8
Plant care (Tues.)	1	0	2	0
Coins (Wed.)	8	8	2	0
New games (daily)*	—	0	—	aver. 5
Library (daily)*	—	0	—	0
Languages				
French	9	10	10	10
Spanish	13	12	12	12

Note: The after-school program ran from 3:15 p.m. to 4:45 p.m. on Mondays, Tuesdays, and Wednesdays. Activity lists were handed out, offering some activities, arts, and crafts for the period 3:15—4:15 p.m., and others—especially the "daily" activities and languages—for the period 4:15—4:45 p.m. Students signed up for any workable combination on each day.
*The daily activities were on a drop-in schedule: a student did not have to come every day—only when he or she wanted to.
**The languages were offered daily, 4:15-4:45 p.m.; students were encouraged to come every day during that period.

Highlights the
second statistical
summary

Now turn to Table 2, which shows the pattern of adult support for the various activities. Let me examine each kind of support by category. We were fortunate to have teacher support in some of the more academic areas such as languages and arts. Parents were especially helpful with the more domestic subjects like sewing and cooking, and also with general activities like games. And outside volunteers from the hobby shops, the Senior Citizens' Recreation Program, and the university's foreign language departments filled out the program nicely. /7

Table 2—Pattern of Volunteer Help

Activity	Teachers		Parents		Outsiders*	
	Fall	Spring	Fall	Spring	Fall	Spring
Crafts						
Macrame					1	
Sewing			4	3		
Cooking			2	4		
Models	1	1			2	2
Woodworking	1	1				
Arts						
Folk dance					2	2
Modern dance					1	1
Videotaping		1			1	1
String art			1	1		
Watercolor	1	1				
Activities						
Chess	1	1				
Plant care			2	3		
Coins					1	1
New games			3	2		
Library	1	1				
Languages						
French	1				1	1
Spanish	1				1	1

*The outsiders included volunteers from the Senior Citizens' Recreation Program, two hobby shops, a videotaping company, and a local coin group. The language teachers came from the university's teacher preparation program.

Shows implications

In some of these areas, however, we are not assured of having continued support. Teachers, for example, were happy to help us launch the program. But let's face it: we are in fact asking them to teach longer hours without pay, as a couple of them noted in their interviews. And, too, the professional outside help from the hobby shops and the videotaping company cannot continue next year. The hobby shop people told us they are under pressure to stay at work. And the woman who runs the videotaping company no longer has children at this school, and so she won't continue. We, therefore, have to find ways of encouraging more outside volunteer and parent helpers.   /8

Transition to first recommenda-tion

With these facts in mind, turn now to our recommendations, which you have on the third sheet. I'll discuss each of the four items in terms of rationale and practicality.   /9

Recommendations from the Curriculum Subcommittee to the Henry Louis Elementary School Parents Association

1. We recommend that more pressure be put on parents to volunteer on a regular basis for work in the after-school program.
2. We recommend that more outside volunteers be sought from nonprofessional sources (the local VISTA program, the service clubs in town, the women's groups in various churches, and junior high and high schools).
3. We recommend that this school seek permission from the school board to offer French and Spanish as regular courses in the curriculum.
4. We recommend that students be more carefully surveyed at the beginning of each term to determine desired crafts, arts, and activities.

Rationale

Number 1. *"We recommend that more pressure be put on parents to volunteer on a regular basis for work in the after-school program."* We are, after all, serving parents—especially those who use the program as a child-care facility—and so therefore they ought to feel some obligations to serve.   /10

Shows practicality and course of action

At the beginning of each term, we should send out a notice with instructions for parents to tell us what services they could offer us. That survey should include a list of times on Monday, Tuesday, and Wednesday, with dates, when one or both could volunteer. In that way, some parents might feel freer to volunteer some time without feeling pressured to work every day, all term.   /11

Shows feasibility by use of example

Uses nonstatis-tical data

We might also indicate that unless parents get more involved, we will have to raise the participation fees for those parents who cannot devote, say, ten hours a term to the program. This sort of strategy has worked well at Martin Luther King Elementary School, which has a similar program; parent volunteers more than doubled when they tried it. And, it's similar to cooperative babysitting arrange-ments, where, if a particular family is not doing their share of sitting for others, they have to pay for services they're using. And, from our interviews with parents who had not participated directly, it became clear that more would make the effort to help if they could schedule in advance specific commitments for particular days.   /12

Second recommenda-tion

Rationale

Examples

Number 2. *"We recommend that more outside volunteers be sought from non-professional sources."* To pick up the slack when the hobby shop people cannot work, we need to tap more volunteers. In addition to the Senior Citizens' Recreation Program, we ought to talk with the local VISTA program coordinator, the service clubs in town, the women's groups in various churches, and the junior high and

Shows feasibility

**Third recommenda-
tion**

Rationale

**Uses practicality
as criterion for
judgment**

**Fourth recommenda-
tion**

Rationale
**Demonstrates prac-
ticality and course
of action**

Backpatting

**Review of cri-
teria and recom-
mendations**

**Call for dis-
cussion of report**

high schools—especially the Future Teachers Associations and the art and drama groups. Increasing volunteers will keep our program costs down, yet provide the services we need.   /13

Number 3. *"We recommend that this school seek permission from the school board to offer French and Spanish as regular courses in the curriculum."* The student and parent response to our after-school program in this area indicates that language instruction ought to become a more important educational goal. I think we could work out a useful arrangement for regular courses. The continuing interest in languages means that parents would support such a move. Several indicated they would meet with the school board if we initiated a meeting. With school board financing, we could enter into an arrangement with the university to get regularly scheduled student teachers as helpers. And, to offset the cost of hiring teachers, we could share two instructors with four other elementary schools wishing such programs, thereby reducing the cost per school.   /14

And the final item—Number 4. *"We recommend that students be more carefully surveyed at the beginning of each term to determine desired crafts, arts, and activities."* As you saw in Table 1, some activities generated no interest at all, even though we thought they would. Such problems could be avoided in the future if we more carefully tapped student—and parent—interests at the outset of a year, thus working from a more precisely determined picture of student desires. Such a move would also help us avoid the embarrassing situation of lining someone up to run an activity for which there is little or no interest.   /15

Overall, then, our committee is most satisfied with what went on last year, and hopes the school is willing to continue the after-school program. From our interview with the principal it's obvious that the staff is likewise supportive. We think our recommendations, however, will make it work even better. The first two recommendations for bringing in more parents and outside volunteers will make it easier for the program to function. The third recommendation for starting regular foreign language classes will add measurably to our school's curriculum development. And, the fourth recommendation for surveying student interests will help guarantee that we serve our clientele—the students—better than before.   /16

If you have questions about the data or the recommendations, the rest of the committee and I will be happy to try and answer them.   /17

Notice the various speaking strategies employed by this reporter. The introduction could be short, because the group was aware of the program and the committee's charge. The *introduction* was devoted primarily to a description of (1) data-gathering procedures (to increase the reporter's credibility); and (2) criteria for judgment (to establish some common ground between the reporter and the audience, and to prepare the way for later recommendations). Within the *body* of the speech, the statistical data were not actually reviewed in detail because the handouts included them. Instead most of the time was devoted to drawing out implications and, more important, to justifying the reasonableness and feasibility of the recommendations. This sort of strategy is a good one for many advisory reports, as most people are much more interested in "bottom lines"—data summaries and recommendations which flow from them. And finally, the *conclusion* of the speech also was short; it functioned primarily to compliment those involved and to open discussion to the audience. In that way, the reporter was able to create a sense of both finishing and beginning: the report itself was over, and it was time for the discussion to start.

Now, we can examine somewhat different strategies employed in a typical explanative speech.

SAMPLE SPEECH: EXPLAINING

Pre-Speech Analysis

Subject:	Marriage contracts
Audience:	A speech class, a campus or community study club, or a premarriage group counseling session
Situation:	Most audience members are not married.
Purpose:	To explain the basic provisions in marriage contracts, thereby indicating how they help couples consider marital obligations and rights realistically
Speaker:	The speaker has read several sample contracts and discussed their benefits with married couples.
Strategies:	1. The speaker stresses how putting marital obligations and rights on paper creates a sense of realism and objectivity.
	2. Audience members likely think their marriages will not end in divorce. The speaker uses a light appeal to fear to make them question that belief.
	3. The speaker helps audience members apply the idea of marriage contracts to their own situations by offering varied examples of sample points to include in a contract.
	4. In this brief speech, the speaker (a) attempts to offer a rationale for employing contracts, (b) outlines basic provisions which should be considered, and (c) gives brief examples where the basic provisions are not self-explanatory.

Outline

Reference to occurrences the audience is familiar with

Introduction of fear to grab the interest of the audience

I Do, But Do You?

Introduction

I. Couples now frequently design their own marriage ceremonies.
   A. For some couples personalized ceremonies are the "in" thing.
   B. People use them in an attempt to make the institution of marriage more directly relevant to their lives and attitudes.
II. Yet, it's doubtful that specially tailored ceremonies will alter the fact that the divorce rate in the U.S. is the highest in the world. Nearly half of our marriages end in alimony rather than matrimony.

Allusion to a way of reducing fear	A. But those beautiful words in the ceremony may become more significant if couples take time to consider how they'll treat each other after the ceremony.
Introduction of the concept to be explained	B. Marriage contracts delineate personal and financial aspects of a marriage relationship. 1. Although the provisions of such a contract are not legally binding, these contracts can force a careful examination of the upcoming relationship.
Tying the idea to a piece of folk wisdom	2. Couples may use these provisions to make their marriages what they want them to be; or, if they cannot agree, then they may choose to avoid a potentially rocky marriage, looking before they leap.

Forecast	III. Let's examine some of the basic provisions of marriage contracts to see how engaged couples may be forced to view marital obligations realistically as they put one together.
	   A. To begin, I'll review some personal questions many couples need to answer.
	   B. Then, I'll discuss some financial obligations worth considering.

Body

First half of the explanation: explaining how personal relationships are discussed	I. Marriage contracts require an engaged couple to ask each other some crucial personal questions.
	   A. One type of personal question involves physical and mental health.
	      1. Besides knowing that your potential mate is in good physical condition, ask about hereditary diseases or mental illnesses in the family.
	      2. Further, it's important to ascertain whether there are compulsive addictions—perhaps to alcohol, drugs, or gambling.
	      3. Health also relates to concerns of childbearing. Can your mate, to his or her knowledge, father or bear children?

Transition	B. The issue of childbearing provides us with the second major area of personal agreements.
	      1. Couples must ask themselves whether or not they really want children.
	         a. If they plan to have them, how many?
	         b. If they can't bear them personally, do they want to adopt?
	      2. Methods of child care also need consideration.
	         a. For example, will the woman be expected to stay home with children under school age?
	         b. If both parents work, how will the responsibility for sick care be shared?
	      3. Third, there are questions about methods of birth control.
	      4. Attitudes toward abortion should also be discussed honestly.

Transition	C. Along with these basic questions about health and childbearing, couples should openly discuss sexual rights and freedoms. 1. Although monogamy is legally mandated in this country, some couples want occasional periods of freedom away from each other.
Careful introduction and tasteful discussion of a potentially disturbing subject	a. If you find this idea disturbing, make sure your partner knows your sentiments.

      b. It is probably also wise to find out how your partner might react if there were infidelity.

  2. Disclosures about past sex life present a tricky problem.

      a. Such disclosures may be important to some people and might aid in a frank discussion of their future sex life together.

      b. However, for some couples, this issue is not relevant and is better avoided.

      c. Each couple has to decide if a discussion of their past sex lives is worth getting into—if they think that it would be constructive or destructive in their relationship.

Internal summary

  D. Although questions about health, childbearing, and sex can be terribly embarrassing to ask—and answer—it is better they are aired before a marriage is underway.

Second half of the explanation: explaining how to discuss finances

II. Assuming these questions haven't short-circuited your future marital plans, you next should discuss some of the financial obligations of marriage.

  A. Couples should examine financial options.

    1. Will the man or the woman or both support the family?

    2. If both are wage earners, how will they answer questions such as these:

      a. Will they pay expenses proportional to their incomes?

      b. How will they handle wage disparities?

        (1) Will a joint checking account be satisfactory?

        (2) Should the couple establish joint savings accounts?

      c. How will the couple distribute wage-earner contributions during unemployment, as in a period of maternity or illness?

  B. Some couples don't stop with these general financial questions, but also prepare a projected monthly budget.

    1. Such a budget helps them determine whether and when to make large expenditures.

      a. Will the budget allow for a two-bedroom apartment?

      b. Can they make furniture payments and car payments simultaneously?

    2. Other questions also can be answered by the projected budget.

      a. How much can they spend on specific items such as recreation, eating out, and gifts for their families and friends?

      b. How much can they save for babies, emergencies, future schooling, and so on?

  C. These are some of the financial questions which ought to be addressed.

    1. Obviously, it's almost impossible for any couple to project actual financial outlays, as we've discussed them, very far in advance.

    2. Accuracy, however, is less important than working through—together —possible arrangements, to head off potential problems.

Conclusion

Summary

I. So, marriage contracts often contain provisions concerning such personal matters as health, childbearing, and sexual arrangements and such financial matters as income, savings, expenditures, and emergencies.

Recognition of possible remaining doubts	A. Some of you may be like the friend who listened to me expound on this topic and then asked, "Aren't these topics awfully personal?"
Easy answer	B. Before I had time to respond, she answered her own question: "Oh wait, I see. That's what it's all about. If you talk about these things, then you really know what you're getting into."
Reinforcement	II. She's right.
	A. Marriages initially seem to be made in heaven, but too many are ending up in hell.
Personal commitment	B. I believe that firmly enough to have gone through this process myself. And if you want to see what the process can produce, I invite you to examine my own contract. [Holds up the contract]

The foregoing outline illustrates four virtues a good explanative speech should exhibit: (1) The speech is framed in *motivational statements*, with reasons (fear of marriage failure and a promise of benefits from interpersonal openness) why someone should listen to the explanation. (2) The speech is carefully *segmented* or partitioned; typical marriage contract agreements are organized under two main heads (personal relations and financial matters), which in turn are broken down into sub-topics for clarity. (3) The speaker is careful to include *internal transitions and summaries* so the audience always knows "where it is" in the enumeration of topics. Those transitions and summaries are especially important for topical patterns, for without them, listeners feel left with a "string of beads"—a series of more or less independent and seemingly unrelated bits of information. (4) And, the speech depends heavily on *examples*. Especially if the ideas have not been considered previously (e.g. management of money) or if they appear threatening or embarrassing (e.g. sexual relations), clear examples are absolutely necessary—to make new ideas concrete and to make controversial ideas less threatening. In all, what could have been an overly complicated speech, in this case, has succeeded in clearly packaging ideas for a student audience.

TIPS FOR PACKAGING AND CLARIFYING IDEAS

Reports and explanations are communicative staples in this culture. Audiences, therefore, usually are quite conscious of their expectations for reporters and explainers. Hence, keep the following guidelines in mind as you prepare and deliver these sorts of speeches.

Tips on Reports

■ *Research the information with great care.* While you may be asked to present only a series of statistical summaries in a short five-minute report, your research must be extensive and solid. You must assemble the material and define the categories with one eye upon your charge and the other on possible follow-up questions. Remember, you will be expected to be an expert. Be prepared to offer fuller data, justifications for your categories, an extended example, or even expert testimony. The reportive speech itself ought to be viewed as only the tip of the iceberg of information you have gathered, not as a mere cube floating on the surface with no visible support.

■ *Include a complete rationale for any recommendations you make.* Use the criteria for judgment your group or audience expects of you as the basis for your rationale. A strong rationale is important for two reasons. First, a solid rationale enhances your *image* or *credibility* because it demonstrates your ability to think through and rationally solve problems. More importantly, if your rationale is a good one, it more likely will be adopted. Remember that audience members, in turn, have constituencies to which they must answer. If audience members act on your recommendations, they must be prepared to explain their actions to the people affected by them. In our outline, the Parents Association members in the audience might have to justify their decisions to other parents, the school staff, the kids who would be taking part in the program, and the school board. By not only making recommendations but also offering reasons, you help your listeners to meet objections and to urge action in the important second step—their appeal to secondary audiences.

■ *Make full use of visual aids.* A report, like any public speech, is both an oral and a visual event. Furthermore, because reports often are pressed for time, you have to be certain that they contain the maximum amount of material in a short period. So, in our sample outline, the committee included two tables of information and a sheet of recommendations. If they had wished to offer other visual information, they could have offered an audiotape of interviews with students; a slide show of the various crafts, arts, and activities; sample videotapes made by students in that activity (or in dance, cooking, etc.); or a list of names and addresses of potential volunteers to be contacted. Indeed, in a reportive speech, one of your objectives often is to let nonvoice media present the information while you carry forward the task best suited to oral communication—building the rationales and appeals for action.

■ *Whatever you do, stay within the boundaries of your report-making charge.* If you are charged with bringing in a factual report, do not turn it into an advisory report. If you're asked to report on today's closing stock market prices, don't offer suggestions on what stocks to buy tomorrow. Conversely, if you've been asked to bring in recommendations on selections for your book club to read next year, don't just list twenty-seven books and then say you couldn't make up your mind. At the least, offer criteria members could use in selecting upcoming attractions—fiction and nonfiction, best new books in biography, history, consumerism, or sports, with rankings within each category. Be sensitive to the boundaries within which you are operating. When in doubt about those boundaries, ask questions.

■ *Be adaptable.* The way you structure your report and the kinds of material you include will vary from situation to situation. In the sample outline, notice that there is very little in the way of introduction (except to clarify the purpose) and even less of a conclusion. In other reports, either or both might be much longer. If many members of the audience are new to the group, you may need to include a more formal introduction, with even more background. If your recommendations are controversial, conclusions will demand more justification. The kinds of information included in the body of the report may also vary. Often statistical summaries or examples are not needed, or time does not allow for them. Do not accept any guidelines as always applicable; be prepared to make variations. You will have to be sensitive to group traditions, rules, demands on time, and the state of knowledge of the audience in front of you.

Tips on Speeches of Explanation

■ *Tie the explanation to the interests, needs, and beliefs of the audience.* As for all good speeches, unless people are actually interested or involved, an explanation is worthless. Notice in the sample outline on marriage contracts the clear attempts to tap the audience's feelings and interests— the use of fear (reference to the divorce rate); the appeal to realism (a common concern these days); and the recognition of individual values (telling audience members to put their own special concerns into the contract). Explanations are no good in and of themselves; they're good only if real people want or need them.

■ *Use concrete detail.* Because we often are called upon to explain unfamiliar or complex happenings, concrete detail is absolutely necessary. For the audience who heard the speech on marriage contracts, much less would have been communicated had the speaker not offered descriptions of sample areas of concern. The speaker could have said, "By writing a marriage contract, two people attempt to agree on their interpersonal and financial relationships before they get married," and then have sat down. It even would have made sense. But it would *not* have allowed members to "see" how a marriage contract works, to visualize specific areas where agreement ought to be reached. You usually can tell if you're including too much or too little detail by reading the feedback you are getting from an audience's movements and faces. If you're not getting feedback, ask for it: "Does everyone understand?" "Is that clear?" Make the two-way process of communication work for you.

■ *Use analogies.* Remember how someone explained gravity to you by swinging a ball on a string around your sunny little head, and how you learned about eclipses with the help of two balls and a flashlight. Explaining the unfamiliar in terms of familiar experiences is often one of your best communicative tools.

■ *Be careful with your vocal tones when explaining.* Our culture is rife with patronizing and pompous explainers. You can turn on your educational television channel in the mornings and see any number of condescending explanations from people who explain with a tone of voice that makes you feel like a four-year-old. And just as bad are some government officials, educators, scientists, and other experts—people who are professing *their* wisdom and *their* social rank by offering explanations sprinkled with jargon and characterized by ponderous delivery and lecturish-sounding voices. Those people are too busy showing off themselves to concentrate hard upon accurately and directly communicating ideas to real people. As you prepare and present an explanative speech, watch out for the two extremes: undershooting your audience (talking down to them) and overshooting your audience (using jargon they don't understand). Aim at the sense of conversationality expected of an articulate person. Keep your audience, rather than yourself, clearly in mind.

■ *Encourage audience questions.* Allowing a question-and-answer period, either in the middle or at the end of your explanative speech, helps the two-way communication process work. To encourage questions from audience members, you must do two things well. First, you must be sure you leave *time* for questions. If you're scheduled to talk twenty minutes and then talk nineteen-and-a-half minutes, you're not doing a good job of encouragement. You're only pretending to invite the audience in. Second, you must build an *inquisitive atmosphere.* You must leave the audience feeling that you are open to questions. If you finish an explanative speech on various ways for financing your first home with, "So there can be little doubt but that land contracts are *the best* way to finance a house. Now, are there any questions?", you've created such an authoritarian atmosphere that only the most brash audience member would dare to ask a question. When giving explanations, don't be afraid to be more tentative, more open to alternative explanations and viewpoints. *Probablys, perhapses,* and *maybes* won't kill you; rather, they'll show you to be an open-minded explainer, secure in your knowledge yet willing to entertain additional data, doubts, and overviews.

■ *Rigorously test your own logic.* This is especially necessary for explanations-how and explanations-why. In Chapter 3, we advanced the idea of "rationality" and presented some tests of logic you can apply to the structure of ideas in your speeches. That, obviously, is an extremely important activity for the explainer. To test the logic of your explanations, you must apply two criteria:

Crucial factors test:

Have you left out any of the crucial factors, or have you stressed noncrucial factors? A speech on Jimmy Carter's victory in 1976 could run into trouble on this account by either underemphasizing the "post-Watergate mentality" (a presumably crucial factor in the election) or overemphasizing his toothy smile (probably a noncrucial factor).

Temporal sequence test:

Is there an important gap in the sequence of events you are portraying as an explanation of some phenomenon? An explanation of the economic crunch currently faced by colleges and universities that ignores the great expansion of faculty and facilities in the mid-1960s has deleted an important consideration.

One of the great virtues of strategic outlines is that they help you visualize the intellectual structure of your ideas. Examining that logical structure is especially important when you are dealing with chronological and cause-effect patterns, both of which are used often in explanative speeches. By preparing an outline and by asking yourself to think of everything you left out, you can do some logic-testing, *before* your listeners do!

That concludes our discussion of information transfer and informative speaking, and prepares us for persuasive speaking. Actually, explanative speeches bridge the gap between informative and persuasive speaking. When you give an audience *facts* to the point that they start seeing the world differently than they did before, and when you offer them *rationales* which account for the world as it is experienced, you are influencing their thinking and perhaps even their behavior. If you're any good at reports and explanations, you're an implicit persuader.

NOTES

[1] For a somewhat more technical yet readable discussion of explanations, see W. V. Quine and J. S. Ullian, *The Web of Belief* (New York: Random House, 1970), Chap. 8, "Explanation."

ASSIGNMENTS

Pre-Performance

1. Divide into small groups for the purpose of considering the following topics. First, decide upon the audience to which each topic will be presented. With the particular audience in mind, proceed to discuss the sources you would use in preparing each reportive speech. In addition, attempt to specify how you would organize any data you might find.

Is a new field house (or other university facility) needed?

Should a traffic signal be installed at a particular intersection?

What is the present condition of local playground facilities?

Is this college's present system of registration adequate?

2. Ask your family and several friends to save their junk mail for a brief period, perhaps two weeks. Examine the mail and study the ways statistics are used or misused. Note your findings in your communication journal.

3. Consult two consumer-oriented publications for information concerning a specific product or line of products. How do their evaluations differ? How thorough do their analyses of the products appear to be?

4. Assume that you are to speak to each of the following groups on the topic of noise pollution. How would you go about explaining this topic to each of these audiences?

a high-school ecology class

residents gathered to protest the building of an auto speedway

a group of merchants with businesses near an interstate highway
a group of students at a meeting of the Pre-Med Club
a city council meeting at which a noise ordinance is to be discussed
members of your speech class

Indicate the general and specific purposes of each speech, and suggest specific ideas which should be incorporated.

5. Choose one of the following topics (or choose from others your instructor provides), and locate at least three sources of material for preparing an explanative speech on the topic. Why, in your opinion, are these good expository supporting materials?

What life will be like in the year 2525
How farm parity functions
Minimum competency testing for high-school graduation
How a Pope is chosen
Why we bury the dead
How presidential popularity polls are conducted
The process of mining the minerals at the bottom of the seas
The why of fermentation

6. Indicate the type of organizational pattern you would use to build a speech on the topic you chose in the previous exercise. (See Figure 2, "Organizing Patterns for Speeches," in Chapter 2.) Defend your choice of type of arrangement, and state the main headings you would use in your talk.

Performance

1. Investigate a local problem. Use the principles discussed in this chapter to explain the nature, dimensions, and causes of the problem. Your four- to six-minute report should include workable solutions, but your charge will not be that of recommending a specific solution. A brief period for questions should follow the speech. Provide your instructor with an outline of your speech.

2. Assume that you have been asked to collect and evaluate information for a particular business or student organization. Choose a topic, and prepare an advisory report for this special audience. Make sure that you reveal the nature of the charge at the outset of the speech, that you are clear about where and how you obtained information, and that the information seems to warrant the conclusions. Time limits for the speech will be six to eight minutes with two to three minutes of questions. You should prepare an outline of the report.

3. Informally report your findings on the use of statistics in junk mail, surveyed in Pre-Performance 2. These reports should stimulate class discussion about statistics as a form of support.

4. Select a difficult concept from one of your other courses, and prepare a four- to six-minute explanation. You should prepare a strategic outline for the presentation. Also, remember the value of visual aids. The following topics may stimulate your thinking:

amino acid configuration in DNA molecules [biology]

systems analysis [political science]

logarithmic charts [mathematics]

5. Choose an interesting sequence of events or a social movement as the subject for a four- to six-minute speech. Make sure that your account can "pass" both the crucial factors and temporal sequence tests. In addition, provide an accurate and vivid description of scenes and participants in the historical account. If you detect a definite change in the history of an era, you should offer reasons for apparent changes. Be sure to develop a detailed outline. You could narrate such occurrences as the building of the U.S. space shuttle program, the rise of Reverend Sun Myung Moon, recent developments in the women's movement, or the development of the American Indian Movement (AIM).

6. Prepare a two- or three-minute speech narrating a personal experience. Your general purpose will be to inform your listeners about what it is like to do something such as backpack in the Tetons, learn to fly, or participate in a large political march. Pay particular attention to use of language and detail, and concentrate on a conversational delivery.

Post-Performance

1. The question period at the end of most performances in this chapter can be especially useful in pointing out problems with a presentation. Think about the questions you received at the end of your report. Was the clarity of some idea questioned? Did your organization of material appear to cause confusion? Did you complete the exercise as assigned?

2. Recall an oral report given in this class which was clear and satisfactorily organized, but shallow in development or use of supporting material. Indicate in your communication journal the type of materials you thought should be added.

3. After each speech for Performance 4, quickly jot down the speaker's main ideas. You may want to take brief notes during the presentation. Give your notes to the speaker. Speakers should summarize the data, and prepare to report (in class or in the communication journal) on problems listeners may have had in understanding the complex concept. Speakers should remember that discrepancies in the comments may be related to factors other than the speech itself.

4. In your communication journal, analyze how two student speakers in your class used rationales. Choose a speaker who offered an effective rationale and one who did not.

PERSUADING

PREVIEW THREE

Audience Psychology

For fifty years now, Americans have been scrutinized by social scientists—sociologists, political scientists, communication specialists, and psychologists of every stripe. And not only have we been scrutinized, but the results of that scrutiny have been applied to all the institutions of our society. TV networks systematically analyze viewer preferences to determine programming hits and failures; politicians survey the beliefs and attitudes of the constituents to help them make decisions on issues and images. But this is not to suggest that we've just been victimized by all of this. Inasfar as the social scientists have taught us how to influence the ideas, attitudes, and actions of our fellow beings, we can become the beneficiaries of their work. Clearly, we can't compress all of the theories about audience psychology into one brief section. But we can convert some of the implications into strategies to use when attempting to persuade others. We'll need to simplify, but that always happens when one gets "practical."

HEART AND HEAD   As early as the sixth and fifth centuries B.C., Greeks began talking about psychology (to them, a natural union of philosophy and medicine). Ever since, theorists and researchers have been divided into the "heart" and "head" camps. Those concerned with the heart have envisioned human beings as driven by "rapture," "drives," "needs,' "motives," "feelings." That is, some theorists view Homo sapiens as *animals,* controlled as are all animals by instincts to survive, to cope, to predict, to belong, to overcome adversity, and so on. Such needs or drives in human beings, of course, tend to become a good deal more complicated than they are in animals. As we have stressed, humans have a great advantage over other animals—the ability to symbolize. Yet the "heart" theorists argue that humans are still basically governed by the same impulses all beasts are—and that these impulses are "bio-basic" (based in biological structures) even though they are "symbolically elaborated."

Those theorists concerned with the head, in contrast, have pictured people as driven by entities they call variously "beliefs," "ideas," "attitudes," "notions," "arguments," "thoughts," "values." These theorists view persons as *rational creatures,* as special beings who have learned to control their hearts or glands with their heads or minds.

There thus exist today two great groups of psychologists. The "heart" theorists are the biological or behavioral psychologists ("rat runners" and behaviorists, as they often are called). The "head" theorists are the cognitive or informational psychologists. Because both have a good deal to say to the arguer and persuader, we will draw ideas and strategies from both groups. In this preview, we will talk about "motives" or "motivational appeals" (thanks to the heart folks) and about "reasoning" and "arguments" (thanks to the head theorists). Because people are both body and brain, you undoubtedly will mix both "appeals" to the heart and "arguments" to the head as you seek to change human thoughts and acts with words.[1]

MOTIVATION AND MOTIVATIONAL APPEALS

It is useful for a speaker to think of people as governed, or at least often put into motion, by drives or motives. What this means might become clear if you consider four events:

Event A: You are walking through a woods on a fall afternoon and hear a loud noise. You jump. Then you say to yourself, "That must have been a gunshot."

Event B: You have been dating a person for some time, going together to films, concerts, picnics. Finally, you decide that tonight you will declare your love, toward the end of the evening. Every half hour or so during the earlier portion of the night, you notice that your palms become clammy, beads of sweat appear on your brow, your heart seems to race, and an unmistakable knot twists relentlessly in your stomach.

Event C: You know nothing about glaucoma. One day a doctor tells your aunt that she has the eye disease. You immediately go to the library to find a layman's explanation of it.

Event D: You have never been much on going to church. One evening, however, you agree to attend a religious meeting and become convinced of the truth of the ideas offered. Thereupon, you devote at least ten hours a week explaining those truths to anyone who will give you five minutes.

These events illustrate four important aspects of motives and motivation:

1. *Motives or drives are bio-basic and can affect you "without thinking."* In Event A, you jumped without thinking the thought, "That must have been a gunshot." Like any other animal, the human must protect itself. Some drives, like the drive for self-protection, are based in your biological makeup; hence your body can react physiologically "on its own."

2. *Motives often manifest themselves physiologically.* The sweat, increased blood pressure and heart rate, and stomachache in Event B attest to the power of fear even in our daily lives. Similarly, people often can "read" emotions in your bodily responses and actions even before you say anything.

3. *Motives can affect your beliefs.* In Event C, you sought information to construct new beliefs because you feared for your aunt (and perhaps for yourself). A motive can be so powerful, as a matter of fact, that a drive (say, thirst) can make you believe in something (a mirage of water) that does not exist.

4. *Conversely, beliefs can affect motives.* In Event D, once you acquired a new set of beliefs-attitudes-values, your motivation changed, driving you even to confront strangers in ways you didn't before.

In each of these four events, then, an inner aim or goal impelled you to act. These inner goals may be called motive needs. More formally, a *motive need* is an impulse to satisfy either a biological urge (protection, safety, hunger) or a psychological-social want (power, belongingness, pleasure). A speaker can appeal to many different kinds of motive needs of an audience—to needs for achievement, adventure, companionship, conformity, creativity, curiosity, endurance, fear, fighting, independence, loyalty, power, pride, reverence, revulsion, saving, sex, sympathy, and so on.[2] *Motive appeals,* then, are a speaker's attempts to raise or create motive needs in an audience. Most motive appeals work psychologically in one of two ways:

Visualization   One common way to raise motive needs is through verbal description of situations you wish your auditors to "see." Public service ads on television, for example, often seek to create feelings of fear and revulsion by showing the viewer the results of excessive speeding—pictures of a swerving car, a crash, flashing ambulance lights, twisted metal, the chalked outline of a person on the pavement. Such visualization helps "spectators" to project themselves into the situation, to feel certain motive needs, and to then change beliefs, attitudes, or behaviors as a result—in this case, to slow down. Ours is a vision-oriented society, and hence verbal depiction or visualization is an extremely powerful, though somewhat indirect, method for tapping motive needs.

Association   A second and more direct use of motive appeals involves associating certain motives with particular concepts, beliefs, attitudes, or courses of action. In the 1960 presidential campaign, then-candidate John Kennedy associated his programs for social legislation with the idea of "the New Frontier," playing upon the voters' motives of adventure and generosity. In 1980, candidate Ronald Reagan worked hard to make voters view him in a certain way, to associate his simple image with notions of honesty, homespun values, and conversationality. More technically, then, association involves verbally tying together a *concept* (the belief or action you wish accepted) with a series of *attributes* (motivating reasons to accept the belief or action).

Motivational theories of audience psychology may seem a bit glandular in their view of human beings as members of the animal kingdom, yet it is possible to turn some of these notions into communication strategies. We will expand upon these strategies especially in the chapters on reinforcing beliefs and attitudes, changing attitudes, and moving an audience to action.

REASONING AND ARGUMENTS   But we all know that people are also rational—at least upon occasion. Even in the face of powerful thirst and the mirage, you can tell yourself that your senses are playing tricks on you; you can learn to deal with deception (the stick only looks bent when it's put in the pond, right?). *Learning* is the key term here, for in an important sense you must learn to reason.[3] Some of that learning takes place *experientially:* after touching a hot stove a few times you arrive at the generalization, "Touching hot things with the hand produces an inordinate amount of pain." Some of that learning occurs with the help of *authorities:* teachers tell you that 1 + 1 = 2 and parents drill into you that lying is wrong. And once you are older, especially, learning can take place *technically* or formally: in high school, you were given theoretical derivations explaining why a triangle has only 180 degrees or why its area is calculated by multiplying one-half its base by its altitude.

Experientially, authoritatively, and technically, you learn generalizations about the world ("whats") and patterns for arriving at generalizations ("whys"). Those patterns are called reasoning. *Reasoning* is a process of connecting something which is known or believed to some concept or idea you wish others to accept. Reasoning patterns have three basic elements: the something known or believed can be thought of as *evidence;* the concept or idea to be arrived at is a *claim* or *proposition;* and the connecting notion is the *inference.* "Patterns of reasoning," then, are habitual ways in which a culture or society uses inferences to connect evidence with claims.[4] While people have proposed several different ways of classifying reasoning patterns in this culture, we will work simply with five basic patterns.

FIGURE III.1 **The Reasoning Process**

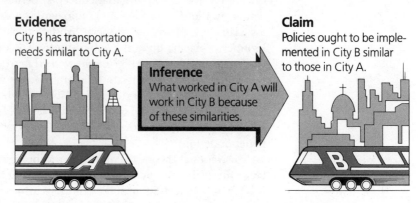

Evidence
City B has transportation needs similar to City A.

Inference
What worked in City A will work in City B because of these similarities.

Claim
Policies ought to be implemented in City B similar to those in City A.

Reasoning from Instances

Often called *inductive* reasoning, reasoning from instances is a matter of examining a series of particular examples or known occurrences (evidence) and drawing a general conclusion (claim). The inference in this reasoning pattern can be stated: "What's true of particular cases is true of the whole class." This represents a kind of mental inductive "leap" from specifics to generalities. So, for example, the Food and Drug Administration will study the effects of cyclamates on a few people and discover a larger than normal incidence of cases of visceral cancer (the examples or evidence). With an inductive leap they'll move to the claim, "Cyclamates can cause visceral cancer in Americans in general," and hence ban them. You use a similar pattern of reasoning every time you drive home during rush hour. After trial and error, you decide that Street A is the best one to take home between 5:00 and 5:30 p.m., and Street B, between 5:30 and 6:00 p.m. After enough instances, in other words, you arrive at a generalization and act upon it.

Reasoning by Parallel Case

Another common reasoning pattern involves thinking, not in terms of generalizations, but solely in terms of closely similar events. Your city, for example, probably designed its transit system or its parking lots by examining the transit systems or parking arrangements in cities very much like it. The evidence was the occurrences in a *parallel* town; the claim was that certain policies ought to be implemented in your city; while the inference ran something like, "What worked in City A will work here because of similarities." As a parent, you employ reasoning from parallel case every time you say, ever so sanctimoniously, "Don't run into the street. Remember what happened to Jamie Johns when she did?" Obviously, you're not generalizing (for not everyone who goes into a street will be struck down). Instead you are asserting that Jamie and your child are parallel cases—that they have enough features in common to increase the likelihood of another accident in the neighborhood.

Reasoning from Sign

A third reasoning pattern uses an observable mark or symptom as proof for the existence of a state of affairs. You reason from sign when you note the rash or spots on your skin (the evidence) and decide you have measles (the claim). The rash doesn't "cause" measles; rather, it's a sign of the disease. Detectives, of course, are notorious reasoners-from-sign. When they discover someone had motive, had access, and had a weapon in his or her possession (the signs), they move to the claim that the person might be the murderer. Your doctor works the same way every time she asks you to stick out your tongue, looking for signs of trouble. These signs, of course, are circumstantial evidence—and could be wrong. Just ask detectives and doctors. The inference, "This evidence is a sign of a particular conclusion," is one you have to be careful with. This sort of reasoning works pretty well with natural occurrences (ice on the pond is always a sign that the temperature has been below 32 degrees Fahrenheit). But reasoning from sign can be troublesome in the world of human beings (as when people take people's skin color as a sign that they are shifty/lazy/dishonest/rhythmical). Yet we often have to use signs as indicators; otherwise we could not project our economy, predict our weather, and forecast the rising and falling of political candidates.

Reasoning from Cause

Reasoning from cause involves associating known antecedents (that which comes before or "pushes") with certain consequents (that which comes after as a result of the "push"). Such cause-effect reasoning is important enough, you'll remember, that it is frequently used as a basic pattern for organizing speeches. Its power derives from the hope we have that our world is a regularized, predictable one in which every occurrence has a cause. Hence, if crime rises in your community, there's an immediate scramble to find the causes—drugs, economic deterioration, inept law enforcement, or bad street lighting. Instead of reasoning from certain effects back to possible causes, we also can reverse the process by reasoning from causes to possible effects. When the Great Plains are threatened with drought, the government moves immediately to head off bad effects by stockpiling grain, by arranging for airlifts of hay for animals, by raising beef import quotas, and by planning for emergency loans to build irrigation projects. The evidence and the claim, therefore, are the identified causes and effects, while the inference is the simple but important generalization, "Every cause has an effect."

Reasoning from Generalization or Truism

A final kind of reasoning pattern, often called *deduction,* is essentially the reverse of reasoning from instances (induction). Even as a child you probably were taught that buying goods in large quantities saves money (the generalization or evidence). Therefore, because discount stores purchase goods in quantity, you will be able to save money shopping there (the claim deduced from the evidence). Or, to take the classic example, because all people are mortal (generalization or truism), and because Socrates is a person, therefore Socrates is mortal (the claim).

FIGURE III.2   **Tests of Reasoning Patterns**

Reasoning from Instances
1. Have you looked at enough instances to warrant generalizing? (You don't assume spring is here simply because you have one warm day in February.)
2. Are the instances fairly chosen? (You certainly hope your neighbors don't think you've got a rotten kid just because he picked one of their flowers; you want them to judge your son only after seeing him in many different situations.)
3. Are there important exceptions to the generalization or claim which must be accounted for? (While it is generally true, from presidential election studies, that "As Maine goes, so goes the nation," there have been enough exceptions to that rule to keep Maine losers campaigning hard even after that primary.)

Reasoning from Parallel Case
1. Are there more similarities than differences between the two cases? (City A and City B may have many features in common—size, location, etc.; yet they probably also have many features in which they differ—perhaps in the subgroups that make up their populations, the degree of industrial development, and the like. Too many differences between the two cases will rationally destroy the parallel.)
2. Are the similarities pointed out the relevant and important ones? (So there are two tads in your neighborhood who are the same age, live on the same block, and wear the same kinds of clothes; but are you therefore able to assume that one is a saint simply because the other is? Probably not, because more relevant similarities would include their home lives, their school backgrounds, their relationships with siblings, and so forth. Comparisons must be made on relevant and important similarities.)

Reasoning from Sign
1. Is the sign "fallible"? (As we noted already, many signs are merely circumstantial, as in the case of the murderer and racial examples above. Be extremely careful not to confuse sign reasoning with causal reasoning. If sign reasoning were infallible, your weather forecaster would never be wrong!)

Reasoning from Cause
1. Can you separate causes and effects? (We often have a difficult time doing this. Do higher wages cause higher prices, or is the reverse true? Does a strained home life cause child misbehavior, or is it the other way around?)
2. Are the causes strong enough to have produced the effect? (Did Jimmy Carter's winning smile really give him the election, or was that an insufficient cause? There probably were much stronger and more important causes.)
3. Did intervening events or persons prevent a cause from having its normal effect? (If the gun's not loaded, no matter how hard you pull the trigger you won't shoot anything. Even if droughts normally drive up food prices, that

might not happen if food has been stockpiled, if spring rains left enough moisture in the soil, or if plenty of cheap imported foods are available this year.)
4. Could any other cause have produced the effect? (Although crime often increases when neighborhoods deteriorate, increased crime rates can be caused by any number of other changes—alterations in crime-reporting methods, increased reporting of crimes which have been going on for years, or closings of major industries. We rationally must sort through all the possible causes before championing one.)

Reasoning from Generalization or Truism

1. Is the generalization true? (Remember how long sailors set certain courses on the assumption that the world was flat, or the number of years parents in this country accepted as gospel Benjamin Spock's generalizations about childrearing.)
2. Does the generalization apply to this particular case? (If a small neighborhood store has a sale, it may well offer better prices than discount houses. Or the old saw "Birds of a feather flock together" certainly applies to birds, but perhaps not to human beings.)

Note that the inference can garner its power from one of two sources: in the first case, it is justifiable because of *experience* (by shopping around a lot we arrived at the generalization); and in the second, the generalization really is a *definition* (i.e., one of the innate characteristics of human beings is mortality). In other words, we accept the first inference because of uniformities in the world, and the second because of ways we use words such as *human* and *mortal.*

These five forms of reasoning are judged "logical" or "rational" in this culture. Because we pride ourselves, often, on logicalness or rationality, we can apply very strict tests of reasoning to each pattern to check for *fallacies* or illogic. These tests are summarized in Figure III.2.

Overall, then, we can certainly accept the cognitive psychologists' attempts to map out ways people in this culture reason, ways they rationally link their beliefs, attitudes, values, and behaviors. There are demonstrable cases when you change your mind or actions when someone points out inconsistencies in your reasoning: "How can you generalize about all high-school principals after you've met only one?" "How can you accept 'loose' liquor laws after you've argued for 'tight' marijuana laws?" "You say you're going to vote for Politician X because she's for reducing taxes, but remember that she's also opposing other causes you fervently believe in." And, again and again, "Practice what you preach." The so-called consistency schools of psychology and audience analysis have explored the power of these sorts of arguments, and they certainly will help us map out communication strategies, especially in the chapters that discuss arguing and refuting.[5]

The human being is often a wonderfully unpredictable beast, thank goodness. Even half a century of dedicated research has reduced none of us to lockstep patterns of thought and behavior. You'll never be able to reach every listener with the "perfect" motive appeal or the "perfect" rational argument. Yet we know enough about audience psychology to give you a fighting chance. We now will proceed to examine those occasions upon which you will employ both appeals and arguments.

NOTES

[1] Fuller introductions to various schools of psychology and their contributions to our understanding of argumentation and persuasion can be found in: Herbert W. Simons, *Persuasion; Understanding, Practice, and Analysis* (Reading, Ma.: Addison-Wesley Publishing Company, 1976); Stephen W. King, *Communication and Social Influence* (Reading, Ma.: Addison-Wesley Publishing Company, 1975); Philip Zimbardo, Ebbe B. Ebbesen, and Christina Maslach, *Influencing Attitudes and Changing Behavior*, 2nd ed. (Reading, Ma.: Addison-Wesley Publishing Company, 1977).

[2] For a fuller discussion of motivation, motive needs, and motivational appeals, see Douglas Ehninger, Bruce E. Gronbeck, Ray E. McKerrow, and Alan H. Monroe, *Principles and Types of Speech Communication*, 9th ed. (Glenview, Il.: Scott, Foresman and Company, 1982), Chap. 6, "Determining the Basic Appeals."

[3] For development of the notion that reasoning is socially learned, see Bruce E. Gronbeck, "On Classes of Inference and Force," in *Explorations in Rhetoric; Studies in Honor of Douglas Ehninger*, ed. Ray E. McKerrow (Glenview, Il.: Scott, Foresman and Company, 1982), pp. 85–106.

[4] The concepts of "evidence," "proposition," and "inference" are developed by Stephen Toulmin (who calls them "data," "claim," and "warrant") as the backbone of the so-called Toulmin Model of argument. See Stephen Toulmin, Richard Rieke, and Allan Janik, *An Introduction to Reasoning* (New York: Macmillan Publishing Company, Inc., 1979) for fuller development of the notions and their use.

[5] The notion of psychological consistency is discussed and developed technically in R. P. Abelson et al., eds., *Theories of Cognitive Consistency: A Sourcebook* (Chicago: Rand McNally, 1968).

CHAPTER 7

Reinforcing Old Beliefs and Values

Americans are joiners. Ever since childhood, you have been urged to join something—the Boy Scouts, the Campfire Girls, the church choir, the school band or volleyball team. To get our political, economic, social, and personal work done, we are constantly organizing ourselves into groups and associations. Those groups provide each of us with part of our identity, as when you tell people "I'm a Sierra Club member," or "I'm a union representative." And, they also serve you by gathering and packaging the latest information, keeping on top of problems and proposals for solutions, dispensing funds and other resources to needy people, playing the watchdog, sponsoring retreats and conferences, and on and on.

America works and plays in groups. But even the most dynamic group or association discovers along the way that its membership declines, that its joiners get tired, that the "cause" gets lost among all of the other causes in society. Periodically, people have to be reminded of why they joined the group, what the services are, and how the group helps them meet their personal goals. More technically, clubs, caucuses, associations, and even spokespersons for more informal groups have to offer *reinforcement*. Reinforcement becomes a matter of recalling the "old" beliefs and values which caused people to join the cause in the first place, and of reinvigorating audiences to the point that they once more contribute their time, energy, and finances to the tasks needing doing.

THE OCCASION AND THE AUDIENCE: WHAT, WHO, WHEN, WHY

Reinforcement speeches are demanded in situations characterized by apathetic "believers," by people who have intellectually and emotionally accepted particular ideas, attitudes, and values, but who now are flagging in their zeal. Very often these people are dues-paying members of social and political organizations. They get involved in a time of crisis; but once that crisis has passed, they just swim along with the crowd. Apathetic believers must occasionally, annually, biennially, or quadrennially be shaken out of their lethargy. Think for a minute of organizations you belong to or have contributed to, and of the occasions when they try to rally your support. Every fall the United Fund hits you to up your contribution, and the Heart Fund or local cancer society does the same. The Sierra Club and Common Cause periodically send out an SOS to their members, when an important state or national bill is up for consideration. Labor conventions are called to remind workers of their plight, and national political conventions are keynoted by fire-eaters who point out the work to be done. In all of these cases, *reinforcement* is taking place. In reinforcement, "believers" are asked to increase or return to commitments they have already made.

The *why* of reinforcement speaking perhaps is obvious. Psychologically, reinforcement speaking is an often-necessary form of *motivation*. While people, in an intellectual sort of way, are likely to say, "Sure, I support the Republican Party," or "Yeah, I believe in Common Cause and its efforts to increase the efficiency of the federal government," they often seem unmotivated. Their assent is there all right, but they don't always act on those beliefs and attitudes. They need to be stirred into action; once motivated, then they may well act upon their accepted beliefs and values.

Therefore, in this chapter, we will be concentrating our attention upon some commonly used strategies or tactics—called motivational appeals— as well as organizational patterns which will allow you to expertly structure those appeals in a useful way.

MOTIVATIONAL MATERIALS FOR REINFORCEMENT SPEECHES

To meet its goal of reactivating old believers, a reinforcement speech contains two kinds of materials:

1. A review of people's original commitments to some set of ideals or programs, together with an examination of the current state-of-affairs; and,
2. A call for renewed effort and recommitment.

Such sub-goals often are achieved by reinforcement speakers through the use of *facts and figures* (which allow them to describe and/or quantify the current situation); *expert testimony* (which can inspire rededication); *examples* (which portray specific aspects of the remaining problems, or which show the believers what the "opposition"—if there is one—is doing); and *comparisons and contrasts* (which compare membership activity now and in the past, or which contrast "our" effort with "their" effort in some area).

But, reinforcement speakers also need to consider, more particularly, techniques of psychological motivation, for that, after all, is the principal barrier-to-action being faced by such speakers. Because reinforcers are seeking to stop stagnation and to push an audience to new levels of activity, speakers use six basic motivational appeals time and again in reinforcement speeches: promises of *reward*, coercive *threats*, psychological *inoculation*, appeals to *legitimacy*, calls for personal *commitment*, and challenges to *action*.

Reward   A desire for reward is an extremely strong motivating factor in humans, and reinforcers use it frequently. Although the reward can be tangible (e.g., increased return on your investment dollar if you buy now), often the rewards promised by reinforcers are intangible and psychological. These psychological rewards can take many forms, including: *praise for past actions*, as when the speaker thanks you for commitments you made during the last organizational crisis; *acknowledgment of present actions*, as when the chairperson of the local United Fund drive expresses appreciation that you've shown up at a planning meeting; and *promise of future gains*, pleasures, or satisfaction, as when the American Cancer Society chairperson visualizes the great social and medical gains to be made if the organization meets this year's goal. Because all of us like tangible profits and psychological strokes, reward is a primary technique.

Threat   The mental opposite of reward is punishment or fear, and hence is an equally powerful tool. You can be threatened by what will happen if you *don't* heed the words of the reinforcer. That threat can take two forms. *Fear appeals* promise some harm to you individually if you don't brush your teeth, stop smoking, prevent the erosion of your neighborhood, or elect a person who will take a hard stand on industrial zoning in your end of town. *Conspiracy appeals* indicate that some group is out to harm or injure the audience as a whole. Reinforcers are especially fond of identifying "conspiracies" because they can strike terror in an audience (but not too precisely, for if we knew the names and addresses of our enemies, we could handle them). So Common Cause fights "big campaign spenders" and "Fat Cats"; the Sierra Club fights "big oil" and "big lumber"; labor unions attack "big business"; and the Young Republicans fight "big government." The size and the presumed pervasiveness of such conspiracies can coerce flagging supporters into renewing their original commitments.[1]

Inoculation   The term *inoculation*, of course, comes from medicine; and its psychological power is analogous to a vaccine's physiological power. Basically, inoculation involves (1) showing an audience a part of the opposition's *ideology* and then destroying it, or (2) taking some *activity* of the opposition and demonstrating how you've already beaten it. So a speaker for an environmental protection organization might say: "The timber industry says that 'clear cutting' in national forests does no harm because they work in only small areas and because they replant; but *we* can point out that. . . ." Or "The coal industry spent $X million dollars in a campaign to get the Iowa legislature to allow it to start strip-mining in southeastern Iowa, but we beat them in a landslide vote." With either technique, the reinforcer is showing the audience a part of the opposition's ideology or actions and then tearing it apart. In that way, the audience is "inoculated" —protected against the propaganda of its "enemies." Inoculation is especially important when the opposition seems to be making inroads into your own organization or ideals. You attempt to inoculate your audience against the opposition's ideas and stop psychological erosion.[2]

Legitimacy   This strategy attempts to make your cause legitimate by demonstrating that "significant others" believe in that cause, product, or candidate, and are acting on its behalf. Appeals to legitimacy can take two forms. *Authoritarian appeals* are employed to indicate that "great" people support the cause. So a mayor is asked to make a statement the day the United Fund drive is opened; a governor or senator urges everyone to get behind the state's tourism program; and the President will address the nation on ways of conserving fossil fuels. *"Bandwagon" appeals* show that not only "big folks" but also the "little guys" are behind a project. Most organizations publish figures of their recent growth—if more are joining, the cause must be good, right? Your local newspaper may publish a picture of the "carrier of the week," to demonstrate that even twelve-year-olds can hustle and make the American dream come true.

Commitment   Once an audience has been reminded of what a cause or organization stands for, a reinforcer inevitably calls for renewed or further commitment. The reinforcer asks the audience to revitalize their beliefs and attitudes for one of two reasons. The *inherent good*—with this appeal the speaker is reminding you that the cause is good in and of itself, as when the representative of the local humane society argues that neutering pets will produce an immediate drop-off in stray and starving animals in your neighborhood. The *instrumental good*—your action now, so you are told, will generate some future good. So, for example, if you continue to believe strongly in an environmentalist organization and act upon those beliefs, one day you'll have a cleaner, a healthier, a more beautiful America. Good reinforcers know that an audience must be put into a ready state, must have attitudes that prepare them to act. The audience must know what to do and why to do it before it is susceptible to the sixth appeal—the call for action.

Action   This, of course, is the crux of the reinforcer's speech. Will the audience renew its memberships, join an action committee, knock on doors, read a book? Will it act? Not automatically. Even if praised, coerced, inoculated, legitimized, and committed, that audience normally needs extremely direct appeals to action. It needs one last psychological kick.

FIGURE 7.1   **Motivational Techniques for Reinforcement Speeches**

Usual Techniques	Persuasive Goal
Reward	
a. Praise for past actions	create feelings of self-satisfaction
b. Acknowledgment of present actions	recognize the current effort being expended by listeners
c. Promise of future gains	hold out real and psychological bait
Threat	
a. Fear appeals	make individuals feel threatened
b. Conspiracy appeals	depict group enemies
Inoculation	
a. Attack on ideology	demonstrate that the enemy's ideas are weak
b. Attack on actions	show that the enemy's activities can be beaten
Legitimacy	
a. Authoritarian appeals	illustrate the support from great personages
b. Bandwagon appeals	illustrate the support from common people (like the listeners)
Commitment	
a. Inherent good	indicate that the cause is good in and of itself
b. Instrumental good	point out that it will generate additional benefits
Action	
a. Death	action must be taken to keep something from dying
b. Growth	action must be taken to keep something increasing
c. Maturation	action must be taken to complete something

That kick can come from three different communicative feet. *Death*—you can urge action because a cause or campaign is dying and should be saved. In 1969 former President Richard Nixon and Vice-President Spiro Agnew began a campaign for the "forgotten American"—later the "silent majority"—as a group of people whose ideals and values were pictured as dying. As a result, public opinion poll ratings for both of them went up, and thousands of Americans supported the executive branch in fights against Congress over Vietnam and social legislation. The "silent majority" rallied in the face of this appeal. *Growth*—you also can call for action because something is growing and should be helped to continue expansion. People who organize neighborhood block associations, for example, often argue in this way: "Half the blocks in this section of town now have organizations. We already are gaining the ear of the city council, but we won't have significant impact on decisions until we can show them that 100% of the blocks are behind us. So won't you join?" This call to join a growing movement makes use of the bandwagon appeal we mentioned earlier. *Maturation*—a speaker can get that last ounce of effort from people by saying that the idea is culminating, and now can be pushed over the top to meet its goal. The United Fund organizers come on strong the last week of a drive; the political volunteer stuffs sample ballots in people's doors the night before the election; and Common Cause calls for one last round of telegrams to congressional delegations before a crucial vote on a key measure. This form of action appeal seems to work because everyone wants to be associated with a winner, a completed goal. Overall, then, you select an appeal for action based on your perception of the stage at which an organization is—near dying, growing, or peaking.

Reward, threat, inoculation, legitimacy, commitment, action—these strategies comprise the bulk of reinforcers' messages.

ORGANIZING REINFORCEMENT SPEECHES

Several of the traditional organizational patterns are available to reinforcers. A *comparison-contrast* sequence allows you to compare, say, a period of high activity and commitment from the past with the current state of do-nothingism and passive commitment in an attempt to rekindle the fires. Or, a *problem-solution* format lets you focus on member or audience slackness as the problem and renewed effort as the solution; or, the lack of commitment can be pictured as a *cause*, with "enemy" inroads and triumphs the *effects* which must be stopped by renewed efforts.

As well, however, some special patterns have been devised for use by reinforcers. As we noted in Chapter 3, "special" patterns tend to be easily adapted to particular characteristics of audiences; hence, they are most useful in reinforcement speeches, where one is attempting to overcome apathy. Let us look at three such patterns.

The *Yes-Yes* Pattern

In this pattern, you organize your message carefully around a series of propositions with which you think your audience agrees. Each time an auditor says *yes*, you have him or her closer to the renewed commitment you desire. The more *yeses*, the better off you are. So, for example, if we organized a speech on a school bond issue on the *yes-yes* pattern, it might look something like this:

   I. Education is the backbone of a democracy.[Yes, of course.]
  II. In this country, the center of education is the public school. [Sure.]
 III. America has been wise in maintaining local control, insuring that
      each community can govern the curriculum, the learning, and the
      facilities. [Yes again.]
  IV. With control comes social responsibility. [Think so.]
   V. Part of the responsibility for local schools involves the guarantee that
      the facilities are adequate to the task. [Sounds good.]

At this point, the speaker is ready to launch the pleas for responsible
provisions. When talking about something as sacred as education, the
yes-yes approach can prove most effective.

The *Yes-But* If you think you're going to encounter some serious opposition, you can
Approach slide from a *yes-yes* to a *yes-but* organization. For example, most insurance
agents these days are trained to use the *yes-but* approach; a typical
insurance pitch nowadays goes this way:

   I. Protection for yourself and your family is something you have to be
      concerned about. [I suppose.]
  II. Most of us just don't have enough money in the bank to provide that
      protection. [I sure don't.]
 III. And how about retirement? We don't really have enough resources
      there, either. [*Yes, but,* how about social security and my company's
      retirement plan?]
      A. O.K., how about them? Inflation will destroy the value of both of
         them.
      B. A catastrophic illness or a change in jobs will finish off the
         retirement plan. [O.K., O.K.]
  IV. Insurance is, overall, the best way of providing both protection and
      future income. [*Yes, but,* how about stock investments, savings
      accounts, land investments?]
      A. O.K., how about them? Let's look at each. . . .

The Motive- Because reinforcement is largely a matter of motivation, the structure of a
Reinforcement reinforcement speech often can be built around the motivational appeals
Approach to reward, threats, inoculation, legitimacy, commitment, and action we
discussed earlier. These appeals almost naturally fall into an organizational
pattern:

   I. Review of past accomplishments of the group/audience
  II. Documentation of current threats to group beliefs, attitudes, and
      values
 III. Call for renewed commitments
  IV. Call for new actions

Notice that this approach (a) centers on the audience's own beliefs, (b) brings into the picture the beliefs and actions of those opposed to listeners' beliefs, and (c) then seeks to dispel apathy by calling for renewal of efforts. It is simple but effective. Because it is used so commonly, we'll use this motive-centered approach for this chapter's sample outline.

SAMPLE SPEECH:　　**REINFORCING**

Pre-Speech Analysis

Subject:	Public financing of political campaigns*
Situation:	A meeting of a local chapter of Common Cause, a citizens' lobby group seeking to streamline and democratize government at all levels. While membership is holding up, fewer and fewer members in this local chapter are showing up at rallies and helping with various projects.
Purpose:	To reinforce the group, sparking it to further individual and collective action
Speaker:	President of the local chapter, well known among the audience for efforts on various campaigns
Strategies:	The speaker employs all of the basic reinforcement techniques—reward, threat, inoculation, legitimacy, commitment, and action appeals—to stir up the believers and revitalize their thinking and acting.

Outline

In Common We Can Win

Introduction

Reward by identifying past successful actions taken by the listeners

I. First off, let me thank the hundreds of you who sent letters and telegrams to our congressional delegation in support of changing laws on financing federal congressional campaigns.
   A. Five out of six of our congressional representatives voted for the recent bill.
   B. Even though it did not pass, your efforts did not go unnoticed; and your messages are being passed on to the House Committee on Elections for further consideration.

Coercion (threats)

II. Even though we have had some successes in this state, there is more to be done.

(Appeals to a presumed conspiracy)

   A. While corporations, banks, and unions by law cannot contribute directly to candidates for federal office, they can set up voluntary political action committees (PACs) to channel contributions.

Forecast

   B. Today, I want to review the operations of some PACs aligned against us, and suggest steps we can take to blunt their power.

---

* The supporting material in this outline is taken from *In Common: The Common Cause Report from Washington* (Spring 1978). Reprinted by permission of Common Cause. Additional updating materials come from "Campaign 80: How Special Interest Groups Use Their Power," *Nation's Business*, June, 1980, pp. 38–41, and "Election Tab: A Billion Dollars, and Rising," *U.S. News and World Report*, 15 December 1980, p. 33.

Body

Documentation of
current problems
(legitimating authorities,
statistical trends)

Credibility of the
authority is established
by reciting facts
gathered by a "neutral"
organization

I. As Fred Wertheimer, Senior Vice-President of Common Cause, has noted, "interest group political giving is a growth industry," and figures from the Federal Election Commission bear him out.

A. Between 1974 and 1976, 650 new PACs were born.

B. In 1977, another 230 new PACs appeared.

C. In just the first two months of 1978, 132 more registered with the federal government.

D. Another 350 new PACs were organized in 1979.

E. In all, by 1980, the last year we had a presidential election, there were more than 2000 PACs ready to spend between $50 million and $60 million.

II. The problem those of us in state Common Cause organizations face is this: The 1974 Presidential Election Financing Act allows little of this money to be channeled into presidential campaigns. Therefore, most of this money must go to congressional and state elections.

Legitimacy (appeals to
an external authority)

A. As the *Wall Street Journal*'s Washington Bureau chief, Norman C. Miller, has written: "The bulk of special interest contributions represents a sort of investment in the careers of incumbent Congressmen and Senators, with the aim of enhancing the influence of the financing groups."

Examples of the
conspiracy

B. The examples supporting Mr. Miller's view of special interest conspiracies are numerous.

1. In 1974, the Senate passed no-fault legislation by a vote of 53–42; but after the American Trial Lawyers Association (which generates income from automobile negligence suits) organized a campaign fund, the bill failed in the Senate, 49–45.

2. The Airline Pilots Union and all major airlines except United and Pan American have been lobbying hard against deregulation of the commercial airline industry. In all, aviation-related interests contributed more than $160,000 to campaigns by October 1977, with 14 of the 23 members of the House Subcommittee on Aviation receiving substantial campaign contributions.

3. Common Cause researchers have discovered that the American Medical Association and Federation of American Hospitals PACs have contributed $73,462 to the campaigns of members of the House Ways and Means Health Subcommittee.

4. Among top PAC recipients were Democratic Senator Alan Cranston of California, who received nearly $439,000, and Democratic House Majority leader James C. Wright, Jr. of Texas, who got more than $293,000.

(Use of a fear appeal to
bring the conspiracy
down to individual
listeners)

Call for renewed
commitment

D. All of this means that those of you who faithfully contribute $5 here, $10 there, in support of reform-minded political candidates are facing financial powers who can swamp your efforts to bring about the demise of special interests, because you can't match their money when reelections come up.

III. It is time to renew your commitment to the efforts of Common Cause and other concerned citizens groups.

(Inherent good)

A. You must rededicate yourself to the goals which got you to join Common Cause in the first place.

(Instrumental good)

B. Such a commitment pays off with an increased sense of self-satisfaction and with the knowledge that your children will participate in a government characterized by open decision-making.

Inoculation to show that opponents can be beaten by committed workers

C. Though PACs are organized against us in all states, we can win.
   1. Our Washington lawyers were in large part responsible for writing the 1974 Presidential Campaign Financing Act, over the objection of big corporations.
   2. State Common Cause organizations led the fights in New Jersey and Wisconsin to pass laws which provide for public financing of gubernatorial, state senate, and state house races. They came within an eyelash (one vote) of getting the California Assembly committee on financing to recommend a similar measure.

Conclusion

Call for Action

I. Most of you have been in this organization long enough to know what has to be done.

(Growth)

A. As our membership continues to grow, we add more and stronger voices to our efforts.

(Maturation)

B. And, we face a crucial test in our own state, where a bill to publicly finance statewide campaigns and congressional races comes up for consideration in one or two months.

Helps audience take first steps by providing a list of specific people to contact

   1. On the sheet of paper which you have been handed are the names and addresses of our state legislators and those of the members of the Subcommittee on Elections. Write them tomorrow.
   2. And when your local state house or senate representatives hold office hours in town—and these are published in the paper—drop by for a little chat on these bills.

Final Appeals

II. Our state organization's motto is a simple one: "In Common We Can Win."
   A. Just as the federal government has reduced the power and influence of PACs on elections, so can our state government.
   B. We can once again have government "of the people, by the people, and for the people" if you'll do your part to make governmental officials unequivocally accountable to individuals rather than groups.
   C. Let's work as hard as we have in the past to keep government open!

Notice in the outline that all of the principal reinforcement appeals were used. They were structured in such a way that listeners first would feel satisfied about their past action, next would discover that a new threat faced them, and finally would know that if they once again became active they could stave off destruction from an organized enemy. This sort of structure—moving from satisfaction through doubt or fear and on to "salvation" through action—is very effective in reinforcement speeches.

Another feature of the outline is worth noting: the speaker was careful to be a credible communicator. He carefully marshalled facts and figures as well as expert testimony to make his picture of the situation believable. And he added specific instances of successful activities from other states (arguing by parallel case) to demonstrate that his listeners had a good chance for future victory. The structure of the speech, as well as its evidence, then, made it a masterful reinforcement speech.

TIPS FOR REINFORCING

■ *Don't overdo the guilt and fear appeals.* As we have seen, reinforcers often play upon the guilt and fears of listeners. Yet, if you overplay your hand, berating auditors for their inaction or painting pictures of disaster in the wake of "enemy" actions, you're likely to run into trouble. Research on fear appeals has pretty conclusively demonstrated that *moderate fear appeals* are more effective than *high-level fear appeals*.[3] Speakers, for example, trying to get people to brush and floss their teeth daily are ill-advised to drag out pictures of mouths running with puss and filled with broken, decayed teeth; revulsion, rather than fear, is the likely reaction, and people work very hard to forget or ignore that which revolts them. Therefore, use appeals to guilt and fear, yes, but don't overstep the bounds of good taste and workaday psychological advice.

■ *Do rely, however, on visualization.* Images, metaphors, and other kinds of descriptive language we discussed in Chapter 4 and Preview Three serve the reinforcer well. Building "verbal pictures"—and even using some actual pictures as visual aids—are important tools for the reinforcer. Graphic detail helps listeners picture scenes, and tends to get them visually involved with your message. Visualization allows listeners to "see" themselves in action, fighting the enemy and winning the battle; that sort of psychological "projection" of self can support the reinforcer's goals.[4]

■ *Maintain a harmonious relationship between yourself and your audience.* Remember that a reinforcer is more or less a group's *representative*; you think like your audience, presumably have the same attitudes and values, and want them to act as you do. You are "one of them," not an outsider. You are the embodiment of the "ideal" audience member, the "perfect believer" in the cause. Therefore, you must do everything you can to stress your close relationship with them: talk in terms, in examples, and in metaphors they'll understand and appreciate. Talk as a friend to friends, not as a morally superior preacher. Stress your commonalities and the results of joint efforts.

■ *Work on your oral syntax.* Reinforcement speeches, at times, seem to demand what we used to call "eloquence," because they must be more or less inspirational. People must be inspired to get off their apathetic duffs and to begin the hard work of fighting the good fight. You need not, of course, be "flowery"—as that will work against you in these days of "plain" speaking. But, you can approach inspirational eloquence in your use of images and metaphors, in your phrasing of motivational appeals, and in your sentence syntax. Many successful reinforcers use short, hard-hitting, parallel sentences, especially, to drive points home. So, a conclusion to a speech telling party members to get back to work for a political candidate might include the following sentences:

> *We must start the political campaign anew. We must register voters in our neighborhoods. We must hold coffees and open houses for candidates. We must raise money for radio, newspaper, and television ads. We must distribute pamphlets in every corner of the city. We must do block-by-block surveys of voters. We must arrange rides to the polls for shut-ins. We must organize ourselves and our efforts as never before if we are to triumph in November.*

Here, short sentences are combined with parallel sentence structure ("We must . . . We must . . . We must . . .") to list the action steps in concise, clear ways. The sentences build in a kind of crescendo to the final goal—"triumph in November."

SAMPLE SPEECH: **REINFORCING**

Pre-Speech Analysis   Let us close this chapter with what has become known as a classic reinforcement speech. In it, you will see all of these "tips" followed to near-perfection: the guilt and fear appeals are present, but under control; visualization can be found, both in the initial section (where the speaker herself is a "living picture" of progress) and in later discussions of party goals; the speaker is highly conscious of her membership in the political party she is addressing, and uses that membership often to remind them of the tasks ahead; and, her sentence syntax borders on the poetic, at times, in her simple, eloquent parallel structures, short sentences, and direct address.

The occasion was a large public convention—the 1976 Democratic National Convention. The speaker was Barbara Jordan, then a member of the United States House of Representatives from Texas; the speech was a "keynote address"—a time when party faithful are reinforced, are called back to work for ideals they believe in. Ms. Jordan fulfilled all those goals, and more. She made use of her own credibility as a politically successful black woman to underscore the main theme of Jimmy Carter's 1976 campaign—a rededication of public officials to the American dream, so much a part of the bicentennial celebrations across the country. Both personal and public appeals, therefore, were united in an electrifying speech.

Democratic Convention Keynote Address
Barbara Jordan

Introduction
One hundred and forty-four years ago, members of the Democratic Party first met in convention to select a Presidential candidate. Since that time, Democrats have
(past traditions)   continued to convene once every four years and draft a party platform and

nominate a Presidential candidate. And our meeting this week is a continuation of that tradition.   /1

But there is something different about tonight. There is something special about tonight. What is different? What is special? I, Barbara Jordan, am a keynote speaker.   /2

A lot of years passed since 1832, and during that time it would have been most unusual for any national political party to ask that a Barbara Jordan deliver a keynote address . . . but tonight here I am. And I feel that not withstanding the past that my presence here is one additional bit of evidence that the American Dream need not forever be deferred.   /3

Now that I have this grand distinction what in the world am I supposed to say?   /4

I could easily spend this time praising the accomplishments of this party and attacking the Republicans but I don't choose to do that.   /5

I could list the many problems which Americans have. I could list the problems which cause people to feel cynical, angry, frustrated: problems which include lack of integrity in government; the feeling that the individual no longer counts; the reality of material and spiritual poverty; the feeling that the grand American experiment is failing or has failed. I could recite these problems and then I could sit down and offer no solutions. But I don't choose to do that either.   /6

The citizens of America expect more. They deserve and they want more than a recital of problems.   /7

We are a people in a quandary about the present. We are a people in search of our future. We are a people in search of a national community.   /8

We are a people trying not only to solve the problems of the present: unemployment, inflation . . . but we are attempting on a larger scale to fulfill the promise of America. We are attempting to fulfill our national purpose; to create and sustain a society in which all of us are equal.   /9

Throughout our history, when people have looked for new ways to solve their problems and to uphold the principles of this nation, many times they have turned to political parties. They have often turned to the Democratic Party.   /10

Body

What is it, what is it about the Democratic Party that makes it the instrument that people use when they search for ways to shape their future? Well I believe the answer to that question lies in our concept of governing. Our concept of governing is derived from our view of people. It is a concept deeply rooted in a set of beliefs firmly etched in the national conscience, of all of us.   /11

Now what are these beliefs?   /12

First, we believe in equality for all and privileges for none. This is a belief that each American regardless of background has equal standing in the public forum, all of us. Because we believe this idea so firmly, we are an inclusive rather than an exclusive party. Let everybody come.   /13

I think it no accident that most of those emigrating to America in the 19th century identified with the Democratic Party. We are a heterogeneous party made up of Americans of diverse backgrounds.   /14

We believe that the people are the source of all governmental power; that the authority of the people is to be extended, not restricted. This can be accomplished only by providing each citizen with every opportunity to participate in the management of the government. They must have that.   /15

We believe that the government which represents the authority of all the people, not just one interest group, but all the people, has an obligation to actively underscore, actively seek to remove those obstacles which would block individual achievement . . . obstacles emanating from race, sex, economic condition. The government must seek to remove them.   /16

We are a party of innovation. We do not reject our traditions, but we are willing to adapt to changing circumstances, when change we must. We are willing to suffer the discomfort of change in order to achieve a better future.   /17

We have a positive vision of the future founded on the belief that the gap between the promise and reality of America can one day be finally closed. We believe that.   /18

(internal summary)

This, my friends, is the bedrock of our concept of governing. This is a part of the reason why Americans have turned to the Democratic Party. These are the foundations upon which a national community can be built.   /19

Let's all understand that these guiding principles cannot be discarded for short-term political gains. They represent what this country is all about. They are indigenous to the American idea. And these are principles which are not negotiable.   /20

Transition into the second point of the speech

In other times, I could stand here and give this kind of exposition on the beliefs of the Democratic Party and that would be enough. But today that is not enough. People want more. That is not sufficient reason for the majority of the people of this country to vote Democratic. We have made mistakes. In our haste to do all things for all people, we did not foresee the full consequences of our actions. And when the people raised their voices, we didn't hear. But our deafness was only a temporary condition, and not an irreversible condition.   /21

Even as I stand here and admit that we have made mistakes I still believe that as the people of America sit in judgment on each party, they will recognize that our mistakes were mistakes of the heart. They'll recognize that.   /22

Projection of future actions which must be taken to keep the ideals alive

And now we must look to the future. Let us heed the voice of the people and recognize their common sense. If we do not, we not only blaspheme our political heritage, we ignore the common ties that bind all Americans.   /23

Many fear the future. Many are distrustful of their leaders, and believe that their voices are never heard. Many seek only to satisfy their private work wants. To satisfy private interests.   /24

But this is the great danger America faces. That we will cease to be one nation and become instead a collection of interest groups: city against suburb, region against region, individual against individual. Each seeking to satisfy private wants.   /25

If that happens, who then will speak for America?   /26

Who then will speak for the common good?   /27

This is the question which must be answered in 1976.   /28

Are we to be one people bound together by common spirit sharing in a common endeavor or will we become a divided nation?   /29

Warning that actions cannot be avoided

For all of its uncertainty, we cannot flee the future. We must not become the new puritans and reject our society. We must address and master the future together. It can be done if we restore the belief that we share a sense of national community, that we share a common national endeavor. It can be done.   /30

There is no executive order; there is no law that can require the American people to form a national Community. This we must do as individuals and if we do it as individuals, there is no President of the United States who can veto that decision.   /31

Listing of action steps (legitimation)

As a first step, we must restore our belief in ourselves. We are a generous people so why can't we be generous with each other? We need to take to heart the words spoken by Thomas Jefferson: /32

Let us restore to social intercourse that harmony and that affection without which liberty and even life are but dreary things.   /33

A nation is formed by the willingness of each of us to share in the responsibility for upholding the common good.   /34

A government is invigorated when each of us is willing to participate in shaping the future of this nation.   /35

In this election year we must define the common good and begin again to shape a common future. Let each person do his or her part. If one citizen is unwilling to participate, all of us are going to suffer. For the American idea, though it is shared by all of us, is realized in each one of us.   /36

And now, what are those of us who are elected public officials supposed to do? We call ourselves public servants but I'll tell you this: we as public servants must set an example for the rest of the nation. It is hypocritical for the public official to admonish and exhort the people to uphold the common good if we are derelict in

(parallel sentences)

upholding the common good. More is required of public officials than slogans and handshakes and press releases. More is required. We must hold ourselves strictly accountable. We must provide the people with a vision of the future.   /37

(parallel sentences)

If we promise as public officials, we must deliver. If we as public officials propose, we must produce. If we say to the American people it is time for you to be sacrificial; sacrifice. If the public official says that we (public officials) must be the first to give. We must be. And again, if we make mistakes, we must be willing to admit them. We have to do that. What we have to do is strike a balance between the idea that government should do everything and the idea, the belief, that government ought to do nothing. Strike a balance.   /38

Let there be no illusions about the difficulty of forming this kind of a national community. It's tough, difficult, not easy. But a spirit of harmony will survive in America only if each of us remembers that we share a common destiny. If each of us remembers when self-interest and bitterness seem to prevail, that we share a common destiny.   /39

(Commitments)

I have confidence that we can form this kind of national community.   /40

I have confidence that the Democratic Party can lead the way. I have that confidence. We cannot improve on the system of government handed down to us by the founders of the Republic, there is no way to improve upon that. But what we can do is to find new ways to implement that system and realize our destiny.   /41

Conclusion

Return to the personalized themes of the introduction

Now, I began this speech by commenting to you on the uniqueness of a Barbara Jordan making the keynote address. Well I am going to close my speech by quoting a Republican President and I ask you that as you listen to these words of Abraham Lincoln, relate them to the concept of a national community in which every last one of us participates: As I would not be a slave, so I would not be a master. This expresses my idea of Democracy. Whatever differs from this, to the extent of the difference is no Democracy.   /42

NOTES

1   On both reward and fear appeals, as well as expert research summaries on each topic, see Erwin P. Bettinghaus, *Persuasive Communication*, 3rd ed. (New York: Holt, Rinehart and Winston, 1980), pp. 145–149, as well as his bibliography; and William J. McGuire, "Personality and Susceptibility to Social Influence," in *Handbook of Personality Theory and Research*, ed. Edgar F. Borgatta and William W. Lambert (Chicago: Rand McNally, 1968), pp. 1130–1187. On the ethics of using reward and fear appeals, see Kenneth E. Andersen, *Persuasion: Theory and Practice*, 2nd ed. (Boston: Allyn and Bacon, Inc., 1978), esp. pp. 155–156, 370–372, and 375–377.

2   The bases for inoculation theory are discussed in William J. McGuire, "Inducing Resistance to Persuasion: Some Contemporary Approaches," in *Advances in Experimental Social Psychology*, ed. Leonard Berkowitz (New York: Academic Press, 1964), pp. 191–229. The view of inoculation taken here is supported by research findings in Demetrios Papageorgis and William J. McGuire, "The Generality of Immunity to Persuasion Produced by Pre-Exposure to Weakened Counterarguments," *Journal of Abnormal and Social Psychology*, 62 (1961), 475–481. Inoculation theory in general is reviewed succinctly in Mary John Smith, *Persuasion and Human Action; A Review and Critique of Social Influence Theories* (Belmont, Ca.: Wadsworth Publishing Company, 1982), pp. 286–296.

3   See the research summarized by Bettinghaus and McGuire in n. 1 above.

4   On the power of "story-telling" and visualization in persuasion, see Donovan J. Ochs and Ronald J. Burritt, "Perceptual Theory: Narrative Suasion of Lysias," in *Explorations in Rhetorical Criticism*, ed. G. P. Mohrmann et al. (University Park: Pennsylvania State University Press, 1973), pp. 51–74; W. Lance Bennett, "Storytelling in Criminal Trials: A Model of Social Judgment," *Quarterly Journal of Speech*, 64 (February 1978), 1–22; and W. Lance Bennett, "Rhetorical Transformation of Evidence in Criminal Trials: Creating Grounds for Legal Judgment," *Quarterly Journal of Speech*, 65 (October 1979), 311–323. See also any number of books on advertising techniques, in your library.

5   "Democratic Convention Keynote Address" by Barbara Jordan, from *Vital Speeches of the Day*, August 15, 1976. Reprinted by permission of Vital Speeches of the Day.

ASSIGNMENTS

Pre-Performance
1. Choose at least a dozen full-page magazine advertisements, and analyze the reinforcing motive appeals they use. What are the most commonly used appeals?
2. Have a salesperson present a "pitch" in class or to a small group of class members designated to report on the saleperson's efforts. In particular, note the way in which motive needs are created and satisfied. If possible, question the salesperson to determine how the contents and organization of the sales pitch were selected.

Performance
1. Write two versions of a brief speech to reinforce. In the first one, use a strong appeal to fear; in the second, a mild fear appeal. Present both versions to an in-class committee of six to eight classmates.
2. Prepare a five-minute sales talk in which you attempt to persuade members of the class to buy a product from you. You might attempt to sell tickets to a specific function, to sell a car, to sell books, and so on.

Post-Performance
1. The audiences for the speeches given in Performance 1 should evaluate which of the two speeches given by each person was the more persuasive and why.

CHAPTER 8

Changing Attitudes

For centuries, the core of communication studies (termed "rhetoric" in earlier epochs) has been *persuasion*—the art of changing people's beliefs, attitudes, values, and behaviors. For most of those centuries, persuasion was considered primarily an art or talent, one a person was born with, even though it could be shaped by master rhetorician-teachers and honed through regular practice. Over the last half century, however, persuasion has increasingly been considered a science rather than an art. As scientist after scientist puts people under statistical microscopes, they create more and more generalizations about human behavior—and ways to influence behavior through communication. These generalizations grace the pages of professional journals and even popularized how-to-win-friends-and-influence-people types of books.

Along with audience psychology, professional persuasion has become big business. Universities and colleges spew forth hordes of trained "practical" researchers who fill jobs with TV networks, religious establishments, public relations departments in corporations, government bureaus, and public utilities. The impact of professional persuaders on our lives caused the then-young social critic Marshall McLuhan to react with horror in his exploration of advertising, *The Mechanical Bride* (1951):

> *Ours is the first age in which many thousands of the best-trained individual minds have made it a full-time business to get inside the collective public mind. To get inside in order to manipulate, exploit, control is the object now. . . . Today the tyrant rules not by club or fist,*

but, disguised as a market researcher, he shepherds his flocks in the ways of utility and comfort.[1]

It is good to keep this vision of mass persuasion—and the havoc it potentially can wreak upon our society—clearly in mind as you proceed through the next two chapters. Ours is a persuading and a persuaded society on a scale never quite seen before on earth. Word-merchants and image-merchants ply their trades for the highest bidder. Communication consulting firms are ready to prepare ads, to offer two-day workshops on instant communicative success, to do an "image analysis" for a fee. There are big bucks in persuasion. All of this means that some important ethical questions are involved, questions we will explore later.

With that brief orientation to our new ground, let us venture into the second major type of persuasive speaking—that of attitude change.

THE OCCASION AND THE AUDIENCE: WHAT, WHO, WHEN, WHY

A speech to *change attitudes* is one in which a person attempts to reorient an audience's conceptions and preferences. In attitude change, you seek to get an audience to look at some idea, person, event, or object either positively or negatively. You have been subjected to attitudinal messages for years, ever since your mother tried to convince you to like spinach or your father gave you lectures on why going to bed early was good for your body. Attitudinal messages express "likes" and "dislikes," "beautifuls" and "uglies," "justs" and "unjusts."

You become an attitude changer any time you either feel some special attachments to the attitudes of others or are seized by a sense of social responsibility. So, for example, parents work hard to make sure their children have "proper" attitudes toward others, themselves, foods, the worlds of school and work, and traditions. The same is true in other contexts, where we all—even teachers—feel a responsibility for the attitudes of friends, organizations, or other elements of society. People will work long hours to convince friends that an attitude of political or religious cynicism is improper and self-defeating. They will attempt to turn around the thinking of members of their book clubs on the issue of "dirty words" in contemporary novels. They'll fight with a friend over the relative value of a particular school major, the merits of musical styles, the strengths and weaknesses of a TV show. In these contexts, you're attempting attitude change because you are committed enough to certain preferences to want to make them public. We all, then, are attitude changers on innumerable occasions in our lives.

Fundamentally, then, communicative attitude change is attempted for two reasons. First, you can feel uncomfortable with particular attitudes held by family, friends, and groups, and hence wish to change them. If you can accomplish that task, you probably will feel a sense of satisfaction at having carried out a social mission. At the same time, of course, you in a sense will validate your own attitudes. If you can get others to prefer things, people, and actions you yourself prefer, then you are strengthened in your own beliefs and feel approved by others around you. Never underestimate the power of approval or validation as a private goal for attitude changers.[2]

The second reason attitude change is often sought is that it can be the first step in reaching other goals. Attitude change is a form of "incipient behavior." If you can get someone today to abstractly change his or her attitudes toward a course of action, tomorrow you may actually get the person to take that action. If you can convince your book club members that the presence of "dirty words" in a novel is no reason to reject such books, tomorrow you may get them to make a peppery book a group project. Overall, then, attitude change is attempted both to reorient thinking and to prepare for future appeals to action.

ATTITUDE CHANGE MECHANISMS

Before we can delve into this subject further, we must stop to consider some psychological theory we've been hinting at throughout this book. Then we can examine specific communicative techniques which are generated by that theory.

The BAV System

We have talked throughout this book about "beliefs," "attitudes," "values," and "behaviors," simply because these concepts are your primary targets as a public speaker. You have been encouraged to recognize beliefs, attitudes, and values in your audience, to adapt messages to them, to build new ones and change old ones. We need now to go farther, to discuss at least one way of visualizing the relationships among beliefs, attitudes, and values.

We can consider beliefs, attitudes, and values as interrelated elements in what we will call a *BAV system*. Think of beliefs, attitudes, and values as existing in concentric circles (illustrated in Figure 8.1). In the center are *beliefs*—your concepts or images of persons, places, ideas, or objects. A belief is the perceptual image you have of your neighbor, the President, New Orleans, the sun rising every morning, stones, playpens, and so on. So you believe your neighbor works for ABC Insurance Company, has two kids, is a member of Kiwanis, and in general is a kind, hard-working, conscientious husband, parent, employee, and friend. Or you believe New Orleans is a well-run, clean city, with unbelievably varied entertainment, efficient harbor facilities, and nearby southern plantations. A belief, then, is the picture you hold of a person, place, or object; the picture is composed of the facts *you* put into it, and it is judged accurate by standards of truthfulness *you* bring to bear. In the next circle are the *attitudes* you attach to those persons, places, beliefs, and objects. You may *like* your neighbor, *distrust* the President, think of New Orleans as *beautiful*, be *happy* that a rising sun will germinate your carrot seeds and tan your body, find stones *useful*, and *detest* playpens as miniprisons for babies. In the outer circles are *values*, your basic orientations toward life—your habitual ways of responding to your world.

FIGURE 8.1   The BAV System

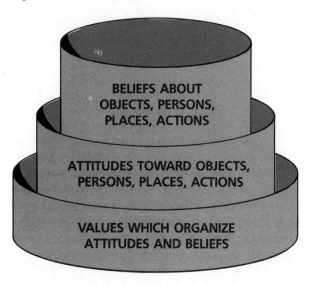

Another way to think of values is to see them as important congregations or collections of beliefs and attitudes. Eduard Spranger, a German scholar, argues that we even can "type" people by which of their "value congregations" are dominating in various arenas of thought and action.[3] Some people are "economic" types, in that they usually think in terms of usefulness or practicality; others are "political," valuing competition, power, and influence; still others are "theoretical," in that they are intellectual, concerned with abstract truth and logical rigor. With some fiddling, we can adapt Spranger's ideas and display a series of value congregations which tend to govern individuals' attitudes and beliefs. (These are illustrated in Figure 8.2.[4])

While you never respond to literally everything in your life from the vantage of a single value, you probably do have some *valuative habits*. If you detest cruelty to people, you'll likely despise cruelty to animals as well, because you look at both from a sociological (humanitarian) value. If you think that making prudent political choices concerning whom to side with in disagreements is the only way to advance in your company, you're likely to look at social and even husband-wife relationships in the same way because you hold a strong political value. If you're a lover of good music and art, you're likely to view questions of environmental protection in the same way—from an aesthetic vantage.

Valuative habits, in other words, represent relatively broad psychological orientations (sometimes called *ideologies*) which members of groups apply to basic aspects of life. They are *response tendencies*, concepts which

---

FIGURE 8.2 **Value Congregations**

1. **Pragmatic values**—values held on the assumption that the end justifies the means, that efficiency in solving problems is more important than abstract considerations.
2. **Political values**—values which seek to establish hierarchies and power relationships among people and institutions.
3. **Psychological individualistic values**—personalized values which stress the care of the individual's own mind and body, aiming at personal satisfaction with who that person is and what that person does.
4. **Sociological values**—values which stress the virtues of human relationships in and of themselves, "other-directedness," humanitarian concerns no matter what the individual or group sacrifice.
5. **Philosophical-theological values**—values which stress commitment to abstract systems of thought and ethics, and commitment to the notion that ideologies, dogmas, and religious doctrines ought to govern behavior.
6. **Aesthetic values**—values which emphasize the importance of form, ritual, and inner appreciation of beauty.

---

people bring to mind when confronted with particular people, objects, and events. And, they can be applied by individuals in extremely wide ways. For example, in 1975 J. W. Prescott investigated a general value he called "bodily pleasure and violence." Under this valuative orientation, he found that people hold "together" in their minds a series of attitudes:

With regard to pain:

1. Harsh physical punishment is good for children who disobey a lot.
2. Capital punishment should be permitted by society.

With regard to sex:

1. Prostitution should be punished by society.
2. Nudity within the family has a harmful influence upon children.
3. Sexual pleasures help build a weak moral character.
4. Abortion is a punishable offense against individuals and society.

With regard to drugs:

1. Alcohol is more satisfying than sex.
2. Drugs are more satisfying than sex.

With regard to politics:

1. Conservatism is better than liberalism.[5]

Note two features of this list: (1) Many different aspects of life—sexual mores, child-raising, crime, consumption patterns, and politics—are being *organized* or "held together" by a dominating value. (2) And, these attitudes become *interlocked*; they have a common "anchor," and hence it is difficult to change any one of them without finding a way to dislodge it from the nest of other beliefs and attitudes. If people have strong valuative orientations, it becomes most difficult to change their attitudes.

Approaches to Attitude Change Within the BAV Model

Yet, attitude change, as we noted, can and does occur with relatively great frequency. The question for you, the student of public speaking who wishes to improve attitude-change skills, is this: how can we use this view of the BAV System to build more workable persuasive speeches?

Return to Figure 8.1 for a second. Note that beliefs, attitudes, and values are arranged in concentric circles. Those circles provide the clue to strategic approaches one can use when seeking to change attitudes. Fundamentally, a speaker can attempt to change attitudes in three ways: (1) You can attack *attitudes directly*, trying to substitute one set of attitudes for another. (2) You can attempt to change attitudes by getting people to *alter their beliefs* about what's "true" and "false" in this world. Or (3), you can urge your listeners to "attach" particular attitudes to *different valuative orientations*. Before we discuss the materials for attitude change, let us briefly examine each of these strategies.

Directly Attacking Attitudes Hammering away on people's attitudes, trying to get them to say "good" when they've been saying "bad," is a time-honored approach to attitude change. We normally use one of two concepts when describing this approach: When *we* do it to people, it's called *education*. When *they*—an evil or malicious "they"—do it to people, it's called *brainwashing* or *propaganda*. Education or brainwashing is largely a matter of repetition, sloganeering, and isolating listeners from other sources of information and influence. Your parents told you over and over that "spinach is good for you," that you should "try it—you'll like it," that "children should be seen and not heard." Seldom did they give you a lot of understandable explanations or clear reasons why you should hold such attitudes; rather, they relied upon their own credibility, their experiences, their ability to cut you off from others who might try to instill different attitudes. (They went so far, in some areas of living, to tell you to "stay away from so-and-so—he [she] is a bad influence.") Not only parents but also teachers in school systems have the same sort of persuasive power over you, at times.[6]

Changing Attitudes by Changing Beliefs Second, you can attempt to change attitudes (in circle 2) by attempting to alter beliefs (in circle 1), because in many instances a change in beliefs will produce a change in attitudes. Suppose, when you think of Yugoslavia, you have a vision of poor, dirty shepherds, crumbling villages, despair and misery, a ruthless Communist dictatorship. If that's your image of (your beliefs about) Yugoslavia, you're likely to have negative attitudes toward it. Now suppose one night you see a travelog about the country. In the film you see sunlit knolls, happy shepherds, Slavs and Croats in clean little villages, dressed up in native costumes at a fair or festival. As the camera moves into Belgrade, you're exposed to modern skyscrapers, industrial expanse, crowds lining the streets for a holiday parade. That travelog will put immediate pressure on your negative attitudes, perhaps forcing you to change your attitudes from positive to negative. Why? Because now you think about Yugoslavia with different facts, with new information—in other words, with reformed beliefs. Your attitudes are likely to follow your new beliefs. Technically, this process is called *psychological differentiation*. You have differentiated—separated and re-evaluated—Yugoslavia from all the other southern European Communist countries, changing your informational base and hence altering your attitudes.[7]

Changing Attitudes by Changing Valuative Orientation As we move from circle 3 (values) to circle 2 (attitudes), we come upon a third approach or strategy for attitude change. You can attempt to get listeners to apply different values to some attitude-object. Think back to our discussion of values in Chapter 2, when we discussed values people attach to the concept of abortion. In the innumerable times you have heard abortion discussed, you've probably heard statements such as these:

> *"Sure, to you abortion is a matter of church doctrine* [religious value]. *Well, to me it's a matter of individual free choice and psychological health* [psychological value]."

or

> *"I don't care how many people in public opinion polls say abortion should be allowed* [political value]—*I just don't think any person is allowed to take another person's, even an unborn human being's, life* [individualistic value]."

or

> *"Medically, it's now possible to grow a human being from a three-day-old fertilized egg* [scientific value], *so how can you stand by that ol' Supreme Court stuff about allowing abortion in the first trimester* [legal-political value]?"

In each of these cases, you see one person trying to get another person to shift valuative orientations, to "look at" some problem in a different way or light. Psychologically, these strategies are called *transference*; attempts are being made to get listeners to "transfer" their attitudes/objects-of-attitudes from one value congregation to another.

With this much as introduction, we now can get more specific about materials one can use in building attitude-change speeches, and then about kinds of organizational patterns which are available to persuaders.

RAW MATERIALS FOR ATTITUDE-CHANGE SPEECHES

Here, as in all other speaking, your basic supporting materials are examples, statistical descriptions, parallel cases, and so on. However, we need to explore in somewhat more depth some techniques for developing these materials in attitude-change speeches.

Selective Description

Selective description is essentially a matter of accentuating the positive. In the travelog example, selective description was at work. The maker of the travelog included in the film only positive images of Yugoslavia; the filmmakers skipped over the pockets of poverty, the food lines, the jails, rain-soaked or starving shepherds. Only information capable of being viewed positively was presented. It's really the same technique your mother used on you when she tried to convince you you'd like to go to camp: "Camp? Ah, you'll love it! Swimming every day, horseback riding, new friends, a candy store, campfires, treasure hunts! I'm sure it will be the most exciting thing you've ever done!" Your wise old mother very carefully avoided bringing up the mosquitoes, K.P. duty, homesickness, poison ivy, and mean older kids. Her description accentuated the positive.

Narrative

You can do more than select the facts; you often can turn facts into a convincing story. Anyone who's watched TV is familiar with this technique. The defense attorney takes the floor, and in a deliberate voice begins, "Let me tell you what really happened on the night in question. My client Ed had just returned home from work, tired, and ready to patch up the argument he'd had with his wife that morning, when the neighbors heard all the shouting. He wanted to make things right with her, so she wouldn't leave him. Well, he walked in to find her on the floor, stunned or dead. He screamed in horror, as other witnesses have testified. Then, he picked her up to take her down to the car, to get her to a hospital. And that's when his neighbor Bob saw him. Thinking Ed had killed his wife and was about to get rid of the body, Bob. . . ." And on the narrative goes, giving us an explanation of the events. Notice two features of that story which all good narratives should contain.

Plausibility As a narrative unfolds, listeners should be able to see how the pieces fit together, and should say to themselves, "Yes, that's what I would have done in those circumstances—that's reasonable."

Motivation Buried in a good, persuasive narrative are the actors' motives. In the defense attorney's story, you've been told that Ed was contrite and ready to seek reconciliation, and that he was carrying his wife's body only because he wanted to get her medical attention. Not only have his actions been made to seem plausible, but his motives are pictured as pure and upright. A good narrative, then, draws us into a story and gives us a particular way of viewing a series of events. And if it's plausible and well motivated, it might even change some attitudes.

Appeals to Uniqueness

There are circumstances when it is difficult to get an audience to buy the notion that a whole class of objects, persons, or whatever—all churches, colleges, politicians, vacuum cleaners, shampoos—ought to be viewed in a different way. In those situations, you can appeal to uniqueness. You can attempt to demonstrate that a particular object, person, or institution contrasts with others like it. You've heard these appeals many times: "*Our* oil company cares." "This is a school with a heart." "The shampoo with an added plus." "This is not just another good cause, but. . . ." "Unlike my opponent, I. . . ." With such phrases, speakers ask you to differentiate between their particular qualities and those you see as characteristic of the whole class.

Appeals to Consistency

We all are susceptible to this appeal, for there's great pressure on human beings to be rational and consistent.[8] Naked inconsistency is almost a sin in this mass-produced, highly organized society. The appeal to consistency can be made in myriad ways, but three consistency appeals are most common. *Temporal appeals* ask someone to maintain now the attitudes they expressed at some other time: "Last year you voted for a liberal candidate for school board, and I hope you will maintain that posture this year." *Objective appeals* tell people to prefer an object or thing because they liked another one similar to it; as the movie ad said in 1978, "If you liked *Jaws*, you'll love *Jaws 2!*" *Authoritative appeals* suggest people ought to like or dislike something because a group or other authority figure does: "As a member of the American Legion, you ought to favor. . . ." "Jackie Jock likes Throwup Pizza and we think you will, too." All of these are asking auditors to make their attitudes consistent—either with their own other attitudes or with the attitudes of other people. The secret, of course, is to convince an audience that those particular attitudes ought to be consistent: that my voting last year and this year should follow the same preferences; that I ought to like one movie because I liked another; that the American Legion or Jackie Jock's opinions are relevant to this issue.

Valuative Shifts

When the insurance sales representative says, "I'm not just thinking of the money involved in this policy, but of you and your family's need for protection," he is seeking a valuative shift. He wants you to look at buying insurance not from a pragmatic vantage, but from a humanitarian one. So, too, as long as this country viewed the Vietnamese war as a struggle between democrats and communists (political value) and our role in the situation as one dictated by the SEATO agreements (ethical value), a majority of citizens supported the war efforts. But when the protesters and others got the society to view the war as a civil war (a different political orientation) that was costing us dearly in terms of money and lives (pragmatic and humanitarian values) to the point that we were aggressors rather than defenders (negative ethical value), we found a way to get out in a hurry. In both of these examples, a valuative shift has occurred. The trick here is to make the preferred value seem legitimate and appropriate. That sometimes is hard to do—ask the insurance agent.

Transcendence A most sophisticated persuasive technique involves *transcendence*—the attempt to make an audience see some object or action from a "higher" value. Anyone who lived through the Watergate era certainly has seen transcendence used, and by both sides. President Richard Nixon attempted transcendence when in 1973 he urged citizens to view his actions as dictated by a need to defend "executive privilege" (which was why he wouldn't release White House records) and "the integrity of the presidency" (which was why he wouldn't answer every little question asked of him). On the other side, the attackers constantly told us that more was at stake than the outcome of the 1972 election or the jobs of a few political flunkies; in grandiloquent words they implored us to see as their "mission" the destruction of "political corruption" and the return of America to a course of "public morality." With that appeal, they won. This appeal was even extended by Jimmy Carter in 1976, as he campaigned, not on this or that specific issue, but on the questions of "trust," "morality," and "love." Lest you think that these attempts to appeal to higher values are limited to politicians, look for them in your own life: "Now, Johnny, I'm only doing this for your own good." "Sure, a new jail will cost this county a few tax dollars, but just think of the ways we've been treating petty offenders in the old facilities." "Enough viewing of prime-time trash. Change channels and watch something aesthetically and intellectually challenging." Because we like to think of ourselves as high-minded and intellectually broad, such appeals to transcendence seldom fall on deaf ears.

Repetition (Slogans, Refrains) At the 1972 Republican National Convention, after then-candidate Richard M. Nixon had delivered his acceptance address to the delegates, a chant of "Four more years! Four more years!" was started rhythmically in the upper balconies of the hall. It continued for a full ten minutes, until the hall fairly shook from the thousands of people chanting with near-hypnotic effect. In a sense, of course, naked repetition is not really "supporting material" in any rational sense of that phrase; but, slogans such as "Four more years!" or jingles such as "At McDonalds, we do it all—for you!" or refrains such as Martin Luther King, Jr.'s "I have a dream" (which was repeated eight times in his 1964 speech to the March on Washington audience) are potent persuasive materials. Slogans, jingles, and refrains "condense" ideas, feelings, attitudes, and values into short, often rhythmic bursts of language which "stand for" entire philosophies, platforms, and ideologies. Repeated phrases beat on an audience, catching them up in the emotion of the occasion and subject-matter; they also are easily remembered by listeners long after the event, and serve as a trigger for someone trying to recall the message. As a speaker, then, while you must be careful not to sound too much like an oily salesperson, you may well find a slogan or refrain which works to your advantage in your persuasive speeches.

Bandwagon Appeals

"Everybody's doin' it, doin' it, doin' it; everybody's doin' it—the Black Bot-tom." Ask your grandparents to sing and dance the Black Bottom for you. (Or, try your parents out on the Twist, Frug, Chicken, Swim, or Mashed Potato. . . .) Fads and crazes run through this country annually; they take the form of appliances (the Fry-Baby), music (bubble-gum rock), clothing (Fry boots), diets (Dr. Stillman's watery weight loss plan), political strategies (walking through one's constituency in search of votes), religions (the Moonies), foods (granola and quiches). As we noted in the last chapter, this is a country of joiners, and hence a bandwagon appeal— asking people to jump on the bandwagon with their friends and neighbors in support of some idea, cause, or way of life—finds fertile ground in America. We all—almost—want to be part of the "in" activity or topic of conversation. Thus, many people change their beliefs, attitudes, and even values in the face of bandwagon appeals, always in search of fun or deeper fulfillment. Do you want your audience to attend next week's symphony concert? Tell them the hall is almost full, there are few tickets left, but they still can get in if they hurry. Or, do you want them to get involved in a charitable fund-raising effort? Mention the campus groups already organizing, and discuss the group activities which will follow the event. Bandwagon appeals should be a part of your persuasive repertoire.

Identification Strategies

We already have discussed authorities; authorities are useful to speakers because listeners often follow the advice and opinions of people they respect. Indeed, all of us listen attentively to people we like and admire—especially if they are "like us." "Identification" is a word used by many advertisers and by social commentator Kenneth Burke to describe person-to-person perceptions of mutual interests, characteristics, and motives. "I was a farm boy myself" is by now almost a cliche for every politician seeking votes in America's agricultural heartland; "I worked on the assembly line myself" springs from the mouth of the senatorial candidate shaking hands at the factory gate; "Yes, I fought in the Big War, so I know what you guys went through and I understand the importance of national defense" can be heard by the candidate patrolling American Legion clubs. Similarly, how many advertisements have you heard or read which begin, "If you're like me, then . . ."—"If you're like me, then you probably face the common problem of occasional irregularity." In each of these cases, the speaker is seeking "common ground," areas of mutual identification between people. Identification strategies can seek many different sources of common ground, including:

- *Common Background:* Appeals to similar youthful experiences, geographical regions ("We're all New Yorkers"), ethnic roots, temporal roots ("Those of us who grew up during the '60s know . . .").
- *Similar Motives:* Appeals to values and motivational springs one person shares with another ("If you believe, as I do, that common courtesy is the cement of human relations," or "As patriotic, red-blooded Americans, we all know that . . .").
- *Physical Characteristics:* Appeals to physiological similarities ("Anyone who's had to battle acne knows . . ." or "You and I both have fought the Battle of the Bulge and therefore know the importance of exercise").
- *Occupational Identification:* Appeals to the values common to (presumably) everyone in a particular occupation ("As teachers, we believe," "As accountants we all know the importance of . . .," or "We're all students in here, and hence have a stake in the issue of tuition increase").
- *Communities of Taste:* Appeals to common interests ("music-lovers," "pizza freaks," "sports car drivers," "M*A*S*H fans," "beer drinkers," "surfers," "those of us who care about our hair").
- *Age and Gender Groups:* Appeals to points of chronological or sexual commonality ("Women know . . .," "As a young person trying to enter the job market, you understand, as I do, that . . .," "Like you, I'm a person over 65, and often wonder why the world treats all of us like fragile crystal, to be carefully put up on the shelf and then ignored").[9]

These, then, are nine sorts of substantive strategies available to persuaders. One final note: It may be helpful to think of these strategies as more or less organized by type of persuasive speech. Look at Figure 8.3 for one possible breakdown.

So, these raw materials are more or less grouped—but do keep in mind that "more or less." One certainly can use appeals to uniqueness, or appeals to consistency, or identification strategies, for example, in *any* persuasive speech. The important point is not to put all of these strategies into tactical boxes, but to understand their psychological force or rationale, and then use any of them when it seems prudent to do so.

ORGANIZING ATTITUDE-CHANGE SPEECHES

Let us move to the question of structuring attitude-change speeches. Yes, we certainly can use many of the patterns we discussed earlier. The *comparison-contrast* pattern is often used by speakers who wish to compare old beliefs with new ones, or the consequences of holding one set of attitudes rather than another. Likewise, many speakers ask audiences to change their attitudes by arguing that the old attitudes cause *problems* which can be *solved* by assuming new attitudes; a speech asking people to re-evaluate their attitudes toward the elderly and their needs could be

---

FIGURE 8.3   **The Raw Materials of Attitude Change**

Primary Persuasive Tactic	Important Appeals
Change Attitudes by Changing Underlying Beliefs (Differentiation)	**1. Selective Description** (constructing verbally a favorable or unfavorable view of the world of beliefs) **2. Narrative** (Constructing a "story" which is plausible to listeners and which contains motivational statements) **3. Appeals to Uniqueness** (distinguishing between your particular object or person and all others seemingly like it)
Change Attitudes by Changing Overarching Valuative Orientation (Transference)	**1. Appeals to Consistency** (asking audiences to apply similar values to similar objects) **2. Valuative Shifts** (encouraging audiences to look at and evaluate something from a different point of view) **3. Transcendence** (telling audiences to think about the "higher" issues involved in some judgment)
Change Attitudes by Directly Attacking the Old Ones (Education or Brainwashing)	**1. Repetition** (building slogans, jingles, and refrains which state the preferred attitudes and "drive out" the old ones) **2. Bandwagon Appeals** (asking people to abandon the old attitudes and to seek the new ones because many other people are doing that) **3. Identification Strategies** (telling people to accept the new attitudes because others "like them" hold those attitudes)

organized in that way. *Chronological* patterns are especially useful when you want to tell audience members how it was that we came to acquire the old (and faulty) attitudes; *spatial* sequences make sense when you wish to point out how widespread a faulty attitude is, or to indicate where it is especially prevalent. So, you might organize a speech on Anti-Semitism in this country either by tracing its roots, or by pointing to particular communities across the country where it has re-emerged recently.

In the speech which follows, you will find a broad-based *problem-solution* format. The speaker assumes that economic and valuative problems are creating negative attitudes toward a proposed bond issue. Those attitudinal problems become the focus of most of the speech; and, then, the proposed solution is depicted as a new set of attitudes toward schools. Note, as well, that the speaker has tried to attack the old attitudes by assaulting both underlying beliefs and overarching values; in other words, two major approaches to attitude change are offered. Finally, you will see most of the substantive strategies we've discussed in this chapter being employed.

SAMPLE SPEECH: CHANGING ATTITUDES

Pre-Speech Analysis

Subject: A $4.75 million school bond issue in Lampasas, Texas*

Audience: The county chamber of commerce, a voluntary association of business firms and individuals interested in the future of the community and the county

Situation: A school bond election, to be held in two weeks, has sparked considerable discussion among the 6,000-plus voters in this school district. Bond supporters have been asked to make a brief presentation at the chamber of commerce meeting.

Purpose: To change attitudes from neutral to positive

Speaker: The speaker is an interested parent, a member of the Committee for the Bond Issue, and a member of the chamber of commerce.

Strategies: 1. The local newspaper and radio station have provided information about school board decisions relating to site, design, and unworkability of alternatives, so the speaker can concentrate on simply selling the idea.

2. Because opponents of the bond issue, calling themselves the Concerned Taxpayers, have stressed the economic aspect, the speaker will (a) attempt to recast the economic issues factually (differentiation), and (b) shift the valuative outlook of the audience from economic to humanitarian values (transference).

3. The speaker therefore will (a) soften the audience in the introduction, (b) attack the opposing financial analysis, (c) stress the importance of a responsible decision, and (d) work on attitudes toward school bond issues from both the factual and valuative sides.

* The "hard" information comprising this speech is based on an actual school bond controversy over a new high school in Lampasas, Texas.

Speech

An Investment in Education
John Wisniewski

Introduction

Reference to occasion
and to previous
efforts and shared
goals

In the past decade we've worked hard in the chamber of commerce—and I've been on these committees with many of you—to attract industry to our community, and although we've succeeded beyond our expectations, the industrial growth has brought some problems.   /1

First mention of
relevant facts

Personal
identification with
audience

In particular, I'm thinking about the overburdening of our school system. This district, contrary to the trend in most areas of the country, is experiencing a sustained growth. The total population of the area served has approximately doubled since the last real expansion of the physical plant—and you business people know what that can mean.   /2

Touch of humor, with
a mention of "duty"

While the chamber can't take credit for raising the local birthrate—at least I don't remember a committee to promote parenthood!—we certainly must take part in planning ways to expand our schools to meet present and future needs.   /3

Forecast

In the next few minutes, I want to discuss two areas: the economic considerations and the positive aspects of the new high school facilities.   /4

Body

Starting discussion
with the foremost
issue

Because we're all "concerned Taxpayers," I'll begin by discussing everyone's favorite topic, money. Now, obviously, we've got to do something immediately about overcrowding. If you've been to the current school during the day, you've seen classrooms with 30 to 35 students jammed in, a lunchroom up for grabs at noon hour, a library where half the kids have to stand because there aren't enough chairs, and a gymnasium which threatens to collapse every basketball game. As a school board survey shows, the over-crowding will only get worse with each entering class.   /5

Selective description
to identify problems
Generalization

"New" economic
facts, tied to the
audience's
experience
Parallel case (with
a hint of bandwagon
appeal)

But of more importance to some of us whose businesses are fighting inflation, the price tag goes up each year we delay in building. With building costs spiraling almost one percent a month, we must build now. We can certainly benefit from the lessons Houston school planners are learning about battling inflation by starting construction projects ahead of schedule.   /6

Internal summary and
visual aid showing
projected tax
increase

Granted then that we must act now, let's look at the money involved. As the table I have here indicates, the bond issue will increase taxes by relatively small amounts.

TABLE 1. PROJECTED TAX INCREASES

Now	After Passage	Increase
$10	$22.08	$12.08
$25	$55.28	$30.28
$50	$110.41	$60.41
$100	$220.00	$120.00

Displays graph to differentiate Lampasas from similar communities— appeal to uniqueness

When we compare these tax increases to those school taxes paid by comparably sized school districts, we find that our debt will still be relatively small.   /7

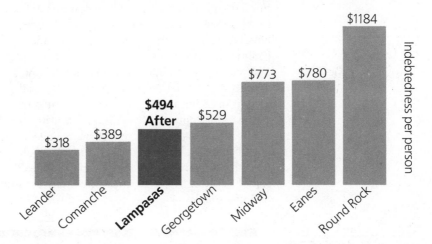

Valuative shift from economic to humanitarian vantage

Narrative, personalizing by reference to listeners' own children

My second consideration is this: If we consider education as an investment in the future rather than as a current cost, then we must be concerned about providing a facility which can adequately serve the needs of our high schoolers.   /8

As you think about a new school, visualize if you can what your children will be exposed to. They'll start their classes each morning with 25 rather than 35 kids in each room. When they go to the library, they'll be in a room which can accommodate 35 more students than the old one could, making it easier for them to acquire the knowledge to survive in this world. When they eat, the new cafeteria will house an additional 100 kids per shift. In the afternoon, as they head into the science class, they'll find ultramodern labs with work space for more than 60 students. Just before they come home, they'll have worked in a gym which can seat all of the students and will have space for both boys' and girls' athletic competition.   /9

Internal summary

I could continue, but you probably have the picture. If not, just ask your own children to paint it in more detail for you.   /10

Conclusion

Personal appeal to urgency

In conclusion, I ask that each of you consider the negative impact on the school district and its economic base if we cannot get the school problem solved quickly.   /11

Appeal to sympathy and shame

Appeal to community pride and concern

Then think about the school taxes and the relatively small impact this bond issue will have on them. Of course, the increase will not be pleasant for you as business people and homeowners. But then, you all know we can't expect something for nothing. A minimal investment in education now, however, will pay off in handsome benefits in the future: expansion will be able to continue, and you'll be proud to have been a part of an uplifting social mission.   /12

Notice the careful structuring of attitudinal appeals through this speech. The speaker has begun with himself and his credibility, progressed through the two most relevant considerations (money and community benefit), and finished with direct challenges to the audience. Because emotions always run high when public money is to be spent on school facilities, emotion-charged tactics have been attempted—selective description and narration (both pictorializing the object of concern), hard-hitting appeals to personal motives (urgency, sympathy, shame), and finally the appeals to community pride. "Community pride" may not be an especially strong motive appeal by itself, but, following as it does the more emotional material, it makes for a fitting climax. The core of the message, therefore, is embedded in description and narration; once those "stories" are told, then the "lessons"—the actual motive appeals—are drawn from it. This sort of structure is not an uncommon one for attitude changers working in narrative modes.

TIPS FOR ATTITUDE CHANGE

It is impossible to summarize briefly every possible piece of useful advice for becoming a more sophisticated and successful attitude changer. So, instead, let us more simply set out our major considerations which social scientists have demonstrated to be controlling elements in persuasive messages. Massive research programs have turned most of these considerations into "iron laws," generalizations demonstrated over and over in the laboratory and in practice.

■ *The law of degrees.* Never try to change attitudes too radically in a single speech. Move your audience by degrees—a little at a time. If an audience is strongly hostile to some notion, it would be foolish to attempt to make them strongly favorable; what's more likely to happen if you push them too far is that your message will *boomerang*, making them even more intransigent. If they're really nasty about the whole thing, simply try to neutralize that feeling today, and hope then that tomorrow you'll be able to carry them along a little farther toward a positive attitude.[10]

■ *The law of saliency.* Much of what we've said about differentiation and transference can be talked about in another way—in terms of *salience*. Making an idea salient means calling to mind some belief, attitude, value, or behavior which the audience already holds, but hasn't really thought about as relevant to a claim. So, if you can make something which I already favor salient, and then attach it to something I've been disfavoring, I may change my mind. In the speech you just read, the attempt was made to make salient the chamber of commerce's interest in new industry—to make that idea relevant to the school bond issue. In our examples of authoritative appeals, you saw a speaker making the attitudes of a *reference group* (the American Legion) relevant to your opinions on some issue. (A *reference group* is a group that is seen as having some power over the thoughts of individuals.) There was also an attempt to make an opinion of an *authority figure* (good ol' Jackie Jock) salient to what kind of pizza you should eat. The law of saliency says that people, objects, or actions we already value can affect us if they can be made relevant to what we are discussing now.[11]

■ *The laws of credibility.* One of the most highly researched areas in communication studies is that of *credibility*—the degree to which an audience finds you a trustworthy, competent, attractive, dynamic human being. If you can find ways of increasing an audience's perception of your trustworthiness and competence, you are much more likely to affect their attitudes. Among the many, many conclusions scientists have settled upon regarding credibility are these:

- Reference to yourself (see the introduction in our sample outline) tends to increase your perceived competence and trustworthiness, while reference to others (authorities) increases your perceived trustworthiness and dynamism.
- If you can demonstrate that you and your audience share common beliefs, attitudes, and values, your credibility will increase.
- Using highly credible authorities increases your perceived fairness.
- Your credibility increases as your speech's organization improves.
- The greater your sincerity, the greater the attitude change.
- The more dogmatic and authoritarian you are, the less likely it is that attitude change will occur.

The laws of credibility are strong ones. You are encouraged to read more on them.[12]

As we conclude this chapter on changing people's attitudes, keep in mind two considerations mentioned at the beginning of this chapter: (1) Just as you can use the tactics and strategies mentioned here on audiences, so also can others use them on you. You therefore should be concerned about attitudinal appeals as both a generator *and* a consumer of persuasive messages. Learn to identify them easily, habitually, for your own self-protection. (2) And, some of these appeals perhaps are ethically suspect. Bandwagon appeals, for example, have been used to lead entire countries to war; selective description, in so far as it ignores some facts, can turn into a lie; identification strategies can be used to introduce considerations (one's ethnic background, gender, personal tastes, etc.) which may well be irrelevant to the question under discussion. We will discuss the ethics of persuasion at the end of Chapter 9.

NOTES [1] Marshall McLuhan, *The Mechanical Bride.* Reprinted by permission of the publisher, Vantage Press, Inc. Copyright © 1951 by Herbert Marshall McLuhan. Copyright © renewed 1979 by Herbert Marshall McLuhan.
[2] For a look at the research on self-approval or self-validation, see Mary John Smith, *Persuasion and Human Action* (Belmont, Ca.: Wadsworth Publishing Company, 1982), Chap. 7, "Group Interaction and Self-Persuasion."

[3]   Eduard Spranger, *Types of Men*, 5th ed. (Berlin: Max Niemeyer Verlag). Reprinted by permission of Max Niemeyer Verlag.

[4]   For an enlarged discussion of interrelated attitudes in people, see Philip G. Zimbardo, Ebbe B. Ebbesen, and Christina Maslach, *Influencing Attitudes and Changing Behaviors*, 2nd ed. (Reading, Ma.: Addison-Wesley Publishing Company, 1977), esp. pp. 50–53.

[5]   From "Body Pleasure and the Origins of Violence" by J. W. Prescott, *The Futurist*, April, 1975, (9:64–74. Copyright © 1975 by The World Future Society. Reprinted by permission. As summarized in and modified by Zimbardo, Ebbesen, and Maslach, pp. 51–52.

[6]   Much of what we are saying here can be fit into the so-called *learning theory* of persuasion, as it is discussed in Herbert W. Simons, *Persuasion: Understanding, Practice, and Analysis* (Reading, Ma.: Addison-Wesley Publishing Company, 1976), pp. 112–113. Cf. Kenneth E. Andersen, *Persuasion: Theory and Practice*, 2nd ed. (Boston: Allyn and Bacon, Inc., 1978), Chap. 16, "Totalitarian Persuasion."

[7]   On differentiation understood as "a change in the object of judgment, rather than in the judgment of the object," see Solomon Asch, "The Doctrine of Suggestion, Prestige, and Imitation in Social Psychology," *Psychological Review*, 55 (1948), 250–276.

[8]   An excellent introduction to the concept of cognitive consistency can be found in Erwin P. Bettinghaus, *Persuasive Communication*, 3rd ed. (New York: Holt, Rinehart and Winston, 1980), pp. 37–49. Or, if you want to learn the theory in detail, see R. P. Abelson et al., eds., *Theories of Cognitive Consistency: A Sourcebook* (Chicago: Rand McNally, 1968).

[9]   The notion of identification is developed most fully in Kenneth Burke, *A Rhetoric of Motives* (1950; rpt. Berkeley: Univ. of California Press, 1969), pp. 19–23, 55–59. We have drawn these strategies in part from Burke's writing; for another useful list of identification strategies, see Akira Sanbonmatsu, "Darrow and Rorke's Use of Burkeian Identification Strategies in *New York vs. Gitlow* (1920)," *Speech* [Communication] *Monographs*, 38 (March 1971), 36–48.

[10]   For a summary of some of the research on "the law of degrees," see John Waite Bowers, "Language and Argument," in *Perspectives on Argumentation*, ed. Gerald R. Miller and Thomas R. Nilsen (Glenview, Il.: Scott, Foresman and Company, 1966), esp. pp. 168–72.

[11]   On the "law of saliency," see Gary Cronkhite, *Public Speaking and Critical Listening* (Menlo Park, Ca.: The Benjamin/Cummings Publishing Company, Inc., 1978), esp. pp. 73–79.

[12]   The "laws of credibility" are most fully summarized in Stephen W. Littlejohn, "A Bibliography of Studies Related to Variables of Source Credibility," *Bibliographic Annual in Speech Communication: 1971*, ed. Ned A. Shearer (Falls Church, Va.: Speech Communication Association, 1972), pp. 1–40.

ASSIGNMENTS

Pre-Performance   1. Consider your attitudes toward the following subjects:

affirmative action   Ford Pinto   political speeches
Russians   marijuana   the CIA

In particular, list the basic attitudes which you attach to the words; attempt to ascertain the value congregations that contribute to those attitudes; and indicate your level of ego-involvement with these attitudes. Would you consider altering any of these attitudes? Why or why not? What would it take to change your way of thinking?

2. Read two or three speeches by Native Americans and comment in your journal about the cultural values expressed or implied in them.

3. Read the speech Senator Edward Kennedy made in defense of his actions in the Chappiquiddick incident. Pay special attention to Kennedy's attempt to restore his credibility. You also may want to read David Ling's "A Pentadic Analysis of Senator Edward Kennedy's Address to the People of Massachusetts, July 25, 1969," *Central States Speech Journal*, 21 (Summer 1970), 81–86. Prepare to analyze in a class discussion Kennedy's use of credibility.

Performance

1. Prepare a two- or three-minute persuasive speech consisting of a single narrative. Design your story to carry the entire weight of changing the audience's attitudes toward the topic you have chosen.

2. Select a topic for an attitude-change speech. Choose two different audiences. Using the same topic, design a two- or three-minute speech for each audience—adapting the speech to meet the needs of each audience. Present the speeches to a committee of six to eight of your classmates. Be prepared to explain the choices you made in adapting the speech to each audience.

Post-Performance

1. After a committee of classmates listens to the presentations in Performance 2, that group will discuss how well each of the speeches matched the needs of the designated audiences.

2. Choose one recent classroom presentation which really held your attention. In your journal, analyze what the speaker did to arouse and maintain attention. Include specific examples to support your conclusions.

CHAPTER 9

Moving to Action

Every TV program, radio broadcast, mass mailing, and newspaper overwhelms us with persuasive messages which demand a portion of our time, our mental energy, and our dollars. So many clever ads and appeals have been made that many people are simply tuning out, refusing to read or listen anymore. The world seems filled with too many pressure problems, bargains, and worthy causes for us to function socially and politically. We tend to become numbed, immobilized. Many of us may be at the point of hollering "That's enough! I quit! Get off my back!"

As we start thinking about moving the uncommitted or apathetic members of our audiences to action, therefore, we confront what has to be considered the articulate person's greatest challenge. Talk is cheap, and almost always has been; and, hard-core commitments from people are very dear. We're simply called upon to be committed to too many different products, organizations, and reforms in this decade. But, before we all sink into a state of despair and paralysis, we must remember some very important facts. New products do come upon the market, and some survive. While many worthy causes slide into oblivion, some do grow to maturity and influence in our society. New politital faces come upon the scene and have impact locally, regionally, and nationally. Yes, the skillful, determined persuader *can* make it. Our job in this chapter is to give you some advice on how to persuade people to act.

THE OCCASION AND THE AUDIENCE: WHAT, WHO, WHEN, WHY

Moving to action is a phrase that applies to two kinds of communicative situations. One situation is characterized by apathetic "believers"; we treated that context in Chapter 7, when we discussed reinforcement speaking.

The second kind of situation in which calls for action occur is characterized, not by apathetic "old" believers, but by doubting, uninformed, or uninvolved audiences. You certainly are familiar with this sort of situation in the new products market. Literally every day soap companies, toy manufacturers, and auto companies attempt to change your buying habits, to get you to try something new. Every year or two another person seeks to put his or her political star in the sky by launching a reformist political campaign. The federal government sponsors public service television, radio, and newspaper ads in an attempt to get citizens to stop wasting energy, to attend public hearings, to order pamphlets on shopping/canning/smoking/ad infinitum. And almost weekly, letters creep into your mailbox from new organizations to promote legal justice, environmental protection, informed voters, congressional efficiency, back-to-basics eduction, and pants for dogs and cats. In such cases, "new" believers and workers are being sought. On these occasions *actuation* is taking place. People are seeking to activate uninformed or even hostile audiences to some social, political, or economic goal.

The *why* of moving to action is perhaps obvious. Moving to action is the final step in launching a campaign for change. For social, economic, political, or personal change to occur, someone must spread the word—must convince others to divert their energies from lawn-mowing and bridge to causes and products. The goal might be as short-ranged as making a profit during the next quarter of the fiscal year, or as long-ranged as social-political revolution. Any society that wishes to avoid stagnation must have enough actuators to keep it progressing. There must be actuators in positions from Washington, D.C., down to local chapters and clubs, who are willing to pound away at their fellow Americans.

Few of us will ever be national chairperson of this or president of the board of directors of that; but we all will be called upon on countless occasions to organize parents, go door-to-door in our neighborhoods, speak up at public hearings, or campaign for a friend. We all need to know about the communicative processes of actuation. Let us examine some of the techniques useful in this enterprise.

RAW MATERIALS FOR ACTUATIVE SPEECHES

Because the audience of an actuative speech may be uninformed or even potentially hostile, the steps involved in constructing one are a bit more complicated than those which make up a reinforcement speech. An actuative speech has three major tasks: creating motive needs, satisfying motive needs, and specifying actions. To fulfill those tasks, the actuator usually takes an audience through six or seven steps. A few words about each of these steps is in order.

FIGURE 9.1   **The Communicative Tasks of Actuators**

Creating Motive Needs
1. *Arousing* appropriate beliefs, attitudes, values
2. Using *motive appeals* to deepen those BAVs

Satisfying Motive Needs
3. Channeling BAVs into specific *plans*
4. Intensifying commitments via appeals to *urgency*
5. Occasionally, answering possible *opposition*

Specifying Actions
6. Pointing out the *first steps*
7. Highlighting the *long-range plans or actions*

Arousal Strategies   Your first job as an actuator is to bring your audience to life, to spark their curiosity or their enthusiasm. The techniques appropriate to this communicative challenge are those we reviewed in Chapter 8, for this job is one of creating beliefs and changing attitudes. Thus it is that a new political challenger inevitably begins by reciting a series of reasons he or she is running—the local government is stagnating, is unresponsive to the people, is pursuing disastrous policies, is overspending (or underspending), is unrepresentative of the wishes of the taxpayers. The politician hopes that those reasons will trigger relevant beliefs, attitudes, and values, and arouse the public to take him or her seriously. Also look carefully over the advertisements for emergent worthy causes in magazines and newspapers. First there is a startling statement: "Would you spend $25.00 a month to see that this child is fed and educated?" There then follows a recitation of facts concerning conditions in that country, with some judgments about those conditions: "a tragedy," "misery," "a blight on the scene of human rights." These are attempts to arouse beliefs, attitudes, and values that are relevant to the issue.

Motive Appeals   A second communicative task ties the aroused beliefs, attitudes, and values to specific motives for acting in order to deepen the audience's reaction: "If we do not throw the rascals out now, the city will be plunged into chaos and bankruptcy [fear motive]." "The smile on this boy's face when he receives a pencil and pad of paper will be worth the few martinis you'll have to forego to help him [shame and self-satisfaction motives]." "Join together with thousands of others like yourself, and . . . [belongingness and companionship motives]." "Big oil can be beaten if we . . . [power motives]." Such appeals reach out to an audience, promising a better tomorrow and fitting the auditor's own motives into the picture.

While it is impossible to list all of the possible motive appeals you might find useful, consider carefully some of the following:[1]

- *Appeal to Achievement*. "The successful businessman knows . . ." "To make maximum use of your talents, act today to . . ." Such appeals depend upon people's interest in making a mark, developing themselves.
- *Appeal to Adventure*. "Taste the High Country!" cries the beer commercial. "Join the Army and see the world" says the local recruiter excitedly. The human soul yearns for release, the human body seeks risk as a way of validating human worth. The call to adventure and excitement is universally appealing.
- *Appeal to Affiliation and Belongingness*. Yet, paradoxically perhaps, we all need others—their presence, their touch, their recognition of who we are. Few can make it in this world alone. Thus, "We care about you . . . ," "Join our group and find fellowship with kindred souls," and "You are one of a few people in this country we're extending this invitation to" are appeals which draw us into groups and causes.
- *Appeal to Conformity*. Similarly, while there are times we wish to strike out on our own (see Appeal to Individuality below), there are other times when we simply want to be recognized as "one of the crowd." Our sense of belongingness can be so overpowering as to make us want to conform—to do what "the others" do. Commercials stressing what "the in-group does," what the "successful businessman wears," what "all true Americans believe" contain potent appeals to conformity. See as well the discussion of "bandwagon appeals" in Chapter 7.
- *Appeal to Fear*. We said enough about fear appeals in Chapter 7 (see "Threats") to have already made the point: Human beings have a broad range of visible and invisible fears—fears of failure, of death, of inadequacy, of harm, of triumph by the other. Fear is a powerful motive, one productive of both good (as when an individual is driven to achievement and bravery) and evil (as when fear-based prejudice produces bestial behavior toward others).
- *Appeal to Generosity*. Generosity is a curious motive. Basically, one assumes, the human being is a selfish individual, and rightly so, for we all want to survive. Yet, when we think of ourselves not as individuals but as group members, then we submerge our selfishness or self-centeredness and bring to the surface our other "face"—our generosity. All appeals to giving, to support of others, to self-sacrifice in the name of group or cultural goals are predicated on the assumption that your *social self* will overcome your *private self* when the occasion demands it. Acting generously makes us feel good personally and wins us public admiration. Thus, the speaker can use this appeal in almost any speech.
- *Appeal to Individuality*. "Be your own person . . . don't follow the crowd." The appeal to "know yourself," "be yourself," and "act on your own" draws its force—like the appeal to adventure—from our struggles to

at least occasionally stand out from the group. In an age of mass media, corporations, and mass society, the appeal hits home.

• *Appeal to Loyalty and Pride.* Not only do we need to belong, however, but we also want (as we shall see in Preview Four) periodically to celebrate our membership in groups and societies. In times of crisis, a speaker can, therefore, call for "tests of loyalty," for extraordinary actions which demonstrate the individual adheres to group standards for belief and action. Similarly, "pride"—in both the group and in oneself—can drive us to collective or individual achievement. Pride in the group tightens one's loyalties; pride in oneself is a prod to personal effort.

• *Appeal to Power and Dominance.* Animals regularly fight for territory, for leadership, for their mates. Human beings, with their animalistic origins, likewise have an aggressive side to them. Sometimes it emerges in acts of physical dominance. Often, though, because we are "civilized," power is found in symbolic forms—in the laws which demand conformity-of-action; in religious dogmas which give authority to preachers, priests, and rabbis; and in our everyday linguistic interaction with others, when we beat them into submission verbally. The metaphors of warfare (as when President Carter called his energy policy "the moral equivalent of war"), the language of competition ("Cancer can be beaten in your lifetime"), and the urge to dominate ("If you want to rise to the top, then . . .") all gain effect because of our primal needs.

• *Appeal to Reverence.* Yet, again paradoxically, we all also recognize our inferiority. We see ourselves inferior to others of superior qualities, to institutions we admire, to nature and the cosmos, and to deities which humble us in their magnitude and eternity. Thus, reverence can take three forms: *hero worship, reverence for institutions,* and *divine worship,* conceived of both religiously and philosophically (as when eighteenth-century philosophers worshipped Nature). Like an appeal to generosity, the appeal to reverence calls for *public* acts, and hence appears in many actuative speeches.

• *Appeal to Reward.* This appeal we already have discussed in Chapter 7; suffice it to say here that after a decade of "me-ism" in this country—as seen in the growth of assertiveness training workshops, transcendental meditation, est, and all of the other "what's-in-it-for-me" movements—appeals to personal reward hit you frequently. Rewards can be materialistic, social, spiritual, or personal. Whatever form they take, they undoubtedly move many listeners to action.

• *Appeal to Shame.* Because you and I often are aware of our own selfishness, and because our parents and even our friends knew they could get us to act if they played upon our guilts, the appeal to shame can be forceful. Watch some TV commercials for laundry products, many of which try to shame you into using them. (Why else should you worry about "ring around the collar"? Why else must you have "whiter whites and bluer blues"?) The appeal to shame, though, works for almost all public causes as well, for we *do* feel guilty about the starving kids in China, our own overconsumption of energy, our unwillingness to give one hours' worth of salary per month to United Way.

• *Appeal to Sympathy.* Shame's companion is sympathy. Shame comes from our recognition of personal fault, and, to overcome that feeling, we reach out sympathetically to others. The appeal to sympathy depends for its success primarily on speakers' abilities at verbal depiction. In attempting to get people to believe that "There, but for the grace of God, go I," and thus to act out of sympathetic understanding, speakers must be able to produce a strong sense of identification (as we discussed it in Chapter 8). That sense of identification is produced primarily by "word pictures," by vivid description and narrative.

• *Appeal to Tradition.* Most of us know that while we live in the here-and-now, generations of others have gone before us. We were born into a society, we didn't create it; we were taught from our most youthful days the traditions of family, of groups, of society-at-large. "Tradition" demands that we act in certain ways in certain situations; and, hence, because we have learned from the beginning that tradition is what makes us human, what makes us Americans or Presbyterians or Hispanics or a railroad family or Gronbecks, we are susceptible to traditional appeals. Appeals to tradition take the "long view," depending upon our willingness to accept the past as guidelines for present and future action.

In many ways, these fourteen and many other motive appeals form the primary materials for actuative speeches.

Plans   In the third place, one must tell audience members what sorts of mechanisms are available for channeling their beliefs, attitudes, values, and motivations into workable plans of action. So you will hear or read such statements as these: "The Bleeker for Councilman Committee is a group of concerned citizens committed to returning local government to the hands of the people." "Save the Children, Inc., is a nonprofit, nationwide organization of professionals and volunteers who are moving into third-world countries for the purpose of. . . ." These communicators, once beliefs and attitudes have been changed, are pointing out what to do about it. Most of us feel alone, small, in the face of great local, national, or international problems, and need the assurance that an organization—one of the keys to contemporary society—is available for solving those problems. "We are not alone," say the articulate persons who call for action.

Urgency   We are also prone to psychological and behavioral inertia. We tend to say, "yeah, yeah!" only to go right back to what we were doing before we heard the speaker or read the ad. An important next step for actuators, then, is to instill a sense of urgency in their audiences: "I'm glad you agree with the goals of my campaign; but remember one thing—it takes people and money to change city government, and that's especially important right now. While many, many volunteers have given freely of their time and riches, we're at a crisis point, and. . . ." "The recent flood and earthquake in Poorland has left thousands homeless and orphaned, without food, clothing, and the other necessities of life. Every day we delay in moving into that country will result in another 900 dead and another 2500 slowly starving to death. You must act now." As an actuator, then, you normally must point out some crisis or potentially pressing problem in need of immediate attention, to produce a sense of urgency about the action you are seeking.

Opposition   Especially if your auditors are hostile or doubtful, you next must deal with other plans or opponents to your operation. Because a new product, politician, or cause is often confronting old products, political machines, and organizations, the actuator may want to tackle the opposition. So, you are told, "My opponent has claimed . . . , but *I* say. . . ." Likewise the conservationist organizations inevitably point out that Big Oil/Big Timber/ Big Coal/Big Government are arrayed against them; that these big interests are seeking to lull the public into thinking that the energy crisis/ environmental crisis/foreign oil crisis is melting away; but that these crises are still ahead of us. Just as one's commitments to beliefs, attitudes, and values have to be deepened by motive appeals, so, too, do people's commitment to a particular course of action—actions which often have to be taken in the face of an "enemy."

First Steps   To start the actuation on the road, listeners must take the first steps. Most sophisticated actuators begin small, seeking a minimal behavioral commitment. Listeners may be asked only to send in a card for more information, to sample a trial size of a product, to read one issue of a magazine absolutely free, to accept a free gift which will be delivered by a sales representative who will "tell you more but without obligation." The first steps are the foot-in-the-door, as well as the bait.[2] If an audience can be convinced to do something or try something which will demand little of their time and money, they may get hooked.

Long-Range Plans   Some actuative speeches conclude with first steps, but others go farther, into a heroic vision of what society will be like if commitments are extended into long-range actions. The rising politician might say: "I ask you only to attend a meeting tonight to learn more about me and this campaign. If you like what you see and enjoy the people you'll be working with, we'll welcome you aboard our team, and let you participate in this citizens' movement. As you lick envelopes, make a few phone calls, leaflet your neighborhood, hold coffees, and contribute in any other way you can, you'll be part of the greatest people campaign this city has ever seen." Notice how motive appeals to belongingness, adventure, and achievement are worked into this picture of longer-range actions and their effects. You are asked to visualize yourself functioning as part of an energetic, worthwhile cause—to add meaning, direction, and purpose to your life. It's awfully hard for audiences to ignore these appeals.

In the process of carrying forward these seven steps, the actuator meets the three goals of an actuation speech: constructing motive needs; pointing to ways of satisfying those needs; and specifying precise actions to be taken. And with luck, an uninvolved, uninformed, or even hostile audience can be turned around.[3]

ORGANIZING ACTUATIVE SPEECHES

Most actuative speeches are organized in any one of several variations on a *problem-solution* pattern. Certainly, a simple problem-solution pattern can be used, where one argues that *x* is a problem and *y* is a solution to it. Usually, though, somewhat more complicated *special* patterns are employed. Most actuators tend to work in multi-stepped patterns which are based on listeners' needs and motivations, and on ways of presenting plans-of-action which meet those needs and depend for success on their motivations. Let us briefly examine a few of the typical patterns.

Dewey's Reflective Thinking Pattern

American philosopher John Dewey, near the turn of the twentieth century, devised a five-step "psycho-logic" which offered a systematic procedure for problem-solving. The procedure assumes that people can rationally identify some problem needing solution, and then "scientifically" search for solutions. A speech built on Dewey's model of reflective thinking would look like this:

I. *Defining the Problem*: What is it that is bothering us? How may it be defined informally or formally?
II. *Analyzing the Problem*: What is the scope, and what are the causes and effects of the problem?
III. *Suggesting Solutions*: What are all (some) of the possible solutions to the problem?
IV. *Evaluating Suggested Solutions*: What are the strengths and weaknesses of each solution? Will they solve the problem without creating other problems?
V. *Selecting and Acting Upon the Solution*: Which, then, is the "best" solution, and how should we go about putting it into effect?[4]

The Product-Sales Pattern

If Dewey's reflective thinking sequence is highly rationalistic in its assumptions, the classic product-sales pattern relies in contrast upon straight-forward, non-rational appeals. Rather than depending upon a rational "logic," the sales model depends upon the creation and satisfaction of subjectively felt needs. While there are many variations on this model, one a speaker could use might run this way:

I. *Opening*: gain the attention of listeners, piquing their interest and curiosity and gaining a hearing for the sales person (e.g. "merely asking for information," as do the telephoners who "simply want to know something about your family" or who offer you wonderful prizes if you can "name one of the Great Lakes")

II. *Needs Assessment:* often through a process of question-and-answer (in cases where feedback can be direct) or through a process of prior audience analysis, attempt to "convince" people that they have a "need" for the product or course-of-action (e.g. as when advertisers attempt to convince you that you stink badly enough to require a deodorant or are so busy that frozen gourmet meals are a necessity for enjoyable family life)

III. *Needs Gratification:* normally through bald assertion, "show" that a product or a cause will fulfill or gratify those needs (e.g. as when you're told that striped toothpaste will both meet your health needs and your social obligations, or when the ad asserts that spending $20 a month on a homeless waif in South America will let you "save a child")

IV. *The Close:* make the person so anxious to gratify the need that he or she will sign on the dotted line or take whatever other action is proposed (e.g. as when you are asked to write today, or to send only a couple of dollars for an "introductory offer")

In other words, the product-sales model—though it needs a little alteration when using it for a speech—is based on the assumption that you have enough guilt or greed in your head to drive you to act on impulse. The needs often are not felt before you're hit with the message; the message attempts to create the need. And, the solution—the action—may or may not "solve" anything big; what's important in this approach is that the auditors "think" needs are being met.

Monroe's Motivated Sequence

In 1935, communications expert Alan Monroe, who'd obviously studied both Dewey's rational decision-making model and sales approaches, came up with a model with rationalistic and motivational dimensions. Monroe's Motivated Sequence assumes that people prefer, psychologically, a systematic analysis of problems and solutions (as did Dewey) *and* that they feel needs which must be satisfied (as does the sales model). The result is a five-step speech organizational pattern:

1. *Attention:* The creation of interest and desire
2. *Need:* The development of the problem, through an analysis of things wrong in the situation and through a relating of those wrongs to individuals' interests, wants, or desires
3. *Satisfaction:* The proposal of a plan of action which will alleviate the problem and satisfy the individuals' interests, wants, or desires
4. *Visualization:* The verbal depiction of the situation as it will look if the plan is put into operation
5. *Action:* The final call for personal commitments and deeds[5]

FIGURE 9.2   **The Need-Action Model for Actuative Speeches**

Creating Motive Needs

I. **Arousing:** Activate listeners' latent beliefs, attitudes, and values on some issue. This step brings an audience into the subject matter.

II. **Motivating:** Use motive appeals to make listeners want to act on their beliefs, attitudes, and/or values. This step makes an audience sympathetic to your point of view.

Satisfying Motive Needs

III. **Channeling:** Demonstrate that some plan of action will satisfy the listeners' aroused desires. This step shows them how to act upon their BAVs and sympathies.

IV. **Intensifying:** Deepen listeners' feelings of commitment so that they want to act immediately. This step insures that audiences move beyond mere mental acceptance of the plan.

Specifying Actions

V. **Pointing:** Indicate the first steps which must be taken. This step focuses audience BAV's and sympathies into concrete steps.

VI. **Highlighting:** Visualize long-range plans or effects of actions. As a conclusion, this step promises a better tomorrow and secures enduring commitment to the cause or project. (In cases when there is direct opposition to your viewpoint and plan, you may need to add another step here—**Answering questions and objections.**)

The genius of this organizational pattern is twofold: (1) It attempts to follow a more or less "natural" psychological sequence, one wherein people become aware of a need, *then* explore its dimensions, *then* seek satisfaction, *then* try to picture how it will work, and only *then* act. The sequence, therefore, is eminently "reasonable" even while being based on psychological rather than logical principles. (2) And, it can be employed in almost any speaking situation, through simple expansion or contraction of its steps. So, if people don't really know about a problem, the Attention step can be enlarged; or, if they don't really understand how the problem affects them personally, the Need step can be dilated; or, if they know the problem all right but have heard far too many bogus solutions (e.g. as in the so-called "farm problem"), then the Satisfaction step can receive emphasis; and so on. To show you the model at work, the sample speech at the end of this chapter is divided into the steps of the Motivated Sequence.

The Need-Action Model

The final organizational pattern we will examine is the one implicitly suggested earlier in this chapter. This model depends particularly on all of the kinds of "raw materials" we have discussed both in this chapter and in previous chapters. Like the Motivated Sequence, this pattern assumes that audience needs must be aroused and satisfied. But, it also (1) recognizes that listeners must be made to feel, not only the adequacy of some solution, but also a sense of urgent commitment, and (2) asks listeners to take both short-range and long-range looks at action steps. The model is displayed in Figure 9.2.

To see this model fully fleshed out, we will use it to organize the following sample speech outline.

SAMPLE SPEECH: ACTUATING

Pre-Speech Analysis

Subject:	Licensing cats
Audience:	Junior Women's Club or a similar group who are likely to be parents of small children
Situation:	A child, recently bitten by a stray cat, is now undergoing the mandatory series of rabies shots. As a result of this incident and the attendant publicity, some concerned citizens have formed a neighborhood committee (the Cat Committee) to push for a local licensing ordinance.
Purpose:	To encourage overt support for the committee and to organize a pressure group
Speaker:	The speaker is one of the organizers of the Cat Committee, a mother, and a cat owner.
Strategies:	1. The speaker doesn't dwell on the recent episode; the facts doubtless have been discussed widely enough.
	2. The speaker asks the person introducing her to briefly explain about the Cat Committee so the speaker can concentrate upon the need and the plan.

Outline	**Bless the Beasts and the Children**

Introduction

Arousal (by referring to the recent episode)

(Creates fear, sympathy)

I. Johnny Dunlap only wanted to hug the nice kitty.
  A. He picked up the stray cat just the way many young kids probably would.
  B. Right after the incident, when I asked my seven-year-old daughter if she'd pick up a cat she didn't know, she responded: "Aw, Mom, cats are nice; they don't bark like dogs do."

(Arousing a sense of shame in the listeners)

II. Johnny's case isn't the first in our community.
  A. Four years ago, another child was bitten by a cat and forced to undergo the same painful series of rabies shots Johnny did.
  B. Why didn't our community act then, in 1978, to protect both the beasts and the children?

Transition and forecast, moving into the body of the speech

III. If we want to bless both the beasts and the children, to save them both from painful or even fatal consequences, we must solve this community problem.
  A. First, I'll discuss the problem.
  B. Then, I'll consider some relatively simple actions this community can take to solve it.

Body

Motive Appeals
(Appeal to fear)

(Appeal to fear and sympathy for children—a fitting move for this audience especially)

I. The problem with stray cats is, as I see it, twofold.
  A. First, we must find ways to protect our unwary kids from unvaccinated animals.
    1. Many kids are going to pet stray animals no matter what we as parents tell them, so why not require tags on vaccinated cats so that the kids can distinguish more easily between the safe and the unsafe cats?
    2. Even a young child is likely to remember whether the cat had a collar and tinkling tags.
    3. And, if the cat can't be found, knowledge about the tags will help a doctor to decide on whether to administer the series of rabies shots.

(Expressing concern for animals, too—almost as lovable as children)

(Appeals to sympathy, fear, and rewards)

  B. Our concern also must extend to our pets.
    1. Prevention is the best medicine, so let's protect our cats from rabies by requiring annual shots.
    2. Tags also can help animal shelter officials and private citizens who might find a cat to return it to its anxious owner.
    3. In addition, if a tagged cat were injured and people could not reach the owner, they could call the veterinarian named on the tag.

Channeling BAVs into *plans* (indicating scope of proposed action)

II. Our community, therefore, needs a licensing law to protect the health and safety of both pets and children.
  A. Most cities our size have a licensing regulation that applies equally to cats and dogs.
    1. The fees could be the same as they now are for dogs: three dollars a year for all neutered males and spayed females, and ten dollars annually for pets of either sex which have not been altered.
    2. Cats, as well as dogs, would be required to wear the license tag when away from the owner's property.

(Practicality of the plan is demonstrated)

    B. Cat licensing could become just as convenient as dog licensing.
       1. To save postage, next year's license renewal form will be enclosed with water bills.
       2. The owner will need to have a vet sign the rabies line, and enclose a check when mailing back.

(Advantages)
(Appeal to reward)

III. A licensing law which includes cats has two additional benefits.
    A. It could contribute to the financial support of the animal shelter so that cat nuisance problems could be handled.

(Appeal to reward)

    B. A cat licensing law would make the animal shelter self-supporting, so that your tax dollars could go for other services and so that those who are using the shelter are the ones paying for it.

Intensifying audience reactions via appeals to *urgency*

IV. No one reacted to the cat crisis four years ago.
    A. Another child, and his parents, have been made to suffer unnecessarily.

(Additional evidence)

    B. And, I'm willing to bet that Johnny Dunlap won't be the only child in the headlines: when the Cat Committee paid a surprise visit to the animal shelter yesterday, we found three more cats being held for rabies observation.
    C. But, if we act now in support of a cat licensing regulation, maybe we can spare other Johnny Dunlaps the risks and pains of rabies shots.

Conclusion

Pointing to first steps ("Easy" first step)

I. I would ask that you do three things:
    A. First, take a copy of the leaflet I'm going to pass around and read it; if you need more information, call me or any of the others whose numbers are listed on the sheet.

("Easy" second step)

    B. Second, please sign this petition that requests the city council begin immediate consideration of a cat licensing ordinance.

Highlighting later, more demanding actions

    C. And third, when the matter comes before the council for final action, we need your presence.
       1. Through a "telephone tree," which we will construct from information on the petitions, we will relay information about that council meeting to you.
       2. And, we will ask you to come to the meeting to support the measure.

(Final vision of "victory" for the cause)

II. With these actions, those of you who are cat owners like me will demonstrate your sense of responsibility. And those of you who are parents will have protected your kids from one more unnecessary hazard.

(Summary of the campaign's slogan)

III. Let's "bless the beasts and the children" today!

This speaker essentially has gone through the six steps to be found in many actuation speeches. (The seventh step—overcoming opposition—has been omitted because opponents probably will not surface until a later date, perhaps at the city council meeting. The speaker did not want to create a sense of deep anger or panic if it was unnecessary.) Given the situation, the speaker wisely concentrated most of her message on the plan, demonstrating that it was feasible, practical, and workable. Such a strategy is especially important if you and your group are going to have to move an additional body—here, a city council—to action in order to achieve your goal. In essence, the speaker was arming audience members with arguments they could use on other people and on other groups. This is called the *two-step flow* of communication: the speaker communicates ideas and attitudes to one audience, which in turn communicates them to others. In that way, messages reverberate through a society. Finally, note the care she took in indicating first steps. They were laid out concretely and clearly, making them easy to follow.

TIPS FOR PERSUASION: THE ETHICS OF IT ALL

There are some other considerations which you ought to confront as you think about moving to action or any other type of persuasion in society. The communication phenomenon of mass persuasion raises certain ethical questions. It is time you faced those issues squarely. The ethical issues which confront you as a persuader fall into two groups—legal issues and moral issues.

The Legal Issues

First off, as a society we are concerned enough about mass persuasion to have written a series of limitations into federal, state, and local statutes. Granted, the First Amendment in the Bill of Rights guarantees you free speech, but only within boundaries. These barriers include such specialized laws as those forbidding "subliminal persuasion" (flashing messages on screens for only mini-seconds as subconscious prods); but since most of you won't have that opportunity, we needn't be concerned about it. You are, though, faced with three other legal restrictions.

■ *Libel.* You are forbidden by law to libel other people, to engage in public fabrication of lies concerning their conduct. Although libel is a favorite tactic of the demagogue seeking to discredit his or her opposition, you can be prosecuted for such wanton character assassination. It is one thing to attack someone's motives on moral grounds, but quite another to accuse them of illegal, unfounded behaviors. Beware.

■ *Truth in advertising.* Federal law also requires that you be able to present independent research demonstrating that any products you attempt to sell publicly do in fact perform what you claim they do. While enforcers of this law—notably the Food and Drug Administration and the United States Post Office—have had time to prosecute only the most flagrant cases of big-company ads for cars, creams, and aspirin and but a few of the "miracle cures" slipped into the back of magazines, the law is beginning to have effect. Persuaders are starting to exercise more care in their claims. To keep within the law, you too will have to avoid exaggerating the facts.

■ *Legal assembly.* While it is considered your constitutional right to publicly assemble and demonstrate for your cause, there nevertheless are state and local ordinances which can control that right. You may well need a parade or park permit. You are liable in most places for any damage to public or private property you—or even opposing forces—incur. Violations of curfews and other laws will often be met with arrest and incarceration. Know the difference between legal and illegal assembly in any area you are working before planning to exercise your right to assemble peaceably.

The Moral Issues

Of more importance are the moral issues persuaders confront, for in these areas there are no automatic penalties and few specifiable guidelines. Three of these issues, especially, have put persuaders in moral quandaries for centuries.

■ *The means-ends dilemma.* Does the end justify the means? "Sure," comes the answer from those of us with righteousness on our side. "Anything we can do to instill a sense of social pride, religious or civic commitment, and 'right' action should be condoned." "Good grief, no!" comes the reply of those who point out what happened during the Inquisition, during the Nazi reign in Germany and the Fascist regime in Italy. For most of us, of course, choices on whether or not to enslave a nation are nonexistent, but even "little" decisions flow from the same dilemma. Do you ignore opposing ideas because you think they might "confuse" your audience? Do you conveniently skip over "bad" information about your product or your organization? When asked a direct question, do you evade it by giving a lecturette on yourself, your proposition's goals, or your company's virtues? In these situations, you are implicitly acting as though your ends justified your means.

■ *Humaneness.* You also are faced with a problem of how to view your audience. Do you visualize them as a glob of clay to be molded in any way you wish? Or as a block of resistant marble which is going to take verbal hammering and chipping? As an ignorant mass hardly deserving of your enlightenment and presence? As a group of coequals, owed all of the consideration and gentle guidance you can give them? Such questions probe your sense of humaneness, the degree to which you see as your mission in public speaking the care and feeding of fellow human beings.

■ *Source of ethical responsibility.* The final moral question, perhaps, is the knottiest of all: On whose shoulders does the ultimate responsibility for ethics in communication rest? Essentially four positions on this question can be taken. Some argue that ethical questions are solely determined by *speakers*—that speakers must never lie, distort, or fabricate; or if they do, they ought to be condemned. That notion is attractive, although we must note that such an absolutist view of ethics ignores situations in which we "allow" speakers to utter less than the truth. We allow parents to spare children grief by holding back some of the facts, as when a loved one is brutally killed. We even let Presidents withhold information when engaged in sensitive negotiations with foreign powers. Some, therefore, answer, "It's the *audience* who is ultimately responsible." This is a sort of "buyer beware" position—one that says if people are gullible enough to be taken in by snake oil salesmen, so much the worse for them. The third position counters, "But, that's not fair, for it lets anyone say anything at any time, and we have a right to some expectations of truthfulness—there are such things as *social rules*." The *social rules* advocate urges that people have a right to expect speakers to adhere to basic democratic ideals and to conform to social expectations. So we accept the fact that campaigning politicians and used-car sales representatives will overpromise and stretch the truth here and there; and we adjust our listening to that fact. But we do not expect a minister, rabbi, or priest to ever alter facts. The problem we face here, though, is this: Who should determine what the situational norms are? The government, as it does with its truth-in-advertising laws? The practitioners (salespeople, preachers, politicians, etc.) of each of the communicative arts?

The final position, then, is a sort of combination of all of the others: moral responsibility is *shared equally* by speakers, audiences, and institutions of our society. *Speakers* have a responsibility to uphold the dignity of public communication and of their audiences, and to treat both with respect. *Audiences* have the responsibility of screaming bloody murder when they have been hoodwinked by an unscrupulous orator. And *institutions* must regulate their people—through such mechanisms as the television industry's "Code of Fair Practice," the Hippocratic oath to govern doctors, the American Bar Association's Ethics Committee, and the like. Actually, this fourth position is the easiest to defend of all of them, for it lets no one off the moral hook. Speakers must have integrity; audiences cannot simply sit back and let messages roll over them; and institutions cannot escape by saying they're only "professional" and not "ethical" groups.

Whatever you yourself think about ethical matters—both legal and moral—you must grapple with them every time you turn on TV or seek to be an articulate person yourself.[6] The stakes are too high not to.

SAMPLE SPEECH: **ACTUATING**

Pre-Speech Analysis   Let us conclude this chapter with a complete actuative speech, one prepared by Todd Ambs of Eastern Michigan University for one of the annual contests sponsored by the Interstate Oratorical Association. Mr. Ambs faced particular problems of audience and setting in preparing this speech on hypertension and heart disease: (1) His audience generally was composed of college students, who undoubtedly felt they were too young to worry about heart disease; and (2) the setting was a speech contest, one where audience members probably were more concerned about their own speeches than about Mr. Ambs' call for action. Notice how he attacks these two barriers to effectiveness. And notice, too, that the speech falls into an organizational pattern—Monroe's Motivated Sequence—we discussed earlier.

Speech

The Silent Killer[7]
Todd Ambs

Attention Step

For many Americans, life can seem to be a maze of numbers. We use many numbers so often that to be without them seems almost impossible. How long could college students survive without their student numbers? How many businesses could operate without a phone number? How many of you have never had use for your social security number? The answers to these questions are easy. But there is one other set of numbers that could set us on the road to preventing an estimated 300,000 deaths and over two million serious illnesses each year, if we would only pay attention to them. For no student number, phone number, or social security number will ever be as vital to you as your blood pressure reading.   /1

The human blood pressure is a veritable measuring stick of good health. Normal blood pressure, that is anything between 90/70 to 140/90, is generally a good indication of normal health. Unfortunately, over 25 million Americans do not have a blood pressure within this range. They suffer from high blood pressure, or hypertension.   /2

Indeed, according to the Department of Health, Education, and Welfare, this year, 310,000 Americans will perish from illnesses whose major contributing factor is hypertension. Two million will suffer strokes, heart attacks, and kidney failure as a direct result of hypertension. Even more startling is the realization that of that 25 million, 11 million aren't even aware of their condition. According to Dr. Theodore Cooper, Director of the Heart and Lung Institute, "Hypertension can be brought under control through proven treatment which is neither unduly hazardous, complicated or expensive."   /3

Need Step

Before we can fully understand the magnitude of the problem though, we need to know what high blood pressure does to the body. When the pressure of the blood becomes too great for the arterial walls, high blood pressure results. This is somewhat like giving your circulatory system a headache. Fatty tissues, salts and fluids build up and the heart must be made to work harder than it should to keep the blood flowing properly. In this case, however, one tiny time pill won't relieve the pressure, or the irreparable damage that follows.   /4

That information may sound familiar to many of you. But then, why is hypertension still responsible for one out of every eight deaths in this country!   /5

The National High Blood Pressure Council attempted to answer that question when they said: "Half of those who have high blood pressure don't even know that they do. Of those who do, only half are being treated, only half again of those have their blood pressure under control. Patients and physicians alike just don't seem to take this condition very seriously."   /6

Such carefree attitudes leave many people's lives just hanging in the balance because high blood pressure has no symptoms. Contrary to popular belief, high blood pressure is not confined to trapeze artists, overactive children, or the Annie Hall's of the world. There is, in fact, no direct correlation between tension and nervousness and high blood pressure. The only way you can tell if you have high blood pressure is to get it checked. As Dr. Frank Finnerty, author of the book, *High*

Blood Pressure—The Silent Killer, put it: "You can look great and feel healthy and have been living for years with the hidden time bomb of high blood pressure doing internal damage to your body." For Bill, a 49-year-old account executive, the time bomb was about to explode. One minute he was walking along seemingly in the best of health. The next he was on the ground clutching his chest. The heart attack would be the last event in Bill's life. He would never know the anguish that his family would suffer when they discovered that high blood pressure, a totally preventable condition, had caused his death. The silent killer had quietly destroyed life again.   /7

A routine physical could have saved Bill's life. And it could save yours. But unfortunately, our hectic, fast-paced lifestyles often provide easy excuses for not getting that needed physical. Lack of time, money, and the ever-popular lack of awareness can all be easy rationalizations for our failure to diagnose and treat hypertension. And our health care systems have failed to adjust to this reality at home, or especially on the job. A recent major manufacturing study found that on the average, businesses spend over $300 per employee per year, for illnesses caused by hypertension. Dr. Andrea Foote and Dr. John Erfurt, the country's leading specialists in hypertensive care, painted the picture in this light: "The current inadequacy of treatment suggests that the problem is a matter of social organization and lies primarily in the inability of the health care delivery system to provide health care for this disease."   /8

And here we reach the apex of the problem. Simple diagnosis must be followed by constant treatment if hypertension is to be controlled. Unfortunately, many people do not continue this vital treatment. Mike Gorman, Executive Director of the Citizens for the Treatment of High Blood Pressure, estimates that at least 50% of those diagnosed drop out of treatment after a few months. One man who had a severe attack of high blood pressure on his vacation came home, followed a steady treatment plan, and brought his pressure down. After a while, he foolishly decided to try foregoing the medication. Within a month, he had a stroke which left him with irreversible brain damage. This man should have known better. He was a doctor, who was about to be nominated to the A.M.A. presidency. Unbelievably, a man who had frequently prescribed treatment for hypertension, and ignored his own warnings! The precautions must be heeded; anyone can be a victim.   /9

Satisfaction Step   Obviously then, the public needs to be made aware of the dangers of hypertension, health care systems should be improved to provide adequate health care for the disease, and finally, hypertensives must realize that constant treatment is essential to effective control.   /10

Thankfully, the goals I have mentioned are not just mere ideals proposed by a few specialists in hypertensive care. In 1972, the National Heart, Lung and Blood Institute organized the National High Blood Pressure Education Program, a program that all of us can get involved in. Their goal is to alert people to the dangers of hypertension through location, diagnosis, and treatment. The results have been astounding. According to the National Center for Health Statistics, 290,000 people leading normal lives today would have died, were it not for the Hypertensive Education Program. Over eight million people now have their blood pressure under control, a 100% increase since 1972.   /11

And it touches all sectors of society, for the Hypertensive Education Program is nationwide. Here in Michigan, for instance, you can contact Steve Renke at the University of Michigan's hypertensive care unit in Ann Arbor, if you want to help.   /12

Visualization Step

But we cannot rest on the laurels of this program. A disease which claims the lives of over 300,000 people annually is hardly under control. Doctors Foote and Erfurt have found that blood pressure control, for employed people, can best be carried out in the work setting. Their Worker Health Program was tested at four different job sites. As a result, 92% of the hypertensives at these jobs have their blood pressure under control, and the cost to the businesses involved has been cut from $300 per employee to $6.21. The program has been so successful that Blue Cross/Blue Shield of Michigan and Connecticut are now undergoing pilot programs of their own, based on the Worker Health Program.   /13

On the local level there are things you can do as well. In 1970, Savannah, Georgia, had the infamous title of Stroke Capital of the World. Today, Savannah has 14 permanent blood pressure reading stations and the stroke toll in that city has been cut in half. A program, like one of these, can work in your community.   /14

Action Step

So often, those of us in forensics use persuasive ploys instead of getting right to the heart of the problem. As a result, we tend to perform, instead of persuade. And you in turn as an audience listen, but don't hear. *Please*, if you do nothing else today, hear what I'm saying. There are people in this country who are dying because they have high blood pressure and there is not enough being done about it. You could be one of the 11 million Americans who has high blood pressure and does not even know it. If you are lucky enough to not be inflicted with the malady of hypertension, certainly someone that you know is. Don't let yourself or someone you know become a number on a fatality sheet. Get your blood pressure checked and save a life, your own.   /15

NOTES

[1]   Certainly the fullest treatment of these and other motive appeals can be found in Douglas Ehninger, Bruce E. Gronbeck, Ray E. McKerrow, and Alan H. Monroe, *Principles and Types of Speech Communication*, 9th ed. (Glenview, Il.: Scott, Foresman and Company, 1982), Chap. 6, "Determininig the Basic Appeals."

[2]   For a discussion of the "foot-in-the-door" phenomenon and the communication research documenting its importance, see Mary John Smith, *Persuasion and Human Action; A Review and Critique of Social Influence Theories* (Belmont, Ca.: Wadsworth Publishing Company, 1982), pp. 149–151.

[3]   The broadest survey, in understandable terms, of research on changing behavior is probably Philip G. Zimbardo, Ebbe B. Ebbesen, and Christina Maslach, *Influencing Attitudes and Changing Behavior*, 2nd ed. (Reading, Ma.: Addison-Wesley Publishing Company, 1977). For a much more abstract and theoretical treatment of these issues, see Donald P. Cushman and Robert D. McPhee, eds., *Message-Attitude-Behavior Relationship; Theory, Methodology, and*

Application, Human Communication Research Series (New York: Academic Press, 1980).

[4]   From *How We Think* by John Dewey, D. C. Heath Company, 1910. Reprinted with the permission of the Center for Dewey Studies, Southern Illinois University at Carbondale. See p. 72.

[5]   The Motivated Sequence originally was advanced in Alan H. Monroe, *Principles and Types of Speech* (Chicago: Scott, Foresman and Company, 1935), esp. pp. vii–x. It still is available fully developed in Ehninger, Gronbeck, McKerrow, and Monroe (n.1 above), Chap. 8, "Adapting the Speech Structure to Audiences: The Motivated Sequence." The description we offer of each step is quoted directly from p. 147.

[6]   As ways into these and other ethical issues, consult the following: B. J. Diggs, "Persuasion and Ethics," *Quarterly Journal of Speech,* 50 (December 1964), 359–373; Douglas Ehninger, "Validity as Moral Obligation," *Southern Speech* [Communication] *Journal,* 33 (Spring 1968), 215–222; Franklyn Haiman, "Democratic Ethics and the Hidden Persuaders," *Quarterly Journal of Speech,* 44 (December 1958), 385–392; Sidney Hook, "The Ethics of Controversy," *New Leader,* 37 (February 1, 1954), 12–14; Richard L. Johannesen, ed., *Ethics and Persuasion* (New York: Random House, Inc., 1967); Wayne C. Minnick, "The Ethics of Persuasion," *The Art of Persuasion* (Boston, Ma.: Houghton Mifflin Company, 1957), pp. 276–287; Thomas R. Nilsen, *Ethics of Speech Communication* (Indianapolis, In.: The Bobbs-Merrill Co., Inc., 1966); Edward Rogge, "Evaluating the Ethics of a Speaker in a Democracy," *Quarterly Journal of Speech,* 45 (December 1959), 419–425; Karl R. Wallace, "An Ethical Basis of Communication," in Johannesen (above), pp. 41–56, as well as his "The Substance of Rhetoric: Good Reasons," *Quarterly Journal of Speech,* 49 (October 1963), 239–249; and Henry Nelson Wieman and Otis M. Walter, "Toward an Analysis of Ethics for Rhetoric," *Quarterly Journal of Speech,* 43 (October 1957), 266–270.

[7]   "The Silent Killer" by Todd Ambs. Reprinted from *Winning Orations* (1980) by special arrangement with the Interstate Oratorical Association, Larry Schnoor, Executive Secretary, Mankato State University, Mankato, Minnesota.

ASSIGNMENTS

Pre-Performance

1. Are there some television commercials which you find particularly offensive? Identify the appeals upon which these ads are based, and attempt to isolate the specific aspects of the appeals that offend you. Have these ads produced a boomerang effect in you? Or after viewing the commercials, have you still purchased the products?

2. The class as a whole should designate some item as a new product to be analyzed and advertised in this exercise. Class members then will work in groups of three or four to prepare a marketing analysis. To do the marketing analysis, each group will determine its target audience (the kinds of people most likely to buy the product). Then the group will decide which persuasive appeals to accentuate in trying to sell the product. Groups also should design some type of advertisement—magazine, newspaper, bill-

board, radio, television—for introducing the new product. After completing these tasks, a delegate from each group will report to the class. The class should discuss variations in and effectivensss of the marketing analyses and the advertisements.

3. What wants and needs would you address if you were attempting to get students at your school to take the following actions:
   a. run for a seat on the student senate
   b. study harder
   c. dance in the annual marathon to raise money for the Muscular Dystrophy Campaign
   d. sign up for a course in the theory and practice of persuasion
   e. attend a seminar on sex differences in communication

4. Think about your use of persuasive techniques, and evaluate yourself as an ethical communicator. Make an entry in your journal in which you disclose your response toward means-ends choices, ethical responsibility, and consideration of audiences. Now, for the next few days keep a diary of your use of persuasion. What does the diary indicate about the actual ethical code you practice?

Performance

1. Select a single topic and develop two four- to six-minute persuasive speeches. Make the first one a speech to reinforce attitudes; the second, a speech to actuate. Half of the class should prepare to deliver the messages of reinforcement, and the other half will present actuative speeches. Turn in detailed outlines for both speeches, and be prepared to explain the aspects you considered in planning both presentations.

2. Develop a four- to six-minute speech in which you urge that some change be made in your hometown. Prepare to explain your communication plan for bringing about the change.

3. Prepare to sell an actual item currently being sold by some local or campus group. Three or four students should choose the same product but work individually to prepare five-minute sales talks. Students should present the sales talks in units and then hold a brief panel discussion in which they analyze the creation and satisfaction of motive needs.

Post-Performance

1. After you have presented the speech in Performance 2, explain your plan for bringing about change. At minimum, include these aspects (mentioned in Chapter 8, Changing Attitudes) in your explanation:
   a. What kinds of commitments are you asking from audience members?
   b. What methods must they use to carry out the action?
   c. What institutions need to be moved in order to achieve the goal?

2. If your class did Performance 3, each of the units should check to find out how many classmates bought their item. The unit's survey also should attempt to uncover apparent reasons for success or failure.

CHAPTER 10

Arguing

Argument is one of those words that stir controversy in and of themselves. In this day of concern for others, the word has highly negative connotations to many people. "Why do you have to be so argumentative?" "Let's discuss this, not argue about it." "You're always trying to start an argument." Such comments come from people who fear that sharp differences of opinion will destroy friends and cripple ideas. On the other side of the fence, however, are those who believe that decisions can be made only through head-to-head combat (for that, after all, was how this republic was founded). There are also those who enjoy taking someone to task, crowing, "Now *that* was a good fight!"

Argumentation, indeed, represents a special species of public communication, in that we often believe it is healthy for *ideas* to be tested, but fear that *persons* may be hurt in the process. Hence, we both love and hate argumentation, enjoy it yet fear it. Such a love/hate controversy surrounds the term, perhaps, because there are different sorts of arguments. Anatol Rappoport, for example, talks about three kinds of arguments: fights, games, and debates. A "fight" occurs when two people are so mad that they wish to psychologically hurt or injure each other, as when two friends are on the verge of splitting up. A "game" takes place between two people who, like chess players, enjoy the process of maneuvering around each other. By advancing arguments the other person can't answer or nitpicking at ideas that person has proposed, points are scored; winning is all in an essentially intellectual exercise of "gaming." But, to Rappoport, a "debate" is a serious and important method for addressing a problem and arriving at a solution. In a debate, both parties advance a proposition or claim, a judgment, or a course of action, and then defend it with all of the facts, values, and criteria for judgment they have available, so as to arrive at the best possible solution for the problem.[1]

Perhaps, then, the reason we sometimes fear argument is that we think of it in terms of the personal—and risky—fight, or in terms of a mere game that combat-lovers play for fun at someone else's expense. Yet, the reason argument has been defended as a mode of decision-making for centuries is that it can become a useful debate between serious participants, both of whom have the good of an organization or society in view. In this chapter, we will be discussing primarily the best that argumentation has to offer, a debate model. Obviously, we will also have to say some things about strategies for self-defense when fighting and gaming situations arise.

THE OCCASION AND THE AUDIENCE: WHAT, WHO, WHEN, WHY

Technically, the word "argument" is ambiguous, because we use it commonly to refer to a unit-of-proof (your first or second "argument" for something), to the process of fighting ("They're having an argument"), and to a rational debate. Because we are concerned with rational debate, with the serious communication process, we define it as follows: An *argument* is a relatively controlled communicative exchange in which good reasons are advanced for believing, valuing, or doing something. Let us look at the key terms in this definition:

. . . Relatively Controlled Often when arguing, you are expected to talk according to *rules*. Sometimes these rules are very formally stated, as when you are operating under parliamentary procedure. Other times, the rules for arguing are merely social conventions. Many audiences, for example, expect you to concede a point to an opponent if you cannot answer it well. Others will boo you if, in the middle of a "rational" discussion, you suddenly start calling your opponent names. In all, public argument takes place in a kind of intellectual fishbowl; the speaker as arguer is setting forth his or her case for public examination in a relatively controlled situation, one in which the audience and social conventions set the rules.

. . . Communicative Exchange In an argument, you normally have one or more opponents, other speakers you are "allowing" to examine your assertions, your reasoning, and your evidence as well as they can. Sometimes that opponent is specified, as in a political debate between candidates for office. At other times, as in a club or chamber of commerce meeting, you don't know who the opponent(s) might be, although you still proceed as *though* you had a direct adversary. That is, an argument is an exchange so you expect someone to attempt to refute you.

. . . Good Reasons No matter what you assert in an argument, you usually can expect someone to challenge or deny it. Your listeners expect you, therefore, to have good reasons for believing, valuing, or doing what you do. In argument, there is an implicit commitment to rationality in this culture. You are presumed to be able to offer evidence in support of beliefs;

an analysis of values in support of criteria for judgment held to; and rationales for why you think any plan of action you advance is feasible, practical, and without serious disadvantages. The demand for good reasons puts argument squarely in the field of the "head" psychologists.[2]

. . . Believing, Valuing, or Doing Fundamentally, you argue with someone else in the light of disagreements over an assertion or claim. This claim may be one of three kinds: belief-claims, value-claims, and policy-claims.

A *belief-claim* is an assertion that some state of affairs exists or does not exist—that some idea is true or not true. "The United States is militarily superior to the U.S.S.R." "Assembly-line work causes mental depression." "Large doses of vitamin C do not reduce the body's susceptibility to colds." "Modular scheduling of work periods in elementary schools accelerates learning." All four of these assertions are belief-claims; the speakers are claiming something is true or false.

A *value-claim* goes one step farther by assigning a value to a belief. A value-claim is an assertion that something is desirable or undesirable, beautiful or ugly, right or wrong, just or unjust. "Contract marriages are good for both partners." "Plea bargaining destroys the foundation of our judicial system." Strict zoning laws harm a city's growth potential." "A management-by-objective system of employee evaluations is just and efficient." In these value-claims, the speakers are expressing a valuative preference.

A *policy-claim* is an assertion that something should or should not be done. "This city should enact a noise pollution ordinance." "The overtime parking penalty should be increased from $2.00 to $5.00." "Our PTA should hold a garage sale to raise money for new band uniforms." "Our city should eliminate the office of ombudsman." In these policy-claims, audiences are being asked to act upon certain beliefs and values.

As a species of oral communication, therefore, an argument normally involves communicative turn-taking in a rational atmosphere, one in which a particular belief, value, or policy is at stake. Throughout an argument (at least in the debate form) there is a sense of formality and control not often present in other kinds of public speaking. A committed speaker *(who)* presents good reasons *(what)* in support of a disputed claim *(when)* in order to achieve intellectual or action-oriented agreement *(why)*—that's argument.

RAW MATERIALS FOR ARGUMENTS

Before plunging into the heart of an argumentative speech, we need to examine the material out of which it is built. The kinds of materials needed are determined by the demand for "good reasons" and by some of the principles of cognitive or rationalistic psychology discussed in the preview. Materials useful in an argument include *definitions, facts, values, actions,* and *logics.*

Definitions   First, of course, anyone who argues must begin with clear and acceptable *words* or *concepts*. Many disputes in this world are merely "verbal" disputes—essentially disagreements over the meanings of words. This is so because the way you define important words often determines how you look at the world—organize it, encapsulate it for examination and action.

The perennial political debate over unemployment is a good example of an argument that rests on definition. *Unemployment* is a term that is usually defined by how it is measured (defining by describing operations, as discussed in Chapter 5). But how should unemployment be measured? By counting every last citizen who's not working during a particular month? By counting only those who apply for federal or state unemployment benefits? By "seasonally adjusting" the figures, to take into account the normal drop when students go back to school in September as well as those workers temporarily laid off when the auto industry is involved in a model changeover? By counting only the "hardcore" unemployed, that is, those who have not worked during the last twenty-seven weeks? The point is, we can come up with quite different unemployment figures, depending upon how unemployment is measured and therefore defined.

The same sort of dispute arises when schools are forced to define *disadvantaged students* or *open learning,* when scientists attempt to define *light,* or when the state legislature tries to write a new *rape* law. How these key words are defined can shape the debate. Without agreements on what we mean by such slippery concepts, we can find ourselves in interminable, meaningless disputes. Often one of your first tasks as an arguer is to offer definitions, in ways we discussed them in Chapter 5. Otherwise, you may never get on to more important matters.

Evidence   Next, arguers have to be concerned with evidence—material your audience will accept as "good reasons." We have referred to several kinds of evidence through the course of this book, especially in terms of the statistical summaries and examples you can offer as evidence in reports. Perhaps you should think of the arguer's evidence as coming in two flavors:

- *Hard evidence* includes factual-type materials: statistics, examples, illustrations, and testimony from authorities who carry weight with auditors.
- *Soft evidence* includes testimony which adds human interest or feelings to an idea, as well as analogies. Some analogies are "literal analogies"—actually parallel cases as we discussed them earlier. Others are "figurative analogies," as when you compare the evolution of the universe with the functioning of a machine or when you compare human development to planting, nurturing, and harvesting foods from plants.

These two kinds of evidence serve somewhat different functions in an argument. Hard evidence provides a rational sense of "proof"; while soft evidence makes your argument seem believable or understandable. Say that you are arguing that your city should build bike lanes to prevent bicycle accidents. Statistics on the drop in bicycle accidents when Jonesville laid bike lanes along major streets add hard evidence to your argument; and testimony from an injured bicyclist (soft evidence) would supplement it with human interest and believability. Most articulate arguers assemble a variety of tested, defensible, relevant evidence for their speeches; for if they do not, an opponent is sure to call for "proof."[3]

Evaluative Criteria   In most arguments, however, mere facts are not enough. It's one thing to recognize that 10.6 percent of the town's population is unemployed, but quite another to get people to do something about it. You first must get them to feel they in fact *want*, need, have motives to do something; and that involves feelings, attitudes, and values—the motivating forces we discussed earlier. Simply put, to get an audience off the dime, you must get at its preferences or what we have occasionally termed evaluative criteria.

As a person bombarded with junk mail, you undoubtedly know a good deal about appeals to attitudes and values. You're told to *feel sorry* for starving children in Asia. You're asked to *feel pride* for your country, and to exhibit that pride by purchasing a 4' by 8' American flag complete with aluminum pole. You've been told it's your *moral duty* to join a wilderness-preserving organization. You're advised to *save $10.00* off the newsstand price by returning a prepaid/no-money-until-later postcard entitling you to the next twenty-six weeks of a popular magazine. Appeals to pity, pride, morality, acquisition and savings—the list of criteria by which to judge some thing or action goes on and on. As an arguer, then, you have to mentally take apart your subject matter and your audience, trying to guess what combination of values and attitudes will link your facts with courses of thought and action you wish the audience to take.

Actions   And, of course, there are the specific actions you wish an audience to take in light of your argumentative speech. Sometimes, the actions are obvious and cause you no special problems in identifying them. When you urge that Mary Jones rather than Ken Brandtson be elected president of your school association, the action is easy to specify—vote for Mary. But, say, when the action involves setting up a board, appealing to a governmental body to change a law, affecting the behavior of others who aren't present (as when you enlist the group to get community members to use a recycling center), you immediately are faced with a host of questions:

• *What kinds of commitments are you asking from audience members?* Can they do it right now (say, vote), or are they committing themselves to post-speech actions such as letter-writing, telephoning, door-to-door visitations, or baking goodies for the sale?

- *What methods must they use to carry out the action?* Further oral communication from audience members to others? Letters to the editor or members of Congress? In-person visits? Or what?
- *What institutions need to be moved in order to achieve the goal?* Should the PTA, the neighborhood or block association, or the chamber of commerce be asked to get involved? Must the legislature act, and, if so, through which of its committees should the appeal be made? Does the press need to be activated? Do you need to find lawyers to bring a class-action suit? Does someone need to lobby the school board or the library committee or the parks and recreation board? If so, when and where do these organizations meet?

Overall, any call for action must be feasible and practicable. You will also need to describe the action carefully, step by step, including a time line. Inertia can set in, because most people act only when it is extremely easy to do so. As the old adage has it, "When everything is said and done, usually more is said than done."

Logics   The word *logic* probably scares most of us, conjuring up visions of complicated proofs and bearded philosophers. "Formal logic" in that sense need not concern us here. The speaker in an argumentative context needs to be more concerned about the overall sense of rationality or reasonableness in his or her analysis. Questions of consistency and relevance to the audience are most important. That is, an audience member listening to an argument or a debate has every right in the world, given our cultural expectations, to apply tests of reasonableness, consistency, and relevancy. We have already discussed testing your overall reasoning patterns. You can also apply tests for reasonableness to the definitions, evidence, evaluative criteria, and actions that make up your argument. These tests are listed in Figure 10.1.

The "logics," then, an audience applies to an argumentative speech belong to them by rights of social expectations. You are expected to meet such tests of reasoning if you are to be considered a proper arguer in this culture.

ORGANIZING ARGUMENTATIVE SPEECHES

Most argumentative speeches, especially those defending value- or policy-claims, use the *causal patterns* we described in Chapter 3. Organizational patterns which stress *problem-solution, cause-effect,* or *effect-cause relationships* are naturally suited to speeches which must define terms or concepts, assemble relevant facts, and offer evaluative criteria upon which listeners' decisions are to be made. They are also, as we noted earlier, the most strongly coherent or rational of the organizational patterns.

Belief-claims, however, because they are so strongly definitional in their emphases, often can be defended with the use of additional patterns as well. *Topical patterns* employing *partial or complete enumeration,* for

FIGURE 10.1   **Additional Tests of Arguments**

Testing Definitions:
• *Are you using language in a reasonable manner?* Is it reasonable to define *unemployment* so as to include every man, woman, and child not working? That is, is it reasonable to expect a private or public plan attacking unemployment to put every single citizen to work? When in doubt, don't be afraid to bring in authorities—expert testimony—to support your understanding of concepts.

Testing Evidence:
• *Are you reasoning fairly and consistently from your evidence to your claim?* When you are using any of the reasoning patterns discussed in Preview III, you need to check the instances, parallel cases, signs, causes, or generalizations that you are citing as evidence. (See Preview III, Figure III.1, for ways of checking your evidence when using these reasoning patterns.)

Testing Evaluative Criteria:
• *Are the values to which you are appealing applicable to your claim?* Upon what basis, for example, should the question of legalized abortions rest? It is a matter destined to raise voices and blood pressures because it ultimately will be decided by determining what values to bring to bear upon the issue. If this country could ever agree on which criteria apply to the issue, the rest would be easy. Be sure you understand clearly what evaluative criteria an audience will "allow" you to apply to the claim you are urging, and be ready to offer motivational appeals which can make your values seem important.

Testing Actions:
• *Is the plan really needed?* O.K., so you've been ripped off by a local store. Do you really need to set up a new Citizen's Complaint Board, or can you use already existing machinery (the Better Business Bureau or small-claims court) to get satisfaction?
• *Is the plan feasible?* Would it actually solve the problem? Would new city buses really get more people to ride them? Is the quality of the present buses really the problem?
• *Is the plan practical?* Could it actually be put into practice? Do you have a workable timetable, the organization of people, the money, and the like, to make it go?
• *Could the plan be put into effect without creating more and greater problems?* So, we could eliminate any potential threat from China by dropping fifteen strategically aimed H-bombs around that country; they would "solve" the problem of China feasibly and practically. But the plan would raise one or two additional problems, from atmospheric radiation to intolerable senses of guilt.

example, are well-suited to belief-claims, because they allow you to divide your belief or concept into its constituent parts for explanation and examination. So, a speech comparing the industrial strengths of the United States and Russia might easily be segmented into such comparative topics as steel production and resources, energy production and resources, labor resources, managerial training programs, etc. But, even belief-claims must be defended in speech structures which leave the audience with a sense of orderliness and rationality.

Let us move on now to a sample outline of a speech that argues for a value-claim. Although this is only a partial outline (presenting only the body of the speech), it does illustrate one way to handle the especially nasty problem of arguing for values, using a cause-effect structure.

SAMPLE SPEECH: ARGUING

Pre-Speech Analysis

Subject:	Road salting*
Audience:	Legislators, city council members, or a local environmental protection and research group
Situation:	The state or local government is holding hearings on road servicing and is looking for citizen input.
Purpose:	To change the current practices in road servicing by attempting to alter values applied in making decisions.
Speaker:	The speaker has studied a series of research reports put out by the Environmental Protection Agency (EPA) and the Michigan Highway Safety Institute.
Strategies:	1. The speaker attempts to destroy the conventional wisdom (general beliefs) on the value of road salting (a) by attacking beliefs already held, and (b) by explaining (through cause-effect reasoning) why a new belief which seems contrary to common sense should be accepted.
	2. The speaker attempts to broaden the audience's definition of "costs" of salting.
	3. The speaker relies upon two highly personalized values, economics and health, to create the motive need of fear.
	4. The speaker employs expert testimony because of the degree to which changes in perceptions must occur.

* The factual material included in this speech outline comes from Charles F. Wurster, "Road Salt Costs You Plenty." Copyright © 1978 by The New York Times Co. Reprinted by permission. Professor Wurster teaches environmental sciences at the Marine Sciences Research Center, State University of New York, Stony Brook. Additional material for this outline (and for Professor Wurster's article) comes from Donald M. Murray and Ulrich F. W. Ernst, *An Economic Analysis of the Environmental Impact of Highway Deicing*, Environmental Protection Technology Series EPA–600/2–76–105 (Cincinnati, Ohio: U.S. Environmental Protection Agency Office of Research and Development, 1976).

Outline	**Take It With a Grain of Salt?**

Body

Definition of effects

1. To understand the many ways road salting affects our lives, we must first of all identify some specific effects it can have.
   A. Too often, we think only of traffic accidents which result from slippery roads.
   B. But road salting has effects on a whole series of economic and health problems.

Expert testimony gives weight to the argument

Factual belief to be changed

   C. As the Environmental Protection Agency points out, those who consider only the effects on accidents are in danger of having a myopic view.
   D. Therefore, what I want to do today is to lay out the full range of possible effects, and suggest ways we should look at them.

Factual belief

II. There is no solid evidence for the claim that salting roads increases safety.

Attacks reasoning from generalization

   A. Attempts to study the usefulness of salting are difficult because the effects of salting are often inseparable from those of plowing and sanding.

Expert testimony

      1. The EPA tends to reject those studies that do not attempt to separate salting from plowing and sanding.

Explains away an exception

      2. The Michigan Highway Safety Institute's study, conducted in Ann Arbor, Michigan, which did deal only with salting, cannot be considered conclusive:
         a. The Michigan study did find that salting tends to reduce accidents.
         b. But it was not conclusive because there was no attempt to take into account the number of storms and the quantity of snow during the year the study was done.

New belief

   B. Salting may well not reduce accidents.

Explanation of its rationality (cause-effect)

      1. One explanation for this may be that, because salt usually permits faster driving and creates a false sense of security, drivers have as many accidents as they had at slower speeds under poorer conditions.

Second explanation of its rationality (cause-effect)

      2. And because salt prolongs street wetness, turns dry snow into sticky slush, and reduces tire traction, it may even contribute to accidents.

The major value claim of the argument. It suggests that, in addition to the value of safety, the values of economics, environmental protection, and health should be applied.

III. But, even if salt is occasionally beneficial in reducing accidents, the long-term costs, ecological effects, and health hazards of using salt outweigh its presumed benefits.
   A. According to the EPA, road salt and its application costs this country $200 million annually.
   B. Furthermore, an estimated $2 billion is spent yearly on repairing corrosive damage to vehicles caused by salt.
   C. And don't forget the $50 million that the EPA estimates for annual destruction of roadside vegetation, particularly shade trees.

Economic value applied

   D. Then, add $10 million for yearly salt-seepage damage to underground cables and lines.

Specific instance

   E. And, finally, there's the $500 million spent to repair deteriorated bridges and other highway structures. The best example is the collapse, several years ago, of New York City's West Side Highway, believed to be caused principally by salt.

Environmental value applied

IV. Heavy salt use can upset the natural ecological balance, damaging soil in near-fatal ways.

Expert testimony

    A. According to the EPA, high salt contamination in soil may lead to drainage conditions in which almost irreversible erosion is likely to occur, and in which only a limited variety of vegetation can be planted.

Cause-effect reasoning

    B. Salt applied to highways also causes a decline in roadside trees and vegetation.

Health value applied

V. And, of greatest significance is the health hazard caused by salt seepage into underground water supplies.

Expert testimony

    A. The EPA estimates that 25 percent of the population in the Snow Belt now drinks water contaminated by road salt.

Specific instances

    B. More specifically, several states have experienced significant increases of salt in ground and surface drinking water.

        1. Over 90 communities in Massachusetts have water supplies with a sodium content greater than 20 mg./liter—the maximum allowed for persons on low-sodium diets.

        2. Over 30 water supplies in Connecticut contain more than 20 mg./liter of sodium, and the number is increasing.

        3. Processing water to remove salt is extremely complicated and expensive, and therefore rarely is done.

Cause-effect reasoning, personalizing the health valuative criterion

    C. Couple these facts with data coming out of recent research into the effects of salt on the human body.

        1. The research indicates that salt intake is a causative factor in hypertension, heart disease, and circulatory problems, as well as in various liver, kidney, and metabolic disorders.

        2. The salt contamination is producing not only fouled drinking water but serious damage to human beings—you.

        [The conclusion of the speech could include a summary, a valuative reinforcement, and suggested alternatives if necessary.]

TIPS FOR ARGUING

We will have more to say about argumentation in general after we discuss refuting an argument in the next chapter—after the whole process of attack and defense has been reviewed. Nevertheless we can offer a few pieces of advice for arguers at this point.

■ *Learn strategies for handling "fighters."* If argumentation is going to remain a viable force in our society, each of us has a responsibility to be sure that arguing does not continually degenerate into fighting. Arguments have a tendency to heat up, especially after a period of time. You try again and again to get some person or group to see the logic and reasonableness in your argument, but they seem intransigent. And often your opponents —most often when your case is a good one!—in desperation will resort to calling you names, to picking on your special interests, and even to referring to your family heritage with an obvious lack of respect. In such situations, it is easy to throw mud back, as political candidates are tempted to do as the election nears. If you succumb to the temptation, argumentation as a decision-making process is the worse for it; your audience, while treated to the fun of character assassination, has seen the commitment to rationality fly out the window. Don't yield. Hold your own temper. Try to turn away the personalized wrath of a fighter (1) by ignoring the person; (2) by judiciously using a humorous response ("If the previous speaker wishes to engage in a name-calling contest, I will be happy to join him in one at the bar"); or (3) by reminding the audience of the purpose of the argument ("The real point at issue here is not my parentage, but the issue of. . . ."). Eighteenth-century English parliamentarians invented the phrase "Measures, not men" to discourage fighting. You would do well to remember that injunction.

■ *Keep an eye out for "gamesters."* When someone is trying to score points at your expense, be ready. If the gamester nitpicks over precise dates, don't be afraid to concede minor points ("You're right: it was in 1976 and not 1975"). Sometimes a gamester tries to drive your conclusions to ridiculous extremes ("Now I suppose you'll want to have salt banned by the Food and Drug Administration!"); in that case, you could gently remind your opponent that you're discussing wholesale road salting and not the virtues or vices of salt in general. Don't let yourself be driven to exasperation or intellectual extremity by a clever gamester. By conceding minor points and by keeping the argument from being taken to extremes, you will emerge a stronger, more credible advocate.

■ *Don't overclaim.* Know the limits of your case. It is all too easy to persuade yourself, sometimes. The more you think about your proposals, the better they seem; you soon are tempted to forget (a) that your evidence is often only partial or nonconclusive (as was that in the road salting outline); and (b) that audiences don't necessarily see the world as you do. In the salting speech, for example, it would have been easy to launch a tirade against the Morton Salt Company and others who have grown rich at public expense; or to urge that the EPA has "conclusively" demonstrated the harmful effects of road salting. The speaker resisted the temptation to overstate the case. A wary audience, when faced by a speaker who overclaims, often moves to a "backlash" position intellectually. In the backlash the audience may reject even the "good" things you say in an attempt to purge your ideas of their "bad" features.

■ *Suggest specific actions when advancing policy-claims.* This has been said already, but bears repeating because it's so crucial. Always remember the principle of *audience inertia*: that audience which is at rest tends to remain at rest. Unless you indicate specific actions, as well as stir them with facts and values, you're most likely not going to get them to act. Do you want them to write a member of Congress? Don't just say it: actually give them a name and address. Do you want them to give blood? Pass out a sign-up card along with times and locations for the bloodmobile. Do what you can to make the all-important first step in some proposed action seem concrete and even easy. (See Chapter 9, "Moving to Action," for more advice on this point.)

■ *Be sensitive to the differences between positive and negative claims.* A *positive claim* asks people to start believing or doing something; a *negative claim* asks them to stop. The road salting example illustrates a negative claim—an attempt to get an audience to *stop* salting roads. Notice what had to happen: the speaker had to clear away misconceptions and unexamined values (the safety value) before introducing the positive features (the "new" economic and health-related values). Especially with outrightly hostile or even mildly doubtful audiences, destroying old beliefs and values is a necessary first step. Defending a negative claim is sort of like swimming upstream: you not only have to propel yourself, but must also overcome a natural current flowing the other way. (We'll illustrate positive claims—getting people to start—in later chapters.)

■ *Maintain an open attitude.* An open attitude is essential for arguers. Argumentation, in many ways, is a *corrective* process. As you and others engage in careful examinations of definitions, facts, values, and policies, you both probably will change a little bit. In the give-and-take of mutual argument, you are bound to be given ideas and notions you had not thought about before. Now, it is inordinately easy to stamp your foot, put on a mask of smugness, and retreat into your own prejudices. If that's your attitude, frankly, you probably ought not argue in the sense of "debate." Only if you are willing to learn as well as teach in an argument will you serve both yourself and society in this form of public communication.

NOTES

[1] For a full discussion, see Anatol Rappoport, *Fights, Games and Debates* (Ann Arbor: University of Michigan Press, 1960).

[2] These notions are expanded in Richard D. Rieke and Malcolm O. Sillars, *Argumentation and the Decision Making Process* (New York: John Wiley & Sons, Inc., 1975).

[3] An enlarged discussion on using "hard" and "soft" evidence appears in Douglas Ehninger, Bruce E. Gronbeck, Ray E. McKerrow, and Alan H. Monroe, *Principles and Types of Speech Communication*, 9th ed. (Glenview, Il.: Scott, Foresman and Company, 1982), Chapter 7, "Finding and Using Supporting Materials."

ASSIGNMENTS

Pre-Performance

1. Work in small groups to develop a list of controversial topics which could be used as subjects for the argumentative speeches in the Performance section. After making the list of topics, discuss how strongly you

feel about some of the topics. How would your degree of ego-involvement with certain of the topics affect your responses to an attack on your position?

2. Work in groups of three or four. Each group should choose a topic as the subject for two brief argumentative stands. Develop one of these arguments with high intensity language and the other with low intensity language, but try to vary the content as little as possible. (See Chapter 4 for a discussion of language intensity.) Reconvene the class as a whole, and present the arguments. Then discuss the effectiveness of the different versions.

3. Read a daily newspaper for at least one week. Choose a problem that is currently being debated, identify the arguers, and delineate the arguments. For example, you could analyze the issues underlying the Arab-Israeli conflict, the passage of tax reform laws, or labor contract concessions in times of recession.

4. Phrase a belief-claim, a value-claim, and a policy-claim in each of these general areas:

> A current municipal or campus problem
> Federal tax laws
> National health care
> Strategic arms limitation
> Day-care centers for working mothers
> Cigarette smoking

Performance

1. Choose one of the controversial topics from the list developed in Pre-Performance 1. Work with another classmate whose ego-involvement with a particular topic differs from yours. Each of you should prepare a three- to five-minute speech in which you state your stand and present a rationale. The two speeches may represent opposite views or may vary only in the degree to which they are both pro or both con.

2. You and another member of the class should prepare an argumentative exchange based on a belief-claim, a value-claim, or a policy-claim. One of you will advocate the claim; the other will oppose it. Use an issue format. That is, meet a few days in advance of the debate to choose three issues that relate to the topic. Each of you should develop a two-minute stand for each of those three issues. Present first the pro, then the con, for each issue.

3. Plan a brief two-person debate using a value-claim. One of you should prepare a two-minute speech of advocacy; the other, a two-minute speech in opposition. Do not discuss your presentation with the other person. After the four-minute debate, switch sides. For the next four minutes conduct an informal exchange by extending your opponent's arguments.

4. Build an argumentative speech approximately five minutes in length. You will be allowed to speak without interruption for the first two minutes. After that, your listeners may ask you questions during the remainder of

your speech. You may refrain from answering irrelevant questions. If you are unclear about the meaning of a question, you may ask the listener to repeat it. Prepare thoroughly, and provide your instructor with an outline of the planned speech. Before giving the speech, you may want to review the tips that suggest ways for handling "fighters" and "gamesters."

Post-Performance 1. After each set of presentations in Performance 1, spend five minutes exchanging questions about the differences in your stands and seeking possible explanations for those differences.

2. If you did Performance 2 using the issue format, attempt to ascertain which of the issues in each debate was most convincing. Does the order in which the stands on an issue are presented have any bearing on which is most convincing? Does the overall order of presentation influence your response to the issues? Explain.

CHAPTER 11

Refuting

If we are a bit gun-shy when it comes to arguing for an idea which might be attacked, we resist even more the idea of rising up and objecting publicly to the ideas of others. And, worse, we often find it absolutely paralyzing when we must respond to someone's disagreement with arguments we've made. The process of refutation seems so personal, so risky, so destructive sometimes, that it often is easier to let pass an opportunity to argue or to answer.

Nevertheless, we must remember that argumentation as a democratic decision-making process demands answerers. Without answerers, demagogues thrive and dumb ideas become law. On many occasions in your life, you simply must discover the courage of your convictions, the fortitude to stand up publicly, in front of friend and foe, and resolutely say "No!" Part of that courage will come from some soul-searching, a review of your own priorities and values in life. And, we hope, part of it will come from an understanding of techniques you can employ in verbally accentuating the negative.

In this chapter, therefore, we will complete our examination of argumentation as a communication process or exchange. We will look at the other half, the answer.

THE OCCASION AND THE AUDIENCE: WHAT, WHO, WHEN, WHY

A refutative speech is one in which a speaker either answers an argumentative speech or rebuilds his or her own case in response to attacks upon it by others. More technically, refutation includes three sorts of verbal-intellectual activities. *Counter-argument* is an answer to someone else's argument. *Rebuttal* is an answer to counter-arguments laid against you. *Reestablishment* goes one step farther, not only rebutting counter-arguments but also rebuilding the arguments you offered in the first place. Argumentation, therefore, is a continual process of offering arguments, countering them, rebutting the counter-arguments, and reestablishing positions in light of attacks. Figure 11.1 pictures the argumentation process.

Suppose that at an office meeting you propose that your division institute a "management-by-objectives" system of employee evaluation. In a management-by-objectives system, each employee semiannually sets a series of objectives to be met over the next six months. At the end of the period, those objectives are reviewed by supervisors in consultation with the employee, to see which objectives have been met and which have not. On the basis of the meeting, new objectives are set and monetary as well as other rewards are dispensed. You *argue* that this system ought to be instituted because it will increase office productivity; because it will involve each employee in decisions about his or her future; and because it will make company expectations more concrete. Someone rises with the *counter-arguments* that management-by-objectives procedures really are mere busywork involving a lot of extra paper and time; that supervisors aren't really interested in having underlings participate; and that job frustration rather than job satisfaction is the more likely result. You then return to the floor, *rebutting* those counter-arguments with the results of studies at other companies very much like your own (reasoning from parallel case): these studies indicate that the paper load is not drastically increased; that supervisors like the idea of being able to pin down precise expectations on paper; and that employees' satisfaction must be increased because job turnover rates usually go down (reasoning from sign). You furthermore *reestablish* your original arguments by reporting on the results of interviews with selected employees in your own company, almost all of whom think the system would be a good one. The process of argument/counter-argument/rebuttal and reestablishment could go on until everyone in the room felt ready to vote.

As the foregoing example indicates, we must dispel forever the idea that only nasty, cantankerous nitpickers engage in refutation. Sure, in a sense you are attacking another person when you are refuting, but of course that is not (or at least should not be) the principal justification for a verbal assault. Essentially you are attacking ideas, not people. Constructive answerers are absolutely necessary for reaching the democratic ideal of tested ideas. If we are to weed out illogic, insufficient evidence, prejudices, and infeasible plans of action, we must have ready refuters in our society. It is for that reason that the United States Senate refuses most of the time to vote for "closure"—the attempt to stop debate ("filibusters")—even when a majority thinks a particular bill is a good one. Our government is committed to a process of full testing and airing of ideas, even if it seems time-consuming upon occasion. The ancient British notion of a "loyal opposition" is rooted in a vision of refuters who support the goal of rational decision making and are committed to using any means available for making their dissatisfactions public.

Obviously, then, refutation is called for any time you think you have

FIGURE 11.1   **The Process of Argumentation**

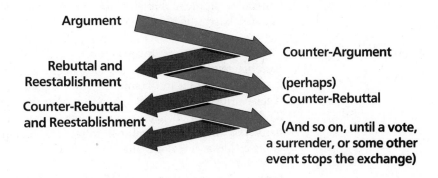

good reasons for *objecting* or good reasons for *maintaining* a position you advanced even after it has been attacked. Even though refutative speeches occasionally degenerate into personalized attacks, you must never forget the general commitment to rationality which must characterize solid argumentation. It often is easier to walk out of a school board meeting than it is to object to one of its policies. It often is tempting to shout obscenities at a politician who advances a seemingly stupid platform. You are encouraged to refute on all of these occasions—any time an arguer has exhibited illogic, insufficient evidence, the "wrong" value, or unexamined plans. It may sometimes seem a bit scary to stand up for your communicative rights, but you are unfair to yourself and to your audience if you do not.

Let us now examine some of the techniques refuters can employ in various situations. These are the building blocks. Because refutation is a complex process, we cannot offer all the techniques that are available to you. You are encouraged to follow up your reading here by examining some additional works.[1] But we can generally arm you with some common refutative weapons.

RAW MATERIALS FOR COUNTER-ARGUMENT

There are two basic approaches you can take in presenting a counter-argument. One approach, of course, is to attack the original argument. A second approach is to build a completely different case. By offering a different and better argument, you are in effect eliminating the other person's argument and replacing it with your own. So, for example, if somebody argues that your city ought to improve its mass transit system by constructing a monorail system, you could counter-argue by proposing instead an expansion of the bus system. Because this sort of counter-arguing is actually building an original argument, it proceeds as any argumentative speech and we need not treat it separately here. Rather, let us concentrate on refutative counter-arguments which are based on attacking an opposing argument. There are three basic elements which you can examine and attack in an opposing argument: *ideas*, *reasoning*, and *language*.

Attacks on Ideas

One mode of attack involves examining the opposing argument for *material fallacies*—faults in the ideas or material used in the argument. Essentially this means examining the strength of the evidence used to reach various conclusions and claims. While there are many different kinds of material fallacies, some are used often enough to be singled out here. Test an opposing argument to see if it contains any of the following faults in ideas. If it does, attack it.

Hasty Generalization ("Inductive Leap") A *hasty generalization* is a generalization made on the basis of too little evidence. Has the opposing arguer really examined enough typical cases to make the claim? Urging the closing of a hospital because two people have successfully brought malpractice suits against it is probably making a hasty generalization.

False Division A *false division* is an attempt to argue that some process or idea can be subdivided in only one particular way, when in fact there are alternative ways to subdivide or there are additional processes and ideas that are ignored in the proposed division. When someone argues that there are only three ways to rejuvenate your community's uptown district, be on the lookout. *Only* is a signal of a possible false division; there well might be other plans which could be considered.

Genetic Fallacy Many people argue for an idea by citing its origins. They may suggest that it is "rooted in sacred traditions" and trace its ancestry back to respected sources. Many people who defended the idea of slavery in the nineteenth century talked about the Founding Fathers and the seemingly racist ideas in the Bible; they argued that because the idea of slavery was in venerated books and events, it therefore must be good. This fallacy in effect suggests that an idea must be true because it's been around in respected places for such a long time. But times change; new values rise to replace old ones. Be ready to point out that knowing the origins of an idea in no way validates (or invalidates) it.

Faulty Evidence Check an arguer's testimony, statistics, causes, and analogies. Is the testimony from a credible, disinterested source or from a person able to actually witness the event in question? And how about statistics: are they up-to-date? Was a survey or experiment done under controlled conditions? (See the example of salting studies in Chapter 10.) Has a false cause been identified? Can the analogy or parallel case really stand up under close examination? Test all aspects of someone else's evidence that you can. Don't be afraid to call for the credentials of an expert, to check out the statistics with those of other experts, to demand that other possible causes be considered, and so on.

Irrelevant Values Check that the values applied in an argument are actually relevant to the situation. This is tricky territory, but one you must enter. It certainly would be economically advantageous for a government to eliminate its welfare programs and to reduce taxes accordingly; but is economic benefit the most important value to consider in this situation? Or are questions of social duty and humanitarianism more relevant? Questions of the relevance of values are hard to answer; yet counter-arguers very often must ask them, to help an audience make a carefully considered decision.

Attacks on Reasoning A second mode of attack is to search an opposing argument for *logical fallacies*—faults in reasoning. We have suggested that consistency is a crucial feature of a person's argument. While thinking through an arguer's proposals, you must constantly ask consistency questions: is the person's evidence consistent with my own experience? consistent with other sources I have heard or read? consistent with evidence in other sections of the speech? Besides inconsistency, the counter-arguer ought to be ready to attack other faults in reasoning as well.

Appeal to Ignorance (*Argumentum ad Ignoratiam*) People often argue with "double negatives" ("You *can't* prove that it *won't* work"). Or they may attack an idea because of gaps in human knowledge ("We can't write laws about euthanasia because we don't know enough about death"). Both of these strategies are appeals to ignorance. Now, of course we usually cannot prove something won't work; but we can counter that argument by pointing to other things which we do know have worked before (parallel case) or by answering one appeal to ignorance with another. Thus if someone argues we can't prove it won't work, we can respond by saying they can't prove it will either. And, in the second example, of course we don't know what medical discoveries will be made in the future, discoveries which might force us to change our medical definition of death. You can counter-argue that if we never acted until we had complete knowledge, we'd never act—and that would be worse. In other words, the second sort of appeal to ignorance (the appeal to gaps in human knowledge) can be answered by appeals to adventure, curiosity, progress, or necessity.

Appeal to Popular Opinion (*Argumentum ad Populum*) Many an argument begins, "Everyone knows. . . ." To see the fallacy in such arguments, just complete that statement with a few which were sustained for centuries: "Everyone knows the earth is flat." "Everyone knows that Blacks are inferior to Whites." "Everyone knows the earth is the center of the universe." Now, there is nothing wrong with systematically assessing public opinion, especially on valuative preferences and priorities; but questions of fact, particularly, are ill-founded on appeals to public opinion. Go after them.

Sequential Fallacy *(Post Hoc, Ergo Propter Hoc)* Literally translated "after this, therefore because of this," the sequential fallacy is one to look for in cause-effect arguments. The sequential fallacy is the assumption that because one event occurred after another, the first must have caused the second. There are no grounds for automatically asserting this cause-effect relationship. So, when the man reached 100 years, a local newspaper asked him to what he attributed his longevity. "I drink a pint of whiskey every morning," he replied. Ah, but many teetotalers reach the century mark, and a good many whiskey sippers die young. Carefully test causal assertions for this sequential fallacy.

Begging the Question *(Petitio Principii)* Begging the question is simply rephrasing an idea and offering that as its own reason. If someone argues, "Marijuana smoking is immoral because it just isn't right," that person has begged the question—simply rephrasing the claim (it is immoral) to form a reason (it just isn't right). "Immoral" and "just isn't right," in this case, are synonymous; and hence one phrase cannot be used as proof for the other. This kind of reasoning also can be called "reasoning in a circle." So, you're in an argument with someone who says that Shakespearean drama is the best kind, and offers as evidence that "the best critics think it is." "Who," you ask, "are the best critics?" The answer which comes back is, in effect, those who prefer Shakespearean drama! Be on your guard for such circular reasoning.

Either-Or (Two-Valued) Logic We often hear, "either it is or it isn't," "either it's good or it's bad," "either you're with us or against us." All of these statements are examples of two-valued logic or *either-or* reasoning. Now, there are contexts in which *either-or* thinking applies; you can say, "Either that's a dog or it isn't." A so-called "A or non-A" ("dog" or "non-dog") argument is perfectly acceptable. But, an "A or non-A" argument is quite different from an "A or B" argument: "Either you're for Proposition 13 (A) or you're against us (B)." "Either we must fight (A) or surrender (B)." *Either-or* thinking often ignores compromises, additional alternatives (good ol' C), or even combinations of both A and B ("I like some features of Proposal A and some of Proposal B"). Counter-arguers often have to break down *either-or* thinking by looking for compromises and alternatives. Many a group member will thank them for that service.

Technical Invalidity Finally, in a logical sense, some arguments are just plain *invalid* or illogical. Technically, invalid arguments are based on faulty inferences; thus their conclusions do not necessarily follow from the evidence. An example of an invalid argument is this one: "Professors influence our kids; and communists attempt to influence them, too. Therefore, all professors are communist." That's fallacious, as you can plainly see if you translate it into common objects (All dogs are animals; all cats are animals; and therefore all dogs are cats). Another invalid argument, termed *affirming the consequent*, looks like this: "If Joe comes, I'm going to the movie. I went to the movie, so therefore Joe must have come." For that argument to be valid, we would have to prove the "antecedent" (If Joe comes), and not the "consequent" (I went to the movie); because I of course could have gone to the movie with someone else. The reverse of this is called *denying the antecedent*. A person might try to say, "Well, Joe didn't come (the denial), so you didn't go." Of course you could have decided to go, anyway, so Joe's nonappearance doesn't "prove" anything. The study of formal logic considers many other examples of logical invalidity. (You can check them out in a good introductory logic book.)

Attacks on Language A final mode of counter-argument is to attack *linguistic fallacies*—faulty use of words. Because word meanings are so slippery, people often use them either sloppily or manipulatively. One of the refuter's jobs is to listen for distorting language. Be especially watchful for the following common misuses of language.

Ambiguity *Ambiguity* is the fallacy of using one word with two or more meanings in the same context. Suppose you heard the following argument: "The end of a thing is its perfection; death is the end of life; therefore, death is the perfection of life." Either something truly profound has been uttered, or else there is a mistake. Probably a mistake, which is this: the word *end* has been used ambiguously, with more than one meaning. In the first statement, *end* means "goal"; but in the second, *end* means "final state."

Nonqualification It is all too easy for people to drop out some important qualifications as an argument progresses. *Maybes, mights,* and *probablys* tend to fall by the wayside. An expert may have said, "Perhaps this is the best answer," or "Plan A would work if Committees X, Y, and Z get behind it." Advocates using that testimony might be tempted to forget about the *perhaps* and the *if* clause. Watch for arguers who delete those little but important qualifying words.

Is-Faults The word *is* is one of the snakiest verbs in English, because it can mean so many different things: "John is a man" and "John is a radical" are grammatically equivalent sentences; but in the first case we are identifying an eternal characteristic of John, and in the second, specifying a changeable attribute of his personality. Be on the lookout for cases in which a speaker is confusing a temporary condition or state of a person or thing with one of its defining characteristics.

Persuasive Definition In the heat of a dispute, many an advocate attempts to win by persuading you to accept his or her own definition of an idea. The two important signals of a persuasive definition are "true" and "really." " 'True' liberty consists of freedom from governmental regulation." "A university education is 'really' a matter of learning a job skill." In both cases, the arguer is attempting to persuade you to accept his or her own definition; for if that can be done, then you probably will have to accept that person's values and courses of action.[2] Keep your ears open.

Name-Calling *Name-calling* is a general label for several kinds of attacks on people, instead of on their arguments. Three name-calling techniques, in particular, are extremely popular. *Argumentum ad hominem* is an attack on the special interests of a person: "You can't offer a fair analysis of the 'right to work' question because you are a union member." *Argumentum ad personam* is an attack upon some personal characteristic of someone: "You are a sniveling liar [or an Irishman or a male]." Even liars, Irishmen, and males occasionally offer solid arguments! *Ideological appeals* give some idea or person a political-valuative label: "The Kaiser medical plan is really communistic socialized medicine and is thus un-American." This appeal attaches a value label to an idea rather than examining its merits and operational faults. Now, of course, it may very well be that someone's membership in a particular organization or their habitual propensity to lie will affect their arguing; yet arguments must be analyzed and destroyed on their own features, not on the personalities and ideologies of the arguer. If you are attacked by this sort of opponent, be ready to point out that name-calling cannot substitute for solid analysis of ideas.

Attacks on ideas, reasoning, and language, therefore, represent the principal weapons of the counter-arguer, together with "constructive" appeals (building a case of one's own). Counter-arguers who can destroy the position of an opponent or present good reasons why a different policy (even the present one) ought to be pursued are in a good position to win.

RAW MATERIALS FOR REBUTTAL

When the original arguer is forced to respond to counter-arguments of the types we have identified, the original arguer can in turn use any of the counter-arguing techniques. Rebutters, like counter-arguers, must be on guard for faulty ideas, faulty reasoning, and faulty use of language. In addition, however, there are other effective techniques for answering attacks in a rebuttal. These, in general, are techniques which attempt to condemn an attacker on his or her own grounds. You often can take the counter-arguer's own words or evidence to regain the upper hand. Five such techniques, particularly, have been proven effective in rebuttal.

FIGURE 11.2   **Refutative Strategies**

Counter-Argumentative Strategies

Attacks on Ideas
Hasty Generalization ("Inductive Leap")
False Division
Genetic Fallacy
Faulty Evidence
Irrelevant Values

Attacks on Reasoning
Appeal to Ignorance
Appeal to Popular Opinion
Sequential Fallacy
Begging the Question
Either-Or (Two-Valued) Logic
Invalidity
    (affirming the consequent)
    (denying the antecedent)

Attacks on Language
Ambiguity
Nonqualification
Is-Faults
Persuasive Definition
Name-Calling
    (argumentum ad hominem)
    (argumentum ad personam)
    (ideological appeals)

Rebuttal Strategies
Reductio ad Absurdum
    Extension
    Analogy
Dilemma
Residues
Turning the Tables
Even-If Responses

Reestablishment Strategies
Restatement
Rebuilding

Reductio ad Absurdum   A technique that often gains you a lot of points with an audience is that of extending someone's argument to its "logical" conclusion—pushing the person's analysis farther in the direction it's already heading, to the point of absurdity. Suppose, for example, that you are arguing to rid your school of heinous required courses. Someone then counters your proposal by saying, "No one should be free until they are fit to use freedom wisely, and that includes students." You could reduce that argument to absurdity in two ways. *Extension* simply pushes the opponent's idea to an extreme: "Therefore, are you saying that since students are not fit to make academic decisions, we should make all of their choices for them, including those in the areas of electives and majors?" *Analogy* (comparing the situation under discussion with another) can be useful if you can show that your opponent's logic does not apply in other situations and therefore does not apply here: "Saying people should not have freedom until they are fit is like saying a person shouldn't go into the water until they can swim. Human beings acquire skills—and wisdom —only through practice." Be careful only that you don't come off as an overly smug or nasty person when rebutting in this way.

Dilemma

The same sort of advice applies when you attempt to put an opponent in a dilemma—a situation in which the person is "damned if he does, and damned if he doesn't." A dilemma offers someone two undesirable choices: "If we join our forces with those of a political party, then we will lose our power and identity; if we don't join them, then we will be ineffective; therefore, either way, we're in trouble." By posing that dilemma, you in effect eliminate the usefulness of discussing relationships between your action organization and political parties—unless your opponent can figure out a way to destroy the dilemma.

Residues

If your counter-arguer has said that there are many other plans for solving a particular problem besides the one you have proposed, you probably can use the *method of residues* (or *elimination*) to rebut the assertion. If you are urging that your city expand its bus service, you might say: "Let's look at the alternatives to increased bus service. Building a monorail system is horribly expensive; increasing the number of parking lots encourages the waste of fossil fuels and will scar our uptown district even more; and subsidized taxi service puts government squarely into a position of interfering with free enterprise. Therefore, an expanded bus service is the only answer [i.e., the "residue"]. You have eliminated all other alternatives, leaving your own idea as the only remaining possibility. This method of residues can be extremely effective in supporting your original position, as long as you're not open to the charge of false division (see above).

Turning the Tables

This technique takes an opponent's argument, testimony, or valuative appeal, and uses that material to answer the argument. While turning the tables cannot be used every day, it can be devastating, as you "hoist him on his own petard." If an opponent quotes economist X as saying in 1980 that increases in salaries for government employees are inflationary, you could respond by noting that this same economist three years earlier had called for increased salaries as a way of keeping the country out of a recession. (You can almost always find areas where economists have changed their minds!) If someone says that the federal Department of Energy has only increased governmental bureaucracy, you might respond by noting that it actually reduced the number of energy bureaus from sixty-plus to one. If an opponent argues that legalizing abortions is inhumane, you might say: "Talk about inhumanity! What is more inhumane than back alley quacks and quick-and-dirty foreign abortion mills?" In this last instance you would be using the opponent's own value appeal and turning it back on his or her position. The effect of such about-faces can be startling.

Even If Responses

You often can use an *even if* response in cases where you can admit an opponent has made a good point (make a concession), but yet can assert that your overall argument still stands. If someone argues against your proposal for new degree requirements by saying that confusion would result, you could respond: "Sure, for a few people the changes will be disconcerting and confusing; but in the long run they will function smoothly, as I've pointed out." In this way, you minimize the importance of the attack, gently concede it, but then proceed to overcome it. You can also rebut some attacks by accepting their validity but pointing out that the good still outweighs the bad. If you are defending modular scheduling in elementary schools, and someone points out that a lot of kids will be lost in the shuffle, you could respond: "Sure, modular scheduling is not a cure-all; and of course there are some kids who function better in regimented classes. Nevertheless, as the studies I quoted have demonstrated, the vast majority of elementary students progress much faster socially and intellectually when they are grouped according to development and ability." The statement, "even if that's true," allows you to show your magnanimity, yet hold your position.

Therefore, in rebutting your counter-arguers, you can respond both with counter-attacks and with techniques that turn opponents' ideas back upon their own heads. Your goal is to rationally demonstrate to your auditors the weaknesses of the other side. Rebuttal calls on your strengths in *negative* argument—your ability to undercut opposing analyses.

RAW MATERIALS FOR REESTABLISHMENT

Psychologically, however, rebuttal probably is not enough. No one wants an advocate to present only negative arguments. Thus you need to balance your *negative* arguments in rebuttal with *positive* arguments in reestablishment. Your original analysis will be greatly strengthened if you can bolster your frontline definitions, evidence, value appeals, and arguments for the feasibility and practicality of your plans. Reestablishment normally uses two techniques: restatement and rebuilding.

Restatement

Sometimes it is enough to remind your audience of what you said or "proved" in your original argument. Especially if several people have spoken since your initial effort, it is good to summarize what you developed earlier. So, you might say, *"First,* I said that . . . , and, in support of that contention, I reviewed. . . . *Then,* I noted that . . . , and quoted X, who said. . . . My *third* reason for proposing . . . was that. . . . And *finally,* I pointed out that my proposal would work because. . . ." If you have in hand a solid outline of your first speech, you'll be able to handle restatement with ease.

Rebuilding

Rebuilding involves bringing in additional evidence, ideas, or authorities to add further support for your original claim. Suppose, for example, you've advocated that your chapter of the League of Women Voters should open a new research project on controlling local gravel pits; and suppose that proposal has been attacked by someone who's said that such control will destroy an important local industry. In your original argument, you might have discussed air pollution, road damage, the destruction of farmland, and zoning problems. Now in your second stand, you might bring in additional evidence, such as studies you didn't mention the first time. You may even present additional arguments, perhaps pointing out that other communities which have tightened pollution and zoning controls have not lost gravel companies. On the contrary, because those companies now better understand what is expected of them, there are better relationships between town and companies in those areas. Such examples of new evidence and arguments rebuilds—and strengthens—your case. To do this, of course, means that the first time around you will have to save some evidence and ideas for later. If you have thoroughly researched your topic and then selected materials for your speech from that research, you probably will have additional support just lying around unused. You'll be surprised how often you'll be able to take material you originally cut and put it to good use later on in a dispute.

Overall, then, the process of reestablishing your position allows you to end on a positive note, one which urges anew that an audience take you seriously and constructively. You'll be able to add further rational and psychological strength to your claim, to increase your credibility with the audience, and to block one final time the opposition's arguments.

**ORGANIZING
REFUTATIVE
SPEECHES**

Counter-arguing, rebutting, and reestablishing—these are the three sub-processes which comprise a full unit of refutation. We have surveyed a number of specific techniques. It will take considerable practice for you to become proficient at employing them in particular situations. But, you can do it if you remember to think in terms of *units,* of "packaged" argumentative structures. Any unit of refutation, whether you are counter-ing, rebutting, or reestablishing, is built around a four-step structure:

- *Step* 1. Cite the idea, piece of evidence, logical inference, or whatever, that you find faulty.
- *Step* 2. State your objection to it.
- *Step* 3. Recite the evidence, reasoning, valuative appeal, or plan which supports your objection (or reestablishes your original position).
- *Step* 4. Return to your introductory point, indicating the "damage" you have done to your opponent's case (or the bolstering you have provided for your original analysis).

With this unit of refutation in mind, let us turn to two brief sample outlines. The first one is a counter-argument; it uses the unitary approach to speech structure only loosely, but it does illustrate several of the counter-argumentative techniques we discussed earlier. The second is built completely on the *unit-of-refutation* approach.

SAMPLE SPEECH: COUNTER-ARGUING

Pre-Speech Analysis

Subject: Raising the drinking age in a state which reduced it to eighteen a few years ago

Claims to be countered: Raising the drinking age would prevent further teenage drinking increases and accidents, and would return control of children back to where it belongs, the parents and the schools.

Strategies:
1. Constructively, the speaker uses an argument from parallel case—reasoning from consistency—to attack the legal foundation of this change in law.
2. The speaker attacks the evidence of the proposer by isolating a sequential fallacy, thereby destroying the cause-effect reasoning in the proposal.
3. The speaker attacks the proposer's "everybody knows" orientation (appeal to popular opinion) by pointing out a false cause and a more appropriate analogy.

Outline

On Maintaining the Legal Drinking Age at Eighteen

Body

Constructive argument

Reasoning from parallel case

I. Raising the legal drinking age in this state would produce legal inequities and inconsistencies.
   A. Eighteen-year-olds in this state have the right to vote and to seek public office, to serve on a jury, to get married without parental consent, to own property, and to sign contracts.
   B. Furthermore, they have acquired a series of responsibilities along with those rights.
      1. They are bound by the contracts they've made.
      2. They are legally accountable for their own actions, accepting the credit and the blame, the good consequences and the bad.

Points out inconsistent reasoning

Destructive attack on opponents' cause-effect reasoning

"Even if" response concedes one point in the argument, but presents reasons why that idea doesn't apply

Identifies the sequential fallacy

Destructive attack on the appeal to popular opinion

"Even if"

Points out a false analogy in the opponents' argument

Offers a "better" analogy

C. This proposal, therefore, would produce legal inequities and inconsistencies. It would be out of step with the other rights and responsibilities we grant to and demand of eighteen-year-olds.

II. Now, in supporting this measure, the advocates point out that in states which instigated an eighteen-year-old drinking law, incidents of drinking among teenagers increased and so did their auto accidents.

A. I will grant that happened, but:
1. The amount of teenage drinking also has increased in states which did not lower the legal drinking age.
2. Furthermore, teenage drinking did not go down in those states which had lowered the drinking age to eighteen and then raised it again.

B. Therefore, we must conclude that the actual legal age for alcohol consumption is unrelated to these social problems; the proposers of this law have given us a "false cause" for this problem.

III. Finally, I must question that "everyone knows" parents and teachers want the drinking age increased.

A. First, the advocates have offered us no evidence that parents and teachers back this proposal.

B. Second, even if they did find some who want it raised, they are forgetting about the challenge of sneaking booze and about the friends who already are old enough to buy liquor.

C. And finally, they urge, rather fancifully, that we should raise the drinking age because to spare the legal rod is to spoil the child.
1. As you might guess, I think that's a false analogy. There's no real tie between legal questions and questions of parental authority.
   a. Parental authority should be exercised no matter what the age.
   b. And it is not the right of the state to take the place of the parent.
2. We might better look to a "real" analogy, one directly related to the consumption of alcohol.
   a. This country experimented with legal constrictions on alcohol during Prohibition.
   b. Such prohibition simply did not work, as we discovered that alcohol consumption really is a social problem, not a legal problem.
3. We therefore would do ourselves and our young adults a better service by channeling our tax dollars into alcohol education programs and rehabilitation programs.

Note that in the preceding outline, the speaker took pains first to offer some constructive ideas of his own. Only then did the speaker engage in direct counter-argument, first by attacking the evidence for the "need" to change the law, and second by attacking the feasibility of the plan. A relatively complete counter-argument was the result.

SAMPLE SPEECH:	**REBUTTING**

Pre-Speech Analysis

Subject:	A new law on food labeling*
Situation:	The speaker has proposed that the current laws on food labeling have to be strengthened, and an opponent has said we already have such laws. It is the first speaker's turn to respond.
Strategies:	The speaker wishes to offer a full, effective unit of rebuttal. The speaker will (a) clarify the point of the disagreement, (b) bolster the evidence, and (c) point out to the audience the significance of the reply. This unit of rebuttal will proceed in the four steps we noted earlier.

Outline	**The Cover-Up**
	Body
Claim to be rebutted	I. My opponent has said that we do not need stricter food labeling because we already have such laws on the books.

Objections	II. I do not agree with her for two reasons:
	  A. First, many standardized foods are not subject to current laws.
	  B. And second, many current labeling requirements cannot be understood by most consumers.

Evidence for the first objection	III. The FDA has identified several cases in which its nutritional labeling requirements need not be met.
	  A. Some 350 products, classified as "standardized foods," are not subject to ingredient labeling laws.
	    1. Their basic ingredients are listed in the Code of Federal Regulations only, so you would have to engage in intensive library research to discover those ingredients.
	    2. And unfortunately, some optional ingredients—for example, thickening agents and caffeine—may be added by manufacturers and yet not be listed in the Code.
	  B. Second, the FDA does not require labeling where "knowledge of the nutrient content of . . . foods and the natural variation of this content is poor."
	    1. Because this regulation allows food composition to be described generically, it is difficult to distinguish between brands and formulas.
	    2. And even worse, because the law does not require standardized serving

* Material for this outline comes in part from Report by the Comptroller General to the Congress of the United States. *What Foods Should Americans Eat? Better Information Needed on Nutritional Quality of Foods,* Government Publication AD–AO83 909/2 80–17 3295 PC AO6/MF AO1, 30 April 1980. [GAO–CED–80–68]

sizes, even if you get general nutrient information you cannot really compare the contents of many foods which meet the "natural variation" criterion in the Code.

    3. And finally, this general provision of the Code exempts data on fiber and some other nutrients important for a proper diet.

Evidence for the second objection

IV. While nutritionists may understand the significance of the lists of vitamins and minerals and grams of protein, carbohydrates, and fat, nutritional labeling on the whole does little to help the average consumer with specific dietary problems or concerns.

  A. The consumer interested in reducing sugar intake may not understand the labels.

    1. Currently, Kellogg's Apple Jacks lists sugar as "16 grams per ounce" instead of "57 percent sugar."

    2. Sugar added by manufacturers is often included with starch, fiber, and naturally occurring sugars as "grams of carbohydrates per serving."

    3. Sugar may be included in the list of ingredients under technical names including "fructose," "dextrose," "lactose," "maltose," or "sucrose."

  B. Another example is the amount of salt in products. Because the government does not require that sodium or sodium concentration be listed on the label, buying for restricted-salt diets proves difficult.

    1. Since a salt-restricted diet calls for approximately 6 grams of salt daily, wouldn't it be nice to know that 2 ounces of Kraft American cheese contains 2.1 grams of salt, Campbell's soups about 2.6 grams per serving, and a dill pickle about 5 grams of salt?

    2. Some of these, I suppose, are obviously high in salt, but others are not.

  C. As a third case, for consumers concerned about saturated fats, the labels once again are inadequate.

    1. Saturated fat usually is listed with other fats under "grams of fat per serving."

    2. In addition, the use of grams may be confusing because such listing obscures the fact that hot dogs, for example, may contain up to 30 percent fat.

Significance of the rebuttal

V. Therefore, until opponents of this measure can show me that the current "truth in advertising" or "public disclosure" laws are sufficient—until they can show me cases where manufacturers have been forced to label the ingredients in standardized foods and to translate all lists of ingredients into ordinary and well-understood categories of information—I think my claim stands.

Then, the arguer probably would go on to further bolster the original case with instances of more products, or perhaps with exemplar laws from other states which have been beneficial.

TIPS FOR REFUTING

We now are in a position to complete most of the general advice arguers and refuters should consider when engaging in the complete process of argumentation as a method for public decision making.

■ *Use a flow chart.* As you know from experience, arguing can become a complicated process, as one speaker after another stands to add considerations to the dispute. You often will find it most useful, therefore, to keep track of arguers, arguments, evidence, plans, attacks, and dumb ideas. If you write your own arguments on a sheet of paper, you can note beside each one what has been said by whom. In that way, later on, you can tell which of your ideas have been attacked and which have not. You will be in a better position to counter-argue, rebut, and reestablish.

■ *Don't offer too many different lines of argument.* Some advocates revel in the shotgun approach to public disputes, blasting away at their opponents with torrents of questions: "Who says so? How do you know? Prove to me it will work. I challenge you to prove that. Aren't we moving too fast? Are we moving fast enough?" And on through ten or fifteen questions. While such a tactic, initially, may seem like a good way to smother an opponent, it often backfires. It is easy for a counter-arguer to say, "Well, gee, I've been asked a dozen questions, and I certainly don't want to bore this audience by responding to them all. So let me, in the next couple of minutes, answer only the three most serious ones." With that response, the shotgunner is dead, for the other person has been given an opportunity to look reasonable and to pick the points of response! Certainly that person will choose to respond to the easiest questions— leaving your strongest points unanswered. A better strategy is to concentrate your attacks; you always can raise additional points later.

■ *Carefully package and group arguments.* Group your arguments, putting your *constructive* arguments in one portion, your *destructive* arguments in another. Group your arguments from cause, from parallel cases, and so on, in one area, and place your attempts to destroy the feasibility of a plan in another. Or you might arrange arguments around definitions, facts, values, or plans. By giving your audience the arguments in prepackaged groups, you make the speech easier to follow and you strengthen your arguments.

■ *Don't overrefute.* This may seem like dumb advice, but consider the possibility of backlash. If you beat an opponent hollow with your words, two sorts of backlashes can set in. You might engender sympathy for your opponent as an underdog, in which case the audience might react positively to his or her appeals to pity and forlornness. Or by engaging in refutative overkill, you might actually make that person's argument seem more viable than it is, causing an audience to think, "Gee, if it takes that many words to jump on that idea, it must be pretty good." In either case, overrefuting can hurt you. As nearly as you can judge, give each idea in your opponent's case neither no more nor no less time than it's worth.

■ *Get in a summary speech whenever time allows for it.* Because arguments can drag on through near-interminable twists and turns, it is advantageous before a vote or final decision to get in one last lick—a summary from your point of view. A summary speech is sometimes hard to do; for in it, you must appear *dis*passionate and "above the fray." If you can systematically review the progress of the argument—the definitions, facts, values, and policy-claims—you will be doing the audience a service. More important, such a review gives you the opportunity to indicate (a) where your side's points still stand, and (b) what's left after all the shouting and scrambling. As you balance your side against theirs, you're in a position to indicate why the scale swings in your direction.

■ *Be gracious in both victory and defeat.* Fits, tantrums, and bloodied opponents have a way of coming back to haunt the victor who crows or the vanquished who cries. You may wish to rise to argue another day, with new opponents and new allies, on new (or recurrent) problems requiring reasoned inquiry. Keep your options open by treating others fairly. And in that way, too, argumentation as a rational decision-making process is kept sacrosanct and protected.

NOTES

[1]   While there are several logic and argumentation books you can examine, we have found the following useful in expanding the treatment of argumentation/refutation offered here and in clearly dealing with notions of strategy. One of the finest (and most readable) logic textbooks available is Irving M. Copi, *Introduction to Logic*, 5th ed. (New York: Macmillan Publishing Co., Inc., 1978), especially Chap. 2 and 3 on language and "informal fallacies." For those wanting a more clever (and maddeningly "strategic") approach to logic, see Nicholas Capaldi, *The Art of Deception* (Buffalo, N.Y.: Prometheus Books, 1971). Among the many books on argumentation and debate, three can especially be recommended for their discussions of refutation: James H. McBurney and Glen E. Mills, *Argumentation and Debate: Techniques of a Free Society*, 2nd ed. (New York: The Macmillan Company, 1964), Chap. 16, "Fallacies and Stratagems," and Chap. 17, "Refutation and Rebuttal"; Richard D. Rieke and Malcolm O. Sillars, *Argumentation and the Decision Making Process* (New York: John Wiley & Sons, Inc., 1975), Chap. 9, "Refutation"; and Douglas Ehninger and Wayne Brockreide, *Decision by Debate*, 2nd ed. (New York: Harper & Row, Publishers, 1978), Chap. 7, "Criticizing Units of Proof," and Chap. 13, "Carrying on the Debate."

[2]   For a fuller discussion of "persuasive definitions," see Charles L. Stevenson, *Ethics and Language* (New Haven: Yale University Press, 1944), Chap. 9, "Second Pattern of Analysis: Persuasive Definitions."

ASSIGNMENTS

Pre-Performance

1. Locate a debate in the letters-to-the-editor section of your daily newspaper by reading that section for a week or two. Look for a letter which sparked a counter-letter which, in turn, called for a rebuttal. Which author does the best job of debating? Why?

2. Locate a piece of evidence to support each of the following statements. Then engage in a class discussion to determine which of the suggested pieces of evidence would best substantiate each statement.

    a. Rapid transit systems can contribute to lower energy consumption.

    b. Business lobbying poses a threat to the consumer interest.

    c. Food additives may be hazardous to your health.

    d. National park recreation facilities are overcrowded.

    e. The movement of women into male-dominated occupations has tended to be very slow.

3. Collect information put out by proponents and opponents engaged in debate of a controversial topic. For instance, examine literature relating to concerns such as gun control, passage of the Family Rights Amendment, or saving the ocean's whale population. Prepare a written report in which you identify the basic arguments. Then survey the types of supporting material used by each side. Note similarities and differences in the use of supporting material.

4. Start a fallacy collection. During the next couple of weeks locate ten fallacies. State each fallacy as it was originally presented, and then explain why it is a fallacy. Although it may be tempting to record ten fallacies from the letters-to-the-editor section of your newspaper, make sure that at least half of these examples come from other sources—advertisements, editorials, radio or television commentaries, and the like.

Performance
1. Develop a two- to four-minute speech in which you support a single issue with carefully chosen evidence. Just before your presentation the instructor will ask a member of the class to refute your speech. That person will present a two- or three-minute speech of counter-argument.

2. Plan to debate using the Lincoln-Douglas format, a type of two-person debate named for these two famous debaters. One debater advocates a claim, and the other opposes it. The advocate speaks for four minutes; the opponent, for six; and then the advocate closes with a two-minute statement. Class members should practice making flow charts of the arguments. (See "Tips for Refuting.") Your instructor may wish to rotate who is making flow charts rather than have the entire audience taking notes at any one time.

3. You and another class member should choose a policy-claim and prepare to debate according to the following format: each speaker talks twice in alternation, four minutes in a constructive speech, two minutes in rebuttal. This, too, provides an excellent opportunity for the class to practice making flow charts of arguments. Your instructor may request that members of the class fill out a shift-of-opinion ballot, to indicate their attitudes (whether in favor, neutral, or opposed to the topic) both before and after the debate. [For a sample shift-of-opinion ballot see Linda Moore, *An Instructor's Guide to Using Principles and Types of Speech Communication, 9th Edition* (Glenview, Il.: Scott, Foresman and Company, 1982), p. 79.]

Post-Performance   1. Analyze one of the debates for which you made a flow chart. How accurate were you in keeping track of arguments, evidence, plans, etc.? If you were not always able to keep track of arguments, was this essentially your problem in being able to quickly record data? Or should speakers have inserted more signposts or presented better organized speeches? Did you find yourself in agreement with the way refuters packaged arguments?

2. Recall an issue, presented in one of the classroom performances, that you did not believe. Write a brief explanation in your journal about why the issue, as supported, was not credible.

3. In listening to a classroom debate, did you find a material, logical, or linguistic fallacy which the person refuting did not spot? Record any such fallacies in your journal, and explain the nature of those fallacies.

CELEBRATING

PREVIEW FOUR

Ritual, Ceremony, and Public Communication

Human beings are social animals. They have survived by some rather specialized aptitudes, particularly the ability to organize into small groups and large collectivities for mutual protection and support. Indeed, groups and social institutions are so important to us that, in most ways, we define our "selves" in "social" terms.

When asked, "Who are you?", each of us tends to respond in social categories: "I'm a college student" (educational institution). "I'm a Baptist" (religious institution). "I'm an Italian" (ethnic collectivity). "I'm a secretary" (work group). "I'm one of the Anderson kids from southern Minnesota" (familial and geographical identification). "I'm a teenager" (age group). "I'm a Republican" (political organization). "I'm an American" (societal roots). All of this is not to say that there's no "real" or "independent" *you* behind or underneath those labels. There is. But, it is to say that human beings tend to think of themselves in terms of social groups or institutions and in terms of the *roles* defined by those groups or institutions.

Any complex collection of people must have rules by which to organize itself, to grant authority, to determine people's expectations for others' behaviors. Those rules often are called *social customs,* habitual ways of looking at and doing things within the group. So, your family may "customarily" say grace before dinner; a classroom instructor before lecturing may "customarily" ask for questions about required reading; a religious organization may "customarily" go through a liturgy of worship;

a political democracy may "customarily" go through a political campaign and an inaugural ceremony when choosing and installing a new president.

Customary or habitual ways-of-doing-things are characteristics of almost all groups, small or large. These sets of habitual behavior are called *rituals* or *ceremonies.* One sub-set of rituals or ceremonials involves public communicative behavior. Every culture, our own included, has sets of *mass social-political rituals,* used primarily to *celebrate cultural identity.* These social-political rituals and the public communication which accompanies them are the focus in Part IV of this textbook.

THE FUNCTIONS OF SOCIAL-POLITICAL RITUALS

Why rituals? Rituals bond the individual to the group. They provide a network for relationships between the individual and society, a network that allows both *a* person and *a* society to benefit. Let us look separately at the benefits to each.

The Social Benefits of Rituals

Think, for a moment, of societies as creatures, as "beings" with lives of their own. Why do social institutions such as political structures, churches, work organizations, social clubs, and the like, "need" rituals and ceremonies? Ritualistic behavior fulfills at least four valuable functions for the group.

Education   Institutions, as we have noted, are enduring cultural structures; most of them existed before you were born, and most will outlive you. Individuals who come in contact with institutions, therefore, need to be educated—to learn institutions' purposes or reasons-for-being, their views of the world (beliefs), their attitudes and values, and their prescriptions for "proper" behavior. In your family, for example, you probably often heard when you were a child that "we" don't do that, or "we" believe this-or-that, or "that's right [wrong]." Such instances of communication were examples of an institution—your family—educating you into the ways of the group. To become a part of the "we," to be accepted fully by "the others," you had to learn how to think and to act *properly.* Groups make you a part of them by such educational processes.

Those educational processes occur in larger social institutions as well. In schools, children are not only taught skills and facts but also how to learn—the proper ways of reading material, of showing and telling about themselves in front of others, of analyzing literature or political institutions. So, for example, you learned not only that the Russian Revolution occurred in 1917, but that it was a bad revolution (unlike the American revolution) because it bypassed democratic institutions; thus, you were taught not only "facts" but also ways of looking at or interpreting those facts attitudinally and valuatively. Your education includes both such political facts and such political values.

Finally, we should note that many of these educational processes become ritualized. Consider, for example, the standard Boy Scout troop meeting. It begins with recitation of the Scout Oath ("On my honor I will do my best; do my duty to God and country; and obey the Scout Law; to . . .") and the Scout Law ("A Scout is trustworthy, loyal, helpful, friendly, courteous, kind, obedient, cheerful, thrifty, brave, clean, and reverent"). Not only does the joint recitation of the Scout Oath and Law bring the group of Boy Scouts closer together interpersonally (see "communion" below), but it also engrains the basic beliefs and commitments of the scouting organization into the heads of individual tenderfoots. Classroom rituals, family rituals, religious rituals, and club orientation ceremonies accomplish the same goals.

Communion As noted, social-political rituals accomplish a second function for the group: they make individuals feel a part of and close to other members of the group and thus strengthen and solidify the group. The old adage, "The family that prays together, stays together," reflects this function, for the family is strengthened by its shared rituals.

To "commune" is to share-together any number of things—common or joint behaviors, a creed or set of beliefs, a history, a sense of the future. Take, for example, a national political convention. Convention delegates commune by sharing *activities* (the nominating and electing of party standard-bearers), *creeds* (the party platform), *history* (speeches reciting the accomplishments of founding fathers and great past leaders), and a sense of the *future* (goals to be implemented in the upcoming campaign and beyond). Indeed, perhaps the primary purpose of a political convention is such communion, for each individual is energized back home in his or her precinct work by having shared these experiences with like-minded individuals from all over the country.

And, as was the case with education, the communal function of ceremonies often is carried out in habitualized communicative rituals. Most religious services, for example, are centered on a liturgy—a pre-programmed series of communicative acts for worshipping together. And, in many elementary schools the day still begins with a Pledge of Allegiance ceremony, which "blesses" civically the communal efforts of teachers and children. Speeches dedicating monuments, bridges, dams, governmental buildings, and the like, also are placed within a ritual ceremony attended by the public; such speaking occasions are characterized by references to what "we" as a taxpaying group and a nation have done together in getting the monuments, bridges, dams, and buildings constructed.

Protection Originally, human beings gathered together for protection from a stronger, hostile environment. And, although we perhaps no longer worry so explicitly about predatory beasts, we nevertheless—at least symbolically and occasionally—band together in groups for mutual protection. New immigrants to a country seek out others from the Old Country to help them adjust to strange customs and living conditions. Political institutions often justify their existence, at least in part, by arguing that other countries or groups are seeking to destroy us. Religious groups offer individuals protection from the evils of a godless world. And even social groups such as dance studios, lonely hearts clubs, weight-control organizations, and the American Legion are attractive because they can protect individuals from, respectively, social clumsiness, loneliness, overindulgent behavior, and civilians who don't understand what it means to fight.

Ritualistically, groups and institutions enact their protective function in many ways. In political conventions, the "enemy"—either another political party or a foreign government—is identified and condemned; the party faithful also are told that if they work unceasingly and remain ever-vigilant, the enemy will be overcome. Likewise, in other political ceremonies—Fourth of July or Memorial Day ceremonies, presidential or gubernatorial inauguration addresses, State of the Union addresses—enemies to democracy or to growth or to happiness are singled out and "destroyed," at least symbolically.

Celebration of the Mystical The group is, of course, larger than the individual. It is larger in two ways: (1) It is *larger physically,* in that it collectivizes the energy and talents of many. (2) More important, it is *larger symbolically* or *psychologically:* because our fundamental beliefs, customs, values, and the like "reside" in the group, it seems endowed with near-superhuman powers.

We emphasize this symbolic largeness in many ways. Most of our governmental buildings are huge, made from (durable) stone, and decorated with paneled rooms, massive desks and elevated podiums, and patriotic icons (flags, the figure of blind justice, seals, constitutional documents). Largeness, too, is created by such activities as presidential motorcades (filled with black, somber limousines or even military mobile equipment), ceremonies occurring on the steps of massive buildings, and such "special" occasions as diplomatic receptions—all focusing our attention upon out-of-the-ordinary power and magnificence of government.

Indeed, we even create a sense of largeness by the language we employ when talking about government. "A" president is a mere mortal, a representative of a political party, a person from somewhere. But, the "Office of the President" is quite a different matter, as though "the office" had an existence independent of the person holding it. We assume that the "office" is wise, sagacious, fair, reverent, moral, compassionate. And, as well, we somehow want to believe that investing "a" president—through an inaugural ceremony—with the "office" of the presidency will automatically "transfer" those characteristics of "the office" to the person holding it. The office is viewed by us as so large and powerful that it can turn a "mere" person into a President with a capital "P."

This kind of symbolic magnitude could be similarly traced in religious leaders, corporate executives, and even family patriarchs or matriarchs. What it symbolizes is the larger-than-life, near-mystical power of the group—the myths and magic we all hope will govern the individuals holding the positions and will protect us in a way we could not do as individuals. We gather together regularly to celebrate those mysteries ritualistically. We "ordain" ministers, priests, and rabbis; we "inaugurate" presidents; we choose "keynote speakers" to tell us truths and to recall our magical powers. On each of these occasions, we celebrate our group's or institution's sources of mystical power.

The Individual Benefits of Ritual

Groups and institutions, then, benefit from ceremonies which reinforce their importance and power. And, individuals also receive important rewards when they participate in mass social-political rituals.

Sense of Predictability Because rituals are habitualized, repetitious from occasion to occasion, and pre-ordained, they are highly predictable events. And although at times predictability can seem empty or boring, it nevertheless is comfortable. We all feel a little more at ease when we know what's going to happen. Moreover, when we have a sense of predictability, we know which of our bodies of knowledge is appropriate and which of our values are being called upon in the ceremony. So, for example, when you participate in a church ritual such as a baptism, you know that your knowledge of sin, of absolution from sins, and of water as a biblical metaphor for cleansing is being drawn upon in the baptismal ceremony. (You also know, of course, that some of your other knowledge about water—such as its specific gravity, its physical properties, the problem of water pollution—is *irrelevant* to the baptismal ceremony. In a ritual, you bring to bear only that portion of your knowledge which is "appropriate" to the ceremony.) We like rituals, therefore, because of their predictability and of our own sense of what is appropriate.

Sense of Role-Satisfaction Closely related to the matter of predictability is that of role-satisfaction. Rituals are important to most of us individually not only because we "know" what to expect and how to interpret what's going on, but also because we know our own roles. In familiar rituals, we know what is expected of us individually, what is expected of our behavior.

When attending a political party gathering, we know when to listen attentively, when to speak, when to applaud, when to cheer. At a wedding, we know when to listen, when to present gifts, when to kiss the bride, when to offer a toast, and when to leave the reception. In each of these ceremonies, in other words, we have strong senses of "proper" behavior—and that is comforting. (If you question this, attend a wedding ceremony in a culture with which you're unfamiliar; you'll notice your own uneasiness, your penchant for glancing around nervously to see what you're supposed to do next.)

As we have noted throughout this book, we all want to fulfill our roles properly, to do what is expected of us. Rituals make that easy.

Sense of Togetherness As we said, groups and institutions attempt to create a sense of communion by drafting creeds, histories, and goal-statements which all group members can know and celebrate. In most groups, though, we go farther than that: we actually do things together to cement the bonds of communion, to make people feel of one substance with each other. One of the functions of ceremonies is to heighten your sense of belonging to a degree where you feel a "part" of other individuals.

Groups and institutions instill this sense of oneness by actually having you do things with other people: you recite together, sing together, eat together, dance together. Scouts undertake group projects; families set up joint rituals such as picnics, trips, and bedtime stories; athletic teams clasp hands. In each of these cases, some specific activity is shared in order to make you feel a part of the others who are there. Sharing increases your sense of togetherness, and that feels good.

Sense of Personhood And finally, ceremonies and rituals allow you to sense very, very strongly "who you are." As we noted, you often define your self in terms of groups and institutions to which you belong—family, political party, church, gender group, age group, occupational group. As you participate in the rites of those groups, you confirm your own identity, and thereby gain a sense of well-being.

That sense of well-being is traceable in part to the fact that you learned the rituals of many groups as a *child;* psychologically, then, when you participate in the "old" rituals you feel the comfort of childhood, when your sense of belongingness probably was at its strongest.

That sense also is traceable in part to the fact that most rituals are characterized by *special languages*—verbal and nonverbal symbols whose meanings you "know" and "understand." A college community shares names for the union, the bookstore, the mascot, the main building, an unpopular course, a regular campus event. Americans have particular meanings for such words as "the American Way of Life," "founding fathers," "government of the people, by the people, and for the people," "checks and balances," "life, liberty, and the pursuit of

**FIGURE IV.1   Communicative Sharing and Celebrating:
The Function of Ceremonies and Rituals**

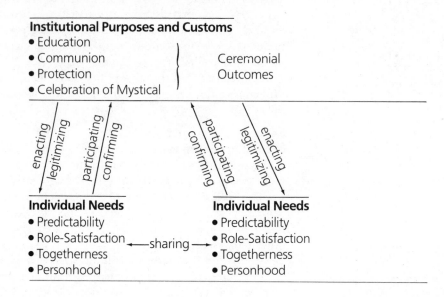

Institutional Purposes and Customs
- Education
- Communion   Ceremonial
- Protection   Outcomes
- Celebration of Mystical

enacting *legitimizing* *participating* *confirming*   *confirming* *participating* *legitimizing* *enacting*

Individual Needs   **Individual Needs**
- Predictability   - Predictability
- Role-Satisfaction ←—sharing—→   - Role-Satisfaction
- Togetherness   - Togetherness
- Personhood   - Personhood

happiness." Some of those languages are nonverbal as well—the school's colors, symbols, and music, or the American flag, the eagle, or the salute. You *know* these special languages, and you gain a kind of satisfaction from knowing that you know them. They're a part of you, and they give you part of your identity.

COMMUNICATIVE CELEBRATION IN SOCIAL-POLITICAL RITUALS

Much of what we have been saying is summed up in Figure IV.1. When people gather together on those special occasions we call ceremonies or rituals, they enter into a complex communicative event. Let us look at each of the parts, at the concepts, more closely.

For groups and institutions to achieve their purposes (education, communion, protection, celebration), and for individuals to meet their needs (predictability, role-satisfaction, togetherness, personhood), particular kinds of communicative messages have to be constructed. Those messages are delivered within a full-blown *ceremony* (which includes the physical setting and its symbols, uniforms, often music, etc.), and often within a tightly organized ritual (the specific acts, responses, and other behaviors of individuals). Because both the group or institution and various individuals have pre-ordained and comparatively distinct roles in ceremony and ritual, the messages both the group and the individual deliver have particular communicative functions behind them.

Communicative Functions of Institutional Messages

The organizers or spokespersons for a group or institution, given their purposes, prepare messages which allow them to *enact* the group's customs and to *legitimize* its authority and power. Let us examine each of these purposes more closely.

Enacting The word "enacting" refers to the process of giving form and substance to fundamental beliefs, attitudes, and values. Take, for example, the notion of parental authority. Most American families believe that parents have a degree of authority which must be recognized and followed by children. We *enact* that belief and attitude in numerous ways. Parents tell their children to be home by 11:00 P.M.; children say "yes," and in fact come home at 10:58 P.M., most of the time. In their words and in their actions, the children *confirm* the belief (see below) at the same time as the parents enact or exercise their parental authority. Both parents and children act out the belief.

In institutional ceremonies, the same sort of enacting and confirming occurs. Individual presidents enact the "office" of the President by issuing executive orders, delivering state-of-the-union addresses, and greeting foreign dignitaries. The scouting organizations enact their commitments to the Scout Oath and Law by ceremonies for awarding rank changes and merit badges.

Enactment, then, is a communicative function. That is, we would have little sense of the group's or institution's commitment to customary beliefs and values if we did not see those commitments "acted out."

Legitimizing Furthermore, every time you watch a group enact its beliefs and values, you are called upon to legitimize them, that is, to recognize the authority and power of the institution or group over you. Thus, when you witness a wedding ceremony and join in on the exchange of vows, you have recognized the power of that religious institution to bless marriages; every time you watch an inaugural ceremony and cheer the new president, you have legitimized government's power to select and institute new leaders.

Legitimizing is a most important communicative function. To understand that importance, think back on occasions when group members did *not* grant the group authority and power. Think of teenagers' fights with their parents over who should have the final say on friends, party hours, and clothing. Those fights were not simply over this-or-that friend, this particular Saturday night, or that blouse. Rather, they were struggles over legitimacy, over who should be making decisions. And, consider the turmoil of the 1960s. As a culture we were wracked with conflicts over legitimacy—Who should be responsible for foreign policy and international war policies? Who should determine university grading and hiring policies? Who should be responsible for the censorship of "pornographic" materials? Whose job is it to protect the environment?

In those controversies, various groups and institutions vied for legitimacy, for the power to enact their beliefs and values legitimately in society.

Communicative Functions of Individual Messages

Individuals, too, of course, have their needs, and hence have their own roles in ceremonies and rituals. Three communicative functions are served by the "messages" offered by individuals. In rituals, individuals confirm, participate, and share communicatively.

Confirming As we noted above, perhaps the central function of individual messages occurs in responses, in individuals' "answers" to institutional messages. Those answers confirm the institution's importance in your life and its authority over you. Sometimes, your confirmation is verbal, as when you pledge allegiance to the flag, when you accept your speech instructor's critique of your last speech, when you tell your parents you'll be home by 11:00 P.M., or when you read from the Torah during your Bar-mitzva. At other times, your confirmation is nonverbal: you remove your hat and put your hand over your heart while pledging allegiance; you nod during the instructor's critique; you actually come home before 11:00 P.M.; you wear a prayer shawl.

In all these instances, you are acknowledging some group's or institution's authority, its claim upon your mind and behavior.

Participating Do you ever cut classes, even when you don't have a "legitimate" reason for doing so? Have you refused to sing the national anthem? Have you skipped church? Have you ever said to your family, "Yes, I know we usually go to Grandma's for Sunday dinner, but I want to stay home this time"? In those cases, you are refusing to participate, you are saying verbally or nonverbally that you have some rights, some individuality, some reasons for ignoring the claims the group or institution makes upon you. Refusing to participate in ceremonies and rituals is a matter of self-assertion, personal decision.

Conversely, participation in the group—going to meetings, singing or reciting the litany along with everyone else, etc.—is just another way you have for confirming the institution's power and authority and for testifying that you as an individual "belong," acquiesce to the group's claims over you. Actually participating in civil ceremonies—Fourth of July celebrations, Martin Luther King Day ceremonies, inaugurations—as well as in religious ceremonies becomes the way you gain the personal benefits (predictability, role satisfaction, etc.) we discussed earlier. Your participation in the rituals is what guarantees that you'll receive the personalized kinds of satisfaction you need.

Sharing Finally, because the individual needs both a sense of belongingness (togetherness) and a sense of group-centered identity (personhood), taking part in rituals tightens person-person bonds as well as person-group bonds. The "acting-together"—which is the guts of group ceremonies—brings you closer to others. As you join with others in both civic and religious ceremonies, singing or chanting together, eating together, pledging together, crowding together in pews or auditoriums or outdoor fields, studying together, and so forth, you overtly share a part of your self with the others. And, they share themselves with you. And so, person-to-person bonds of commonality are established and reinforced in the joint participation that comprises public ceremonies. And thus, the human animal, like all other animals, is made to feel the closeness and the security that person-to-person identification can provide.

Rituals, and larger ceremonies, always have been and probably always will be important parts of your lives. You may even be called upon —perhaps often, if you're any good—to be more than a participant-observer in ceremonies. You may well be called upon to speak at the special occasions for which we design and execute our rituals. The chapter which follows will focus on four different kinds of occasions— tributes, dedications, keynotes, and inaugurations—which occur in group and institutional settings. We will focus on these four occasions because they offer us four different kinds of group celebrations—tributes which honor persons, dedications which honor ideals and achievements, keynotes which honor group membership, and inaugurations which honor new leaders. In other words, in these four speeches for special occasions we will be able to identify speech content and organization broadly yet specifically. The demands upon the Articulate Person will be great, but so will the chance for positive effect on others.

CHAPTER 12

Celebrating and Remembering Special Occasions

The more groups you belong to, the more often you are called upon to join in some "special occasion." Special occasions represent brief breaks in a group's day-to-day activities. During those breaks, you are asked to pull back from the hubbub of daily activity, and to think seriously about the group's goals, accomplishments, traditions, leadership, and claims upon you. Those breaks are avowedly *ceremonial*; that is, they're normally attended by special decorations for the room or arena, elevated podiums, often posters and placards, perhaps special clothing requirements, liturgies or other kinds of verbal rituals—and speeches.

We're a culture that talks our way through special occasions. Special sermons are given at christenings, confirmation ceremonies or bar-mitzvahs (both "rites of passage" into adulthood), weddings, special religious holidays, and funerals. While a president delivers many speeches during a term of office, none are so special as inaugurals, state-of-the-union addresses, thanksgiving proclamations, and other ceremonies-of-state. Mayors and governors dedicate memorials or monuments, dams, new government buildings, and the like. College presidents give commencement addresses and state-of-the-university speeches. Social action group leaders report annually on the previous year's and the next year's programs, and sometimes preside over initiation ceremonies for new members. Political organizations and other action groups hold conventions, replete with keynote speakers, and often sponsor one- or two-day conferences and workshops for the public. On all of these occasions, the sorts of speeches we'll be taking apart in this chapter are delivered.

Because we already have discussed the who/what/when/why of special occasion speaking in the Preview, let us first introduce the raw materials for celebratory speeches, and then examine typical organizational patterns.

RAW MATERIALS FOR CELEBRATORY SPEECHES

While any number of different kinds of materials can be employed in celebratory speeches, some kinds appear again and again. This is because special occasions demand the "long" and the "high" views, that is, a look at past/present/future and an elevated contemplation of goals, values, and accomplishments. Therefore, one usually finds celebratory speeches riddled with *narratives, valuative statements, metaphorical statements,* and *mythic statements.*

SAMPLE SPEECH:

CELEBRATING

Pre-Speech Analysis

This speech, given by then-General Douglas MacArthur on May 13, 1962, shows how these materials can operate. MacArthur became a war hero as the Supreme Allied Commander in the Pacific during World War II. He left the Army in a disagreement with President Harry S Truman over U.S. policy in Korea, although his image as a hero was not tarnished even then. He addressed the Congress in his famous "Old Soldiers Never Die" speech in 1951, to a thundering ovation. Finally, at age 82, he was called back home, to West Point, to receive the Sylvanus Thayer Award for service to his country. The tribute was to him, but he turned the occasion around to pay tribute to West Point and its traditions. We will use this speech to illustrate various kinds of supporting materials.

Speech

Farewell to the Cadets[1]
General Douglas MacArthur

As I was leaving the hotel this morning, a doorman asked me, "Where are you bound for, General?" And when I replied, "West Point," he remarked, "Beautiful place. Have you ever been there before?" /1

No human being could fail to be deeply moved by such a tribute as this, coming from a profession I have served so long and a people I have loved so well. /2

It fills me with an emotion I cannot express. But this award is not intended primarily to honor a personality, but to symbolize a great moral code—the code of conduct and chivalry of those who guard this beloved land of culture and ancient descent. That is the animation of this medallion. For all eyes and for all time it is an expression of the ethics of the American soldier. That I should be integrated in this way with so noble an ideal arouses a sense of pride and yet of humility, which will be with me always. /3

Duty, honor, country: those three hallowed words reverently dicate what you want to be, what you can be, what you will be. They are your rallying points to build courage when courage seems to fail, to regain faith when there seems to be little cause for faith, to create hope when hope becomes forlorn.   /4

Unhappily, I possess neither that eloquence of diction, that poetry of imagination, nor that brilliance of metaphor to tell you all that they mean.   /5

The unbelievers will say they are but words, but a slogan, but a flamboyant phrase. Every pedant, every demagogue, every cynic, every hypocrite, every troublemaker, and, I am sorry to say, some others of an entirely different character, will try to downgrade them even to the extent of mockery and ridicule.   /6

But these are some of the things they do. They build your basic character. They mold you for your future roles as the custodians of the nation's defense. They make you strong enough to know when you are weak and brave enough to face yourself when you are afraid.   /7

They teach you to be proud and unbending in honest failure, but humble and gentle in success; not to substitute words for action; not to seek the path of comfort, but to face the stress and spur of difficulty and challenge; to learn to stand up in the storm, but to have compassion on those who fall; to master yourself before you seek to master others; to have a heart that is clean, a goal that is high; to learn to laugh, yet never forget how to weep; to reach into the future, yet never neglect the past; to be serious, yet never take yourself too seriously; to be modest so that you will remember the simplicity of true greatness, the open mind of true wisdom, the meekness of true strength.   /8

They give you a temper of the will, a quality of the imagination, a vigor of the emotions, a freshness of the deep springs of life, a temperamental predominance of courage over timidity, of an appetite for adventure over love of ease.   /9

They create in your heart the sense of wonder, the unfailing hope of what next, and the joy and inspiration of life. They teach you in this way to be an officer and a gentleman.   /10

And what sort of soldiers are those you are to lead? Are they reliable? Are they brave? Are they capable of victory? Their story is known to all of you. It is the story of the American man-at-arms. My estimate of him was formed on the battlefields many, many years ago, and has never changed. I regarded him then, as I regard him now, as one of the world's noblest figures—not only as one of the finest military characters but also as one of the most stainless.   /11

His name and fame are the birthright of every American citizen. In his youth and strength, his love and loyalty, he gave all that mortality can give. He needs no eulogy from me or from any other man. He has written his own history and written it in red on his enemy's breast.   /12

But when I think of his patience under adversity, of his courage under fire, and his modesty in victory, I am filled with an emotion of admiration I cannot put into words. He belongs to history as furnishing one of the greatest examples of successful patriotism. He belongs to posterity as the instructor of future generations in the principles of liberty and freedom. He belongs to the present—to us—by his virtues and by his achievements.   /13

In twenty campaigns, on a hundred battlefields, around a thousand campfires, I have witnessed that enduring fortitude, that patriotic self-abnegation, and that invincible determination which have carved his statue in the hearts of his people.   /14

From one end of the world to the other, he has drained deep the chalice of courage. As I listened to those songs, in memory's eye I could see those staggering columns of the First World War, bending under soggy packs on many a weary march, from dripping dusk to drizzling dawn, slogging ankle-deep through the mire of shell-shocked roads; to form grimly for the attack, blue-lipped, covered with sludge and mud, chilled by the wind and rain, driving home to their objective, and, for many, to the judgment seat of God.   /15

I do not know the dignity of their birth, but I do know the glory of their death. They died unquestioning, uncomplaining, with faith in their hearts, and on their lips the hope that we would go on to victory.   /16

Always for them: duty, honor, country. Always their blood, and sweat, and tears, as we sought the way and the light and the truth. And 20 years after, on the other side of the globe, again the filth of murky foxholes, the stench of ghostly trenches, the slime of dripping dugouts, those boiling suns of relentless heat, those torrential rains of devastating storms, the loneliness and utter desolation of jungle trails, the bitterness of long separation from those they loved and cherished, the deadly pestilence of tropical disease, the horror of stricken areas of war.   /17

Their resolute and determined defense, their swift and sure attack, their indomitable purpose, their complete and decisive victory—always victory, always through the bloody haze of their last reverberating shot, the vision of gaunt, ghastly men, reverently following your password of duty, honor, country.   /18

The code which those words perpetuate embraces the highest moral law and will stand the test of any ethics or philosophies ever promulgated for the uplift of mankind. Its requirements are for the things that are right and its restraints are from the things that are wrong. The soldier, above all other men, is required to practice the greatest act of religious training—sacrifice. In battle and in the face of danger and death he discloses those divine attributes which his Maker gave when he created man in his own image. No physical courage and no brute instinct can take the place of the divine help, which alone can sustain him. However horrible the incidents of war may be, the soldier who is called upon to offer and to give his life for his country is the noblest development of mankind.   /19

You now face a new world, a world of change. The thrust into outer space of the satellite spheres and missiles marks a beginning of another epoch in the long story of mankind. In the five-or-more billions of years the scientists tell us it has taken to form the earth, in the three-or-more billion years of development of the human race, there has never been a more abrupt or staggering evolution.   /20

We deal now, not with things of this world alone, but with the illimitable distances and as yet unfathomed mysteries of the universe. We are reaching out for a new and boundless frontier. We speak in strange terms of harnessing the cosmic energy; of making winds and tides work for us; of creating synthetic materials to supplement or even replace our old standard basics; to purify sea water for our drink; of mining ocean floors for new fields of wealth and food; of disease preventatives to expand life into the hundreds of years; of controlling the weather for a more equitable distribution of heat and cold, of rain and shine; of space ships to the moon, of the primary target in war no longer limited to the armed forces of an enemy, but instead to include his civil populations; of ultimate conflict between a united human race and the sinister forces of some other planetary galaxy; of such dreams and fantasies as to make life the most exciting of all times.   /21

And through all this welter of change and development your mission remains fixed, determined, inviolable. It is to win our wars. Everything else in your professional career is but corollary to this vital dedication. All other public purposes, all other public projects, all other public needs, great or small, will find others for their accomplishments; but you are the ones who are trained to fight.   /22

Yours is the profession of arms, the will to win, the sure knowledge that in war there is no substitute for victory, that if you lose the nation will be destroyed, that the very obsession of your public service must be duty, honor, country.   /23

Others will debate the controversial issues, national and international, which divide men's minds. But serene, calm, aloof, you stand as the nation's war guardians, as its lifeguard from the raging tides of international conflict, as its gladiator in the arena of battle. For a century-and-a-half you have defended, guarded, and protected its hallowed traditions of liberty and freedom, of right and justice.   /24

Let civilian voices argue the merits or demerits of our processes of government: whether our strength is being sapped by deficit financing indulged in too long; by federal paternalism grown too mighty; by power groups grown too arrogant; by politics grown too corrupt; by crime grown too rampant; by morals grown too low; by taxes grown too high; by extremists grown too violent; whether our personal liberties are as firm and complete as they should be.   /25

These great national problems are not for your professional participation or military solution. Your guidepost stands out like a tenfold beacon in the night: duty, honor, country.   /26

You are the leaven which binds together the entire fabric of our national system of defense. From your ranks come the great captains who hold the nation's destiny in their hands the moment the war tocsin sounds.   /27

The long, gray line has never failed us. Were you to do so, a million ghosts in olive drab, in brown khaki, in blue and gray, would rise from their white crosses, thundering those magic words: duty, honor, country.   /28

This does not mean that you are warmongers. On the contrary, the soldier above all other people prays for peace, for he must suffer and bear the deepest wounds and scars of war. But always in our ears ring the ominous words of Plato, that wisest of all philosophers: "Only the dead have seen the end of war."   /29

The shadows are lengthening for me. The twilight is here. My days of old have vanished—tone and tints. They have gone glimmering through the dreams of things that were. Their memory is one of wondrous beauty watered by tears and coaxed and caressed by the smiles of yesterday. I listen vainly, but with thirsty ear, for the witching melody of faint bugles blowing reveille, of far drums beating the long roll.   /30

In my dreams I hear again the crash of guns, the rattle of musketry, the strange, mournful mutter of the battlefield. But in the evening of my memory always I come back to West Point. Always there echoes and reechoes: duty, honor, country.   /31

Today marks my final roll call with you. But I want you to know that when I cross the river, my last conscious thoughts will be of the Corps, and the Corps, and the Corps.   /32

I bid you farewell.   /33

Historical Narratives

As we said, many celebratory speeches ask audiences to take long views, to see their places within the stretch of human history. Historical narratives can be employed to give an audience both that sense of historical sweep as well as a sense of their own place within it. MacArthur begins his breathtaking historical narrative in paragraph 14: "In twenty campaigns, on a hundred battlefields, around a thousand campfires, I have witnessed that enduring fortitude, that patriotic self-abnegation, and that invincible determination which have carved his [the American soldier's] statue in the hearts of his people." From there, he recalls his remembrances of World War I (paragraphs 15–16) and World War II (paragraphs 17–18). Judiciously (given the circumstances of his retirement), he avoids mention of the Korean Conflict, and moves to 1962 (paragraphs 21–25). He finishes the narrative with an implicit look toward the future (paragraphs 26–29), exhorting the cadets to hold fast to their commitments summarized in the speech's refrain, "duty, honor, country."

The use of historical narratives allows speakers to (1) emphasize timelessness, (2) offer valuative interpretations of events, and (3) associate this particular audience with both the timeless elements and the institutional values. MacArthur has achieved all three of these goals. Further, if one can use words and allusions as effectively as he did, one can paint vivid pictures into which audience members can project themselves. Thus, many celebratory speeches, like this one, can be organized around historical narrative.

Valuative Statements

To pay tribute to people and organizations, a speaker usually must be able to praise purposes, goals, and valuative commitments. These represent enduring features of human impulses and organizational urges; they are what people and organizations "stand for." Thus, we saw a barrage of valuative statements in Barbara Jordan's speech to the 1976 Democratic Convention earlier in this book, and, once again, we find MacArthur's speech overflowing with valuative references. Notice that the speech is filled with such words as "pride," "humility," "duty," "honor," "country," "temper of the will," "imagination," "vigor of the emotion," "temperamental predominance of courage," "joy," "inspiration," "strength," "love," "loyalty," "patience," "modesty," "patriotism," "enduring fortitude," "invincible determination," "indomitable purpose," "will to win." And, you also find references to negative values—"deficit financing," "federal paternalism," "power groups grown too arrogant," "politics grown too corrupt," "crime grown too rampant," "morals grown too low," "taxes grown too high," and "extremists grown too violent." These serve as negative reinforcement, holding the audience's visions to the higher and positive values.

Seldom will you be called upon to so fill your discourses with valuative statements; but you always will be expected, in celebratory speeches, to make the group's values explicit and laudatory.

Metaphorical Statements

As we noted in Preview II, abstract concepts are difficult to define, difficult to clarify for people unfamiliar with them. One way to make the abstract more concrete and more sensate is through the use of metaphor. A metaphor associates the abstract or unknown with the concrete or the known. It has the power, therefore, to clarify ideas and to make them compelling. That MacArthur realized the power of metaphor is obvious from the start (paragraph 5), when he refers directly to "brilliance of metaphor." He then goes on to use them:

• *Paragraph 7:* To discuss the power of "duty, honor, country" as motivating concepts, he uses *construction metaphors*, talking about the concepts' ability to "build your basic character" and to "mold you for your future roles."

• *Paragraph 8:* To stress the importance of strong character, he offers a *climatological metaphor*, "to face the stress and spur of difficulty and challenge; to learn to stand up in the storm, but to have compassion on those who fall."

• *Paragraphs 15, 19, 24, 27:* To endow the cadet with higher purpose, MacArthur presents *religious metaphors*. We are told that the soldier has "drained deep the chalice of courage"; that he is "required to practice the greatest act of religious training—sacrifice"; that he has "defended, guarded, and protected its [the nation's] hallowed traditions of liberty and freedom, of right and justice"; and that he is "the leaven which binds together the entire fabric of our national system of defense." (The good general perhaps should be forgiven the mixing of religious metaphor—the leaven—and the construction metaphor of weaving in that last reference.)

• *Paragraphs 26, 30, 31:* To emphasize contrasts, he relies upon perhaps the most popular metaphor of all, *light/dark metaphor.*[2] We are told that the soldier's "guidepost stands out like a tenfold beacon in the night"; that, for MacArthur, "The shadows are lengthening for me," as "The twilight is here." This leads him into the powerful and haunting "night" metaphor—the dream—in paragraphs 30 and 31.

You can find additional metaphors in the speech, water imagery, metaphors-of-motion, and of course "the long, gray line" itself. When a special occasion speaker reaches for the difficult-to-understand, the result is usually a variety of metaphors very much like these.

Mythic Statements

Myths, in an important sense, are "fictions," stories filled with heroes and villains, vile beasts and heavenly saviors. You have heard myths since you were a child. They are important for all cultures, because they recall the grandest impulses of the cultures—its explanations for "who" the cultures are, where they "came" from, the purposes which guide them, the behavioral standards they impose upon members of the cultures. Myths "encode" the basic reasons-for-being of cultures. Some myths are religious, like the stories in the Bible. Others are secular, like the stories of George Washington and Abraham Lincoln learned by every American child. These are fictional in the sense that they contain elaborated narratives which may or may not be factually "true"; but in another sense, they are the most "real" aspects of a culture, because they contain the values to which everyone is expected to aspire as a social being.

MacArthur's speech to the cadets is filled with mythic statements. "The soldier," the perfect cadet, is portrayed in the historical narratives of World War I and World War II soldiers, in the constant vision of his "professional career." He is depicted as one who makes the ultimate sacrifice if necessary, one who stands above the petty political turmoils of any age, one who is willing to "suffer and bear the deepest wounds and scars of war" (paragraph 29). He is shown to be a genuine hero who displays "those divine attributes which his Maker gave when he created man in his own image" (paragraph 19).

The general also identifies the villains in the mythic battle between Good and Evil. Some villains are "unbelievers"—pedants, demagogues, cynics, hypocrites, and troublemakers—who "downgrade them [the soldier's commitments] even to the extent of mockery and ridicule" (paragraph 6). Others are the "civilians"—politicians—who plunge the country into "controversial issues" (paragraphs 24 and 25). And, of course, some are "warmongers," those who push a country into war where the soldier must sacrifice all (paragraph 29). These villains reinforce MacArthur's vision of the pure military hero (who cannot be an unbeliever, a civilian-politician, and a warmonger and still be committed to the Code of Honor); and, the villains and their description force the cadets to constantly look "upward," not "downward," toward the purest values and motives.

A group's or institution's "myths" must be recited periodically, to keep the collectivity progressing toward its noblest future. In summary, MacArthur's Farewell to the Cadets did just that. It blended narrative, valuative, metaphorical, and mythical statements into one of the greatest displays of eloquence this century has seen. Its supporting materials are well worth further study and emulation.

ORGANIZING CELEBRATORY SPEECHES

While there are many kinds of celebratory speeches, in this chapter we will concentrate upon four types:

1. Speeches to offer tribute (honoring a person)
2. Speeches of dedication (honoring ideals and accomplishments)
3. Keynote speeches (honoring group membership)
4. Inaugural speeches (honoring a new leader)

Speeches of Tribute

Speeches of tribute seek to celebrate a person and that person's accomplishments. They are given regularly during political campaigns, at retirement dinners or other ceremonies recognizing the end of someone's service to a group, at funerals, and occasionally at the beginning of someone's tenure in office. Speeches of tribute try to fulfill two specific purposes: (1) *to honor the person*; and (2) *to highlight the personal qualities members of the audience should seek to emulate*. That is, the audience should come away from a tribute sensitive to both the accomplishment of the object-of-tribute and the attributes members of the audience should seek to cultivate in their own lives.

Because either of these specific purposes can be the more important, there are two basic organizational patterns for speeches of tribute, patterns which have been standard since the late days of the Roman Empire.[3] One pattern is essentially chronological, concentrating upon the honoree's biography; the other is essentially topical, with a list of desirable personal attributes forming the topics.

Chronological Pattern The chronological pattern is used when the speaker wishes to focus attention on the person being paid tribute. Elements from the honoree's background are selected to highlight accomplishments and to emphasize desirable personal qualities. Obviously, one cannot tell the "whole" story. Rather, specific incidents are drawn out of the personal history, and woven into a "story" which gives audience members insight into the individual and guidelines for their own behaviors. So, a typical chronological pattern looks like this:

Introduction
I. Reasons the person is being honored
II. Forecast of the biographical review, emphasizing that audience members will learn something about the person's accomplishments and about goals they should set for their own lives

Body
I. Family background (emphasizing either hurdles the individual had to overcome or opportunities the individual had to seize)
II. Early turning points in the person's career (emphasizing challenges or early signs of greatness)

III. Important stages in the person's career of service (emphasizing the qualities of mind and character which influenced or inspired others)
IV. Final rundown of accomplishments and honors

Conclusion
I. Listing of "lessons" the audience can learn
II. Eloquent tribute to the person being honored

Topical Pattern If the stress is more on the qualities-to-be-emulated than upon the greatness of the person per se, then a topical pattern is called for. Biographical references to the honoree will undoubtedly be made, but in a different manner: the major topics are the attributes or qualities; and the biographical references are illustrative or supporting materials, used to instill a sense of importance for the attributes. Thus, a typical topical pattern for tribute runs as follows:

Introduction
I. Reasons the person is being honored
II. Statement that the qualities which have made the person important and effective in life deserve emphasis for the audience

Body
I. First quality (together with exemplification from the person's life)
II. Second quality (etc.)
III. Third quality (etc.)
IV. [Additional qualities, with exemplification, within reason]

Conclusion
I. Summary of the qualities, and the benefits they have given to those who have come into contact with the honoree
II. Eloquent tribute to the person being honored, with exhortation to the audience to emulate the person

When using a topical pattern, be sure (1) not to draw out the speech by referring to too many qualities, and (2) to select only a few of the incidents from the honoree's life, to keep the speech moving forward crisply.

Speeches of Dedication   The dedicatory speech is strongly audience-centered. The thing being dedicated—a monument, a building, a dam, or whatever—in a sense is an "excuse" for praising the audience. The monument, after all, has little to recommend itself to the listeners; it is but a lump of granite or steel. It does, however, represent the aspirations and accomplishments of the listeners (and, sometimes, the artist who molded it). In that sense, the dedication is an excuse for reviewing the listeners' fundamental hopes, fears, beliefs, values, and achievements. The smart dedicatory speaker will praise, ultimately, the audience rather than the work of artists and artisans. The purpose of the dedicatory speech, therefore, is twofold: (1) *to indicate what the monument or edifice stands for literally and metaphorically;* and (2) *to* *celebrate the group's accomplishments and ideals.* Three organizational patterns—chronological, causal, or topical—may be appropriate.

Chronological Pattern If you wish to stress primarily group accomplishments, a chronological pattern, once more, is most useful. It allows you to introduce the speech by saying that the group or subculture has come a long way since its founding, to list in chronological form specific accomplishments in the body of the speech, and then to conclude the speech by pointing to monument, building, sculpture, plaque, or whatever as a fitting representation of those accomplishments. This was the pattern preferred by the man who perhaps was this country's greatest dedicator, Daniel Webster. While his language was a bit flowery by today's standards, his use of chronological reviews of national accomplishments is worthy of study.[4]

Causal Pattern A simple variation on the chronological pattern is one which employs a causal pattern. Here, one pictures the group's or institution's current greatness and accomplishments as results (effects) of past effort and sacrifice (causes). A sample outline in the causal pattern could take this form:

Introduction
  I. Description of the object being dedicated
  II. Assertion that it represents a marking of the group's achievements and goals
  III. Assertion that it is the result of many factors which brought about those goals and accomplishments

Body
  I. First cause (emphasizing the group activities and impulses)
  II. Second cause (etc.)
  III. [Additional causes, as appropriate]

Conclusion
  I. Summary of the efforts which served as causes to the present results or effects
  II. Return to the object as the embodiment of those accomplishments
  III. Exhortation to the audience, urging it to continue the hard work and sacrifice into the future.

Topical Pattern Finally, just as you can single out personalized topics around which to organize a speech of tribute, so also can you emphasize the qualities of mind and of performance represented in the object-to-be-dedicated, qualities you hope the audience members will emulate. The resulting speech outline would look exactly like the one we drew up for a topical speech of tribute, except that you would draw your supporting or illustrative materials, not from someone's biography, but from the group's or institution's history.

Keynote Speeches

Like dedicatory addresses, keynote speeches focus strongly on the audience. Yet, they differ in an important respect: while the dedicatory address tends to focus on *past* effort and *present* accomplishments, the keynote speech tends to survey the present scene and then project *future* efforts which must be made by the listeners. Keynote speeches usually are given at conventions or conferences to direct future-oriented strategies and projects. They represent a taking-account of the present and exhortation to future actions. They are given by people we presume have the vision to understand our present circumstances and to predict future greatness (or trouble) depending upon how we act. Two purposes characterize keynote speeches: (1) *to review present circumstances*, and (2) *to lay out a programme of action to ensure continued accomplishments*. Given these purposes, keynotes tend to be organized either chronologically or causally.

Chronological Pattern The elements of a chronological pattern are visible in Barbara Jordan's 1976 Democratic Convention keynote. (See Chapter 7.) She uses both her presence as a Black female politician and the bicentennial celebration of 1976 to review accomplishments of the Democratic Party, to assess progress on key human issues facing the party, and to project future actions the party must take to fulfill its duty to the country. As you can see from her speech, the chronological pattern serves her purposes of keynoting easily and effectively. She is able, through it, to pat people on the back and to spur them to further effort.

Problem-Solution Pattern It also is tempting to keynoters to adjust the chronological pattern slightly, turning it into one of causal patterns—the problem-solution sequence. If you do that, the keynote address outline looks something like this:

Introduction
  I. Praise of the audience for bringing the group or institution to its present level of accomplishment and effectiveness
  II. Challenge to it to continue such efforts into the future because problems still remain

Body
  I. First problem (discussing its causes, the progress already made, and work remaining to be done)
  II. Second problem (etc.)
  III. [Additional problems, being careful not to list so many that the task seems impossible or people feel their accomplishments are being belittled]

Conclusion
I. Review of the problems, stressing that they *can* be solved in our lifetime if we all work
II. Final vision of the group's worthy goals, and the need to be ever attendant to ways the group can achieve them

In the problem-solution format, there is one more possibility: in discussing problems, you may wish to review the efforts of "the enemy" or others working at different purposes. The enemy and enemy efforts may well be part of the problems. Be sure that you picture the enemy as conquerable through the group's continued efforts; otherwise, they may be tempted to give up.

Inaugural Addresses   Like the keynote address, a speech of inauguration has a future-oriented focus. An "inauguration," after all, is a beginning, and hence must look forward. If a keynote address celebrates group membership and the commitments which arise in the future for that group, the inaugural focuses more particularly on a leader's future commitments—on commitments the leader hopes the audience will approve, even bless. So, an inaugural address, in many ways, is the reverse of the tribute. The tribute looks back to someone's efforts and accomplishments, while the inaugural looks toward future programs and commitments.

Almost inevitably, an inaugural has two purposes: (1) *to acknowledge the transfer of group leadership*: and (2) *to characterize the program the new leader will pursue.* These purposes are so traditionalized or customary in inaugurals that speeches by new leaders almost "must" take the following topical form:

Introduction
I. Recognition of dignitaries in the audience
II. Acknowledgement of the transfer of leadership, with thanks to the group for having put its trust in the new leader (and, in the case of political elections, an exhortation to the group to put the animosities of the campaign behind it and to look to the future)

Body
I. Review of one set of problems facing the group (e.g. in a presidential inaugural, say, foreign problems)
II. Review of another set of problems facing the group (e.g. in a presidential inaugural, say, domestic problems)
III. Call for renewal of spirit and effort in the solution of these problems, with the new leader's pledge of vision and energy in their solution and a call for group members' efforts as well

Conclusion
I. Thanks again for the trust others have put in the new leader
II. Invocation of divine help or group help in carrying out the new program[5]

FIGURE 12.1   Overview of Celebratory Speeches: Temporal and Human Focuses

Human Focus

	Individual-Centered	Group-Centered
Past/Present	Tribute	Dedication
Present/Future	Inaugural	Keynote

(Left axis label: **Temporal Focus**)

Most persons offering inaugural addresses avoid becoming too specific in their proposals. They are, after all, primarily trying to instill a cooperative spirit in the group and a confidence that they, the leaders, have the vision to lead. Specific proposals might cause the group to divide into factions, might even reduce confidence in the new leader. So, these speeches are truly ceremonial or ritualistic in their broad focus on ideals and values. They retain a focus on ideals, and the leaders' understanding of and willingness to abide by those ideals.

We now have examined briefly the raw materials and organizational patterns appropriate to celebratory speeches. To help you visualize the similarities and differences we have stressed, examine Figure 12.1. To be sure, all of these speech types talk about the past/present/future and all of them are audience-centered in an important sense. Yet, there customarily are variations in human focus and temporal focus, and these are noted on Figure 12.1. Think about those differences.

TIPS FOR CELEBRATING SPECIAL OCCASIONS

■ *Steer a middle course between flowery and plain language.* In the nineteenth century, an "oratorical" style was used in speeches on special occasions. In the twentieth century, we have a strong penchant for a "plain" style—except, perhaps, on special occasions. Part of what makes them special to many listeners are moments of eloquence, of finely turned phrases, compelling metaphors, mythic references, literary allusions, and the like. Be careful not to go too far in that direction, however. In the first place, it is most difficult to deliver flowery sentences well, simply because you're not used to talking that way. And in addition, listeners are very good at picking out anything in your oral presentation which rings hollow. So, steer a middle course: do not be afraid to search out an appropriate metaphor, vivid imagery, well-wrought verbal pictures; but, do not present your listeners with a constant diet of swollen language, for their ears are simply not used to rich verbal repasts.

■ *Keep your attention on the occasion and the audience, not yourself.* As you build dedicatory, inaugural, appreciative, or keynote addresses, you may be tempted to show off, to focus attention on yourself rather than on the occasion. It's easy to do, really: it's easy to use high "highs" and low "lows" in your speaking voice, like an evangelical preacher; it's easy to use a dictionary of familiar quotations in order to string together several pithy ideas; it's easy to wait for applause after a particularly nicely worded phrase; it's easy to swing your body around the room in grandiloquent nonverbal expressiveness. Avoid those temptations and concentrate instead on emphasizing the cultural importance of the occasion. Do remember Gettysburg: Edward Everett gave the "principal address" at the cemetary in 1863. It was long, eloquent, finely tuned. Lincoln's was only about four or five minutes long, contained only three or four metaphors, and came out of him in a simple way. How many of you have ever heard about or read Edward Everett's grand oration?

■ *Leave them wanting more, not less.* The average presidential inaugural address, these days, contains only about 1500 words—maybe six pages of double-spaced type.[6] If the President of the United States can launch a four-year political program in that length, think what you can do in half that space and time! When speaking at ceremonies, avoid the natural urge to take advantage of a captive audience. Choose your words carefully, try not to crowd in too many ideas or references, do your job crisply—and then sit down.

The burden to "be articulate" perhaps is never greater than it is on celebratory occasions. The challenge of such occasions is unmistakable. But, the rewards almost always far outweigh the risks, hard preparatory work, and troubled sleep.

THE END AND THE BEGINNING . . .

With this final call for moderateness, sensitivity to audience, and efficiency, we come to the end of *The Articulate Person*. We've come back around to where we began, to a brief vision of the kind of human being and communicator the articulate person is. We have inspected the communication process as a system; gone through nine steps for constructing any piece of oral public communication; examined techniques for packaging information while defining, demonstrating, reporting, and explaining; unearthed the persuasive burdens borne by a reinforcer, a changer of attitudes, an actuator, an arguer, and a refuter; and, noted the demands upon all speakers called upon to help their group or society celebrate and remember special occasions.

These communicative purposes and settings represent the demands this culture places on active adults seeking to serve themselves, people on the job, people in the neighborhood, public causes, and government. These purposes will be achieved in particular settings or contexts for communication, however, only if you harken back to Preview I. The considerations and techniques herein discussed will be worthless unless your audience sees in you an articulate person worth listening to. The call for honesty, authenticity, openness, concern, and so on, was not made merely to start this book on a high plane. That summons was there because, ultimately, mere technical communication skills are not maximally effective without a likeable, trustworthy, committed human being showing through them. As you close this book, you are given one last piece of advice: go back to the beginning, and review the standards against which your society will measure you. If you attain those standards, you indeed will be an articulate person.

NOTES

1   "Farewell to the Cadets" by General Douglas MacArthur reprinted by permission of the MacArthur Memorial. For an analysis of MacArthur's speaking in general, see Stephen Robb, "Pre-Inventional Criticism: The Speaking of Douglas MacArthur," in G. P. Mohrmann *et al.*, eds., *Explorations in Rhetorical Criticism* (University Park: Pennsylvania State University Press, 1973), pp. 178–190.

2   On the importance, even centrality, of light-dark metaphors to public discourse, see Michael Osborn, "Archetypal Metaphor in Rhetoric: The Light-Dark Family," *Quarterly Journal of Speech*, 53 (April 1967), 115–126. If you like that, also read his "The Evolution of the Archetypal Sea in Rhetoric and Poetic," *Quarterly Journal of Speech*, 64 (February 1978), 1–22.

3   In Roman rhetoric, two "special occasions" forms for speeches were developed. The *encomium* was the speech of praise, and it tended to focus on biography. The classical religious homily *(antiquus* or *tractatus)* focused on "lessons to be learned" or themes.

4   Your library undoubtedly will contain many different collections of Daniel Webster's speeches. In those collections, look under the headings "occasional" or "ceremonial" addresses, to find such speeches as his "First Plymouth Oration," "First Bunker Hill Address," "Adams and Jefferson," "The Character of Washington," "Second Bunker Hill Address," or "The Addition to the Capitol." These are admirably analyzed in W. Sandra Nickel, "Daniel Webster—A study of the Nineteenth Century Commemorative Address," unpub. Ph.D. dissert., University of Iowa, 1976. You can get it on Interlibrary Loan or in microfilm from University Microfilms, Inc., Ann Arbor, Michigan.

5   For a review of standard forms in inaugural addresses, see Donald L. Wolfarth, "John F. Kennedy in the Tradition of Inaugural Speeches," *Quarterly Journal of Speech*, 47 (April 1961), 124–132.

6   Noted in Wolfarth, p. 125.

ASSIGNMENTS

Pre-Performance   1. In the library, find at least one ceremonial speech by Daniel Webster. Examine it carefully in the terms we have suggested in this chapter, looking at its narratives, valuative statements, metaphorical statements, and mythic references. Use the material you have found to write a short essay, either "Daniel Webster's Approach to Ceremonial Speechmaking" or "Beliefs, Attitudes, Values, and Myths: Daniel Webster's Conception of His Audiences and Their Society."

2. Page through several issues of *Vital Speeches of the Day*, looking for ceremonial speeches. (Alternatively, see if your library or instructor has a copy of Wil A. Linkugel, R.R. Allen, and Richard L. Johannesen, eds., *Contemporary American Speeches; A Sourcebook of Speech Forms and Principles*, 5th ed. [Dubuque, Ia.: Kendall/Hunt Pub. Co., 1982].) Follow the instructions for Pre-Performance 1 in analyzing a ceremonial speech you find.

3. Hold a discussion in class on the topic, "Contemporary Standards for Ceremonial Eloquence." Among all of the rhetorical techniques reviewed in this textbook, which (1) seem appropriate to ceremonial speaking, and (2) can be employed by ceremonial speakers without seeming "phony" to contemporary audiences?

Performance   1. Interview a class member, and, on the basis of what you learn, offer a speech of tribute to the person in a three-to-four minute speech. As suggested, use either a chronological or a topical pattern, and be ready after the speech to defend your choice of pattern.

2. Assume you are dedicating some building, piece of artwork, or other prominent feature of your school or community. Prepare and deliver a five-minute speech of dedication, either concentrating upon things the monument, building, or artwork "stands for," or focusing on what the group has accomplished in erecting the edifice or statuary.

3. Assume your campus is hosting a conference on "The Importance of Public Speaking in the 1980s and Beyond." Assume you are to prepare and deliver an eight-minute keynote speech. Using principles you have learned in this class and examples from your contemporary cultural environment, construct a keynote address.

Post-Performance   1. If you did Performance 1, ask five classmates who generally are familiar with the person you offered tribute for to critique your speech: Did you capture essential qualities they have noticed in this person? Did you achieve a useful balance between personal detail and public behavior? Did they learn anything about qualities-to-be-emulated?

2. If you did Performance 2, ask others familiar with the building or piece of public art to critique your speech: Did you capture the spirit of the object? Did you praise well enough the sacrifice of those who were

responsible for it? (Alternatively, write a critique of the speech of someone who dedicated a building or community feature you know well, asking and answering those two questions.)

3. If you did Performance 3, ask your instructor to analyze and evaluate the principles and examples you selected for attention. Did you capture the essential, even crucial, communication themes of this age? Might you have done better to emphasize others? (Alternatively, if the whole class—or major portions of it—did Performance 3, as a group write down the principles and examples which were presented in all of the speeches. Did everyone come away from the course with the same sorts of impressions of what's important about public speaking? Why or why not?)

APPENDIX

Groups, Committees, and Teams

An ever-present fact of life for each of us is the *group*. Beginning with the family group, we move through the stages of life connected to a succession of teams, gangs, clubs, societies, leagues, and organizations. All of this group activity occurs in part, of course, because Americans tend to be voracious joiners, a clannish society perhaps compensating for the variegated mixture of social, ethnic, and economic classes which comprise our citizenry. In the group we find ways to reintegrate ourselves, to discover who we are and what we have in common in a land of strangers.

Another reason the group is a powerful force in our society is that it can perform a vast array of important functions for the individual. We can even classify groups by the types of dominating functions they play in our lives:

• *Learning and study groups.* In school, in our neighborhoods, in city government, we rely upon learning or study groups to unearth, share, and organize the welter of information which bursts from libraries, computers, books,

articles, and special-interest publications. If each of us were responsible for our own unearthing, sharing, and organizing of information, we'd never make it through this world.

• *Decision-making and problem-solving groups.* Within large organizations, decision-making and problem-solving groups are called into existence whenever a business or bureau needs recommendations in a hurry on what to think or do. When in doubt, appoint a committee.

• *Activation groups.* Even more specialized committees, activation groups have the job of putting into operation the edicts sent from a study or decision-making group. Thus, a firm will appoint an activation team to launch a new marketing strategy; a political party will assemble a team to run a fund-raising raffle; and a pressure group will authorize a committee to meet with city council members.

• *Therapeutic groups.* Formally or informally, therapeutic groups have become commonplace in our society. They range from the casual kaffeeklatsch, which allows you to ventilate your feelings with close friends, to the highly structured training sessions associated with Transactional Analysis (TA), "est," and Adlerian counseling. These groups offer the input of others to help you come to grips with your "self," to deal with your feelings and experiences, to reset your mind when it tilts.

Because they are conglomerations of often radically different individuals, groups have been known to produce inferior, unenlightened, even foolish results. Such problems, however, have not yet diminished the importance and persuasiveness of the group in our society. If anything, the spectacular failure of some groups tends to show that the articulate person is badly needed in our institutionalized culture. Our reliance upon the committee, the group, and the team cries for competent people ready to do their parts to guarantee that group-centered endeavors are productive.

By now you have participated in enough groups, committees, and work teams to know that group communication processes demand of you many of the skills we have reviewed throughout this book. In many ways group communication is quite similar to other public speaking arenas and has similar requirements.

1. *You must have something to say.* Like any audience, a group demands that those who speak have something worth saying and are prepared to say it intelligently. If members discover that a particular group produces nothing but empty talk and half-formed notions, they'll drop out, physically or psychologically. So don't be a group sponge. If you do your share of the requisite research, thinking, and formulation, chances are that others will, too, and the group experience will be mutually satisfying and ultimately productive.

2. *You must be willing to say it.* In every group, there are those who tend to say a lot, and others who are reticent about speaking up even when they are prepared to make a genuine contribu-

tion. When your society or group needs you, you simply must be willing to step forth and talk. Whether haltingly or smoothly, in a few brief moments or at some length, you have a responsibility to serve your culture and committees with public remarks. Especially in a small group, where the responsibility for ideas and actions is spread among relatively few people, you must overcome your natural desire to be only a follower. Know what you can say, and don't be afraid to say it.

3. *You must cast your messages clearly and concisely.* Just as we have urged you throughout this book to organize and compress your thoughts when speaking in public, so, too, must you package your group messages. Set your ideas in sentence or propositional form; add supporting materials where they are needed; use introductions and conclusions; and pay attention to your wording. Just because you might be sitting down instead of standing up, or talking with people near instead of far away, is no reason to forget the requisites of a good public message. The only real difference in this regard is length. Normally, group talks are more highly compressed than public addresses, simply because group members are more dependent on each other to arrive at some common understanding or joint behavior. Such interdependence often demands that you talk in shorter spurts; that you let others join in, modify, and react to what you are saying; and that you move on to new topics when you have finished. So, you often don't talk as long in groups—but you certainly must talk as well.

4. *You must set clear goals.* Your general and specific purposes in group communication are the same as those which characterize any public message. In groups as well as behind lecterns, you are essentially seeking to inform or to persuade. More specifically, you will be expected to define fuzzy concepts, to demonstrate plans of action, to report on research you have done, to explain complicated processes, to argue for your beliefs, to refute those with whom you disagree, to change the attitudes of

unbelievers, and to move laggards to action. Furthermore, in groups you will probably have both short-range and long-range goals, both public and more personal aims. Each time you chime in on a group discussion think through your goals carefully. Keeping them in mind will help guide some of the communicative choices you make when talking aloud.

In many ways, therefore, group discussions call for the same range of skills as speaking publicly in any other arena. Nevertheless, group discussions also have a series of features which make them somewhat different from other communicative occasions.

Most of the special demands on group speakers arise from the interdependence of group members. Because you as a discussant are sharing the thinking, formulating, talking, evaluating, decision making, and acting with others, you face additional challenges. We can label these challenges the five cardinal principles of group communication.

1. *The principle of the common good.* Most groups you will join at work or leisure exist to be shared by all. Therefore, everything a group thinks about, does, recommends, or acts upon should reflect a sense of common benefit: the good that is generated by a group should be shared by all. To make the principle of the common good a fact of group life, you have responsibilities to see that no one is unnecessarily hurt, that every member's voice is heard, that goals are clear and are acted upon. Only in this way will the common good be served.

2. *The principle of shared control.* Every member in a group is responsible for guiding the intellectual and emotional life of a group. Customarily, certain individuals are designated as leaders or chairpersons, but everyone shares responsibility for guidance. All group members have a need and an obligation to ask questions, to draw out nontalkers, to probe for additional information, to slow down the obsessive talker, to advance and defend ideas. In the phrase of

John Dewey, everyone is responsible for a group's "psycho-logic," the way thinking should progress. See Chapter 9 for more on Dewey.

3. *The principle of constructive conflict.* People are people and not computers, so disagreements of both a personal and a conceptual nature are usually present in a healthy, open group. Again, every member of the group shares responsibility for handling conflict. Here, discussants often are in a dilemma: if they try to suppress conflict too early, competing points of view and creative solutions to problems may not be fully aired. Early suppression can lead to a dictatorial atmosphere and premature judgment. Yet, if a disagreement drags on too long, the discussion can turn into a personalized vendetta, with wounded spirits and little progress. When conflict arises, everyone in a group has to help treat it constructively—to deflect hostility in order to focus on the issues at stake. Handling or managing conflict will be discussed in detail later in this Appendix.

4. *The principle of resolution.* Because groups usually are oriented toward one or more of the goals we identified earlier, members must attempt to find satisfying resolutions to questions or problems. All must join in reaching agreements about information, problems, solutions, and actions to be taken. This cooperation means that everyone is responsible for offering *summaries*, in order to learn what common agreements have been reached. If disagreements persist, all must attempt to determine if more information, additional analysis, or other plans of action will help everyone reach *consensus*. Most groups seek consensus, general agreement on a piece of information, solution, or plan. If disagreements continue, then groups may be forced to seek *majority rule* by voting. Whether a group operates by consensus or by vote, all must contribute summaries, evidence, feelings, and other support which steadily move the group to some sort of resolution.

5. *The principle of common commitment.* Every time group members join a discussion, they

implicitly make a wide range of commitments to others. They sacrifice a part of their personal prerogatives to think and act as an individual, and make a commitment to consider and work with the views of others. This understanding does not mean, of course, that you must disregard individual thoughts and feelings which deserve to be expressed. It does mean, though, that under pressure, you may occasionally have to surrender on something. At times, you will have to regard your commitment to the group as more important than your commitment to your own head.

Whenever you're a member of a group, a committee, a caucus, or a team, then, you're ultimately in the business of *facilitating*. And being a facilitator demands that you use almost all of the communicative skills we have reviewed in earlier chapters, and that you meet the special requirements of good group communication. We'll discuss those special requirements in terms of the skills you will employ as a group participant and those you will need when you are the group's leader. Such a division between "participant" and "leader" is in many ways an artificial one, for everyone in a group shares leadership in successful committees and discussions. We will use the distinction, however, because it allows us to talk about communicative tactics and techniques from two points of view.

DISCUSSING

The nature of your communicative tasks in groups is complicated by the fact that, as a participant, you really are focusing in three directions at once: on yourself, on others in the group, and on the group's task. Because you're looking simultaneously in these three different directions, participating in a group can be tricky business. If you lose sight of yourself, you're a pawn. If you forget about "them," you're a tyrant. And, if you ignore the task, you'll

probably have to attend yet another meeting. In essence, as a discusser, you must engage in a mental juggling act, keeping track of your self, of others, and of the group's progress toward its goal. How can you do all that and remain sane? As you prepare to participate in a group, and as you actually take part in a discussion, the following suggestions may help guide your thinking and your communication.

Knowing and Revealing Your Self in Discussions

Selfishly, let's begin with you. You have both rights and responsibilities as you consider your own head and heart. The following suggestions include both head and heart:

Preparing Obviously, you must enter a discussion prepared to participate. This may mean actually reading the month's assignment in a book club, or scanning recommended articles and reports for a business meeting, or working out a "telephone tree" for an action group about to launch a public campaign. Getting intellectually ready for a discussion guarantees two things: first, it will ensure that you are able to offer positive contributions, and hence uphold your end of the bargain that groupness represents. And second, it protects you from glib-but-shallow sales pitches, silly proposals, ignorant allies, and overpowering opponents.

Getting Background on Others You ought to have information not only on the topic, but also on the other participants. This may not be a problem in a group which has a history, but it certainly can be in newly formed work teams and committees. The more you know about others, the better able you'll be to separate the curd from the cream, to anticipate the sources and strengths of your opposition, to know how to object without hurting someone's feelings, to guess at how tenacious various individuals will be. You'll know whom to trust, and how far. Ask around.

Introducing Ideas As a discussion is proceeding, you must calculate how and when to introduce ideas, opinions, and feelings that you have. That's the only way you can be true to your self. Several tactics for introducing ideas have proven successful:

Hitchhiking. You can link up your idea with an idea that someone else has stated. It seems perfectly natural to say, "Carl said that we needed to consider the impact of this proposal on our clerical staff, and I agree. As a matter of fact, I've done some thinking about this problem, and. . . ." In this way, you build on someone else's notions, and probably gain an ally.

Summary. Or, "So far, we've isolated three causes for declining school enrollments. And, I think they're accurate. But, I wonder if there isn't a fourth reason. . . ." In this tactic, you give everyone who has contributed to the discussion a psychological stroke, and then seek to move the discussion into new territory—yours.

Shift in viewpoint. Consider: "We've looked at the problem of child abuse from the perspectives of the child and of the abusing parent. What about those teachers, doctors, social workers, and other professionals who suspect they've seen a case? What's their role in all this?" This sort of introductory statement, once more, recognizes the ideas and feelings of others while it allows you—with the group's blessing—to interject your own position.

Disagreement. And then there is: "Now, Jean, I certainly can understand why you think no more parking ramps should be built downtown, but I think you've examined only two of the factors involved. Before we reach a decision on the issue, I think we must look at two additional factors. . . ." In this way, you express your disagreement softly. You leave Jean with the feeling you're accepting her analysis and integrity, and yet you give yourself

an entering wedge. In all these tactics, take care that your remarks actually fit with what has been going on.

Listening to and Evaluating Others To protect yourself in a discussion, you must be a rapt and careful listener. You must be able to see through the swarm of words from an eloquent advocate. You must be sure you don't have mistaken impressions, for the consequences of misunderstanding can be great, both interpersonally and intellectually. To protect yourself and to understand the full implications of what others say, consider the following listening techniques:

Questioning. Ask polite questions of others: "I didn't follow that; could you repeat it?" "Can you translate that for me?" "I'm curious—where did you read that?" If you phrase the question in terms of your own needs, you won't seem to be suggesting that the other person is unclear or incorrect. Questioning in this way is relatively non-threatening.

Rephrasing. To check on your own listening abilities, and to make sure you know what position you're disagreeing with, try rephrasing another person's ideas: "Let's see if I followed you. First you said that . . . and then you noted that . . . , right?" Putting someone else's ideas into your own words protects you and can save the group time, especially if others also need the "translation."

Recording. And, of course, take notes. If, say, you're in a decision-making group and the discussion becomes prolonged, by the time you arrive at a solution stage people may well have forgotten all the problems to be solved. Keeping track throughout the discussion will save embarrassment and make your own contributions useful later on.

Reacting to Disagreement and Criticism Not only must you carefully evaluate the ideas of others, but you should be mentally ready to react to their analyses of you.

Your first impulse, of course, is to protect your own ego and feelings. Time and again, it may seem that others misunderstand you, imply that you're not too smart, and pick on you. And you want to fight back. Resist that temptation, and instead be the debater. Focus on the disagreement rather than the personalized attack. This goal can be accomplished in several ways:

Interpreting. "Now, let's see if I can figure out what part of my analysis you're having trouble with." By focusing on the substance of the disagreement, you're telling the group that you want to ignore personal innuendos and keep the group as a whole on track.

Turning the other cheek. In all humility, you could say: "I'm sorry what I said bothered you so much, Fred. Let's see if we can resolve this issue." Poor Fred looks pretty bad after this response, and you can come out more highly credible.

Confronting the attacker. Especially if another person seems to be disrupting and attacking everyone, you (and the rest) may have to confront that person directly: "Now, Janet, you're really feeling your oats this morning, blasting out in all sorts of directions. Is something wrong? Are we irritating you? Is something that we're doing or saying stirring you up? What can we do to make you more comfortable and to get on with the task at hand?" In thus confronting a particularly nasty person, you are extending the group's good wishes and sympathy, and trying to return to the group's common task. And, with all three of these techniques, you are protecting your self, which usually is essential to your own sense of well-being.

Taking Care of Others in Discussions

Your second focal point is the other members of the group. Without that focus, you won't be doing your part to keep them happy and productive. A supportive social-emotional atmosphere, even in times of disagreement, is a must. There are many ways to build a supportive atmosphere.

Stroking It never hurts to give psychological "strokes" to other group members. It costs you little (unless your pride and ego get in the way), and it keeps everyone working and playing together. "That's a great idea!" "Thanks for the suggestion. It makes me see this question in a different light." "That's beautiful, Ralph." Such personal reactions to others show mutual trust and support.

Criticizing Constructively It doesn't hurt, either, to do a little stroking even while you're disagreeing with someone. There are ways to fight ("That's the dumbest thing I've ever heard!"); and then there are ways to criticize constructively. These can involve (a) bringing in additional *authorities* to erode the other person's position; (b) politely cataloging *facts* which have been ignored; (c) introducing alternative *statements of value* ("You look at this as a political question, but I wonder if it's not more a matter of human rights"); and (d) calling for a discussion of the *implications* of an idea ("I think your plan sounds decent, but do you think it will alleviate the first problem we mentioned?"). The important point, as you communicate your criticisms, is to go as far as you can in de-personalizing the disagreement. If possible, keep the focus on *authorities* (who do the attacking instead of you); on the *facts* (which we would love to think speak for themselves); on *value* positions; and on the hard-headed *implications*. Such a "real world" orientation is less personal and less threatening. As a matter of fact, it might even keep the group progressing toward its goal.

Accepting Correction Not only must you be able to disagree positively with someone else's misrepresentation or misunderstanding of you but you'll do the group a lot of good if you can gracefully accept other's positions and ideas as correctives to your own. It is tempting to be the gamester, and to fight back inch by inch. But if you see the basic logic of someone's analysis, or if you note that group opinion is running counter to your own, you'll have to surrender—or leave. Your ego cries out, "You fools! One day you'll see my wisdom!" But your sense of commitment to others demands: "OK, I'm still having a little problem with all this, but if the rest of you think we should try, then I'll certainly go along." Or, "I didn't realize some of those implications of my proposal, Paul. Thanks for pointing them out. Are there other proposals that won't have those bad effects?" In this way, you'll live to fight another day. Be sure, of course, to give your own analyses a fighting chance first; don't fear disagreement in itself. But if you must pull back, do so in a manner which will create respect for you and support for the others.

Being Patient Perhaps patience is the essential quality in your focus on other group members. You're often forced to be an extraordinarily saintly, patient person while discussing. Just as you think you yourself have carved out a piece of truth and wisdom, so does everyone else. Work hard at allowing them— even forcing them—to show you the error of your ways. Ask them to repeat, to go further, to extend. What they say may even be good! Especially with somewhat hesitant or reticent people, you often must gently prod them along, even if you know your own ideas will triumph. Patience is a small price for ultimate victory; it might actually produce a good suggestion or two; and it certainly will promote a positive social-emotional climate.

Achieving the Group's Goals in Discussions

Finally, you must focus on the goal or task of the group. We often think, perhaps wistfully, that it's the leader's job to keep a discussion

moving forward. Of course, it is (as we'll see in the next section). But leaders often need help, occasionally miss important points here and there, sometimes get flustered, and perhaps let the group get bogged down in an overextended discussion of some issue. While there is usually a person named "leader," "leadership" must be shared by all participants from time to time. It includes some responsibilities we already have suggested. Others are strictly procedural matters to which you should be attending.

Knowing the Agenda An *agenda* is an agreed-upon list of tasks to be accomplished or questions to be answered in a particular session. Know it. Know when it is appropriate to bring up a matter you're interested in. If necessary, as the group is about to begin, ask the others whether or not some idea you want to talk about is appropriate to the agenda. If it doesn't appear to be, ask if it can be inserted somewhere. Knowing the agenda, in other words, allows you (and the rest) to keep the discussion orderly and progressive, and tells you something about timing your remarks. (See the following pages for more.)

Asking Procedural Questions Never be afraid to ask questions about what's happening in a discussion: "Are we still on point three, or have we moved to point four?" "Is there some way we can resolve this question and move ahead?" "Can we consider the feasibility of Art's proposal before we move on to Brenda's?" Such questions can seem inordinately naive, and, if asked with a sneer in your voice, could reflect badly on the leader. Yet, sometimes naive questions are absolutely necessary in order to keep the group activity direction-oriented.

Summarizing As you may have noticed, summary is a theme of this chapter— summarizing your own position, summarizing those of others, and here, summarizing so that the group can keep progressing. A good summary allows you to check bases, to see what's been agreed to and what remains to be done. Summaries form the intellectual junctures in a discussion. They can be simple: "Now, as I heard you two, Jack said this and this, and Bob said that and that, right?" Or they can be elaborate attempts to trace through the whole of a discussion so that members have it clearly in mind before you adjourn. Summaries can be oral. In organizations especially, they're often written and checked by others, to become minutes of a meeting. They're useful to you, and with luck, to the others as well.

Arbitrating Another important leadership function which should not fall solely on the leader's shoulders is that of arbitrating disputes. Being the peacemaker is sometimes risky business, for both parties may go for your throat. Yet if a discussion is going to be mutually supportive and satisfying, and also productive, then each person occasionally is going to have to help it get over intellectual and emotional rough spots. Sometimes you can arbitrate by offering a *compromise*: "O.K., is it possible for us to accept a part of Proposal A and a part of Proposal B, and forge those parts into a new Proposal C? It might go this way. . . . " At other times, you're going to have to call for *clarification*: "Now, Bill, you think Ron's idea is defective because of this. And you, Ron, seem to be saying that Bill has missed the point about the riverfront land, right?" By pointing out the ideas in conflict rather than the personalities in conflict, you perhaps can deflate it. You may occasionally have to offer a *gentle reprimand*: "Whoa! If you two don't quit arguing with each other, we'll never get done in an hour! Let's see if we can get to the nub of the matter here." By thus holding out the standards of efficiency and expediency, you may succeed in getting two people to clarify, to remember the rest of the group, and to charge ahead.

Participating in a discussion can be a tre-

mendously rewarding and efficient way of making your own ideas and feelings public, of learning new information and perspectives, of making key decisions at work or at home, and of implementing plans or proposals. You will achieve maximum satisfaction and gain, however, only if you constantly keep in focus yourself, others, and the task. Monitor all three focal points steadily.

LEADING A MEETING

Therapeutic, learning, decision-making, and activation groups all place somewhat different demands upon leaders. And groups can range from informal get-togethers to highly formal sessions governed by parliamentary procedure. Thus we cannot give you specific advice on leading every kind of meeting. You will have to be content with some general procedural and communicative advice, which you will have to adapt to particular situations. In all meetings, however, a leader's job falls into three phases: *pre-meeting preparation, running the meeting,* and *post-meeting evaluation*. By examining a leader's responsibilities in these three phases, perhaps the burdens of leadership can be somewhat lightened.

Phase I: Pre-Meeting Preparation

As a leader, your principal job throughout all three phases is to operate as a facilitator. While leadership in general is diffused among all members of a group (because all are responsible for helping produce a quality end-result), nevertheless "the" leader has special duties. This is especially true in Phase I, pre-meeting preparation. Group members are counting on you to do what you can to make the actual discussion, committee, team, session, or meeting function smoothly. While your tasks will vary with the precise goal and the degree of formality of the group, they may well include some of the following:

Announcing the Time and Place

You probably will be responsible for getting information about the meeting to interested parties. This may include contacting the group members (one hopes you got telephone numbers on a sign-up sheet earlier), making sure the room or facility is open and available, letting the press know of the meeting if it's open to the public. It's a small task, but a crucial one.

Assembling Background Material

You may also have to get some general materials ready for the meeting. In a book club, the thoughtful leader looks up information on the author or on the issue being discussed, to orient the group. The business team leader digs through old files, to find out how the firm last approached this question and to unearth pertinent cost-benefit statistics, sales histories, or whatever. For an in-class symposium, the leader may assign specific tasks to the other members—sources to cover, kinds of articles to read, topics on which to be prepared. If these sorts of background activities are carried out carefully, you'll save the group a lot of frustration and wheel-spinning during the actual discussion.

Constructing an Agenda

Even if the topics for the upcoming meeting were announced in the previous meeting, a group usually needs more guidance than that. That guidance often takes the form of an *agenda*, a structured list of topics, questions, resolutions, and the like. Agendas vary, obviously, in detail and length; their completeness depends on the specialization of the group and the expertise of its members. While there is no foolproof way to build an agenda, we can suggest some general guidelines. Let's look at some examples for the three primary types of meetings: learning, decision-making, and activation meetings.

Note some features of these agenda. The first one is cast in *question* form (see Figure A.1). The use of questions encourages other members to be more directly involved in making procedural decisions. Questions suggest that matters are open for group decision making, and are not dictated in advance by the leader. Sometimes, however, as a leader you're expected to make some hard decisions before the meeting. Often organizations desire short meetings conducted by a trusted leader. If such authority has been delegated to you, then your agenda probably will contain, not questions, but topics or propositions. A *topical* agenda can specify particular matters, reports, ideas, or proposals to be discussed in an orderly manner (see Figure A.2). A *propositional* agenda is often used in formal organizations which depend upon parliamentary procedure, majority rule over controversial matters, and the like (see Figure A.3). It forces ideas to be cast in "official" language which probably will be recorded in minutes, in archives, or in bylaws. Because of its formality, a propositional agenda is usually set up in large activation groups such as monthly meetings of university faculties or annual sessions for stockholders.

Whatever type of agenda you as leader build, be sure that it suits the group's wishes and traditions, and that it is open-ended enough to allow room for additional items which members may want to introduce during the actual meeting. It is also wise, if possible, to circulate your agenda ahead of time, so that members can become familiar with it. That will save the group time; and if someone wants to object to it, may avoid potential fights.

Final Check of Arrangements

Just before the meeting is about to take palce, you as leader may have to check on the facilities one last time. Are the seating arrangements conducive to discussion? If there are microphones, are they working? Are the refreshments prepared? And so on, in all, making sure your meeting isn't problematic because you have overlooked the "little" details people expect leaders to care for.

Phase II: Running the Meeting

With careful preplanning, you should have little trouble actually running the meeting. During the discussion itself, your primary jobs are to keep it progressing toward its goal and to serve the participants in whatever ways you can. To carry out these two jobs, you probably will have to use some of the following communication techniques in each stage of the meeting.

Beginning the Meeting You of course will have to start the meeting. This may involve nothing more complicated than a "Can I have your attention, please? It's time we begin." In other settings, you may have responsibilities for opening remarks, a short speech orienting the group to the meeting's purpose, the procedures you will follow, and the like. (See the sample agenda.) Prepare opening remarks carefully, so

---

FIGURE A.1   Learning Group Agenda, in Question Form

Introduction: Remarks by the leader to orient the group and background the topic.

Analysis: In this step the group generally explores the question: decides how to subdivide it, narrows it, and puts the topics in order.
1. Into what major topics should the question be divided?
2. Should some of these topics be cut away or held off for another time?
   a. Do we already know enough about some of them?
   b. Are we so ignorant of others that it would be useless to attempt discussing them?
3. In what order should we consider the remaining topics?

   [A good, clear summary ought to be utilized here.]

Investigation: Now, the core of the learning discussion begins.
1. What terms or concepts need definition or explanation?
2. Topic by topic, what factual information should be introduced (and by whom, if you have assigned tasks)?
   a. Is the factual information complete enough?
   b. Does it make sense in terms of individual group members' personal experiences?
3. Topic by topic, can the group achieve consensus on any generalizations, cause-effect relationships, general operating principles, or whatever?
   a. Can the group agree on some propositions?
   b. What reasons prevent it from reaching agreement on others?

Summary: Final statement by the leader, with others joining in to make sure it is complete.

FIGURE A.2 **Decision-Making Agenda, in Topical Form**

Defining the problem: After an orientation by the leader, the group begins (in the Dewey model we discussed in Chapter 9).
1. Proposed definitions of problematic concepts [You would list them in an actual agenda.]
2. Proposed parameters for the discussion
   a. Topics to be considered
   b. Topics to be ignored

Analyzing the Problem: Here, the problem or situation is explored, seeking to discover its scope, its causes, its effects.
1. The problem's scope and size
   a. First aspect of the problem
   b. Second aspect [etc.]
2. Causes of the problem
   a. First cause
   b. Second cause [etc.]
3. Effects of the problem
   a. Effects, say, on business
   b. Effects, say, on government
   c. Effects, say, on social relationships [or whatever areas the leader or group deems important]
      [A solid, fair summary is desperately needed at this point.]

Suggesting Solutions: Here, group members propose solutions, and the leader is expected to keep track of them.
1. Suggested solutions
2. Impact of the suggested solutions
   a. Aspects of the problem they would solve
   b. Advantages and disadvantages of the solutions
3. Ways of grouping the suggested solutions for comparison

Evaluating Suggested Solutions: In the fourth step, the leader wants to make sure all relevant criteria are applied fairly to each proposal.
1. Kinds of solutions (economic, political, social, etc.)
2. Ability of each solution to meet the problems [You may get rid of some in this way.]
3. Special problems or disadvantages raised by each solution [Throw out others on this criterion.]
4. Special advantages of other solutions [Rank these solutions higher.]
5. Possible combinations of best features of the remaining solutions [You may generate your winner in this way.]

Selecting the Final Solution: Here the leader must strictly referee, helping the group decide if it can reach consensus or if it must vote.
1. Reaching a consensus on criteria for selecting the final solution
2. Decision on mode of selection: consensual agreement or vote

as not to embarrass yourself, not to forget anything, and *not* to drone endlessly. You're a facilitator, not an orator. If this is in fact a formal meeting of an organization, you may have to begin it in the usual parliamentary fashion:

1. Call to order
2. Review of the minutes of the previous meeting
3. Report from any committees or officers scheduled
4. Review of "old business" (considerations carrying over from the previous meeting)
5. "New business" (new resolutions and considerations)

Whatever the situation, begin the meeting crisply and clearly. Your group will appreciate your sense of organization and your concern that they have time to talk.

Leading the Discussion Once the discussion is launched, you ought to stay out of the substance of it as much as possible. Think of yourself as an interested troubleshooter. You're watching for confusion, omissions, conflict, procedural tangles, and the like. When you see any of these sorts of problems, only then do you move in. In most groups, you have several major responsibilities during the discussion.

Bringing out reticent individuals. Except in the most formal groups, you ought to be on the lookout for nonparticipants, people who hang back because they are hesitant or because talkative souls are dominating the group. "What do you think, Harry?" is a simple but effective way to bring someone out. If that doesn't work, you may need to add a bit of encouragement: "Harry, you're the person here closest to our problems in Missouri. We really could use your thoughts." If you still get no response, move on, looking back at good old Harry periodically to see if he's ready to talk yet.

Summarizing at key points. Another essential job is that of objectively summarizing particular ideas, conflicts, analyses, and agenda items. A summary from a leader does several things for a group: (a) It shows them you

---

FIGURE A.3   Activation Group Agenda, in Propositional Form

Introduction: Depending upon the formality of the group, the leader may orient the group by reminding it of previous discussions or meetings in which the various propositions were discussed. And, if parliamentary procedure is to be used, the leader may review the principal rules for speaking, voting, and other procedures.

Propositions or Resolutions: If this is a formal parliamentary session, resolutions (in the form you see below) will be introduced, debated, perhaps amended, and voted upon. If it is less formal, there will be less rigid forms for matters under discussion.
1. Resolved, that this committee approve Plan A.
2. Resolved, that a subcommittee be formed to raise the necessary money, by the usual means, to implement Plan A.
3. Resolved, that this subcommittee report back to this committee in six months to report on progress.

are a fair leader, summarizing both sides of a dispute cleanly. (b) It gently reminds them to finish off a particular point and move on. (c) It catches up members whose minds have drifted off to other matters. (d) And, if well done, it can push a group to a decision. To make summaries accurate and well structured, take careful notes.

Tying down the key facts, generalizations, and cause-effect relationships. Even though you try to stay out of the discussion as much as possible, often you are needed to fill out the factual picture, to go after a particularly obvious causal relationship no one has mentioned, to intrude a valuative perspective needing consideration, and so forth. Now, you certainly don't want others to think you're running the meeting with a heavy hand, so if possible, you probably will want to draw out the missing information, relationship, or value from the participants. Tact is all-important, and if you're going to make a statement, you might even want to ask the group's permission: "Excuse me, but I was reading an article last week bearing on this point, and I wonder if it would be all right for me to. . . ." Otherwise, you can go to open calls for information: "Has anyone come across material on . . . ?" Or you might refer to a previous discussion: "During last week's session, someone mentioned that. . . . Is that idea appropriate here?" A leader can always make a direct reference to a document members supposedly are familiar with: "So far, we've not said anythng about Appendix B in the Jackson Report. Should its recommendations be considered now?" Try to leave the matter up to the group; you thus preserve your objectivity and impartiality.

Handling conflict. All of the methods for handling conflict that we reviewed earlier are applicable here: de-personalizing it, using outside authorities to undercut positions, trying to get the participants in the melee to settle it themselves, and referring to the need for dispatch. A leader is in a delicate position when it

comes to conflict. On the one hand, a leader realizes that conflict can be creative and can lead to group-generated agreements. Conflict is absolutely necessary for testing ideas and exploring positions, feelings, and proposals. On the other hand, if it becomes dominant and personalized, it can destroy a group. The skillful leader watches—watches to see if it's getting too heated, watches noncombatants to see if they are getting bored, scared, or frustrated, and watches the clock. Then the leader moves in gingerly, with something like: "O.K., you two certainly have demonstrated how complex and touchy this issue is. We really, however, must keep progressing, so how about the rest of you? Now that Jack and June have explored this idea fully, what do you think? Does anyone else have an opinion on it?" If you can succeed in getting the rest of the group to pick up on the controversy—and, perhaps, resolve it—your job is done. Go to harsher measures only if the combatants won't quit. Try to slow down the dominating individuals and more equitably spread the communicative load. Reprimand if necessary, but only in the name of the group itself.

Terminating the discussion. It is the leader's job to terminate the discussion. You must find a way of ending it positively. Your greatest ally in all this, of course, is the clock: "Excuse me, but even though I'm finding this discussion fascinating and enlightening, we've got to quit in five minutes. Any last word or two before we break?" Beyond actually stopping the proceedings, the articulate leader moves to a summary: a summary of what's been discussed and decided, what remains open, and what is left to be treated in another session. A round of thanks (naming names, even) never hurts. A clear wrap-up sets important notions in members' minds, getting them ready for further consideration or discussion at another time.

Leading the actual discussion, therefore, really doesn't involve too many tricks or strategies of communication. As long as you are a careful listener, one sensitive to the intellectual and emotional processes which are developing, you can handle it easily.* Keep your head working and your heart dispassionate, being warm but firm.

Phase III:
Post-Meeting Responsibilities

Too many leaders forget that, once a meeting is over, there often are post-meeting responsibilities they must carry out. Some of these duties are courtesies (thank-you notes to the parliamentarian, for example). Others are economic (paying the bills if hall rental and catering were involved). Other important details have to do with the ongoing life of the group or organiza-

---

* The word "easily" can be used only if you're not in charge of a meeting governed by formal *parliamentary procedure*. If it is, you'd better purchase one of the simplified guides to parliamentary forms (there are several good ones), and learn about "main motions," "amendments," "points of information," "motions to postpone, table, recall," and so on. Parliamentary procedure can be learned quickly, through study and observation.

tion (minutes of the meeting, plans for the next meeting, refiling of materials used, reports to others in the organization of the type we described in Chapter 6, or evaluations to be passed on to your successor).

Because, as leader, you are in so many ways responsible for the social-emotional and substantive life of the organization, be sure you dispatch such duties with aplomb. Members should receive minutes of the meeting within a week so they will remember and understand the salient features of the discussion you can only hint at in the minutes. Thank-you notes leave a good impression, and probably prod the receivers of them to render good service the next time the group meets. The news release you want to peddle as a result of the meeting should get to the press the next day so your group's decisions, recommendations, or actions will be timely news. Finish off your post-meeting duties quickly. It will pay off in what you get done and in how people think of you.

Being a leader, as you can see, demands forethought, anticipation, organization, impartiality, sensitivity, and a truckload of good sense. By spacing your tasks, however, you can serve your club, organization, or group as an articulate leader.

INDEX